THE LAST GENTLEMAN

THE LAST GENTLEMAN

Thomas Hughes and the End
of the American Century

To Dianne Spencer

BRUCE L. R. SMITH

With warm regard,
Bruce Smith
January 2022

BROOKINGS INSTITUTION PRESS
Washington, D.C.

Copyright © 2021
THE BROOKINGS INSTITUTION
1775 Massachusetts Avenue, N.W.
Washington, D.C. 20036
www.brookings.edu

All rights reserved. No part of this publication may be reproduced or transmitted in any form or by any means without permission in writing from the Brookings Institution Press.

The Brookings Institution is a private nonprofit organization devoted to research, education, and publication on important issues of domestic and foreign policy. Its principal purpose is to bring the highest quality independent research and analysis to bear on current and emerging policy problems. Interpretations or conclusions in Brookings publications should be understood to be solely those of the authors.

Library of Congress Control Number: 2021945711

ISBN 9780815738909 (pbk)
ISBN 9780815738916 (ebook)

9 8 7 6 5 4 3 2 1

Typeset in Sabon LT Pro

Composition by Elliott Beard

To my brother Bob, who has kept the faith.

Contents

Acknowledgments		ix
Prologue		1
1	Beginner Boy	7
2	Teacher's Pet	14
3	Student Federalist	22
4	With Bowles and Humphrey	34
5	Bowles in Congress	45
6	The 1960 Presidential Election	59
7	The New Frontier	78
8	Intelligence and Covert Operations	98
9	The Cuban Missile Crisis	116
10	Diplomacy	132
11	The Overthrow of Diem	151
12	The Gulf of Tonkin Crisis	175
13	The 1964 Vice Presidency	196
14	The Humphrey-Hughes Memo	207

15	Point of No Return	228
16	Speaking Out	247
17	The Most Turbulent Year	262
18	London	286
19	Carnegie: The House That Hughes Built	301
	Epilogue	326
	Notes	335
	Index	357

Acknowledgments

Many friends and colleagues have assisted me in the research for this book. I owe a special debt to Tom Hughes for his assistance over the six years involved in writing the book. Having a live subject has obvious advantages for a biographer. Yet dealing with a live person, especially a friend, also poses challenges. Tom's broad understanding made it possible for me to navigate the challenges while taking advantage of the opportunities.

Tom Hughes's story seemed to follow logically from a biography I published in 2015 (*Lincoln Gordon: Architect of Cold War Foreign*). That book told the story of America's "greatest generation," which won World War II and built the peace afterward. I viewed events then from the vantage point and the life of one of the important players of the "supporting cast"—that is, those who did much of the work but whose contributions often went unrecognized. This new book, I thought, would tell the story of the generation that followed—the "new frontiersmen," or those, in John F. Kennedy's famous metaphor, to whom the torch of leadership had been passed. I would tell the story via the life and career of Tom Hughes, a key participant and an important observer and chronicler of the period.

While the careers of Lincoln Gordon and Tom Hughes had similarities, the differences were more significant. Gordon was an Ivy league professor who came from the Eastern foreign policy establishment and who had little interest in and less aptitude for politics. He left politics to the leaders he served. Gordon had a simple and deep-rooted faith in America as a bulwark against fascism and communism and a force for good in the world. The public, he believed, should generally defer to the knowledgeable elites who could best identify and serve the national interest. And to Lincoln

Gordon this was manifestly so regarding the complex issues of foreign and security policy.

In contrast, Tom Hughes came up in the world of politics and saw his mission as helping his fellow midwesterners to abandon isolationism and then to remain committed to a U.S. leadership role in the world. This was never an easy task for a nation with a short attention span and an aversion to long-term international obligations. Hughes had a deep understanding of how much foreign policy depended on a broad base of public support. He was anti-communist but had a nuanced view of America's role in the new postwar era. A self-styled "prairie populist," Hughes had to fight his way into the Eastern foreign policy establishment, only to find that the establishment had splintered into warring factions and was crumbling beneath his feet.

In telling this story, I have relied heavily on Tom Hughes's recollections of events and on interviews with many of his friends and colleagues. I have known a number of them myself so that I could bring to bear my own perspectives as well. I had complete access to Tom's voluminous papers and drew on them extensively. I often cite my sources simply as the "TLH papers," since the papers were not arranged into boxes, file numbers, folders, and so forth, as would be the case with professionally archived files. Tom's papers now reside in their permanent home at the Library of Congress, where they are being processed. I have occasionally taken small authorial liberties with direct quotations for the purposes of clarity and syntax.

When I began this project in the spring of 2015, the Carl and Vera Schmidt Foundation of Rochester, Minnesota, kindly assisted with two start-up grants. I am grateful in particular to Warren West, a Schmidt Foundation trustee, for his advice and encouragement.

William Burns, president of the Carnegie Endowment for International Peace before he left to become CIA Director in the Biden administration, arranged for Carnegie to act as host and fiscal agent for the Schmidt Foundation grants. Jin Wang of the Carnegie staff skillfully handled the administrative arrangements.

John Prados of George Washington University's Security Archives read the original draft of this book for the Brookings Institution with great care. I owe him a special debt of gratitude for his invaluable comments, which greatly improved both the book's content and its presentation.

The Cosmos Club Writers Group, chaired by Howard Newman, commented on several draft chapters. I am grateful to the members of the group for their reactions and suggestions. I must also thank the members of the Cosmos Club's American History Study Group, which I chair, who offered helpful comments.

I first worked for Brookings in the summer of 1960 as a graduate student research assistant and it has been my professional home for much of the period since then. I would like to take this occasion to thank the friends and colleagues I have had the pleasure to know and to work with at various times in the past sixty years. In particular, I thank the members of the team that has helped with this book. Bill Finan has been an understanding and encouraging publisher. Cecilia González has skillfully managed the book's production and allayed my concerns and anxieties along the way. Laura Mooney and her colleagues at the Brookings Institution library were unfailingly helpful in tracking down references and obtaining copies of materials.

Brett Geranen, computer guru, helped me to cope with numerous computer problems and to untangle the snarls that inevitably seemed to arise. Robert de Lapeyrouse, whom I first met when he was a volunteer reader from the Columbia Lighthouse for the Blind, has generously read for me and has been a friend for many years. Marjorie Crow and Joan Kennedy copyedited early drafts.

Elise, my wife of fifty-seven years, has been a valued collaborator in the research and careful reader of drafts. She read the entire manuscript several times, saved me from many errors, and pushed me to make the book readable. I am sorry that I have taken so much time and attention away from her.

My brother Bob took a special interest in the book from the start. His enthusiasm, support, and advice kept me motivated. He supplied many useful insights and lifted my spirits when I felt discouraged. We had pleasant visits together to a number of historical sites and archives in southern Minnesota where Hughes family papers were located: the Blue Earth County Historical Society, the Nicollet and Brown County Historical Societies, the University of Minnesota Mankato archives, and the Carleton College archives. Bob's daughter, Liz Prokosch, acted as research assistant on my visits to the Minnesota Historical Society in St. Paul, an institution co-founded by Tom's grandfather Thomas Hughes. For his encouragement and support of this and many of my efforts, I dedicate this book to my brother Bob.

Responsibility for the judgments made about the people and events in the book is of course mine alone. Errors large and small and other shortcomings are my responsibility, too—an assertion not likely to be seriously disputed. I hope I have done Tom Hughes justice in this biography and that I have told his story in an engaging fashion. I hope also that I have added something to what is known about the events, issues, and the times in which Hughes served the nation. Whether these hopes have been realized is for my readers and not for me to say.

Prologue

On Friday, February 12, 1965, Thomas Hughes, assistant secretary of state and director of the Bureau of Intelligence and Research (INR), telephoned his old friend and former employer, Hubert Humphrey, the vice president of the United States, with an urgent message:

"The die is cast," he told Humphrey.

The time for action on Vietnam had arrived, said the usually understated Hughes. There was urgency in his voice. The United States was on the brink of making a horrible mistake. If the president agreed to the Pentagon's bombing campaign, it would be difficult to reverse course. The bombing would inevitably lead to the commitment of ground troops. The president should instead, Hughes urged, pursue a path toward negotiations.

The bombing campaign, code-named Rolling Thunder, would not be a one-time retaliatory strike, like the Tonkin Gulf action. Rolling Thunder would be continuous and hard hitting, totally unlike the "pinpricks," as some described the earlier bombing and South Vietnam's covert shelling by PT boats against the North.

"Tam," said Humphrey (this was the boyhood name Tom's old friends and family still sometimes used), "can you fly down here to Georgia and brief me?"

Hughes and Humphrey huddled for most of Saturday and early Sunday morning, discussing how the vice president should make the case to President Lyndon Johnson against escalating the war. On Sunday afternoon, Hughes drafted the "personal-eyes only" memorandum that Humphrey would present to the president. The memo approach might not work, Humphrey said, but it would get LBJ's attention.

The bombing campaign, advocated in a joint memo by Robert McNamara and McGeorge Bundy, had been presented to President Johnson in late January. Johnson, like John Kennedy before him, was impressed by Defense Secretary McNamara's crisp style of presentation: an avalanche of statistics and the apparently hard scientific evidence. The defense secretary most characteristically represented the analytical, problem-solving style of decisionmaking that had marked the New Frontier. Johnson had retained Kennedy's national security team. McNamara was "the national symbol of scientific and managerial progress, the embodiment of rational policymaking, the very model of technocratic expertise."[1]

Thus persuading President Johnson to shift strategy and embrace negotiations leading to the U.S. disengagement from Vietnam would not be easy. It would mean going against McNamara, the Pentagon, and the Kennedy legacy. But Humphrey was buoyed by the great electoral victory that he and Johnson had just won, the greatest presidential victory to date in American history. The Minnesotan was also touched by the friendly attention he had had with the president in the period up to and following the inauguration. Humphrey thought that he and LBJ had never been closer.

In many conversations with Tom Hughes since the election, Hubert had excitedly noted that the president had given him a virtual carte blanche to reorganize the State Department. In keeping with the loyalty oath LBJ demanded from him in the summer of 1964, Hubert believed he was observing Johnson's wish that he speak frankly in private when he had something important to tell the president.

Hubert could not and would not argue in McNamara's style. He would not try to rebut the McNamara-Bundy proposal by citing body counts, infiltration rates, weapons captured, and other numbers. His argument would be based on history rather than statistics. He would speak to the president in personal terms as a friend and as one politician to another.

Humphrey could not have been more mistaken in his assessment of the situation. The Humphrey-Hughes memo utterly failed to sway LBJ, though it was one of the most impressive documents of the whole Vietnam War. Johnson was furious with Humphrey. In Washington, no good deed goes unpunished, and LBJ was at his most vindictive in reacting to the memo. He relegated the vice president to the presidential doghouse, where Humphrey languished for a year. Humphrey was excluded from all important Vietnam policy discussions and even demoted from some domestic issues. The president also humiliated Humphrey in countless small ways.

McGeorge Bundy said years later that the memo "broke up" the relationship between president and vice president. The Johnson-Humphrey relationship, he said, "went sour faster than any in the two-hundred-year history of the troubled relationships between presidents and their vice presidents."[2]

The memo was a dramatic point in Tom Hughes's government career. It was indicative of Tom's general role. He was always near the center of the action but as an adviser rather than the ultimate decisionmaker. Like Samuel Pepys in his day, Thomas Hughes knew everyone and used that knowledge to enhance his own and his bureau's standing in the intelligence community. He was both a participant in and a fastidious chronicler of events. He recorded everything that caught his eye. His diaries, records, and notes, as well as his vivid recollection of events, were of great assistance to me in compiling this biography. They give us memorable insights into one of the most turbulent and critical periods of twentieth-century American history.

As the foreign policy establishment, which he had worked so hard to join, was crumbling beneath his feet, Hughes grasped more fully than his contemporaries what was happening. He understood the forces that were transforming the international landscape and changing the nature of diplomacy.

Tom became deputy director of intelligence for the State Department rather suddenly, a week after the failed Bay of Pigs invasion. Two years later, he was appointed director, when his predecessor and good friend Roger Hilsman became assistant secretary for East Asia, including Vietnam. Hughes's background and experience prepared him perfectly for the intelligence role, and he proved to be a skillful manager. The job of intelligence chief combined his love of foreign affairs and his belief in the importance of knowledge for policymaking. He used his position adroitly to keep himself involved in the action.

In a city of towering egos, Hughes was a midwesterner with a modest demeanor and a sly wit. He certainly was as ambitious as others who were drawn to the excitement of Washington, but he had the good sense and innate civility to keep his ambition under control. Tom had a penetrating intellect, but his self-deprecating manner disguised it. People enjoyed his company. He was a gentleman, courteous, polite, and respectful of others, but certainly no prude. He was not in the least self-righteous. He was fun to be with and rather worldly in his outlook.

Tom Hughes was born old. He was perhaps something of a throwback to an earlier era, an Edwardian or German aristocrat like his Hohenzollern ancestors. He was an art collector, amateur historian, essayist, musician, raconteur, and a lawyer, though one who found the actual practice of law dull and much preferred diplomacy and public service.

This book tells the story of Tom Hughes's rise from a small town in Minnesota to the corridors of power in Washington. He later became a major figure in the foundation and think-tank world and continued to interact with policymakers, mostly in an effort to correct the problems and mistakes he had observed during his own government service.

The book is both history and biography. Hughes's story is also the story of his generation, of the Americans who succeeded the great leaders of the World War II and postwar era. The greatest generation defeated Nazism, reconstructed the shattered economies of Western Europe, and fashioned a stable world order. The great wartime and postwar leaders have been celebrated in the media, the scholarly literature, and the popular culture, occupying an almost reverential status in the popular imagination. History has treated Hughes's generation less kindly. The successors to the postwar leaders have been blamed for allowing, or causing, things to fall apart. Dean Acheson grandiosely entitled his memoir of the postwar era *Present at the Creation*.[3] Tom Hughes never wrote a memoir. Had he done so, he might have called it *Present at the Dissolution* and explored the breakdown of America's domestic politics consensus and of stability of foreign policy that occurred in the 1960s.

In 1968, with an eye to history, Hughes commissioned an independent "self-study" to evaluate the INR's intelligence efforts during the Vietnam War. Hughes was unaware at the time of the similar but more elaborate project to study the Pentagon's decisionmaking on Vietnam, commissioned by Defense Secretary McNamara. *Time* magazine, in 1971, mentioned the INR study and dubbed it the State Department's version of the Pentagon Papers. But Hughes's study remained classified until 2004, when it was finally declassified and published online by the National Security Archive of George Washington University.

Hughes, upon the publication of the State Department study of the INR and Vietnam, assessed his and his bureau's role in these terms: "In retrospect, as the INR study shows, those of us who worked here on Vietnam in the 1960s have the ironic satisfaction of knowing that most of our forecasts have been vindicated by history. We can only lament that, while we were heeded, we were unable to persuade, sway, or prevail when it came to the ultimate decisions."[4]

As president of the Carnegie Endowment for International Peace from 1971 to 1991, Hughes sought to correct the problems he had observed in his government service. As his first project at Carnegie, he sought to reform the Foreign Service along more democratic lines. He launched a program to open up the foreign policy establishment by linking insiders with outside experts through seminars and academic exchanges.

He sent many promising young Carnegie staffers into the Carter administration. Carnegie provided a home for others, where they could recharge their batteries for temporary periods before returning to government or taking up foreign policy positions in think tanks and universities. Hughes made a point of trying to restore the unity and morale of the foreign policy elites estranged by the Vietnam War.

Tom Hughes twice turned down appeals from President Jimmy Carter to return to government as director of the Central Intelligence Agency. He saw his role at Carnegie as offering a better opportunity to promote a civilized dialogue on foreign policy and to build a new, bipartisan, and professionalized foreign policy establishment. Sadly, the Washington think-tank community in the 1970s and 1980s began to reflect the same partisan divide that was increasingly evident in the nation's politics.

Tom continued to be one of the most respected leaders in the foundation world, wrote regularly for Carnegie's journal, *Foreign Policy,* and served on many NGO boards. He retired in 1991, on the eve of the First Gulf War, when many pundits were declaring an end to history. Hughes knew better.

The collapse of communism would, instead, betoken a return to the traditional problems of American foreign policy. A unipolar world meant to many that America had no serious enemies and could impose its will on the world. To Hughes, always a deep skeptic on U.S. involvement in the region, the Middle East was a dangerous terrain for United States military forces. History had not come to an end.

Indeed, with the discipline imposed by the Cold War gone, the prospects of lesser conflicts were bound to increase. But these were problems Hughes would leave to his successors at Carnegie, the Pentagon, and State Department.

Harris Wofford, Tom's oldest friend, a presidential adviser, and former United States senator, lamented the absence of his friend's voice in the foreign policy debate in 2006:

> As I see it, Tam's special and great achievement, aside from wit and warmth and salt that comes with him, out of him, over the years, is the view of the world he has honed and expanded and cultivated, and offered to the powers that be and the rest of us. It is the broadest, most accurate, and wisest one I know. His and our failure is in not finding ways and means to make that view of the world more widely known, understood, and adopted by the powers that be. America and the world would be far better. It is the vision without which people are now, and in so many years of our lifetimes, perishing.[5]

Tom Hughes saw American foreign policy as the product of the conflicting forces and the competing values of liberalism, pluralism, and democracy. This complex process led to a foreign policy in which there are no final victories or victors—but no ultimate defeats, either.

In his career, both in war and in peace, Hughes navigated the unclear boundary between politics and expertise, between specialists and generalists, and between the worlds of open and closed politics. Politics at home inevitably constrained what the nation could and should do abroad. Foreign policy professionals had to operate on a base of public support. Policy was nuanced, but politics was not. The questions Hughes dealt with were at times novel but more often were like the ancient political and ethical dilemmas cast in new garb. Rapid technological change had vastly complicated the world that political leaders faced, but they could seek some solace and guidance from the past.

Hughes and his generation learned the lesson that America is fallible, that world leadership comes with burdens and frustrations, and that American military power should be used cautiously. These are lessons that are worth relearning.

1

Beginner Boy

The air was heavy on that August morning in 1862, hanging like a blanket over the cabins in the small Welsh settlement of Cambria, Minnesota. The village was ten miles southeast of the more populous German settlement of New Ulm. Other towns were scattered nearby along the Minnesota River in the southwestern part of the state. In the stillness that morning, something began to stir that caught the attention of Henry Hughes, one of Cambria's respected settlers. His son Thomas sensed something, or perhaps he only felt his father's anxiety. Was it a rumble in the distance, the air carrying the sound of distant voices? The boy's memories were jagged when he tried to recall years later exactly what had happened. More distinct sounds came at some point, he recalled, including the beating of drums. But perhaps that was the next day, when the family fled to Mankato and they could actually see the smoke from New Ulm.[1] He could not be sure, but he painted a dramatic picture when he told the story.

As the elderly Thomas Hughes (1854–1934) retold the story to his grandson, Tam, as the family called him, on Sunday afternoons in front of the crackling fire, every detail and every turn in the narrative was vivid and palpable. The narrative was fresh, even if the children were hearing it for the tenth time. Every Sunday Grandfather Hughes would tell stories of Indians, settlers, and the frontier adventures that were part of his early life. The family's escape from the Indians in the summer of 1862 was a favorite of little Tam and his friends. The old man's face lit up as he described the expression on his own father's face that day long ago. The family was herded into the woods. The father led them deeper and deeper into the forest, pushing past prickly bushes, over fallen trees, and through piles of leaves and damp moss until the light became dim.

Tom's grandfather understood the urgency of his own father's actions. The Indians had been more visible and bolder lately, sometimes knocking on the door and asking for food; at other times, a face would suddenly appear at a window and then disappear. The grown-ups would talk in muffled tones and change the conversation if the children approached. A few weeks earlier, on August 5, a scuffle had broken out at the Upper Sioux trading post, the Yellow Medicine Agency. Fighting with the Indians was narrowly averted by extending credit to them or simply giving them badly needed supplies. The supplies being held in the government warehouse there already belonged to the Dakota by treaty. An agent named Galbraith, from the Bureau of Indian Affairs, refused to release the supplies to save himself the inconvenience of a double accounting entry when the government's gold payment for the supplies arrived. But the Indians, who came from their home at Big Lake, were on the verge of starvation; they broke into the warehouse and took the food that they were meant to receive.

Grandfather Hughes's full understanding of what would be known as the Dakota or Sioux War of 1862 came much later, with his painstaking research and the publication of his monumental historical works, including *Indian Chiefs of Southern Minnesota* (1927), *Old Traverse des Sioux* (1929), *The History of Blue Earth County* (1909, with his good friend Major General D. Brown), *The History of the Welsh in Minnesota* (1895), and *The Semi-Centennial of Mankato* (1903), and his sketches, notes, speeches, outlines, and voluminous other writings.[2] The elder Thomas Hughes became the first great historian of Minnesota. His boyhood encounter did not make Grandfather Hughes an enemy of the Minnesota Indians. Instead, he became an ardent defender and an advocate of making peace with the Indians.

The Dakota War or Sioux uprising of August 1862 cost the lives of some 600 settlers and soldiers and at least 100 Indians, including the thirty-eight Dakota (or Lower Sioux) braves who were hanged together in Mankato in December of that year.[3] President Lincoln issued the order for the hangings after paring down substantially the list submitted to him by the army. The hanging on the day after Christmas remains the largest simultaneous mass execution in the nation's history. The Hughes family witnessed the hanging of the warriors, including the notorious Cut Nose, one of the instigators of the uprising. In a dispute some years earlier, Cut Nose's nose had been bitten off by John Other Day, an Indian who later rescued many settlers caught in the uprising. The nose episode came in a dispute years before John had converted to Christianity and adopted the habits of the white man.[4] Grandfather Hughes was eight years old when he witnessed the mass hanging. He never specifically wrote about the hangings in his scholarly books, but there is no doubt the eight-year-old boy was affected by what he saw and that it helped to form his commitment to the peaceful settling of disputes.

Grandfather Hughes was more than a storyteller and raconteur. He was also a moralist, an activist, and an advocate of Indian causes, and his stories always had a moral. Usually, the moral was peace: the Indians and the settlers had to respect each other and learn to live together in peace. The war with the Indians made matters worse. His grandfather had also lived through the Civil War and told stories of his uncles, who had fought, and some perished, in that war. Grandfather Hughes hated war and always made that clear to Tam.

The Hughes family had good fortune on its side and emerged unscathed from the 1862 crisis, fleeing to Mankato under the leadership of Henry Hughes, eight-year-old Thomas's father. Mankato was the only logical choice and the only safe escape route. Henry rounded up a group of settlers to join him and his family, for, as postmaster of Butternut Valley, appointed by President Lincoln, Henry was a leader of the community. Henry's younger brother, John Henry Hughes, stubborn and a family oddball, refused to leave. He told Henry that he had never had any problems with the Indians and would read his Bible and put his trust in the Lord.

When the family arrived in Mankato, they discovered to their astonishment that John Henry was there.

"Brother, I see you changed your mind," said Henry.

John Henry explained that he had opened his Bible and chanced upon a passage that he took as a sign to depart and join the others. The family never knew how John Henry got to Mankato ahead of the rest of them.

The battle with the Indians never got to Mankato but raged on for eight days to the north at numerous points along the Minnesota River. Reinforcements rushed to the fighting to reverse the tide of battle, which initially favored the Indians. Troops were scarce on the frontier as the country's attention was fixed on the Civil War.

The visit of Little Crow and other chiefs to President James Buchanan in 1858 had resulted in a new agreement with the Indians updating the 1851 Treaty of Traverse des Sioux and had thus seemed to consolidate the framework that guaranteed peace. This optimism was not shared by the Indians. Their fears were not without foundation, since the treaty laid the basis for a vast influx of settlers. At the beginning of the decade, there were approximately 7,000 Indians in Minnesota and an equal number of settlers. By the end of the decade, the settlers had increased to 200,000, and the Indians had been crowded into reservations, which, under the 1858 agreement, amounted to only about half the size of the land allotted under the Treaty of Traverse des Sioux. The system of federal payments and annuities, which was supposed to compensate the Indians for their loss of hunting lands, was marked by delays, corruption, and maladministration, producing resentment and instability. This undercurrent went largely unnoticed or was ignored by the majority of the settlers.

The Indian uprising thus caught the settlers by surprise. With more concerted military action, the Indians might well have routed the settlers all along the Minnesota River and followed the river straight up to St. Paul, capturing or killing Governor Alexander Ramsey and creating pandemonium. President Lincoln would have been forced to send major reinforcements and face an even graver threat than the uprising posed. Finally, however, on September 23, 1862, the Indians were defeated at the Battle of Wood Lake and three days later some 1,200 Dakota men, women, and children surrendered to the army.

The Indians' tactics failed, in the end, for the same reasons that they had entered into the war in the first place. The war appeared to have been precipitated by the theft by several Indians of a few eggs from a white store owner. The incident escalated into violence and led to the killing of a white family. The four Indians involved in the incident were members of the Creek Band, a group of malcontents of the Upper Sioux. The braves reported to Elder Red Middle Voice and Chief Little Six, urging that war be declared immediately on the white settlers. Little Six decided that an alliance with the Lower Sioux tribe would be necessary in a war and sought an audience with Chief Little Crow. Little Crow convened a war council and invited Chief Wabasha and Chief Mankato, leaders of the two other Lower Sioux tribes, to the council. Decisionmaking in the Dakota tribes was decentralized and democratic; this included fateful decisions of war and peace. Chiefs could order their braves neither to fight nor to desist from fighting. Little Crow and Chief Wabasha were strongly opposed to war, but Chief Mankato backed the majority of braves, who favored war.

The 1862 uprising in Minnesota was not the end but the beginning of the Indian wars. Little Crow and many of his followers escaped into South Dakota and carried on the fight with the U.S. Army for years. The Sioux had their biggest victory when they killed Colonel George Custer and his entire company at the Battle of Little Big Horn in 1876. But the army pursued them relentlessly, and they were weakened by hard winters, starvation, and disease. The remnants of Little Crow's tribe were annihilated by the army in December 1890 at Wounded Knee.[5]

The Indian wars continued into Thomas Hughes's adulthood and he began to research and interview Indian chiefs, which came to fruition later in his major historical works. But he did not set off on an academic career or to follow the path of a professional historian. His accomplishments were all the more remarkable because he was a busy man of affairs and town father of the bustling Mankato. He was a gifted amateur, something like a David McCulloch, Ron Chernow, or Walter Isaacson of our own day. Moreover, English was not Hughes's first language. The Henry Hughes family spoke Welsh at home.

Hughes went to Carleton College, where he was first in his class, beating out Thorsten Veblen, who was class salutatorian, and becoming the first Hughes to attend the college in a long line of family members who have been enrolled since then. Hughes also met his wife at Carleton. She was in the class behind him and was a gifted artist. She sketched many of the Indian chiefs she met with her husband and her sketches appeared in a number of his books.

After graduating from Carleton, grandfather Thomas Hughes studied as an apprentice in the Mankato chambers of a local lawyer, Judge Waite, and became a leading practitioner in Mankato. Hughes's two sons, Burton and Evan Raymond (known as Raymond), also went to Carleton College as well as Harvard Law School, and like their father returned to Minnesota to live and practice law. Raymond Hughes became his father's law partner, and he and his wife Alice and son Tam went to live with his grandfather in 1927 after the death of Thomas's wife.

The elder Thomas Hughes founded the historical society of Blue Earth County and the archives at Mankato State Teachers College (later a branch campus of the University of Minnesota). He cofounded and helped to build the Minnesota Historical Society into one of the leading institutions of its kind. He deposited many of his notes, along with the records of his and his wife's families, with the society, and he served on its board of governors for many years. Raymond followed his father as a leading citizen of Mankato and served on the boards of many of the organizations founded by the elder Hughes.

Tom Hughes, the subject of this biography, was born to Raymond and Alice Lowe Hughes on December 11, 1925, and was christened Thomas Lowe Hughes. Tom, or "Tam" as his grandfather Hughes nicknamed him to honor the mostly Scottish ancestry of Tam's other grandfather, Dr. Thomas Lowe, moved with his parents into his grandfather's large house in 1927 at the age of two. Grandfather Hughes, lonely after the death of his wife, decided it was a good idea to invite Raymond and family to live with him and eventually inherit the house. It was a good arrangement. The elder Thomas Hughes became especially fond of his grandson and lavished his attention and affection on the boy.

The bonding between Tam and his grandfather was evident early in this affectionate letter from the elder Thomas to a friend, Mrs. Adelaide Skillman, describing his loquacious little grandson:

Feb. 13th, 1928
Mrs. Adelaide B. Skillman
Northfield, Minn.

Dear Adelaide:
Presume you may wonder how we are getting along at Mankato. We are doing about as usual. I am in fair health and Raymond, wife, and little Tam are all doing as usual.
Tam can talk all day long. Is very busy with his games and is a great company for us. There is nothing that he can't talk about these days. His vocabulary is as fully as great as Webster's ever was, but it is sometimes difficult to understand his pronunciation, but that does not bother him a bit. He keeps chattering away about everything under the sun. He is greatly interested in Mother Goose these days, and every night he brings the book to me to read to him, and the little chap seems to have learned the entire book from beginning to end and can repeat it and put additions to it, too. . . .
Very truly yours,
[signed] Thomas Hughes.[6]

The grandfather, who worked in his study every night, kept three-by-five-inch cards as he wrote his books, and Tam imitated this practice. Tam began to write as a young boy. His efforts at composition included this poem written at age four.

> **Some Day**
> *I'm just a little Beginner boy.*
> *But I shall grow up one day,*
> *Into a great big man like Dad,*
> *Then I'll have more to say.*
> *[signed] Tam Hughes, age 4.*[7]

Raymond and Alice Hughes were loving parents, giving their son every opportunity and encouraging him in his interests. They took pride in their son, as most parents do with their children. But they had a feeling that their son was somehow different from most other children, that he was gifted, that his achievements at school and outside of school were unusual. They made every effort to cultivate his interests and talents.

Both Grandfather Hughes and Tam's maternal grandfather, Dr. Thomas Lowe, probably had an even greater impact on Tam's development and early life than Tam's parents had. Tam was also close to Burton Hughes, Raymond's brother, and considered him his favorite uncle. His family as a whole had a great influence on the young boy and anchored him firmly in the values of his native state. In his eighth-grade autobiography at Lincoln Junior High, Tam declared that history was his favorite subject. On the dedicatory page of the fifty-three-page autobiography, Tam wrote: "To my grandfather Hughes, the historian and author, this book is respectfully dedicated. T.L.H."[8]

Tam Hughes was very much a Minnesota boy. But while his parents, grandfathers, and favorite Uncle Burton spent their lives in Minnesota, Tam followed a different path. He moved away from his home state to the nation's capital, where he toiled in the broader arena of national and international politics.

2

Teacher's Pet

Mankato, located about sixty miles southwest of Minnesota's Twin Cities, had a population of about 10,000 at the time of Thomas Lowe Hughes's birth. The Twin Cities were a cultural magnet for the Hughes family. Tam and his younger sister, Marianne, traveled frequently with their parents to concerts, plays, and festivals in Minneapolis and St. Paul. The Hughes children enjoyed more social capital and had a cultural upbringing that was more cosmopolitan than most of their Mankato peers.

In an oral history many years later, Hughes described his circumstances in these terms: "Even though those were the years of the Great Depression, my youth was more or less problem-free—lots of good schooling, lots of devoted attention, and lots of opportunity."[1]

This was certainly an accurate description, as far as it went. But the family records, fastidiously kept by Tom's mother, Alice, and retained by Tom along with his own diaries and papers, show more fascinating details and provide evidence of Tom's precocity. He was a teacher's pet, much praised and admired by his teachers from grade school through high school. Judging from the rave comments of his doting instructors, Mankato's schools had never quite seen his like.

He was also a musical prodigy, giving public piano recitals as early as six to an audience of family, friends, neighbors, and news reporters. Reporters were usually included not merely for the sake of small-town camaraderie but because Raymond Hughes liked to act as a kind of communications director or public relations man for his son. Raymond made sure that all his son's exploits duly made their way into the *Mankato Free Press*.

The boy's musical training suffered a setback when his music teacher fell in love with the town's piano dealer. The couple eloped and went off to Chicago to make a new life. Tam continued his piano lessons but on a less regular basis. He took time off to play the bassoon in the high school's marching band. No meeting of the local Kiwanis Club took place without Tam playing the piano and the businessmen lustily singing their old favorites. When Tam was a high school senior, his role changed. He now gave speeches on world affairs to the local business leaders.

There were early signs of Tam's interests in genealogical studies, stamp collecting, and rare coins. By eight he had a stamp collection of 2,000 items, some of which came from the correspondence he undertook with his relatives abroad. As war clouds gathered in Europe, the boy sought firsthand reports from friendly relatives in Britain.

The boy's genealogy efforts were directed initially to his paternal family. The Hughes family had emigrated originally from Wales to Ohio. Parts of the family then spun off and moved to Minnesota. Tam corresponded with several families in Wales and later visited them, while studying as a Rhodes scholar in Oxford.

Tam's genealogical studies took a big leap, though, and shifted toward the maternal side when he discovered Grandfather Lowe's German art treasures. Dr. Lowe had hidden the treasures in his attic and had generally played down his German ancestry in response to the anti-German atmosphere of World War I.

Tom Hughes's lifelong interest in the Hohenzollerns resulted from his discovery that he was distantly related, on his mother's side, to the German royal family. Tom began his correspondence with Kaiser Wilhelm II at the age of twelve. He typed out a letter to the kaiser, then living in exile in Holland, explaining that he was an American scholar writing a history of the Hohenzollerns. Over seventy years Tom received some 300 letters from the Hohenzollern family, including a few from Kaiser Wilhelm II and his wife Hermine.

Young Tam Hughes was not kidding when he told the kaiser that he was an American historian writing about the Hohenzollerns. By the age of fourteen he had completed two volumes of a projected three-volume history of the Hohenzollern family. Each volume was 400 pages and was self-published in hard cover. After his retirement as president of the Carnegie Endowment of International Peace, in 1991, Tom Hughes returned to his Hohenzollerns, writing articles about the family for scholarly journals and corresponding with the kaiser's grandchildren and great-grandchildren.

Tam's failure to complete the third volume of his projected trilogy on the Hohenzollerns can be attributed to a new passion: his interest in high school debating. This interest blended into, and was subsumed by, the Student Federalist project. Tam traveled all over the state of Minnesota, and in neighboring states, to compete in debate contests. He was the Minnesota debate champion. His most formidable competitors were Emmy Lou Lindgren, of South St. Paul, and Walter "Fritz" Mondale. Emmy Lou (her name was later changed to Clare) became Tam's partner in launching the midwestern chapters of the Student Federalists. Fritz Mondale, whom Tam debated a number of times in high school, became a friend who would move in and out of Hughes's life over the next seventy years.

Tam's precocity was evidently manifested at an early age to his teachers. Petra Lien, a young woman of Norwegian ancestry, was Tam's fourth-grade teacher. She missed him when he moved up to the fifth grade, so she decided to teach him Norwegian during the lunch hour. She told Tam, "You're wasting your time taking an hour at lunch. Give it a half hour, come back here, and I'll teach you Norwegian for the rest of the lunch period."[2] She gave him the Norwegian grammar she had used as a child. She worked with him during the lunch hour throughout the school year. Though Hughes had lost over the years most of what he learned from Miss Lien, at the age of ninety, prodded by a guest at a dinner party, Tom recited the Lord's Prayer in Norwegian.

But Tam had also developed early a certain whimsical quality and a measure of self-understanding. In his eighth-grade autobiography, written as a class assignment, he observed that "from the tales I hear at home, I must have been quite a burden." He described a large birthday party given by his parents for his third birthday. He was "so excited that I didn't know quite what to do, so I went to the kitchen and got an apron and sat on the floor and started playing with it, paying no attention to my guests or anything else."

At a slightly later age, Tam confessed, he and his cousin Ned had soaked Grandmother Hughes's wallpaper with a new squirt gun. His grandfather, Tam noted, was "quite disgusted with this stunt." The gentle self-mockery only enhanced the quality of the autobiography in the eyes of his teacher, Miss Ila Flathers. She returned the paper with this notation: "Thomas, this is the best autobiography that has ever been written in my classes. I hope you will have many more happy events to record. Sincerely, IF [initials of Ila Flathers]."[3]

Miss Flathers was a neighbor of the Hughes family, living one and a half blocks away. She became a frequent dinner guest at the Hughes household on Sunday evenings.

Tam was evidently so enthused by school that he launched a pedagogic career of his own at the age of nine. He "published" a series of five historical studies: "History of the English People: A Complete History of England Up to the Time of George V," "History of the French People," "A Short History of the Life of Napoleon," "The United States before the American Revolution," and "History of the United States since the Revolution." The books, which ranged in length from fifteen to twenty-four pages, were to be used as textbooks. On a back page, under the heading "Other Books in This Series," the titles of other books to come were listed. The author's name appeared on the title page: "Thomas Lowe Hughes, Age 9, copyright 1935," along with his address, 513 Byron Street.

Each book was a multimedia presentation of text (neatly typed with no typos or misspellings) and pictures cut out from magazines and pasted onto the pages. An example of the text is this charming paragraph: "Frederick's name, Barbarossa, meant Red Beard, for in those days it was the custom to give kings nicknames that described them. Frederick was quite old when he started out on the Third Crusade. But he never reached Jerusalem, for in crossing a stream on the way he was drowned. So much for Frederick, the third king."[4]

Evidently Tam felt a responsibility to disseminate his findings to classmates. He was not content to be a scholar who merely published his works and left his readers to do as they chose. He contrived a set of questions to be used as study guides and enrolled an informal class of thirty neighborhood kids, making them take a quiz based on the questions and the textbooks. It is not recorded how the neighborhood mothers reacted when they saw this Tam Hughes kid, the teacher's pet, arrive with homework for their children.

Tam apparently ran out of steam as a schoolmaster and decided to leave the teaching to his teachers. He did not entirely abandon pedagogy, though, for not long after dropping his classes he pioneered a version of ROTC for a smaller group of highly motivated classmates. Each child had to don a World War I uniform and drill in the barn behind the Hughes home, under the command of Captain Tam Hughes.

MUSICAL CAREER

Music was a big part of Tam's upbringing and became a lifelong passion. At the age of four he began piano lessons. By six, he had progressed to his first public recital, playing a Chopin ballade in his own home to an audience of sixty-five neighbors, family friends, and Mankato musicians.

In April 1933, when Tam was seven, the local paper carried a story with the heading "Master Tam Hughes Presents Piano Recital at Home." The article declared that

> with the sweet simplicity of childhood Master Tam, seven-year old son of Mr. and Mrs. E. Raymond Hughes, 513 Byron Street gave a piano recital at his home Saturday afternoon at 4 o'clock before a large group of friends. He played twelve numbers from memory with fascinating musicianship and with his tiny fingers produced the mu-

sical theme of each selection with unusual understanding. "America" given as the finale brought the listeners to their feet.[5]

There is a photo of Tam in a family album at eight or nine seated at and dwarfed by the grand piano. Dressed in a suit, he is looking directly into the camera. The expression on his face is not that of defiance or fear. It is a matter-of-fact expression, perhaps of composure and self-confidence. It seems to say: You think I can't play? Just wait.

The names of his piano teachers, and the dates of their service, were carefully recorded in his eighth-grade autobiography, up to the elopement of his favorite piano teacher. Love, as Tom liked to quip when he looked back on those days, intervened and dealt his musical career a mortal blow. It was not quite a mortal blow, however. He continued to take lessons and to practice the piano. He played the piano in the high school orchestra, which he and another student also conducted.

When Tam also joined the high school marching band, he played the bassoon, a large and rare wind instrument nearly six feet long. He had to march in a row by himself, lest he knock over one of his classmates with the ungainly instrument. He considered but abandoned the idea of becoming a professional musician.

However, he continued to play the piano at parties and to entertain friends, as he did at college and at Student Federalist parties. While in high school, his performance as pianist at the weekly meetings of the Mankato Kiwanis Club enabled him to get to know and be on a first name basis with every business leader in the town. The Kiwanis made a practice of singing old favorites and patriotic ditties at their meetings. Tam's services as accompanist made him popular. His playing helped him win the hand of his second wife, Jane Casey, in 1995, when he wowed her with his rendition of "Wien, du Stadt meiner Träume" ("Vienna, City of My Dreams").

ART COLLECTOR

In 1937, at the age of twelve, Tam was visiting his Grandfather Lowe, who was a "prairie physician" living and working in the small town of Pipestone in the southwestern corner of the state.[6] Lowe also served as mayor of the town for three terms. In 1936 Lowe was elected to the Minnesota State House of Representatives, telling friends that he relied for his majority on the votes of constituents he had delivered as babies.

Grandfather Lowe often took Tam on his rounds to the local hospital, hoping that Tam might one day become a doctor. From time to time he passed on to Tam old medical instruments no longer in use at the hospital.

Tam became fascinated with medicine. In the section of his youthful autobiography entitled "My Future," Tam declared that he wanted to follow in his grandfather's footsteps and become a doctor.

Whereas Grandfather Hughes was a Republican and a devout Congregationalist, Dr. Lowe was a Democrat and was not religious. The two grandfathers were polite and correct in their dealings with each other but were never close.

The boy felt comfortable with both of his grandfathers and from an early age seemed to have a knack for getting along with different kinds of people. Tam's father was a Republican and Tam's mother was a Democrat, like their fathers. Tam had no difficulty in viewing politics and personal relations as separable. On his visits to Pipestone, however, there was something about Grandfather Lowe that puzzled the boy. Lowe was jovial and outgoing, unlike the more reserved Grandfather Hughes, and easily mingled with people like the skillful politician he was. But Tam felt that he was hiding something.

Tam's instincts were accurate. Dr. Lowe's ancestry was three-quarters Scottish and one-quarter German. As a politician he was at pains to hide or play down his German ancestry during the tense days of World War I and as Germany was once again threatening the peace of Europe.

Tam noticed that Grandfather Lowe had made a mysterious reference to his attic on occasion and then had quickly changed the subject. He had deflected Tam's inquiries in evident discomfort. This, of course, only whetted the boy's desire to find out what was going on here. On this particular visit to Pipestone, Tam found himself alone in the house with his mother's sister, Margaret Lowe. Aunt Margaret lived with her father and acted as housekeeper, cook, and keeper of Dr. Lowe's schedule. The boy's curiosity got the better of him, and he decided to take up the subject of the attic.

"Aunt Margaret, what does grandfather have up in the attic that he doesn't want to talk about?" Tam asked.

"Well, I don't know," she replied. "But let's find out. I have the key."

The two attic explorers were amazed by what they found: a vast trove of paintings, prints, portraits of German nobles, maps, busts, bronzes, vases and porcelains, objets d'art, dozens of letters, ledgers, diaries of Schlaberg ancestors, coins, and historical records of the family. The collection originated with Dr. Lowe's maternal grandfather, Charles Frederick Schlaberg, a German nobleman and a direct descendant of the Hohenzollerns in the male line.

Schlaberg was the father of Wilhelmina Lowe, Dr. Thomas Lowe's mother, and a descendant of the Prussian royal family. The romantic life of Charles Frederick Schlaberg is described in Tam's youthful autobiography.

Inspired by his grandfather's collection, Tam broadened his genealogical studies beyond his paternal ancestors to the more glamorous maternal side, including, in particular, the Hohenzollerns. The idea of writing a biography of the Hohenzollern family came to him. To that end, he began his correspondence with the kaiser and other Hohenzollerns whom he now recognized as his own distant relatives. The more than 300 letters he received now reside in the Hughes-Schlaberg collection at Yale University.[7]

The boy's correspondence with the kaiser had one unforeseen consequence. The FBI visited the Hughes household early in World War II to investigate reports of subversive links with Germans. Raymond Hughes was able to assure the authorities that his son's epistolary efforts were merely the result of Tam's youthful enthusiasm for genealogical research. Out of curiosity years later, when he was chief of intelligence for the State Department, Hughes asked William Sullivan, deputy director of the FBI, if his FBI file had shown any suspicious youthful activities. Sullivan assured him that his record was clear, except for an association with the well-known radical Harris Wofford.

Tam's interest began to shift again at about age fourteen, when he had finished the second volume of his projected three-volume history of the Hohenzollerns. He was drawn toward more contemporaneous matters. His compulsive writing habits, however, continued. He began a diary in 1939 but gave it up, he liked to quip, when his life became really interesting. His last diary entry was at the end of December 1960.

From 1939 until 1960, he typically made at least a one-page entry each night, describing the day's events in his diary. He especially liked to record his first impressions of persons he had met. The diary was originally a small four-by-seven-inch notebook, written on both sides of the page. There was frequent underlining of points he thought were important. Later, a larger five-by-eight version became necessary. Each booklet covered one calendar year. The entries showed obvious signs of being rushed during the 1960 presidential election, when Hughes was frantically busy writing speeches for Chester Bowles and John Kennedy, drafting the Democratic platform at the 1960 Los Angeles convention, and campaigning.[8]

RESOLVED: A WORLD GOVERNMENT

In the early 1940s, Tam's new passion in high school was love of debate. This became almost a vocation rather than an avocation. Mankato High School in Tam's first year had a new teacher and debate coach, Alois Kiefer, who inspired Tam to join the debate team. Kiefer quickly recognized in Tam Hughes the makings of a talented debater. Tam responded with enthusiasm to Kiefer's attention and became the anchor of Mankato's championship debate team.

The team was instantly competitive in meets across the state and the wider Midwest region. Hughes made some seventy speaking appearances during one school year. He spoke more than anyone else on the team, but each team member made a serious commitment of time. Mankato won the state championship in Tam's senior year, debating the negative of the proposition, "Resolved: that there should be a world government."

Debate opened a wider world of action, organization, and leadership for Tam. He developed talents that would serve him well in his career. These included not only his exceptional skill as a speaker but the ability to work at a furious pace, to network constantly, and to impress authority figures with his work ethic. At the end of his junior year, Tam received a letter from the executive secretary of the National Forensic League informing him that he had earned more than 100 points, elevating him to the ranks of the best school debaters nationally. At the end of his senior year, he hit the jackpot: he received a congratulatory letter from Senator Karl Mundt (R-S.D.), president of the National Forensic League, telling him that he had compiled 209 points, the highest total of all U.S. high school debaters that year. When debate coach Al Kiefer left Mankato to take a job in Wisconsin in Tam's senior year, Tam became the de facto coach of the team. With the school's blessing, he recruited the debaters, trained them, and organized the team's schedule.

The team's most formidable opponent was usually the much larger South St. Paul High School, which had long been the state's debate powerhouse. The South St. Paul team was led by the attractive, energetic, and gifted Emmy Lou (later Clare) Lindgren, who was one year younger than Tam. The debaters were a band of brothers and sisters who fiercely competed with one another but had a good time doing it. It was not long before Tam Hughes became romantically involved with Emmy Lou Lindgren.

Emmy Lou and Tam were not only romantically involved, they also became partners in a venture that consumed most of their time and attention for the next several years. This venture, the launching of the Student Federalists, would have a large impact on their lives. The fortunes of the two became linked with those of a dashing New Yorker, Harris Wofford, who was a high school student in Scarsdale, New York. Hughes, Wofford, and Lindgren became the leaders of the Student Federalists, a national organization that advocated for world government. As Gilbert Jonas, the historian of the Student Federalists, observes, "These three—Wofford, Hughes, and Lindgren—dominated the Student Federalist leadership until 1946, when Wofford and Lindgren entered graduate school . . . and Hughes went to Oxford as a Rhodes Scholar."[9]

3

Student Federalist

A group of Minnesotans—politicians, public officials, and private citizens—played important roles in the fight against isolationism before World War II.[1] They were alarmed over a possible repeat of America's mistake in not ratifying the League of Nations after the World War I. Some were especially interested in the postwar international architecture, inspired by and following in the footsteps of Minnesota native Frank Kellogg, President Herbert Hoover's secretary of state and the author of the Kellogg-Briand peace pact of 1928.

Having the right enemies was helpful to the internationalist cause. Politicians such as Senators Gerald Nye of North Dakota and Henrik Shipstead of Minnesota, influential figures who had backed the congressional investigations in the 1930s of war profiters who supposedly had misled America into World War I. The investigations had produced the neutrality legislation that forbade the United States from selling arms to belligerent nations. This legislation would presumably help keep America out of future European wars. The neutralists wanted our defense efforts to focus on the Western Hemisphere. In practice, the neutrality legislation prevented the United States from assisting Britain and France against Nazi aggression.

Surprisingly, a driving force in Minnesota's move toward internationalism was a group of youths. The leader of the group was Tom Hughes. Tom had dropped the "Tam" by this time: the nicknames confused people, and he was tired of explaining that his grandfather on his Welsh side had given him the nickname. Tom cofounded the Student Federalists, a national student organization that attracted wide publicity behind the cause of a new League of Nations to keep the peace.

Tom was president of the Student Federalists from April 1944 through September 1945, the organization's heyday. He blended state politics with the larger national picture. Initially, the Student Federalists seemed headed toward becoming an arm of Harold Stassen's presidential campaign of 1944. The Hughes family was close to the Stassen family, and Raymond Hughes was a longtime political ally of Stassen's. In the summer of 1943, Tom and his friend Emmy Lou Lindgren founded a Students for Stassen organization. Tom was in touch with Warren Burger, Stassen's campaign manager, on how the students could best serve the Stassen cause.

The Student Federalist leadership trio—Harris Wofford, Hughes, and Lindgren—were upper-middle-class youths from Republican families. Harold Stassen appealed to them because he was the most internationalist of the Republican politicians.[2] Wofford, in one of his first letters to Hughes, declared, "Your governor has inspired all of us. I'm not up on Minnesota politics, but certainly Mr. Stassen has taken an admirable stand for federation—for principles which we are unitedly working for. I hope you are as proud of him as we are."[3]

Hughes gradually cooled on Harold Stassen, however, in part because of divisions within the Minnesota Republican Party. Senator Joe Ball split from his fellow Republicans over support of Governor Thomas E. Dewey, of New York, as the Republican nominee in 1944 (after it was clear that Stassen's own candidacy was going nowhere). Stassen, anxious to maintain his standing in the party, stayed loyal to Dewey. Senator Ball, whom Tom Hughes had recruited as one of the earliest backers of the Student Federalists, decided that Dewey was not enough of an internationalist. Ball therefore broke with his fellow Minnesota Republicans and backed Franklin Delano Roosevelt's reelection bid in 1944. Tom Hughes sided with Ball, partly because of Ball's strong support for the Student Federalists.

But Tom had another, more compelling reason for supporting FDR's reelection bid. He had fallen under the sway of Hubert Humphrey, a fast-rising star of Minnesota's Democrats, whom he had met early in 1944. Tom and his fellow Student Federalist leaders were all to move leftward and become Democrats.

Tom explained his own transition in a letter to Steve Benedict, a close Student Federalist friend, apropos of the 1945 San Francisco Conference on the United Nations:

Dear Steve,
 Had lots of fun at the Frisco Conf. . . . You would have loved it. Saw our boy Harold [Stassen] in action. . . . God, did you ever see

anyone who could pick up the publicity that guy can. . . . I've cooled a little on Harold. Haven't time to go into it now. Also some tremendously interesting developments in Minn. Politics—Stassen vs. Ball, Stassen pro-Shipstead, strong Democratic Farmer Labor movement is threatening the whole Stassen outfit. . . . Strong Dem. Leadership, of strong liberal but not radical type. Mayor of Mpls [Humphrey] is top man; got to know him quite well. In fact he offered me the state chairmanship of the young Democrats the other day—a position which could be quite something. . . . Turned it down for the time being, but am working on it behind the scenes.[4]

Hughes's energy and organizational skills fit perfectly with the charisma of Harris Wofford. Both men were aided by the good sense and political instincts of their partner, Clare Lindgren. The three combined put the Student Federalists on the map. They formed the leadership triumvirate that built the Student Federalists into a successful, if short-lived, national organization.[5]

THE BIRTH OF THE STUDENT FEDERALISTS

The Student Federalists had a romantic beginning. According to legend, Harris Wofford, a high schooler from Scarsdale, New York, was taking a bath and listening to the radio. His favorite program ended, and something came on that displeased him. He switched the station deftly by stretching his arm across a chair. Luckily, he did not knock the radio into the bathtub and electrocute himself. He managed to switch stations without fumbling with the dial. He found a public affairs program featuring Clarence Streit, a former *New York Times* reporter. Streit had a book calling for a political union of Western democracies modeled on American federalism to fight Nazi aggression.[6] At the same time, he had founded the advocacy organization, Federal Union Inc., to lobby for the draft and for rearmament.

With the country now fully engaged in the war, the mission of Streit's organization had to change. Streit's radio broadcast touted a new edition of his 1939 book and recast the mission of Federal Union Inc. The focus now shifted to the need for a new League of Nations after the war. This was music to Harris Wofford's ears. Harris jumped out of the tub and immediately wrote a letter to Clarence Streit. Harris proposed to form a youth adjunct of Federal Union Inc. to lobby parents and others for the cause of peace via world federalism.

The exact nature of that world federalism was not entirely clear to either Wofford or Streit. Streit envisioned a Western organization of the United States, Canada, Britain, France, the low countries of Europe, Australia, New Zealand, and Scandinavia. Whether the defeated Axis powers would be included was left unclear, as was the potential inclusion of Third World nations. Wofford, who had gone on a world tour as an eleven-year-old under the tutelage of his well-to-do Southern grandmother, wanted to include India. Harris had visited India on this tour, and he believed it would become independent of the British empire after the war. The two men, however, would not quibble over the exact form of the world federalism they favored. That would have to be based on postwar circumstances.

Streit was bowled over by the sophistication and aplomb of the young Wofford when they met. The sixteen-year-old youth was already six feet tall, spoke quietly with a soft, slightly Southern accent (acquired from spending time with his Southern relatives), and bore himself with great dignity. The young man had the stamp of a leader.

The Wofford family moved in high circles. Wofford's father was the CEO of New York State's largest insurance company, and his parents had many prominent friends. Wofford's proposal for a youth arm of Federal Union Inc., Streit believed, would generate favorable publicity and could possibly assist in fund-raising.

For Wofford, the worldly former reporter would provide useful counsel and contacts to help get the Student Federalists underway. Wofford proceeded on two tracks. He formed a number of chapters of high school students in and around Scarsdale, riding around on his bike like a modern Paul Revere sounding the alarm. With Streit's assistance, Wofford was written up in the national press as a bold new champion of peace.

The second track was to raise funds and to build a network of support among prominent New Yorkers and other notables. Harris had stationery printed, identifying himself as the founding president of the Student Federalists, followed by a list of dignitaries who were members of the Student Federalist advisory board. His own home address was given as the headquarters.

Other adults were as impressed by the young man as Streit had been, and Harris quickly proved adept at fund-raising. He did not raise funds for the Federal Union Inc., however, but kept what he raised for his own organization. Harris was not certain what to do with the funds but had a vague vision of expanding the Student Federalists nationwide. Quite naturally assuming a CEO stance like that of his father, Harris took the publicity in stride and promoted himself and the Student Federalists as if he were born to the task.

In December 1942, Clarence Streit received another letter from a teenager. This one came from a high school student in Mankato, Minnesota, and bore the same message: Tom Hughes wanted to champion the cause of peace via some kind of alliance of youth with Federal Union Inc.

Streit was delighted by this development, for Minnesota was a hotbed of isolationism, as reflected in the political posture of Senator Henrik Shipstead. Streit followed the formula he had used with Harris Wofford and welcomed the youth to the cause. Promoting internationalism would be even more important in the Midwest than in New York: on the East Coast, one was largely preaching to the choir. Streit put Tom Hughes in touch with Harris Wofford and suggested that they join forces.

Tom and Harris began to correspond regularly. With Harris offering avuncular advice, Tom made rapid progress. He formed a Mankato student chapter in January and, with the help of Clare Lindgren, his friend from South St. Paul, set up a Twin Cities chapter of the Student Federalists.

Tom shared Harris's instincts for publicity. He moved swiftly to sell himself and the fledgling Student Federalists to John Cowles, publisher of the *Minneapolis Star and Tribune* and a chain of newspapers across the Midwest. Cowles helped Hughes to enlist a host of prominent business figures, politicians, and well-wishers as backers of the students.

By the summer of 1943, though they had not yet met, Tom and Harris had formed a warm epistolary friendship. They could even banter a bit as they reported on their respective activities. In June, Harris wrote, "Dear Tam, Thanks for your swell letter. Although you in Mankato have been beating us in several things in the last few months, we in Scarsdale plan to beat you in the fund raising drive. . . . In the East many of us are beginning today to put all our hopes on Stassen."[7]

The two youths finally met in Peoria, Illinois, at the annual convention of Federal Union Inc., held on November 11–13, 1943. Harris and Tom, seventeen, and Clare, sixteen, hobnobbed with the various luminaries in attendance but spent most of their time planning for the future of the Student Federalists.

Tom's diary for November 11 records his impression of Harris: "The train from NY with the Scarsdale crowd arrived at 1:00 p.m. Finally met Wofford. What a fellow! An all-around whiz." Then Tom added modestly, "I myself introduced Streit for his speech to the convention with a few well-chosen words and apparently I made a good impression. Elected SF Vice President."[8]

Harris was equally impressed with Tom. Evidently, Harris was also smitten with Clare. Thus began the working partnership and romantic triangle of the three leaders of the Student Federalists.

STUDENT FEDERALIST PRESIDENT

Tom Hughes was elected president of the Student Federalists, succeeding Harris Wofford, on April 1, 1944. Harris had paved the way for Tom to succeed him by making sure that Tom chaired all of the working sessions. The election took place on the conference's last day. The event was billed as the organization's first national convention and took place on the Columbia University campus in New York City. In attendance were 202 delegates from twenty-two states. The convention was the result of hard organizational work and fund-raising by the leadership trio, aided by a large number of other Student Federalist recruits, both high school and college students, from across the country. The delegates adopted a platform, "A Challenge to the Elder Generation," drafted by Tom.

The platform stated that America's youth were demanding that political leaders begin planning seriously for the peaceful postwar world. The international system was to be built around a United Nations. This time, America would not stand aloof but would take a leadership role in the new UN.

In his role as Student Federalist president, Tom did not spell out the specifics of the new world order. His aim was to put the issue on the national agenda, seeking allies wherever he could find them. He did not want to put anyone off by specifics they might find objectionable. As an individual, though, Tom was beginning to find his personal footing. He would later describe himself as "a self-conscious liberal with Midwestern populist roots."[9]

In the meantime, Hughes had entered Carleton College in Northfield, Minnesota, and was completing his first year. He majored in international relations. Hughes had been extremely busy in his senior year in high school, but that was nothing compared with his college schedule. As a college student, he juggled a number of different roles and responsibilities, including his Student Federalist work, full-time academic studies, and part-time employment at the dorm to pay for his room and board. He managed all of this by unusual self-discipline but also by charming his professors and the college administrators into supporting his extensive off-campus activities.

He typically rose at 5:45 a.m. to set up breakfast at the dorm (when he was in town). He then attended classes most mornings, studied and handled his considerable correspondence, and had a hurried dinner around 6:00 p.m. More study would follow in the evenings. He invariably wrote his impressions of the day in his diary. He usually did not get to bed before 1:00 a.m.

He was not so much the big man on campus as the big man off campus. The college was unusually accommodating to him. In the spring term of his freshman year, for example, Hughes was absent from campus from March 25 to early May, a period that included final exams. The college arranged for Tom to take his final exams in German and biology at American University in Washington, D.C., where he was working on Student Federalist business.

His travel schedule was hard to imagine. Student Federalist travel records show that, starting with the Peoria Convention in November 1943, Hughes made twenty-nine trips in 1943–1944. Sometimes he traveled on his own, and at other times he was accompanied by Wofford or Lindgren or both.[10] For 1945, the figure was twenty-six, but the trips were sometimes very long. He spent much of the summer of 1944 setting up the Student Federalist's office in Washington, D.C. He was also on the road for extended speaking tours. In the course of one trip to Canada in the summer of 1944, Hughes spoke to a total of more than 10,000 Canadian students.

Tom's presidency lasted from April 1944 to the end of August 1945. His term as president marked the peak of Student Federalist activity. The organization now had a Washington office with a fulltime director for lobbying purposes and as a liaison with federal government officials. It also had a monthly journal, the *Student Federalist*.

Steve Benedict, one of the original Student Federalists, was the journal's editor. The journal carried articles written by Hughes, Wofford, other Student Federalists, and outside experts and also carried news items. The journal enjoyed a significant circulation. It was sent to the membership, about 4,000 at the time, and also distributed to the membership of the Federal Union Inc. Anyone who made a donation got a subscription. The Washington office estimated that the journal enjoyed a total circulation of close to 40,000 in 1945, a surprising figure, even if it was probably an exaggeration.

Tom made appearances at the platform committees of both the Republican and the Democratic national party conventions in 1944. For his presentations, he drew on his platform, "A Challenge to the Elder Generation," which was more hortatory than ideological. He politely chided party leaders for failing to support the League of Nations and called on them to plan now for a new United Nations.

Tom sent his father a telegram on June 22, 1944, excitedly describing the session with Senators Robert Taft, Warren Austin, and John Bricker and other leading Republicans. He reported that they listened to him politely for ten minutes. He also had a separate one-on-one meeting with Senator Bricker, the sponsor of the Bricker Amendment, designed to curb presidential power. Hughes directed his father to make sure that the *Mankato Free Press* announced his forthcoming July 4th appearance on the *America Forum on the Air,* where he and Steve Benedict would debate two students opposed to world federalism.[11]

The original Student Federalists were not cautious careerists out to pad their resumes. The first-generation Student Federalists were largely young, middle-class or upper-middle-class, and WASP (white, Anglo-Saxon, and Protestant). There were few students from ethnic minorities and few older or married students. Almost none came from working-class backgrounds. The original members were certainly ambitious, but their primary motivation was to save the world. In the process, they would live life to the hilt.

With the end of the war, many veterans who attended college on the GI

Bill became active Student Federalists. They helped to usher in a second phase of the Student Federalist movement. The second generation of postwar Student Federalists became more inward looking and more narrowly concerned with student and youth issues like a traditional interest group.

The high point of Tom's presidency probably came in October–November 1944 at a planning conference that he convened to chart the future path for the organization. Fifty delegates gathered in Chicago to hear Tom's statement of goals. The delegates dedicated themselves to creating a Federal World Democracy "even if it took fifty years of hard educational work." To achieve that lofty goal, the delegates outlined a six-year program of education and action. They proclaimed the following goals to be achieved by 1950: 100,000 student members, 30,000 teacher members, and 25,000 student leaders, to be trained in yearly summer camps.[12]

These goals were clearly utopian. Student Federalist membership reached its peak in 1946 at an estimated 5,000 students in some 150 chapters across the country.[13] But Tom Hughes and his friends thought big. On November 11, 1944, the anniversary of the World War I armistice, the Student Federalists under Tom's leadership declared a World Government Day. The group's leadership team also pledged to sell 10,000 copies of *Great Union*, a new book by David Cort, a *Life* magazine editor, published by the Federal Union Inc. The book laid out the practical steps to be taken once the military victory over the Axis powers had been achieved.

The future looked bright for the Student Federalists. The young people had evidently seized their opportunity. They had made themselves a force to be reckoned with in the national political arena, or so they thought. The United States and other Western governments by this time, however, were now beginning to plan seriously for the postwar world. With the U.S. government finally preparing for the future, what role was left for the student?

In February 1945, Hughes asked for and was given permission to take three weeks off from his classes to attend the San Francisco Conference on the United Nations, representing the Student Federalists. The San Francisco Conference marked a turning point in Hughes's views on student (and world) federalism. He was dismayed with the performance of many of the groups calling themselves world federalists. He wrote in a July article in the *Student Federalist*: "I would not be frank if I did not tell you that by their methods and actions at San Francisco, with the exception of Clarence Streit, they [world federalists] contributed little to Conference progress and measurably . . . [hampered] their own future effectiveness."[14]

Being invited to San Francisco as the Student Federalist president should have been a moment of great pride for Tom Hughes. The world's leaders were assembled to plan for the postwar world. The Student Federalists had a seat at the table. But the conference discussions convinced Tom that the

Student Federalists' moment had passed and that others—the real politicians and the powerful interest groups—were taking over. As the war was coming to an end, the Student Federalists were getting a pat on the head and were being shoved aside.

DEMISE OF THE STUDENT FEDERALISTS

Hughes was enthralled by the spectacle of the San Francisco Conference, with so many nations, world leaders, diplomats, and other notables in attendance. Yet he could scarcely comprehend the sheer number and variety of organizations claiming to be part of the world federalist movement. There were at least 2,500 private citizens present, in addition to the forty-nine official governmental delegations. The numerous causes that were championed made for a circuslike spectacle. There were fifty plenary sessions in all and numerous committee and subcommittee meetings each day.

The assorted delegates and the observers worked hard during the day and partied hard every night. The atmosphere in the off-hours resembled that of carnival season. Lord Halifax of the United Kingdom was said to have brought twenty-five cases of his own special Scotch whiskey plus a supply of cigars. Tom Hughes took a day off from the conference to attend a Student Federalist conference at Mills College. He found the Mills conference stimulating and the after-hours private session with the attractive conference leader even more so.[15]

One obvious lesson of San Francisco for Tom was that there was no unity among the family of organizations operating under the banner of world federalism. The Clarence Streit wing had an Atlanticist orientation. Others favored Roosevelt's Four Freedoms as the goal to be guaranteed for all nations. The world federalists concerned with the fate of Third World nations demanded an end to colonialism. Signs of the Cold War to come were discernible in nearly every debate.

Tom was caught up in a whirl of activity on his return from San Francisco. Before leaving for San Francisco he had won first place in a Minnesota oratory contest with a speech called "The Century of Henry Wallace." In March 1945, he won second place with the speech in the national competition of original college oratory. The speech, subsequently published in pamphlet form, impressed Hubert Humphrey, now mayor of Minneapolis, who arranged for Tom to have lunch with Wallace that summer.

In April, Hughes gave the eulogy for Franklin Delano Roosevelt at a convocation of Carleton College students. Hughes's skills as a speaker brought him an invitation to share the stage with Minnesota politicians, including Governor Ed Thye, at the inauguration of the new Carleton president, Lawrence Gould. Tom's witty and erudite talk outshone the politicians' performances and won him the friendship of the new college president,

Lawrence Gould, who came to regard Hughes as the ablest student of his entire tenure at Carleton and years later tried unsuccessfully to recruit him for the college's presidency.

On February 8, 1946, in Concord, New Hampshire, Hughes delivered a fiery keynote address at a meeting he considered the most important in the Student Federalists' history. He called on his fellow members not to "waste our energies by misdirecting them" and to eschew "atomic hysteria." He deplored the endless debates about goals while the practical means to accomplish anything were being neglected. Two things are required, he declared, for the new world order: "a world-wide monopoly of physical force through a political system" and "the effective economic and social development that a world of change demands."

What mattered, Hughes told his Student Federalist colleagues, was getting results by participating in real politics and solving real problems. Making threats, issuing utopian demands, and posturing will not work: "Our decisions on how we will implement our ideals will *work* if we decide whether we shall become policy determiners or mere irritants."[16]

Tom's paper argued that Clarence Streit's original formulation in *Union Now* no longer fit world conditions. The book had focused solely on the Western world and finessed the question of how to reform the United Nations system. This was a clear break from the man who had been so important for the Student Federalists, and it was not taken lightly. But Hughes could not have been pleased with the course of events. By breaking with Streit he had accomplished nothing more than throwing a log on a fire that consumed them both.

In February 1947, at a conference of world federalist organizations in Ashville, North Carolina, Clarence Streit's Federal Union Inc. was abolished and its membership absorbed into a new umbrella entity, the United World Federalists. Cord Meyer Jr., a poet, a war hero who had lost his left eye at Guadalcanal, and a former aide to Harold Stassen, became the head of the new organization. Meyer had a distinctly different view of world federalism from that of Clarence Streit. Streit resigned and severed all ties with the new entity.

The Student Federalists became a division of the United World Federalists. While they were initially given autonomy, the new parent body gradually asserted tight control over what the students could say and do. It was not long before Wofford and Meyer clashed. Students began to resign in protest over the tactics of the United World Federalists. What was left of the Student Federalist division was reorganized into the National Student Association, an umbrella organization with no clear mission.[17]

PERSONAL DECISIONS

The fall of 1946 was the start of Tom's senior year at Carleton College. It was time for him to think seriously about his future. He did not want to be a politician, but he clearly wanted to be in politics. He needed to be privy to the excitement of the political world and wanted the opportunities it offered for public service. The connection with Hubert Humphrey reinforced his interest in American politics—state, local, and national. In the midterm elections that fall, he volunteered to work for the Democrats as a coordinator for the races in southern Minnesota.

More immediately, graduate study was a necessity and required a decision. Law school was one likely prospect for him. This had been the path chosen by his grandfather, his father, and his uncle Burton. But Tom had another idea. He decided to apply for a Rhodes scholarship. Minnesota was a small state, and he could enlist the support of his prominent Student Federalist backers, his professors, and Carleton president Lawrence Gould. His efforts were successful. In December 1946 he learned that he had won the Rhodes.

With the prestigious scholarship in hand, he could now pursue any courses he wanted in the spring term before departing for Oxford in the fall. This left one other delicate issue, which was potentially the most important issue of all. That was the question of his relationship with Clare Lindgren. For some three years Clare had swung back and forth between Tom and Harris in the Student Federalist leadership's romantic triangle. She admired and felt close to both men but was unwilling or unable to choose between them.

All three understood the situation and even managed to laugh at themselves from time to time. But it could not go on forever. The situation briefly threatened to become even more complicated when the new Student Federalist president, Sterling "Coke" Prentice, also became enamored of Clare. He launched a campaign to woo her. Quickly sizing up the situation, however, Prentice decided that discretion would be the better part of valor. He left the battle for Clare's affection to the two current combatants.

While thrilled by the Rhodes, Tom decided that it was time to resolve where he stood with Clare. He told Clare that he was nervous about taking the Rhodes if it meant losing her. Tom had previously asked Clare to wear his pin, a custom which in those days meant "going steady." However, it also implied that an engagement could follow. Clare had hesitated, asking for time to consider and to assess her feelings toward Harris. The situation remained ambiguous, but Clare and Tom were still exchanging long and passionate letters. Now Tom hinted that he might have to give up the Rhodes. He would be away for two years. She still had a year left at the University of Minnesota. Clare, an extremely level-headed person, seems to have resolved the situation. She told Tom that the Rhodes was a tremendous opportunity that no one could afford to pass up. She would finish her studies and he would take the opportunity of his well-earned Rhodes. The future would take care of itself.

Whatever happened between her and Harris, Clare told Tom, was uncertain. Prompted by Tom's declaration that he would forgo the Rhodes for her, Clare told Harris that "there is a great intangible electric spark about the way I feel toward you that doesn't exist with anyone else." However, "there is a big question mark in my mind about us—which has quite an effect in my attitude toward Tam. . . . I quite frankly don't think I'm the kind of person that could get along with your kind of person. I could love you a great deal, but 90% of the time I'd be miserable." Clare, in any case, told Harris apropos of Tom giving up the Rhodes: "I of course told him that was the most foolish thing I'd ever heard."[18]

As it turned out, Tom did accept the scholarship, and Harris did win the girl, albeit two years later. Evidently Clare and Harris still had problems to work out. The "spark" ultimately prevailed over the "99% miserable." They married in June 1948. Tom was away in England and his parents, Raymond and Alice, who had grown close to the Lindgrens, represented the Hughes family at the wedding in South St. Paul.

Harris and Clare remained Tom's closest and best friends over their lifetimes. Tom's and Harris's careers intertwined at nearly every turn. In January 1996, at a memorial service for Clare at Bryn Mawr College (where Harris had been president for ten years), Tom gave an affectionate eulogy that brought tears and smiles to the faces of the many old Student Federalists friends at the service. Harris, Tom quipped, had changed Clare's name twice, once informally, when he changed her name from Emmy Lou, and once legally when he married her. The first name switch had created some confusion in the newspaper reports of Student Federalist activities. Newspapers reported on the careers of what appeared to be two girls from South St. Paul, apparently each other's doppelganger. One story would note that Minnesota teenager Clare Lindgren had visited Eleanor Roosevelt in the White House. Another might report that Emmy Lou Lindgren of South St. Paul discussed youth issues with Eleanor Roosevelt in the White House. These two young women seemed to be crisscrossing the country trying to outdo each other.

Tom visited Clare in the hospital on one of her last days and brought along a sheaf of yellowed newspaper clippings reporting on the adventures of the rival St. Paul girls. Clare managed to smile, and she pronounced the epitaph for the Student Federalists: "We were funny people."[19]

4

With Bowles and Humphrey

Tom Hughes, as a U.S. Air Force Judge Advocate General officer, was qualified for a discharge from active duty after the July 1953 armistice ending the Korean War. He jumped at the chance for an early release but decided to stay in the Air Force reserve. Tom's commanding officer told him that he would grant the release if Tom served in a public sector role for the time remaining on his original tour of duty.

As a stroke of luck, Tom heard from Harris Wofford just as he was seeking the discharge. Harris asked if Tom was interested in a job as assistant to former governor Chester Bowles, succeeding Harris in the position. Harris and Clare were moving to Washington, D.C. Having graduated from Yale Law School, Harris was leaving New Haven to take a job as associate with the prestigious Washington law firm of Covington and Burling. Tom was interested, and Bowles was happy to certify to Hughes's commanding officer that Hughes would be working in a public-service capacity.

LORD OF THE MANOR

Working with Chet Bowles was one of the happiest periods of Tom Hughes's life. Hughes and Bowles became and remained close friends and political allies, a relationship that continued until Bowles's death in 1986.

Tom summed up his 1954–55 time with Bowles in a 2011 oral history interview:

I rented the Woffords' garage apartment in New Haven and began commuting to Essex, about an hour from New Haven. At the rather grand estate with its commodious house, ample lawns rolling down to the river, and the yawl anchored at the dock, I embarked on several months of an idyllic, almost 18th century style existence. I worked on draft chapters of the next Bowles book . . . , helped prepare frequent foreign policy articles for the *New York Times Magazine,* organized a series of appearances for Connecticut TV, and, with secretarial help, drafted or answered much of the heavy Bowles correspondence.[1]

Bowles wrote books, considered himself a politician-intellectual, and had many friends on the Yale faculty. Having served as U.S. ambassador to India in the Truman administration, Bowles knew many diplomats at the United Nations. They often visited the Bowles home in Essex, Connecticut, which was only about an hour and a half's drive from New York City. Krishna Menon once visited Essex at the request of Prime Minister Jawaharlal Nehru. Ravi Shankar played the sitar at social evenings.

Leading politicians from across the country were frequent guests. The press regularly stopped by to interview Bowles. Tom got to know these people and enjoyed the soirees at the Bowles estate.

When Chet and his wife, Steb, traveled, Tom babysat the house and felt like the lord of the manor. Tom sailed on Chet's yawl, entertained friends, and had just the light duties of answering Bowles's mail and fielding press inquiries. His time at Essex had its dark moments. In April 1954, after Hughes learned that his father had been killed in a car crash, he heard the further bad news on a trip home to console his mother that she might have to sell the family home to make ends meet. But the Mankato State Teachers College's board of trustees came to the rescue. In recognition of Raymond's long service on the board, the trustees appointed Alice to the post of college librarian. She happily served there until her death in 1967.

MARRIAGE

After a year living in New Haven and working at the Bowles's home in Essex, a new chapter of life began for Tom. Tom met and fell in love with an attractive and intelligent New Haven woman, Jean Reiman. She was a reporter for the *New Haven Register* and a political activist. At thirty, Jean was just slightly older than Tom. A graduate of Vassar, she was a forceful, outspoken, and extroverted personality that complemented his own, more reserved nature.

Tom met Jean at a party in New Haven. They were both single and slightly older than the rest of the crowd. They were at a stage of life where they were ready to settle down. Tom asked what Jean did. She told him that she was a reporter. What was she working on now, he inquired? She was writing a series on small liberal arts colleges.

"Well," Tom said. "I went to a small liberal arts college I bet you've never heard of—Carleton College in Northfield, Minnesota."

"It so happens that my last article was on Carleton College. Would you like a copy?"[2]

She sent him a copy, and they started dating. She talked easily about herself, her job, her boss at the paper, and the leading political personalities in Connecticut. Because Jean was the drama critic at the *Register*, she and Tom traveled together around the state attending productions at the state's numerous summer festivals—a pleasant aspect of their courtship.

Jean's political interests also especially appealed to Tom. As a liberal Democrat she was a great fan of Chet Bowles. She knew Connecticut politics well and could tutor Tom on the quirks of the state's politicians. She had once run, unsuccessfully, for the state legislature in a Republican-leaning district. She had nonetheless done well, garnering more votes in the Republican district than Governor Abe Ribicoff, who was running at the head of the Democratic ticket. She always jested with Ribicoff when they met, telling him that she would be happy to give him political advice when he needed it.

Jean was also friendly with Republicans. She was a favorite of her boss, the publisher of the *Register*, who was a prominent Republican. She started her days at the paper by reading him the *Wall Street Journal*, since he was almost blind.

Jean was also a friend of Dorothy Bush, the wife of Senator Prescott Bush. Mrs. Bush wrote a weekly column for the *Register* describing her activities as a Senate wife and commenting on Washington's social life. Jean edited Dorothy's columns, which were very long; Jean had to edit them mercilessly. Somehow she managed to stay on good terms with Dorothy while whacking off 60 to 70 percent of Dorothy's prose.

Tom and Jean married in 1955. Chet Bowles was best man, and Harris Wofford was an attendant. Clare, for some reason, chose not to attend. Chet and Steb threw a lavish party at their home for the young couple, with Tom's mother and sister, Jean's mother, many friends of the couple, Bowles neighbors, and other guests enjoying the evening.

The wedding ceremony took place at the Yale University chapel. One of her colleagues at the *New Haven Register* had the bright idea that Jean's honeymoon would make a great feature story, and so Tom and Jean took their honeymoon in the company of a reporter and film crew. The story never ran, but Tom and Jean had an abundance of honeymoon pictures. Tom, now a husband, began to think seriously of his future.

WASHINGTON ON THE HORIZON

Tom, as noted, had been hired to do research for Bowles's books, articles, lectures, and preparation for his TV show. Chet came up with the idea for a new book shortly after Tom arrived on the scene in spring 1954. Tom initially spent much time on the book, *The New Dimensions of Peace*.[3] A new style of politics was emerging, the book asserted, and was replacing the traditional notions of power politics.

But Chet soon found another and more important role for Tom. He asked Tom to travel the state with him, meeting state politicians and important constituents. The aim was to assess the chances for success when and if Chet ran for office again. To be useful to Chet, Tom knew that he needed a crash course in Connecticut politics.

In retrospect, Chet told Tom, he considered his worst decision as governor had been to appoint his former partner William Benton, of the advertising firm Benton and Bowles, as interim senator instead of one of the Connecticut politicians who desperately wanted to be named. This had exacerbated every subsequent political decision that Bowles faced.

Indeed, Tom's initial exposure to Connecticut politics was eye-opening. Tom considered himself a hard-headed political veteran, but he was taken aback by the differences he saw between Minnesota's and Connecticut's politics. In sharp contrast to Minnesota's high-principled and "good government" style, Connecticut voters cast their ballots in ethnic blocs (Italians voted Republican, the Irish voted Democratic, Jews were Democrats, and so on). Party bosses played the dominant roles in choosing candidates.

The Minnesota style of issue-oriented politics was distinctly unlike the bare-knuckled, transactional style of Connecticut's politics. Bowles, Hughes surmised, would have fit better in Minnesota than here. Connecticut seemed to Hughes a state too small for the outsized ambitions of a large cast of political heavyweights. And Bowles, a patrician WASP with high principles and an intellectual approach to issues, was the odd man out.

Chet passed on the gubernatorial race in 1954, though Tom had recommended strongly that he run. Chet's view was that the Connecticut governor's office did not give him the ideal platform for influencing national and foreign affairs. Tom argued that, even if Chet were most interested in having a national voice, the Hartford office would provide a better platform than remaining in Essex as a private citizen.

In 1955 Bowles deemed that 1956 would not be a good year for the Democrats. He therefore decided to pass up a shot in 1956 for a U.S. Senate seat from Connecticut. With Dwight Eisenhower likely to win reelection, Chet reasoned that even if he won the nomination for the Senate, an effort that almost certainly would be contested, he would face an uphill battle in the general election. His opponent would be the popular Republican incumbent, Senator Prescott Bush.

Bush had consolidated his position in Connecticut politics. He had lost his attempt at a Senate seat by only 1,000 votes in a special election against William Benton. But Bush went on to win another special election, this one occasioned by the death of the Democratic incumbent, Brian McMahon, the principal author of the important 1946 atomic energy legislation. Bush then served ably in the Senate. Given Bush's solid record and Ike's presence on the ballot, Bowles considered that beating Bush in 1956 would be a long shot.

Hughes had looked forward to a campaign. He relished the prospect of being a top aide to Chester Bowles in office. Chet's decision against running in 1956 removed those hopes for now. Chet would not be eligible to run for anything until 1958. Absent the immediate political challenge, Tom began to chafe at his role. Jean also goaded him to think of spreading his career wings.

In the summer of 1955, not quite out of the blue, an attractive offer came from Max Kampelman, Hubert Humphrey's legislative counsel and closest aide. Max called to ask if Tom would be interested in joining Humphrey's staff as legislative counsel. Max had decided that support of his growing brood of children required more income than his government salary afforded. He planned to go into private law practice in Washington.

In his memoir, Max described Tom Hughes as "young but mature, balanced, and wise. Extraordinarily bright and an excellent writer, he was from a small town in southern Minnesota. While foreign policy was his main interest, he had an inquiring mind and broad knowledge of domestic issues."[4]

For his part, Tom knew Max well, having worked with him in Humphrey's Senate office in the summer of 1951. Earlier, Tom had been well aware of Kampelman's role when Humphrey was mayor of Minneapolis: Max had mobilized the Jewish community of Minneapolis behind Hubert's candidacy and then had run Humphrey's fair employment board to ensure minority rights, the first such entity in the nation. Although ostensibly designed to protect the rights of Black Americans, there were few Blacks in Minneapolis or the Twin Cities then, and the board actually had the role of integrating the Jewish residents into the leadership ranks of the community.

Max was an interesting man. Born in New York to Jewish immigrant parents, Max had migrated to Minnesota during World War II to take part in a hunger experiment at the University of Minnesota. Max was a conscientious objector and volunteered for the hunger experiment to escape from the boredom of a camp for objectors in upstate New York. He thence became an adopted Minnesotan, completing both a Ph.D. in political science and his law degree at the University of Minnesota.

In searching for his successor, Max immediately thought of Tom Hughes. Max had been impressed by Tom's summer work in the Humphrey office several years earlier. The 1951 summer assignment had gone well—so well that it had extended part-time into the fall. Tom was able to integrate the project into his legal studies with sponsorship of several of his professors. Furthermore, Max knew that Humphrey would be receptive to Tom's appointment.

The offer of the summer job had resulted from a chance reunion of Tom with his old friend, Hubert Humphrey, the junior senator from Minnesota, who had been elected to the U.S. Senate in 1948. Tom was unhappy for most of his first year at Yale Law School (1949–1950). He found his studies excruciatingly dull, nothing like the broad issues he wrestled with at Carleton and at Oxford. He had also broken up in the fall with a girlfriend, Mary Morris Gamble, which had not enhanced his morale. Matters improved with the moot court proceedings in the spring term. Moot court revived his competitive instincts, and he won the competition.

But this was not enough to alter his resolve to return to Minnesota for his second year of law school. Tom worried that his education was posing financial burdens on his family. His sister, Marianne, was attending Carleton College, and his father was now covering the costs of two kids in college at the same time.

Hughes took his second year of legal studies at the University of Minnesota Law School. This proved to be a good decision. His father appreciated the gesture, and his mother liked having him near home. Tom took the required courses and had several of his classes with a Yale professor who was visiting for the year at the law school.

In the winter, back in Minnesota, Tom suffered from recurrent colds. During the spring term, a bout with the flu put him into the university hospital. As a stroke of luck, his neighbor in the next room was Senator Hubert Humphrey, who was in the hospital for a hernia operation. The two men spent many hours discussing politics, the Senate, and legal practice.

Humphrey proposed that Tom come to Washington and work for him over the summer. Hubert had in mind a project involving the Senate Committee on Labor and Public Welfare. This fit in well with Tom's legal studies and his intellectual interests.

Tom enjoyed the experience as a Senate staffer. He drafted a committee report that interested several of his Yale professors. Tom meanwhile had decided to return to Yale for his third and final year in law school, when the university gave him a proctor's job in an undergraduate dorm. The job carried light duties and room and board plus tuition.

Now, in 1955, the chance to return to Washington and to Humphrey's office was enticing. Many old Student Federalist friends were in Washington, including Harris and Clare Wofford, Steve Benedict and Coke Prentice in the Eisenhower White House, Gil Jonas running the American Friends of Vietnam, and others. Washington was an exciting place for young professionals, very sociable yet with a small-town feel.

Tom and Jean made a trip to Washington to reconnoiter, staying with Max and Maggie Kampelman at their large house in Chevy Chase, Maryland, on the outskirts of the District of Columbia. Max was frank in warning Tom about the downside to the job. He told Tom that working for Humphrey would be demanding, especially so for Tom as a newlywed. There were long hours and the pressures of short deadlines. Hubert sometimes imposed unreasonable burdens on the staff. There were also personal animosities among the staff, which Hubert did not like to deal with, leaving such unpleasant matters to fester unless Max resolved them.

Forewarned, the newlyweds decided to take their chances, and Tom accepted the offer. He would come as soon as he was free; October was settled on, if this timing was acceptable to Chet. As a sign of the less pleasant side of the job, Tom ran into trouble negotiating with Herb Waters over the salary. Waters was one of Humphrey's first staff members, dealing mainly with agricultural issues and Minnesota politics. He had ill-defined managerial duties but was a notably poor manager. Indeed, he was the source of many internal problems.

Tom wanted a salary of $9,000, but Waters balked, saying that $8,000 was absolutely the top limit. The dispute nearly derailed the appointment. After much wrangling, and the diplomatic intervention of Max Kampelman, a compromise was reached at $8,500.

Money was always tight in the Humphrey office. Raises were hard to come by. Hubert's salary as a senator at the time was $22,000, impossible for him to live on. Humphrey was not an independently wealthy man. He and his wife, Muriel, had to raise four children, maintain residences in Minnesota and Chevy Chase, and do a modest amount of entertaining for him to function as a senator. Hubert was thus forced to supplement his Senate salary with $30,000 in speaking fees, which meant that he was frequently on the road.

BUSY SENATE YEARS

The Humphrey offer presented no problem to Chet Bowles. Chet was well known, and much admired by his peers, for his ability to spot talent. He took an interest in promoting the careers of those who worked for him. Furthermore, Hubert and Chet were friends. They were ideological bedfellows at the liberal end of the Democratic Party spectrum. Chet was happy because he would now have good ties in Congress and a stronger Washington presence.

Humphrey, meanwhile, had strengthened his own position by persuading President Harry Truman to appoint Republican governor Luther Youngdahl, Hubert's likely and most formidable 1954 rival, to the federal bench. Hubert thus easily won reelection in 1954 against a weak Republican opponent.

More important for Tom, Humphrey's fortunes in the Senate were on the rise generally. Hubert was originally an outcast with Southern colleagues because of his ringing civil rights speech at the 1948 Democratic convention. Hubert gradually won over his Senate Democratic associates by dint of his hard work and cheerful disposition. Humphrey's rise was significantly aided by the fact that Majority Leader Lyndon Johnson had taken a shine to him being a link to the Senate's liberals.

Humphrey's office was the busiest in the senate, busier even than the office of the majority leader. Hubert poured forth a seemingly endless stream of legislative proposals, negotiated constantly with Senate colleagues, and backed liberal causes of every kind. Hughes did the staff work for what later became the Peace Corps, the Arms Control and Disarmament Agency, the Food for Peace program, the Youth Conservation Corps (modeled on the New Deal's Civilian Conservation Corps), and amendments to the Development Loan Fund.

Hubert also proposed a host of measures dealing with health care (the model for Medicaid), civil rights, federal aid to education (reflected in the National Defense Education Act of 1958), better housing and aid for the homeless, the test ban, and full employment. Tom did the staff work for these measures. Indeed, most of the New Frontier's domestic policy programs originated in the Humphrey office and were later picked up by John Kennedy.

The typical office schedule for many senators in the 1950s, and especially for those with safe seats, was 8:30 a.m. to 5:00 p.m. The staff hours for most Senate offices were relaxed when the Senate was not in session. For the Humphrey office, however, as Max Kampelman had warned, the work routinely went into the dinner hour. And, as Max had warned Tom, when Humphrey was in town, the hours could run even later. Hubert was interested in everything and dreamed up legislative initiatives on a dazzling array of issues.

Hubert liked to have a beer after work at the Carroll Arms, the legendary old hotel located just two blocks from Humphrey's Senate office. The Humphrey party would take seats at the opposite end of the large dining room from where Senator Joe McCarthy, having been censured by his Senate colleagues, was drinking himself to death, accompanied by a few of his remaining hangers-on.[5]

Since Hubert's interests were broad, Tom's duties were broad. As new legislative counsel, Tom was encouraged to take initiatives of his own. One such Hughes initiative was the "paired votes" system. By this device, Humphrey and another senator could neutralize their opposing votes on a measure by agreeing to be absent for a floor vote.

On a bill amending the electoral college, Hughes studied the bill and recommended that Humphrey oppose it and pair with a proponent favoring the bill. Humphrey mildly reproved Hughes, saying that, of course, he opposed this bill, but merely opposing it was not enough. A press release should be issued spelling out why Humphrey was opposed.

Humphrey, though more congenial and informal than most of his Senate colleagues, insisted that his staff follow strict rules and practices. He demanded, for example, that every letter from a constituent be answered within one day, an unreasonable requirement that led to two letters having to be written: the first letter would explain that the letter had been received, and the second, an actual response, would be sent at a later time. Humphrey, who at times demanded impossible deadlines, got results.

One memo of January 1956, labeled from "Senator to Tam Hughes," observed that veterans groups were strongly opposing the Hoover Commission recommendations on the Veterans Administration. Tam was directed to look into the background of disability payments for veterans and lay out the rationale for legislation that would ensure full access of veterans to VA hospitals.[6] Here, Humphrey was sketching out his proposal, which would be an early version of the Johnson administration's Medicaid legislation.

On February 15, 1956, Humphrey issued elaborate instructions to "Tam, Bill [Connell], and Herb [Waters]" on how the office should handle appropriations bills.[7] The bulk of this work fell on Tom, since he handled the domestic appropriations bills on health, education, welfare, labor, and the State Department. Herb Waters took care of bills coming from the Department of Agriculture. Bill Connell was to handle public works projects in Minnesota and other Interior Department measures.

Staff members were supposed to follow the course of all legislation sent by the various executive departments to the Appropriations Committee. They were to prepare a press release indicating Humphrey's position on each bill and any amendments Humphrey would offer.

Staffers should also ensure that the press release was covered in the local Minnesota papers. The press release should not automatically favor increases in appropriations because "we do not want to look like spendthrifts." The press release should always give a clear rationale for an increase or decrease in an appropriation.

When action on a bill was completed in committee and on the floor, the staffer should prepare another press release indicating what happened and claiming credit if the committee or the full Senate adopted any Humphrey-proposed amendment.

Hughes's interest in foreign policy benefited from and reinforced Humphrey's own interests in the area. Lyndon Johnson put Hubert on the Senate

Foreign Relations Committee and asked him to follow John Foster Dulles's actions closely. Humphrey became an incisive critic of Secretary of State Dulles and garnered much favorable publicity in the process.

Humphrey was also a member of the U.S. delegation to the UN General Assembly, and this stimulated his long-standing ties with international volunteerism. "People, Peace, and Progress," the title of a speech Humphrey delivered in 1958, summed up the interrelated themes that drove his public career.[8]

When a visiting student asked him in 1963 what he had done that was important legislatively, Humphrey replied,

> Well, there is nothing around which everyone calls "the Humphrey program" or "the Humphrey Act." But I like to think I've had an effect on many pieces of progressive legislation in the past several years. And there are some, I think it is fair to say, I initiated. I am most proud of three: my work for the Nuclear Test Ban Treaty, the Food for Peace program, and the Peace Corps.

He added a fourth achievement in 1964: "the strongest civil rights act approved by Congress since the Reconstruction years after the Civil War."[9]

Tom Hughes attended the 1956 Democratic convention with Hubert. Hubert believed that Adlai Stevenson had promised to name him as the vice presidential nominee, and Tom saw Humphrey's bitter disappointment at losing the nod. Adlai had allowed himself to be outmaneuvered by Estes Kefauver into throwing open the nomination to the convention, reneging on his promise to Hubert. But Humphrey was not a good hater, and he bounced back to support the ticket. Hubert told Hughes that Eisenhower, despite his heart attack, would defeat any Democrat in 1956.

Tom knew that Hubert was seriously interested in the Democratic nomination for president in 1960. This prospect had a worrisome effect on Hughes. He was concerned that Humphrey did not have the funds, the campaign staff, or the "laid-back style that was suited for the age of television. The notion of working on a losing presidential campaign contributed to a sense that it was time for Tom to leave the Humphrey office. Tom thought he should do so before 1959, since preparing for 1960 would be in full swing by that time and any departure then would be viewed through a political lens. His leaving would attract unfavorable notice and be written up as a close aide abandoning a sinking ship. Hubert would never forgive him.

Tom was, in fact, worn out after three years of running Humphrey's busy office. He was fed up dealing with the staff's personality conflicts, which Humphrey left for him to manage. The personnel problems Max had warned him about were never resolved. Then there were the constant late hours. His own growing family responsibilities made this aspect of the job increasingly difficult. In December 1956, Tom and Jean's son Evan was born, and a second son Allan was born in early 1959.

In 1958 Tom and Jean had bought a house and moved from Old Town Alexandria to Chevy Chase, Maryland. The prospect of practicing law did not appeal to him. He had enjoyed the trial work in Las Vegas during his first year in the Air Force and appellate work in San Antonio later, but he could not see a whole career of this. While waiting for the result of his bar exam in Minnesota, he had worked with his father on a case before the Minnesota Supreme Court. Tom cherished this experience because of the quality time with his father it afforded before Raymond's sudden death two years later.

As he reflected on his position, Hughes concluded that the kind of job he wanted was one that was like the one he now had with Humphrey. Only this time, if it were possible, he wanted more regular hours and better pay. Chet Bowles's victory in a November 1958 House of Representatives election in Connecticut solved the problem.

5

Bowles in Congress

Chet Bowles won narrowly in November 1958 after a tough race in Connecticut's Second District, a traditionally Republican district. Bowles thereupon became an elder political leader, like a latter-day John Quincy Adams, having abandoned his hopes for higher office. The idea of a congressional seat for Bowles emerged after the bitter pill of his losing the Democratic nomination for the U.S. Senate. Bowles lost an acrimonious three-way convention fight involving his former partner William Benton, himself, and Thomas Dodd, a battle eventually won by Dodd.

Bowles coveted the Senate nomination in 1958 because he thought this to be a good year for the Democrats. Both Connecticut's party chair, John Bailey, and Governor Abraham Ribicoff supported Dodd for the Senate in 1958. Dodd was Catholic, and Ribicoff, who was Jewish, wanted a Catholic on the ticket, for balance. Bailey and Ribicoff also feared that if Dodd lost his bid at the convention, he would force a primary fight. It was not beyond Dodd, out of sheer malice, to bring the house down on their collective heads.

Bowles had bowed out gracefully with a concession speech that was well received by the delegates. He thus won points even from his erstwhile detractors.

Tom Hughes flew to Hartford to attend the convention, staying with Chet and Steb. He participated in planning and implementing the convention strategy and returned to Washington shortly after the convention. He later learned what happened next.

Several days after the convention, John Bailey and Abe Ribicoff devised a plan for Bowles to run for Congress in Connecticut's Second District. If they could persuade Chet to run, this would at least partly heal the wounds from the convention. Furthermore, it would greatly strengthen the ticket.

In urging Bowles to run, the party leaders promised to deliver the nomination to him without further effort on Bowles's part. Bowles was initially unimpressed by the offer, still smarting from the Senate rebuff, but he gradually warmed to it. Ribicoff and Bailey forced the withdrawal of the luckless prospective nominee and installed Bowles as the candidate. Not one to enjoy the nitty-gritty of politics, Chet Bowles took no notice of the shenanigans and pretended to be surprised. He announced that he would bow to the leaders wishes and, as a loyal soldier, would accept the party's draft.

Bowles asked Tom to join him and run his congressional office if he won the general election. Bowles was not enlisting Tom for day-to-day office management (which he knew had become an irritant to Tom in the Humphrey office). Rather, Chet told Tom, he sought Tom's policy advice and his talent for strategic thinking. As chief of staff, Tom would get the top salary $12,500, a considerable improvement over what he was getting from Hubert.

Chet confided to Tom that he intended to serve for only one term. Chet intended to be heavily involved in 1960 presidential politics, either as a dark horse candidate or supporter and campaigner for the party's nominee. If he were appointed to a senior State Department post in a Democratic administration, Chet wanted Tom to go with him in an important role.

BOWLES-HUGHES TIES

Hughes had never fully left Bowles. Chet frequently telephoned Tom at the Humphrey office to get an update on developments in Washington. He gave Tom frequent rundowns on the latest twists in Connecticut politics. Chet visited his friend Hubert often and would call Tom to arrange the meetings. Similarly, Tom never really left Hubert when he rejoined Chet. Bowles and Humphrey were close friends, and Hughes continued to serve both men.

The easy relationship between Bowles and Hughes was illustrated in an amusing episode during the 1956 presidential campaign. Chet, campaigning hard for Stevenson after the 1956 Democratic convention, heard reports that General Douglas MacArthur had been privately bad-mouthing Eisenhower to friends and associates.

Stevenson's headquarters surmised that MacArthur might be ready to endorse Stevenson and sent Bowles to assess the general's intentions. Bowles invited Hughes to join him on this visit to the general's penthouse at the Waldorf Astoria in New York City. The two emissaries from the Stevenson camp duly paid a call on MacArthur. Ushered into "the presence" by a MacArthur aide, Bowles exchanged pleasantries for a few minutes and then got to the point.

He had heard reports, Bowles told the general, that MacArthur had reservations about Eisenhower's leadership qualities. Were these reports accurate?

"Yes, that man Eisenhower is plain incompetent. Always has been. Knew him well. He was with me in the Philippines, as you know. All he did was play Bridge. Still doing it. What a disaster!"

"Well, general, if you feel that strongly, would you consider endorsing Governor Stevenson in the campaign?"

"Endorse Stevenson? Oh, hell no! That would be worse than disaster! Be serious, Mr. Bowles," said General MacArthur.

With that, General Charles Willoughby, MacArthur's aide, showed the two Stevenson emissaries the door. Back at street level, Bowles remembered what Eisenhower had once said about MacArthur: "He was the best actor I ever served under."[1]

Hughes aided the Bowles campaign for Congress as best he could from Washington. He sketched out for Bowles how to organize the congressional office and discussed the issues to be pursued in the campaign and implemented afterward, if Bowles won. Tom followed the campaign closely and supplied Bowles regularly with draft speeches and campaign ideas. It was understood that if Chet won, Tom would join him. The decision, it seemed, had already been made somewhere along the line in their collaboration on the congressional bid. Bowles does not quite tell it this way in his memoir. He states that he merely solicited Tom's advice on candidates to run his office, and that it was Tom who declared "Why not me?"[2]

LEAVING HUMPHREY

Still, it was not going to be easy to leave Humphrey. Tom had known Humphrey since he was eighteen. He had first worked with him in the 1944 FDR reelection campaign. He worked for Hubert again in 1951 and had left Bowles to become Hubert's legislative counsel in October 1955. That transition had been easy. This one would not be.

Tom was moved by a letter Hubert had sent him in April 1945. Hubert said, "You have gained quite a reputation for being a sound thinker and a capable speaker. All of us recognize your leadership ability, and are looking forward to the day when your voice will be heard in this state. . . . I consider it a real privilege to know you, and I trust we will see each other as often as possible."[3]

Hughes knew that politicians had elephantine memories. They never forgot or forgave a slight. Even Humphrey, more amiable and forgiving than most in public life, remembered who did or did not go to the airport to greet him on returning from a trip.

Tom's time with Humphrey had been an exhilarating experience, despite the job's irritants. In most respects, the work had suited him perfectly. He had gotten to know every key Senate aide and many senators. Tom had learned much about the Senate's procedural arcana and even more about the major issues. To be effective, Hughes believed, a legislator had both to see the big picture and to understand how the details shape that picture. Humphrey, initially disparaged by the Senate elders, had gained the respect of skeptical colleagues.

Tom, for example, saw how Senator Robert Kerr, a longtime champion of big oil, had sought out Humphrey after the two had clashed on the Senate floor over the oil depletion allowance. Kerr congratulated Humphrey for his analysis of the energy bill's details. Kerr told Humphrey that he had learned a great deal from his discussion of depletion allowance. The Oklahoman became an ardent admirer of his Minnesota colleague. It was not merely substantive policy details that Tom had learned from Humphrey. More important was the lesson that the real politicians—the senators that mattered—behaved toward their colleagues in a gentlemanly fashion.

In this connection, Humphrey's relationship with Lyndon Johnson intrigued Hughes. The majority leader recognized Humphrey's qualities and considered him his major link with the party liberals. The outsized personality of Lyndon Johnson was a source of fascination for Tom. Johnson, in a moment of frustration, had once kicked Hubert in the shin, causing a nasty bruise and swelling. Humphrey had jokingly pulled up his pants leg and showed reporters the bruise as proof of his loyalty to the majority leader.

This was not quite the gentlemanly behavior Tom observed in the usual behavior of senators. Johnson had a dark side that was frightening. Tom could see that the kick had hurt Hubert more in the ego than in the shin. Hughes's diary entry after meeting Johnson for the first time was "very Southern, very dominant, very firm handshake."[4]

As he prepared to leave Humphrey and the Senate, Tom recalled other scenes involving Johnson. Some were scenes that Tom witnessed himself, and some had been relayed to him by Humphrey. A favorite was the time Hughes was conferring with Humphrey in the Senate chamber just after Senator John Kennedy had delivered a major speech denouncing colonialism and specifically lambasting French policy on Algeria.[5]

As Humphrey and Hughes were walking from the Senate chamber, Johnson approached and asked Humphrey what he thought of Kennedy's speech. Before Hubert could respond, Lyndon observed, his face crinkling into a big smile, "I think Madame Alphand [wife of the French ambassador] won't be playing the zither for Jack anymore."[6]

Another favorite story for Hughes, told to him by Humphrey, was Johnson's theatrical removal of the elderly Theodore Green (D-R.I.) as chair of the Senate Foreign Relations Committee. Johnson called an urgent meeting of all members of the committee, at which he waxed eloquent on the virtues of the ninety-year-old senator as the elderly Green sat nodding in his chair. Johnson declared that he always felt greatness whenever he was in the presence of Chairman Green. To his distress, the majority leader solemnly told the assembled senators, Green had expressed the desire to resign his post.

Fortunately, however, Green would stay on in the Senate. Johnson called on the senators to express their appreciation for Green's outstanding leadership. As each senator in turn expanded on the tributes of his predecessors, Green's contributions took on Lincolnian dimensions.

Then an unexpected departure from Johnson's script occurred. Senator George Aitken (R-Vt.), evidently misled by all of the tributes, declared that perhaps Green should reconsider and withdraw his resignation. Startled, Johnson turned to Green and suggested that he should perhaps step into the hall to think the matter over.

"Think what over?" said Senator Green.

"Your resignation," said the Majority Leader.

"Resignation? What resignation?" said Senator Green.

Taking Carl Marcy, the committee's staff director, by the collar, Johnson whispered, "Take this old fart out into the hall and make sure he doesn't retract his resignation."

Johnson then proceeded, without oratory, to appoint Senator J. William Fulbright (D-Ark.) as chair of the Foreign Relations Committee.[7]

"The whole time I was with Humphrey," Hughes remarked to me once, "I never had lunch or dinner alone." There were always meetings with individual senators, groups of senators, the chief aides to senators, sessions to prepare for hearings, negotiations with executive branch officials, protocol meetings or lunches with embassy officials, press briefings, private conversations with reporters, luncheons with important visitors, or myriad other events.

Hubert and Muriel Humphrey were generous with their hospitality, frequently entertaining Tom and Jean Hughes. Tom drove to work many mornings with Hubert and Hubert's next-door neighbor, George McGovern, as well as sometimes with Gene McCarthy, a representative in Congress before his 1956 election as Minnesota's junior senator. Hughes admired and liked both Humphrey and Bowles. He wanted to remain on good terms with both of them. He considered Bowles to be a more interesting man and perhaps this showed. This was all the more reason why Tom wanted to assure Humphrey that they would stay in close contact.

Key staffers never entirely leave their bosses unless there has been a personal breach. Reciprocity of favors binds them. The formal employment contract is merely a step in a larger process of human relations and is usually less important than the informal ties.

With this in mind, Hughes drafted a lengthy letter of resignation filled with expressions of gratitude to Humphrey. Hubert was away in Europe on an extended trip and was expected to finish up by meeting Premier Nikita Khrushchev in Moscow (a seven-hour marathon meeting, as it turned out, that boosted Hubert's standing at home).

Tom did not want to surprise Humphrey on his return home. It would be most unfortunate if Hubert found the office turned upside down and with no one in charge. He arranged to have lunch with Max Kampelman to get Max's advice on how to proceed.

Tom explained the situation to Max and showed him a draft of the letter to Humphrey. A key passage of the draft noted, "In addition to my deep appreciation for the many valuable experiences I have had in the office since 1955, I want to add this: I hope you will continue to feel perfectly free to call upon me at any time for any special assignments I can perform. . . . I personally want to continue to keep in frequent and close contact with you."[8]

Hughes was aware that the dual loyalty to Bowles and Humphrey might create trouble down the line. But navigating conflicting loyalties is the essence of politics. Tom wanted to help ease the transition for Hubert. What did Max think?

Max observed, "I thought this might be on your mind when I noticed that Chet won his House race."[9]

Hughes and Kampelman discussed the staff situation and the problems Hubert would face in finding Tom's replacement. Kampelman observed that Hubert's main problems resulted from his own failure to fire Herb Waters long ago. Of course, this was difficult because Waters had been with Humphrey for a long time. Max was planning a trip to France and had a dinner engagement scheduled with Hubert. He would personally deliver Tom's letter of resignation and try to reassure Hubert. When Max gave Tom's letter to Hubert in Paris, he assured Hubert that Tom would stay until the end of the year and would help out with the transition.

Although Hubert apparently took the news of Tom's departure in seemingly good grace, Hughes's diary entries for November 1958 paint a more nuanced picture. Hubert wrote to Herb Waters that he was "upset to have Tam's resignation." But he could understand since he knew that Tam was very close to Bowles. Moreover, "have profited by having him three years and I am glad he is staying through December."[10]

Hughes received a "letter from HH written in Geneva, friendly but brief."[11] The Hughes diary also recorded that "Max saw HH in Paris. He found him 'very disappointed but still friendly.' Muriel seemed to be taking an understanding view."[12]

When Humphrey returned from Europe, he and Muriel were invited to dinner at the Hughes home. Hubert and Tom discussed the staff situation at length. The meeting was friendly, but Hughes believed that Humphrey was still upset.[13]

Max Kampelman concluded, on reflection, that Tom had been doing the work of two people. Therefore he should be replaced by two people. Since Tom was a liberal but got on well with conservatives, Max thought that the two replacements should have different ideological views. Humphrey followed Kampelman's advice in making two new hires. Unfortunately, in Max's view, he hired the wrong people.

Humphrey's decision was "a bad move but entirely predictable."[14] The two men Humphrey hired were Allard Lowenstein, a fiery New Yorker from the far left wing of the Democratic Party, and Ernest Lefever, a conservative and staunch anticommunist from the party's right wing. Lefever was a defense hawk and one of the early neoconservatives.

The arrangement did not work out quite as Max or Hubert had intended. The two replacements loathed each other and quarreled constantly. They took their grievances to Tom Hughes. Al would have lunch with Tom one day and complain bitterly about Ernie, calling him a reactionary Neanderthal, a McCarthyite, a racist, homophobic, and so on. The next day Ernie would have lunch with Tom and assail Al as a lunatic leftie who might as well be on the Kremlin's payroll. Lowenstein lasted for some eight months and then quit to return to New York. Lefever stayed longer but was not an effective staff member, never in sync with the liberal atmosphere of the Humphrey office.

BACK TO BOWLES

Hughes rejoined Bowles in January 1959. Bowles believed that to accomplish anything legislatively, he would have to exploit his image as an elder political leader. This meant that he would have to be somewhat aloof from parochial concerns. He would also have to act quickly before the 1960 presidential race dominated everything.

An immediate legislative goal for Bowles was to seek reforms in foreign aid and economic assistance programs. Bowles was realist enough to know that he could not stand completely aloof from politics. He wanted to be assigned to the House Foreign Affairs Committee and the Subcommittee on Western Europe, which handled foreign aid. Hughes assisted by approaching Humphrey, who contacted Lyndon Johnson, who got his friend Sam Rayburn to ensure that Bowles got his wish. Speaker Rayburn assured the new elder representative from Connecticut's Second District that the full weight of the Speaker's office was employed to prevent an upstart from seeking the spot that had been set aside for the distinguished former governor and ambassador to India. The Speaker told his new friend Bowles, "I was approached by one of your Connecticut colleagues—I can't remember his name" [it was Don Irwin]—"who had the temerity to seek an appointment to that committee because he spoke Spanish. I was pleased to inform him that that place was being reserved for Connecticut's senior statesman, Chester Bowles, and that he should know better than to try to upstage a worthy gentleman."[15]

The next day Bowles received a similar call from John Bailey, the state party chair. Bailey explained that Representative-at-large Frank Kowalski had coveted a berth on the Foreign Affairs Committee. Kowalski, said the chair, thought he was entitled to the seat "as a matter of right."

Bailey, not to be outdone in declaring his support for Bowles, had taken care of the uppity representative-at-large. Bailey harbored some resentment toward Bowles ever since Bowles as governor had turned down his entreaty in 1949 to be appointed interim U.S. senator. But political logic now triumphed over personal animosity. Bailey now declared, "I'm glad to tell you, Chet, that after my little talk with him, the ambitions of your Polish colleague have ceased to exist."[16]

As a representative from Connecticut's Second District, Bowles was obliged to follow closely the defense budget and to support the Navy's plans to base more submarines in his district. Hughes, as a member of U.S. Air Force Reserve Unit 9999, commanded by Senator and General Barry Goldwater, kept Bowles informed on defense issues. As he had done with Humphrey, Hughes wrote letters for Bowles to the Pentagon inquiring into a matter of interest to veterans or other constituents. Then, while on reserve duty in the Pentagon, he would answer the letters.

This showed Bowles's interest in the issues and his ability to achieve results for his constituents. Whether or not this practice was entirely in line with separation-of-powers doctrines, it proved to be good politics for Bowles. Congress was in the process of reassessing its own role in foreign policy in light of growing criticisms by Democrats of John Foster Dulles's brinkmanship and other policies. It was both good policy and good politics for Democrats on the House and Senate Committees on Foreign Relations to attack the Dulles brothers while casting Ike as aloof and unaware of what was happening in his administration.

Early on, Bowles worked closely with the Kennedy office in the Senate on regional New England concerns, but he quickly moved into broader cooperation. Bowles undertook with Senator Kennedy a series of unglamorous but important amendments to the Mutual Security Act. Furthermore, Chet Bowles made a major effort to reform the U.S. Treasury's Development Loan Fund, a program designed to help the poorest Third World nations. The foreign aid agencies were not accustomed to having members of Congress take a sympathetic interest in foreign aid.

Hughes, a lawyer skilled in statutory language and adept in arcane Senate procedures, won the admiration of the foreign aid administrators. He was offered an attractive post with the Development Loan Fund, with a salary roughly twice his congressional pay. Bowles offered to intercede with

Treasury Secretary Douglas Dillon should Hughes be interested in moving to Treasury. Hughes decided to stay put.

For Hughes, the pace of work with Bowles was more agreeable in personal terms than it had been with Humphrey—at least for a while. The pace quickened as the presidential race began to take shape. Tom's assessment that his hours would be more manageable with Chet than with Hubert did not entirely pan out.

As someone who had made his fortune in the advertising business, Chet Bowles had a near obsession with simplicity and precision of language. He tinkered endlessly with speech drafts and press releases. This was no surprise to Hughes, who knew Chet's habits from his earlier work in Essex.

Chet did not, like Humphrey, require that every letter from a constituent be answered the same day. Humphrey had a habit of perusing the desks of his staff for unanswered letters before going home. Bowles was a good executive. However, Bowles had no sense of a normal workday. He might call aides at any time and hand out assignments. One Sunday, Bowles had an idea for a speech on Africa and had Tom paged at the Chevy Chase Swimming Association pool. He wanted Tom to begin work on the draft immediately. Hughes's diary recorded "another weekend shot."[17]

FOREIGN POLICY

Tom Hughes buttressed his growing reputation as a foreign policy intellectual in April 1959 with an article, his first in a major journal, for *The Reporter*. Max Ascoli, the magazine's publisher, commissioned Tom to write the article on Congress and foreign policy. In the article, Hughes discussed Congress's reappraisal of its own role in foreign policy, drawing heavily on his experience in the Senate (writing most of the article while he was still with Humphrey). Hughes asserted that the congressional reassessment was shifting the initiative on key foreign policy issues from the executive branch to Congress.[18] Senators who were emerging as important players in foreign policy included J. William Fulbright, chair of the Senate Committee on Foreign Relations, Mike Mansfield, Hubert Humphrey on arms control, John Stennis, John Kennedy, and Stuart Symington on defense preparedness, Joseph Clark on human rights, and liberal Republicans such as Thomas Kuchel on Latin America and Jacob Javits on the Middle East and foreign aid issues.

With the death of John Foster Dulles in May 1959, Christian Herter, a Republican and former governor from Massachusetts and a longtime Bowles friend, became secretary of state. This change improved the climate for bipartisan cooperation between Congress and the State Department. The election, however, soon brought politics back into center stage and dominated the foreign policy debate. Bowles and Herter carried on a dialogue of sorts out of the public spotlight but not on the controversial issues that dominated the campaign. After the election, Bowles and Herter worked together closely on transition issues as the designated officials of the incoming and outgoing administrations.

Bowles liked foreign travel and found it useful to bring Hughes along on trips. Tom had traveled widely in Europe as a Rhodes scholar and regularly traveled abroad with his Air Force reserve unit. The unit, made up of representatives, congressional staffers, and senior Pentagon executives, traveled at least once a year to Europe or the Middle East or to a major command in the Far East. They usually had the opportunity to discuss issues with foreign leaders.

Tom was particularly interested in Western Europe and had urged Bowles to get himself appointed to the Subcommittee on Europe of the House Committee on Foreign Relations. This appointment would balance, Tom suggested, Chet's well-known interest in India and the Third World. Once installed on the subcommittee, Chet worked out a plan for an extensive trip.

In September 1959, Bowles and Hughes embarked on a European trip with stops in Tunisia, Yugoslavia, Germany, France, and England. Hughes's contacts in Europe were helpful. Tom arranged for Bowles to meet with Willy Brandt and other politicians in Germany and with Jean Monnet in Paris and to have him address a meeting of Rhodes scholars in England. Bowles also met with Sir Isaiah Berlin and other British politicians, labor leaders, and intellectuals.

The unusual stop in Yugoslavia stuck in Tom Hughes's memory. Bowles decided that a visit to Marshal Tito was important since the Yugoslav ruler was emerging as the spokesperson of the nonaligned nations. Bowles presumed that Tito's stature was similar to that of Nehru, whom Bowles had known well in India. Bowles was prepared to admire Tito greatly. The trip encountered some unexpected logistical problems and seemed to be jinxed from the start.

The entourage had to travel to a U.S. Air Force base at Pula, on the Adriatic, and transfer to a motorboat to Brioni, the island where Tito spent his vacations. They then had to travel by jeep to Tito's Hapsburg villa.

Dodging camels, giraffes, elephants, and other animals that were gifts to Tito from his nonaligned friends, the jeep at length arrived at the villa. The party was greeted by Madame Broz, Tito's redoubtable wife, and was eventually rushed into the leader's presence. Tito was dressed in a baby blue uniform à la Herman Goering. It was adorned with medals, and Tito carried a field marshal's baton.

The conversation turned to the whereabouts of John Blatnik, Tito's wartime buddy and now a Minnesota representative. The guests were enveloped in a cloud of smoke from Tito's chain-smoking. Hughes contributed bits of trivia about Blatnik and Minnesota politics, while lighting one cigarette after another for his host. Hughes's diary suggests that Bowles was revising his opinion of the Yugoslav ruler: "Bowles' expression suggested that a quick reassessment might be taking place."[19]

THE PRECAMPAIGN CAMPAIGN

The early days of 1959 for Hughes were something of the calm before the storm. There was time for reflection and legislative achievements. Bowles worked well with his congressional peers and also with the Eisenhower administration. Bowles had friends, such as Douglas Dillon at Treasury and Christian Herter at State, who were happy to work with him. Hughes's contacts in the White House staff with old Student Federalists as well as his former colleagues in Senate offices helped Bowles to navigate Washington's choppy waters.

Hubert Humphrey offered avuncular advice to his friend Chester Bowles (for some reason, Hubert never used the name "Chet"). Tom Hughes arranged a luncheon soon after Bowles arrived in Washington, where Bowles, Humphrey, and Hughes enjoyed a pleasant conversation. Bowles remarked casually that he had never been part of such a huge organization as the House of Representatives, with all 435 competing for attention. "Chester," Hubert said, "Don't worry. If you just keep kicking higher than the others in the chorus line, you'll be noticed."

Chester kept kicking higher and was noticed.

By the end of 1959, however, the story was not how high the individual members were kicking. The opposing political armies were prepositioning their forces for the political battles of 1960. The focus was on the fortunes and the fate of the candidates and the strength of their campaigns.

The leading candidates for the Democratic nomination in 1960 were all from the Senate: Kennedy, Humphrey, Symington, and Johnson. Estes Kefauver had simplified things by bowing out. Former governor of New York Averell Harriman might have been a formidable candidate, but his loss to Republican Nelson Rockefeller in 1959 eliminated him.

The old rule that governors had a natural edge as presidential nominees had long since been overturned. The leading candidates for the nomination in both parties now increasingly came from the ranks of politicians with national exposure. On the Republican side, Vice President Richard M. Nixon was a solid favorite for the nomination.

Hubert Humphrey officially launched his campaign on December 30, 1959, as the first out of the gate. Jack Kennedy followed closely in early January. Stuart Symington scrambled to be the third. Adlai Stevenson coyly let it be known that he might be amenable to a draft, though he was not a declared candidate. He had little support left in the party, though, and even his old friends, such as Chet Bowles, did not think he was suited to be president. As Tom Hughes described Bowles's thinking then,

> After 1956 Chet had come to the conclusion that Adlai should not be president, even if he had a chance to win in 1960.... Even apart from the two defeats, many people, I think including Chet, had over the years reached the conclusion that Adlai was not cut out to be president, that there was more love of language than substantive commitment, that the aspiration was more social and cultural than based on deeper matters of policy, that the bonafides of his interest in the poor, the black, the Third World, were in doubt, and that the countryside of Illinois and the salons of Manhattan had far greater appeal—not to speak of London.[20]

Harris Wofford, who had once been a fervent Stevenson admirer, found Stevenson indifferent and distracted when trying to brief him on civil rights and now turned strongly against him. Wofford told Tom that he did not want Adlai as either president or secretary of state.

When Hughes told Max Kampelman, in November 1958, that he was leaving Humphrey for Bowles, their conversation inevitably touched on politics.[21] Max explained that he and Hubert had discussed Hubert's running for president. Humphrey had been cool to the idea but had gradually changed his mind.

A politician does not wake up one morning and decide to run for president. The decision emerges from a process more than from a sudden revelation. It is a calculus involving a mix of ambition and opportunity. Mulling over the odds of success and the costs of failure produces an inclination, which gradually hardens into resolution. The candidate must see a realistic path to the nomination and then to victory in the general election. So when Hubert asked for his advice, Max told Tom, he had warned Hubert that running would present an enormous challenge on a number of fronts.

Humphrey needed fund-raising, a significant upgrade in his staff, and an experienced hand to run the campaign. Max advised Humphrey to seek out the advice of Jim Rowe, a well-known Washington lawyer with broad political experience in Democratic politics. Rowe was Kampelman's next-door neighbor, and Rowe's law partner, Tommy "the Cork" Corcoran, was Lyndon Johnson's personal attorney. Humphrey had authorized him, said Kampelman, to sound out Rowe about Johnson's intentions.

Rowe went to see Lyndon, with whom he was on close terms, and asked if he intended to run. Johnson turned the question back to Rowe. What did Rowe think of Lyndon's chances? Rowe told Johnson he had three strikes against him: he was a Southerner; he had had a heart attack; and he represented big oil. Any one of these could be a disqualification. The three together added up to nearly insurmountable odds. Lyndon agreed and told

Rowe he had no intention of running. Rowe took this assurance at face value. The way was cleared for Rowe to work for Humphrey.

The Humphrey strategy was to compete in five primaries: South Dakota, the District of Columbia, Wisconsin, West Virginia, and Oregon. Kennedy had the resources to contest Humphrey everywhere but would be circumspect in where to fight him. He would avoid South Dakota and the District of Columbia because of Hubert's strength there.

The Symington strategy required that the primaries produce a mixed result, with Humphrey and Kennedy neutralizing each other. This outcome would result in a deadlocked convention. Since Symington would not have campaigned against anyone and was friendly with all parties, he would be the natural compromise candidate the party could rally around against Nixon.

John F. Kennedy had both strong advantages and serious liabilities as a candidate. The popular philosopher and communications scholar Marshall McLuhan had invented the concept of the "cool" style as the perfect demeanor for politicians in the age of television.[22] The cool and telegenic Jack Kennedy seemed the ideal candidate for the television age.

Among Kennedy's advantages were the family's name and the political legacy that extended back to his maternal grandfather, John "Honey Fitz" Fitzgerald. The Kennedy family patriarch, Joseph P. Kennedy Sr., was a force to be reckoned with, but he had many enemies. His isolationist and pro-German stance in the early stages of World War II had made him anathema to the liberal wing of the Democratic Party. Joe Sr. had reportedly once asked Harry Truman why he supported "that crippled son-of-a-bitch [FDR] that killed my son Joe." Truman replied that if Joe Kennedy ever talked like that again, he would throw Kennedy out the window.

Jack Kennedy's liabilities included his health (he suffered from Addison's disease) and his religion. As a Catholic, he faced what were considered at the time major electoral liabilities. Finally, some believed that Jack, like his father, stood for nothing but personal ambition.

The Kennedy strategy for the nomination boiled down to keeping the lid on the health problem, cultivating the press and gaining publicity, competing and winning key primaries, and winning over the party leaders and big-city bosses. The aim was to build up on the basis of primary victories a large lead in delegates for a first-ballot nomination. It would be important to avoid a brokered convention.

Humphrey would be the main opponent in the primaries, and Johnson, Symington, and possibly Stevenson would be the main dangers in a brokered convention. In general, Kennedy needed to make gains among the constituencies—party liberals, minorities, young people, and academics—that were opposing him. For that purpose, an ideal figure would be the one distinguished Democratic liberal who was not a candidate himself: Chester Bowles.

As a Connecticut politician, Chet Bowles was within the Kennedy sphere of influence and would be forced to back Kennedy for the nomination. All of the other Connecticut politicians committed to Kennedy early. Bowles, who was on cordial but not close terms with Kennedy, let it be known that he would support Kennedy. This was not good enough for the Kennedy camp. They wanted a formal endorsement and such public appearances as the Kennedy people deemed appropriate.

On October 10, 1959, Chester Bowles spoke publicly for the first time about his own plans and voiced his support of Kennedy for president in 1960. He did so in speeches at the Milwaukee World Affairs Council and at the University of Wisconsin. In a press release the next day, Bowles summarized his position in a series of points. He declared that he did not "intend to seek the Presidential nomination. I expect to run for and win reelection to the House of Representatives." He would be a delegate to the 1960 national convention in Los Angeles as a Kennedy delegate, and "an enthusiastic one. I believe that his unique abilities will enable him to become a great President."[23]

So far, so good from the standpoint of the Kennedy people. Then the trouble started. For some unaccountable reason, Bowles veered off from his endorsement of Kennedy into effusive praise for Hubert Humphrey. Hubert, Bowles apparently declared, was uniquely qualified to carry "the message of Democratic liberalism throughout the length and breadth of this land. Surely no other Democrat of our time can perform this service with greater conviction, knowledge, or persuasiveness."

What kind of endorsement of Kennedy was this? Bowles also said that outsiders should not inject themselves into any Kennedy-Humphrey race lest they divide the party. What did this mean? The translation, as ascertained by the Kennedy people, was that Bowles would not campaign for Kennedy in any primary in which Hubert was running against Jack. This was appalling.

Bowles, while seemingly telling his supporters around the nation not to organize any demonstrations on his behalf, was actually leaving the door open for a dark-horse Bowles candidacy. All of this added up to serious trouble.

Talks to clear the air began in earnest. The principals—Kennedy and Bowles—politely circled the issues. Some kind of formula might be found that would deepen Bowles's engagement in the Kennedy campaign, with Bowles becoming Senator Kennedy's principal foreign policy adviser.

This was the kind of hard-nosed negotiation that Jack Kennedy, floating imperturbably above the fray, preferred to leave to the enforcer, his brother Bobby, and to the enforcer's enforcer, Ted Sorensen. The tough negotiation would be conducted at the Tom Hughes–Ted Sorensen level.

6

The 1960 Presidential Election

Why Chet Bowles, a respected party elder with a New Deal lineage, would appeal to the Kennedys was obvious enough. He could be the bridge they needed to the party liberals. The Kennedy forces were relieved when Chet finally made his expected public endorsement of their candidate. But when they examined what he actually said, they were in shock.

The tone of Bowles's endorsement seemed completely wrong. There was too much praise for Humphrey and not enough for Kennedy, and the assurances of support for Kennedy were not very reassuring. Ted Sorensen immediately let this be known to Tom Hughes.

Hughes was used to dealing with various members of Kennedy's staff. He worked variously with Ralph Dungan, Dick Goodwin, Fred Holborn, Mike Feldman, and Ted Sorensen, depending on the subject at hand. When Kennedy was pleased, the Bowles-Kennedy ties would be handled by the principals themselves. When there was trouble, Kennedy would turn matters over to his brother Bobby or to Ted Sorensen.

Ted Sorensen was not only a gifted speechwriter for John Kennedy but also a skilled negotiator. Ted was to play an important role at the Los Angeles convention, negotiating with Neil Stabler of Michigan to secure the swing state's delegates for Kennedy at a key point. Sorensen's intellect was never in doubt. He had a first-place finish in his law class at the University of Nebraska's College of Law. Ted was the most liberal of those in Kennedy's inner circle, and he could manage diplomatic finesse when it was called for. But diplomatic finesse was not the tactic used in his negotiations with Tom Hughes about the Bowles role in the campaign.

HUGHES-SORENSEN NEGOTIATIONS

Sorensen approached the Bowles issue as the representative of the front-runner demanding obeisance from a supporter. Kennedy, the candidate, needed and was demanding loyalty from Bowles. If Bowles wanted to be considered for secretary of state, it went without saying that he had better play ball.

First, Bowles must drop the idea that he would not campaign under any circumstances against Humphrey in a primary contest. If Bowles was supporting Kennedy, he must support Kennedy unreservedly. Then Bowles must stop going around the country praising Humphrey. He must reach out to minorities, academics, and party liberals on Kennedy's behalf. Furthermore, Bowles must discourage, not encourage, his own supporters from staging so-called spontaneous demonstrations when he went on speaking tours.

Hughes responded that Bowles was indeed reaching out to party liberals and would do more once Kennedy had launched his formal candidacy. Bowles was trying to discourage his supporters from staging demonstrations. As to campaigning in primaries, Hughes argued that their bosses—the principals—were talking directly, and that the two of them, he and Ted, should not muddy the waters by questioning what the principals had apparently already decided.

Chet Bowles, in his fashion, was direct and unequivocal in stating his intentions. As Hughes said later, Chet was "very honest and explicit in his conversations with both Humphrey and Kennedy. He told Humphrey that . . . his own first choice for President would be Humphrey. However, Chet had reached the conclusion that Hubert could not win, and he told Humphrey that. He told Kennedy the same thing."[1]

Nor did Chet mince words about participating in the primaries, even though this was the main concern of the Kennedy camp. Chet told Kennedy, "I will work for you. . . . But one thing I won't do is something you are going to want me to do, which is to campaign actively against Hubert personally in West Virginia or Wisconsin."[2]

Sorensen and Hughes generally knew what their bosses were thinking and saying to each other. They read, or wrote, most of the letters that were exchanged between the principals. Sorensen probed for weaknesses, even when it was clear that he had reached an impasse with Hughes.

When threats did not succeed, Sorensen shifted to blandishments. Sometime in December 1959 the notion of a joint Kennedy-Bowles press conference emerged at which Chet would be named JFK's chief foreign policy adviser for the campaign. Hughes and Sorensen were instructed to begin working on drafts of the letters that would be exchanged and a joint press release that would be issued.

Reaching agreement on the exact wording of the letters and the press release proved difficult. Hughes surmised that the problem lay with Kennedy's caution about implying that Bowles, in becoming chief foreign policy adviser for the campaign, was thereby becoming secretary of state in-waiting. That might offend Adlai Stevenson and complicate the problem of outreach to other party liberals, one of whom (such as Harriman) would be in the running for the State Department post.

The proffer to Bowles of the campaign's foreign policy advisership had to be important (enough, perhaps, to get Bowles to campaign against Hubert). But Kennedy did not want to signal that Bowles was his clear choice for secretary of state. Sorensen and Hughes, in their drafts, were unable to square this circle.

THE DNC KICK-OFF DINNER

The Christmas and New Year's holidays interrupted the work as well as the preparations for Kennedy's official announcement of his candidacy. There was also the need on Bowles's side to prepare for his participation in the January 23, 1960, kick-off dinner for the presidential campaign, sponsored by the Democratic National Committee. The gala event postponed the Kennedy-Bowles press conference.

The committee's dinner was the brainchild of its chair, Paul Butler, and featured more than 1,000 guests from around the country. Virtually every major Democratic politician in the country attended the event. The only notable no-show was Adlai Stevenson, who was out of the country on business for a legal client. Chet Bowles was the toastmaster and master of ceremonies for the evening.

President Harry Truman gave an opening address, followed by Governors Pat Brown of California and G. Mennen "Soapy" Williams of Michigan and Senator Stuart Symington of Missouri. The latter two were billed as program speakers. They were followed by four featured speakers: the Honorable John F. Kennedy, U.S. senator from Massachusetts; the Honorable Lyndon B. Johnson, U.S. senator from Texas; the Honorable Robert B. Meyner, governor of New Jersey; and the Honorable Hubert H. Humphrey, U.S. senator from Minnesota. Chester Bowles would introduce all speakers and preside over the event.

Hughes wrote opening remarks for Bowles, brief blurbs about the speakers, and a number of jokes that were always called for on such occasions. The event was vintage American politics: a mixture of high purpose, grandstanding, and good-natured, if slightly ribald, jocularity. Bowles played his part well, according to Hughes, though "he refused to gavel for silence so he himself could be heard."[3]

Overall, the event was the "best evening of its kind I have ever attended.

Kennedy and Symington also at their best," Hughes reported. But the star of the evening was Humphrey: "Humphrey was sensational—by far the best. . . . I had tipped off HHH earlier in the day to Chet's introduction. (Horatio at the Bridge—Hubert Horatio Humphrey)."[4]

THE KENNEDY-BOWLES PRESS CONFERENCE

Bowles, meanwhile, was growing more confident that matters would work out with Kennedy, despite Chet's reluctance to campaign against Humphrey. Hughes's diary for January 18, 1960, noted, "Chet is full of go go go. He is talking a good deal about what further work he should do for Kennedy, and how he should respond to the pressure for him to do more. Clearly, he is going to refuse to do any direct campaigning against Humphrey (as in Wisconsin)."[5]

On January 26, Hughes recorded that "Chet had lunch with Kennedy in Georgetown—a relaxed two-hour talk over martinis—the best one he has had with Jack. Chet increasingly impressed. Intellectual curiosity, tough mindedness, confidence. Chet reports to me that Jack wants him to serve in a capacity 'similar to Dulles in 1948 and 1952'. . . Nothing specifically said about Secretary of State but clear implication."

Hughes further noted that "Jack understands and fully accepts the predicament with Hubert and his unwillingness to go into Wisconsin . . . but Chet will work for Kennedy in any other way."[6]

Kennedy assured Chet that John Bailey and Abe Ribicoff's early support would not prejudice Chet's own standing in a prospective Kennedy administration. Kennedy and Bowles left it to Hughes and Sorensen to work out the details for the press conference, to be held at the earliest practicable opportunity.

On February 6, the Hughes diary noted a

> long and good lunch with Ted Sorensen. [but] Pressure on Chet to go into Wisconsin and California. I told Ted that he knew very well that the one restriction on Chet's activity was his unwillingness personally to oppose Hubert anywhere. Ted protested but I reminded him that Jack and Chet had discussed this question thoroughly and agreed. I added that it was clear why they were pressing it, but not clear why they were pressing it after we had made our position equally clear.[7]

Bowles agreed, however, to write a strong endorsement letter for Wisconsin newspapers and to have pictures of Bowles with Kennedy displayed all over the state.

Still, there was some resistance in the Kennedy camp. Bowles felt it necessary to have another exchange of letters with Kennedy. He went through the issues again in a four-and-a-half-page letter on February 12, which

Kennedy must have found fatiguing. Chet discussed the history of his relationship with Stevenson and Humphrey, describing them as old comrades. "Let me start by saying in all honesty that if you were not seeking the nomination, I would be. . . . As I told you when we first talked in December, Jack, the one thing I cannot do is personally to campaign in opposition to Hubert or Adlai. I cannot suddenly oppose nor appear to oppose those people with whom I have worked closely for years."[8]

He concluded by asserting that to campaign against one of his liberal friends could create bitterness and might split the party. Kennedy apparently decided that the whole affair had gone on long enough, and on February 17 he answered Bowles definitively:

Dear Chet:

I am delighted with the completion for officially announcing your role in my campaign. . . . I know that this will be a big boost to my candidacy, and I know your advice and support will be invaluable throughout the campaign. . . .

I understand completely your letter of February 12. I do not want you to be embarrassed in your relationship with any other Democratic contender—or even to feel embarrassed about turning down any request from this office, which you feel you must decline. I think now that we have a clearer understanding of your role, there is less likelihood of that happening—and I know that you will understand, should further requests be forthcoming that you cannot accept, that we are making them only to obtain the maximum benefit of your support. . . .

I know your desire to help is sincere, and I know your help will be invaluable. . . .

Sincerely,
[signed Jack]
John F. Kennedy[9]

On February 23, 1960, the Kennedy-Bowles press conference finally took place. Kennedy announced that Bowles would be the campaign's chief foreign policy adviser. The crowd of reporters was disappointingly small, and the conference was somewhat anticlimactic.

Bowles arrived at "Kennedy office at 9:00 a.m. [Had] 10 minutes with Jack. Friendly and in good humor about Wisconsin."[10] The two men "discussed Walt Rostow's draft of defense speech," with Bowles taking a more dovish posture and arguing against a proposed $3 billion increase in defense spending. Kennedy eventually went for Rostow's recommended increase.

The press conference sought to frame the campaign's important policy issues. The pursuit of peace was a major overall theme. The collection of

Kennedy speeches from 1956 to 1959, *The Strategy of Peace*, was published in March, almost simultaneously with the press conference, to burnish Kennedy's image as a serious thinker on important foreign policy and defense issues.

Along with a series of "gaps"—the poverty gap, the economic development gap between rich and poor nations, and a leadership gap by the Republican administration—the "missile gap" was featured for the first time as a Kennedy campaign theme. The missile gap was the invention of columnist Joseph Alsop based on inputs from Stuart Symington. The Missouri senator was the unofficial defense candidate in the Democratic field.

Kennedy embraced the concept, not wanting to cede territory to Symington. It became clear later that Bowles's views were in conflict with the hardline positions of JFK's defense advisers, especially Walt Rostow and Paul Nitze. This conflict would become a sensitive issue later in the campaign.

The struggles between the Bowles peace wing and the Nitze-Rostow camps, already evident, were to mark the campaign, as Kennedy was simultaneously a hawk and a dove as the campaign evolved. He argued, as he had in his speeches in *The Strategy of Peace*, that the Republicans had neglected the nation's defenses. But he also insisted that Ike's administration failed to pursue arms control and disarmament.

The Kennedy-Bowles press conference, in any event, was considered a success by both Kennedy and Bowles. It was more low-key than the parties had expected, given the labors that had gone into it. The Bowles office thereafter focused on the outreach to the party liberals. The Kennedy camp rapidly shifted its attention to the critical primary battles.

CRITICAL PRIMARIES: WISCONSIN AND WEST VIRGINIA

Kennedy's good humor about the forthcoming April 5 Wisconsin primary, displayed in his conversation with Bowles before the press conference, gave way to anxiety as he returned to the campaign trail. The Kennedy forces counted on a decisive win in Wisconsin. Kennedy, in announcing that he would run in the Wisconsin primary, made much of the fact that he was contesting Hubert in his own backyard. Wisconsin would be their first head-to-head competition.

Early indications were that Kennedy would have a decisive victory. Polls by Louis Harris, Kennedy's pollster, showed Kennedy running strongly. The use of polls was a Kennedy innovation. Wisconsin would have twenty-eight votes at the convention, half allotted to the overall popular vote winner and half distributed on a district-by-district basis among Wisconsin's ten congressional districts.

Kennedy's strategy called for him to enter as many as seven primaries. Most of these, though, were not contested. Kennedy had to win in Wisconsin, the first state where he would face Humphrey. If Jack failed, he might be finished. Absent a convincing victory, he would need to demonstrate electoral strength elsewhere to win over the party bosses. If he entered the convention with 600 or more delegates, the chances were good of reaching the 761 votes necessary for a first-ballot nomination.[11]

Thus Kennedy was shocked to discover that his lead in Wisconsin had suddenly evaporated. The new scientific polling showed him trailing in some districts and running even in others. What happened, JFK asked? They discovered you were Catholic, he was told.

The situation called for an all-court press by the Kennedy team. Another effort was made to enlist Bowles to campaign in the district of the University of Wisconsin. Sorensen turned to Harris Wofford to pressure Bowles.

Harris told Bowles: "Your name is everywhere being used against Humphrey and for Kennedy. . . . Surely you knew that when you made your decision."[12] Bowles stood firm. His personal campaigning probably would not have changed much. Kennedy won in the end what to him, his backers, and many political pros was a solid victory: he took 56 percent of the popular vote to Humphrey's 44 percent and won in six of the ten congressional districts.

Tom Hughes recorded in his diary for April 5, "Wisconsin primary JFK won 3-2. A major leg up for him. HHH should withdraw but he hasn't. More fighting statements. HHH carried Madison where Chet was asked to campaign."[13]

The press, normally JFK's reliable ally, was focusing on the Catholic vote. Kennedy's poor showing among Protestants was highlighted. Although Hubert had won only in the districts next to Minnesota, the press noted that Humphrey had done well in districts with a large Protestant vote. Kennedy, it was reported, had shown strength only among Catholic voters.

Humphrey ran well in a number of districts, winning four of the ten districts and narrowly missing in a fifth. Nonetheless, the result was a clear victory for Kennedy and it came in Humphrey's backyard.

Humphrey was in debt for $18,000 after Wisconsin, a considerable sum for a man lacking independent wealth. Hubert had fought a good fight and could bow out gracefully. The Kennedy forces debated whether they wanted Hubert in or out of the May 10 West Virginia primary. With Humphrey out, a Kennedy victory would lose its luster. On the other hand, a loss would be devastating. A poll taken early in the year by the pollster Lou Harris showed Jack with 60 percent of the vote to Hubert's 20 percent in West Virginia's most populous county. Unfortunately, a new poll taken to confirm the earlier result showed a dramatic shift: a 60 to 40 percent edge for Humphrey. Again, the voters had apparently discovered that Jack was a Catholic.[14]

The Kennedy team concluded that Humphrey should be encouraged to enter the West Virginia race. A Kennedy win would knock Humphrey out of the race and put the Catholic issue to rest. Arthur Goldberg was sent to persuade Hubert to drop out of the race. In sending Goldberg the Kennedy forces knew what they were doing.[15] Goldberg was one of the few people Hubert ever thoroughly disliked and a visit by him would anger Hubert and cause him to stay in the contest. Tom Hughes's diary for April 18 noted, "Arthur Goldberg seeing Hubert today to get him to withdraw. But this will just put Hubert's back up again."[16]

The Kennedy machine was at peak efficiency under Larry O'Brien. O'Brien deployed an army of 7,000 volunteers, flooded the airwaves with testimonials to Kennedy's heroism, and sent out 40,000 copies of a *Reader's Digest* article on Kennedy's heroics on PT 109. The campaign organized phone banks and added local notables (especially county sheriffs) to the Kennedy payroll.

Humphrey was put on the defensive from the start by declarations from Kennedy backers that anyone considering a vote for Hubert must be an anti-Catholic bigot. The theme of the month-long campaign was well established before Kennedy went on television to speak directly to the religious issue. The choice, he stated, was between Americanism, fair play, and tolerance, on the one side, and anti-Catholic bigotry, intolerance, and un-American nativism on the other.

How much money the Kennedy forces spent on the West Virginia primary can never be determined. Estimates vary, but all observers agree that Kennedy vastly outspent Humphrey, by a ratio as high as ten to one.[17] The Justice Department later investigated the charges of campaign finance irregularities but found insufficient evidence for any charges.

Four former Kennedy aides and supporters spoke at a May 10, 2010, event sponsored by the JFK Presidential Library to commemorate the fifty-year anniversary of the West Virginia primary. The aides acknowledged their big edge over Humphrey in finances. However, they insisted that other factors were decisive, such as Kennedy's handling of the religion issue and his appeal to women and young people. Panel member Charles Peters, a journalist, one-time West Virginia politician, and publisher, quipped that a sheriff told him at the time, "Sure, Kennedy paid me, but I would've supported Kennedy anyway because my wife and daughter made me." Kennedy, when questioned by reporters during the campaign about his father's spending, had a disarming quip: "No, definitely not true, no lavish spending. Dad has made it very clear that he is not willing to pay for a landslide."

But what the patriarch got was, in fact, a landslide, which knocked Humphrey out of the race and all but sealed the nomination. Kennedy got 236,000 votes to Humphrey's 152,000, a winning percentage of 60.8 percent.

Chet Bowles thought that Hubert might now endorse Kennedy, but he did not raise the issue with him. Tom Hughes, hearing from his former colleagues in Humphrey's office that Hubert was facing the fight of his political life in his reelection campaign for Senate in Minnesota, arranged for Bowles to send a strong telegram of support to Humphrey headquarters. Humphrey's reelection campaign gradually picked up momentum, and he won a close fight with his Republican opponent, Clark McGregor.

MORE ROLES FOR BOWLES

On April 16, 1960, Tom Hughes's diary noted an announcement from the Democratic Party chair, Paul Butler, that "Chet would head the Democratic platform committee . . . [a] move that was greeted with popular acclaim."[18]

Bowles embraced the role with gusto. He planned a series of public hearings with party members across the country. The organizational burdens fell on Hughes, but he got the chance to meet party leaders from all over the country.

Hughes enlisted the help of his friends Harris Wofford and Abe Chayes, from the Kennedy staff, in drafting the platform. Bowles himself was active, especially in drafting the short version of the platform. Chet presented this version to the delegates and used it for a brief film he broadcast to a national television audience.

Citing the technical requirements of preparing the film, the Bowles team declared that the platform could not be amended or further edited. This was the last time the authors of a major party's platform got away with having no amendments because of alleged technical difficulties. The platform was a great success, and Bowles was widely praised for his leadership of the committee.

However, delegates were allowed to offer amendments to the longer printed version of the platform at hearings before the start of the convention. The platform's most important section called for major new legislation on civil rights. On July 10, Hughes's diary said of the Platform Committee, "Dramatic day at Ambassador West. Finished most of platform by 3 p.m. and started civil rights, then Abe read it through and then asked Senator Sam Erwin, who declined to comment."

Erwin then delivered a dramatic speech, saying, "Our South, like the Irish, has suffered at the hands of history [but] need not suffer the final humiliation. . . . But I realize that you people in the North have serious problems to deal with too."[19] Erwin complained that the national party chair had no trouble appointing Eleanor Roosevelt to the committee but ignored the South. In the end he accepted the civil rights section as drafted. Four deletions were proposed that would weaken the section, but they were defeated by a vote of sixteen to four.

On July 11, the full platform committee met to approve the print version of the platform: "Chet was terrible as Parliamentarian and chairman. We had to get John Blatnik to substitute for him and he was not much better."[20] The committee amended several of the foreign policy planks but left civil rights intact.

Hughes remembered Lyndon Johnson's prediction that passage of the 1957 Civil Rights Act would lead to further legislation. The Democratic Party, in committing itself to major new action on civil rights, took an important next step along that path. Hughes read over, made a few minor edits, and delivered the printed version of the platform to the printer.

The short ad and the long version were combined into one pamphlet by having the text in two different font sizes: large, bold print for the version Bowles delivered to the delegates and national TV audience, and the smaller printed sections sandwiched within the large text. Hughes noticed that there was no title, so he added one: "The Rights of Man."[21]

Bowles meanwhile continued to shower Kennedy with drafts of proposed speeches, suggestions for campaign moves, reports on world trouble spots, the text of press releases, and other documents. Bowles and Hughes never quite knew what happened to their efforts once they had sent them off to the candidate.

The working environment around Kennedy seemed chaotic. Bowles's requests for meetings were often ignored or lost in the frenetic pace of the campaign. Hundreds of advisers, it seemed, were trying to gain access to the candidate. Being chief adviser on foreign policy meant only that Bowles was free to compete with a host of other self-appointed or officially designated advisers who were similarly seeking to gain the candidate's attention.

On the most critical decision of the convention, however, JFK was clearly in charge and was decisive, though he heard from every party element. Apropos of the choice of Lyndon Johnson, Hughes's diary for July 14, 1960, reported on the "parade of politicians to JFK suite. The northern governors, Chet, Soapy, etc., expected to oppose Lyndon and most did. Then Bobby was sent down to tell Lyndon. . . . Bobby came back upstairs. Only to find that the [Jake] Arveys, [Carmine] de Sapios, and [David] Lawrences who were expected to oppose Lyndon instead welcomed him. So the basic decision went in Lyndon's favor."[22]

COORDINATING THE BOWLES AND KENNEDY STAFFS

The efforts of the Bowles and Kennedy teams overlapped, which sometimes produced a certain amount of confusion. Harris Wofford, of Kennedy's staff, at times borrowed material that Tom Hughes had prepared for Chet. Hughes noted, "HW went over my . . . drafts for Chet and copied several of the jokes for JFK speeches. . . . He also purloined for Kennedy my Emerson's 'Party of Hope' quote which I hoped to use for Bowles's new book. So I seem to be working for JFK through HW now, in a certain way."[23]

Staff conflict, though, could sometimes be serious. The response to the U-2 crisis in May 1960 was a case in point. The handling of the crisis by the Kennedy team was a case of crossed wires and confusion in the chain of command. A May 8 entry in Tom's diary noted, "U-2 shootdown [by] USSR. Explosive diplomatically and politically. The summit at risk. Chet was first to comment on TV on *Meet the Press* at 8:30. At station with him."

Bowles issued an extensive statement the following day, criticizing the lack of coordination in the government. As the crisis deepened, Bowles wired Kennedy in Oregon that he must talk to him by phone. Chet "told him imperative he speak out before Adlai on summit, which is collapsing today."[24]

Kennedy agreed but then apparently misspoke, for "Kennedy announced in Oregon that Ike had our 'sympathy but not our respect'—a distorted radio report, it turns out, for what JFK really said was . . . 'From our allies we have merited sympathy but not respect.'"[25] Feeling somewhat burned but needing to appear thoughtful, Kennedy authorized Bowles to prepare a speech for him on the whole U-2 situation. The speech was to be delivered on the Senate floor.

Chet was told that he could have the services of Harris Wofford to help in preparing the U-2 speech for Kennedy. Harris prepared a draft after conferring with Chet, as was the usual Bowles practice. Tom then edited the draft. As usual, Chet went over this version and undid the work of his aides. Bowles then became dissatisfied with his own extensive editing and dropped the whole thing into Tom's lap for a complete rewrite.[26]

Tom had a difficult time with the U-2 rewrite because he and Harris disagreed on the substance. Harris wanted the speech to disavow any further U.S. U-2 flights. Tom opposed the suggestion; he wanted options to be kept open for national security reasons. To halt all U-2 flights would make Kennedy look weak.

Bowles vacillated between his aides. Eventually, a satisfactory draft was prepared and sent to Kennedy, and the team waited to hear when, or whether, JFK would deliver the proposed speech on the Senate floor. Then, on May 25, "Chet had another difficult conversation with Sorensen today. No comment volunteered on Chet's draft on U-2. When asked, S. replied, 'Oh, I think some parts of it may be useable.'"[27]

Chet acquired, or rather seized, the further assignment of liaison with the Eisenhower administration and in effect created a "shadow government" in the event of a Kennedy victory. Chet began having regular meetings with Secretary of State Christian "Chris" Herter, who gave him classified briefings on foreign policy developments. Bowles initially resisted the classified briefings on the grounds that classified information only added "2 percent" beyond what was available in public sources. But Kennedy wanted to give signs of cooperating fully with the administration.

So Chet, who was an old friend of his New England neighbor Chris Herter, from their days as governors of adjacent states, was happy to take on the role of insider privy to secrets (as a member of the House Foreign Affairs Committee, Chet had a top secret clearance). Chet was able to do this discreetly by having drinks with Chris Herter at Herter's Georgetown home. The arrangement later gave Bowles the lead role in postelection planning for the transition at the State Department.[28]

Aside from the particulars of his role, there was a deeper problem. Chet Bowles, a courtly man who made a regular practice of being polite and even ingratiated himself, at times, with his foes, did not like Jack Kennedy's style. More important, he did not trust Kennedy. Bowles's basic feelings toward the man, who was his ticket to the policy role he coveted, were revealed to Tom in a moment of frustration: "Chet called with more on his JFK visit. His overall conclusion on Jack: here is a man who is all politics and power. More intellectual curiosity than Ribicoff, smarter than R., but basically and orally identical. No principles. No conviction that couldn't be shaken if circumstances indicated."[29]

POSTCONVENTION BLUES

Kennedy had hoped that liberals would swing over to his side after the convention. Instead, the Stevenson forces and liberals, in general, sat on their hands. They were doing so either for strategic reasons (trying to force Kennedy into an endorsement of Adlai for secretary of state) or because they distrusted Kennedy, or both.

Eleanor Roosevelt, despite her errant son Franklin's embrace of Kennedy in West Virginia, indicated that she would likely not vote if JFK were the nominee. Adlai went back to his farm and pouted, leaving to his law partner George Ball the task of responding to Kennedy's importuning. The nomination of Johnson for vice president shocked the liberals and added to the problem of winning them over.

Thus Chet Bowles, as the house liberal, was granted a new lease on his political life. He took it upon himself to meet with Eleanor Roosevelt, Adlai, Hubert, and other liberals to persuade them to be more active in the campaign. He reported back to Kennedy on the steps he was taking, but his reports were mostly of meetings, not of results.

A particular problem arose with Bowles's efforts to energize Stevenson supporters—a problem that placed him in an untenable position. Stevenson's supporters were holding out for a signal that Adlai would be named secretary of state. They had in mind a William Jennings Bryan–style scenario, with Stevenson, as the party's elder leader, entitled to the senior cabinet post. Since Bowles was waging his own campaign for secretary of state, he could hardly recommend that Kennedy pledge, if elected, to nominate Stevenson for the post. Kennedy from time to time made comments to the effect that considerations of party unity might dictate the choice of Adlai.

Bowles's new book, *The Coming Political Breakthrough,* was published by Ballantine Books soon after the convention. The book won Chet fanfare and public acclaim. He appeared on TV and made the case that the nation was on the brink of a new era.[30] He declared, somewhat prematurely, an end to the Cold War and proclaimed that a more peaceful international order was within reach. At home, the era of divided government that had characterized the Eisenhower years would be a thing of the past. The Democrats, by winning both the Congress and the presidency, would usher in a new era of dynamic, activist liberalism. The book, Hughes observed, "electrified the Democratic Party." Tom Hughes thought that the book was a tailor-made introduction to the John F. Kennedy policy.

This kind of publicity was as helpful to Kennedy as to Bowles, but Bowles's access to the news media was not always welcomed by the Kennedys. Hughes's diary records the many times he was called on the carpet by Kennedy lieutenants Feldman, Goodwin, and Sorensen, who complain of Bowles's leaking stories to reporters. Bowles was criticized for going beyond his mandate and taking positions without authorization. Bowles was accused of being a publicity hound.

Tom wondered whether

> Chet's obsession with writing and speaking . . . will endear him to Jack. . . . [Chet] is admired in academic circles as a good public relations exponent of mutually held positions. But this also means that he has no independent academic standing of his own. His overlay of sentimentalism, fuzziness and imprecision may not endear him to Jack on greater exposure. . . . As an infighter, he may fall between the two stools of politics and professionalism. He is neither. Rather like Jack himself, he is a broker between the two.[31]

A crisis and near rupture in the Kennedy-Bowles partnership came early in August over the question of whether Bowles should run again for Congress. Bowles told Kennedy that he was concerned that a reelection campaign of his own might harm his ability to be effective to Jack. Chet asked Jack if they could have an exchange of letters to help explain to Chet's constituents why he would not seek reelection.

"Sure," said Jack.

Then nothing happened. When Chet raised the matter again, Jack appeared to have forgotten what he had said or else to have changed his mind. Jack now told Chet that it would be a mistake for him to give up the House seat. Chet could easily win reelection, Jack told him, by ten days of campaigning. He would still have plenty of time left over for the presidential campaign. This alarmed Chet, for it suggested that he might end up forgotten as a backbencher in the House. Even worse, he could lose, be cast off by Kennedy, and end up with nothing.

Averell Harriman and David Bruce were evidently also campaigning hard for the State Department post. Bowles confided to Tom that Abe Ribicoff might also be interested in State. Ribicoff had told Kennedy that he would not call a special election to fill the Bowles seat if Bowles did not run. Ribicoff was determined, he told Chet, to do everything he could to keep Chet in Connecticut. He said that duty demanded that Bowles stay put in the House of Representatives.

But Chet surmised that the governor wanted to enhance his own chances for a cabinet appointment. Kennedy had said naming Ribicoff and Bailey to high positions in a Kennedy administration would not jeopardize Bowles's chances.

Kennedy had assured Bowles, Ribicoff, and Bailey separately that he would not be guided by state quotas in appointments. Ribicoff, Bailey, Bowles, and Benton were all major politicians from Connecticut, a small state with too many politicians for its size. But Kennedy could not possibly ignore geography completely in his appointments. Bowles told Tom that he had had an unpleasant conversation with Ribicoff, which drove him to abandon the campaign for a few days. Chet needed to "walk in the woods with Steb."[32]

Kennedy's reluctance to the exchange of letters apparently stemmed from a JFK conversation with reporter William Lawrence of the *New York Times*. Lawrence had written an article about the race between Stevenson and Bowles for secretary of state. He had predicted that neither man would actually get the nod. If an exchange of letters occurred, as Bowles had requested, Lawrence told Kennedy that he would write an article saying that this advantaged Bowles over Stevenson. Bowles had no knowledge of this conversation and persisted in his efforts to get Kennedy to agree to the exchange. Kennedy finally told Chet the letter exchange was off; it would be up to Chet himself to decide whether to run.

Ted Sorensen and Tom Hughes had tried to exchange draft letters at one point. Bobby Kennedy's concurrence was required before Jack would sign. The problem was that the drafts Tom produced proved, one after another, to be unacceptable to Ted and Bobby. Finally, a draft was produced that seemed acceptable, but a weekend summit of Kennedy's inner circle at Hyannisport decided that any letter at all was bound to antagonize Stevenson.

Bowles decided that he would not run for the House again. He would issue his own statement, and he purchased TV time on the two stations in his district to explain his decision to the voters. He told the voters that if offered a position in a Kennedy administration, he would accept the appointment. Since he did not intend to serve the full term, he felt obliged to give the party and candidates the time to prepare for the November election. The statement was issued on August 11 and broadcast on TV a few days later. He received favorable publicity for explaining his intentions to the voters.

LATE MOVES IN THE CAMPAIGN

Chet's sense of relief did not last long. Hughes had feared that Chet's close association with JFK would not necessarily produce mutual confidence. Kennedy's patience with his chief foreign policy adviser seemed to wane with greater exposure.

The intensity of the campaign made it increasingly difficult to reach the candidate as he campaigned across the country. Bowles hatched the idea of Kennedy making a short trip to Europe to confer with French president Charles de Gaulle, West German chancellor Konrad Adenauer, and several British leaders. The trip would be unannounced and have a dramatic impact, Bowles argued, neutralizing the Nixon claim to political stature as sitting vice president. Stevenson was consulted and opposed the idea. Kennedy finally rejected the proposal as "too gimmicky."

On August 30, Bowles received a shock when Paul Nitze paid a call on him. Nitze told him about the new Nitze-led task force on national security. Chet had no idea what Nitze was talking about. What task force had been created, and what was its role? Kennedy had told no one, Nitze said. The Nitze group was to team up with Senator Henry M. "Scoop" Jackson's Senate study group, which was to review and recommend solutions to national security problems before a new Democratic administration took office. The move would be announced the next day.

Hughes's diary noted that Chet "then saw Kennedy, and JFK half apologized for the Nitze move. Blamed it all on Scoop Jackson, said he hadn't read the press release carefully. The task force didn't amount to anything, etc. Jack expressed great disquiet over Adlai and said he wasn't helping at all in the campaign, told Chet to tell Adlai (!) to get busy and bring his supporters along."[33]

Chet decided to talk things over with Adlai and invited him for dinner at his rented Q Street mansion in Washington. Adlai "was very nervous, sparring, and hard to talk to. At least until he had two martinis and then it went smoother. They discovered they had both been assigned to the same things—laughed about it and decided to divide the job."[34]

The two old friends decided that they had been had by Kennedy. They worked out a modus operandi to deal with Nitze if Nitze proved to be troublesome. Since neither Chet nor Adlai accepted JFK's assurances about the Nitze appointment, Hughes was sent to find out the real meaning behind

Nitze's appearance on the scene. What Tom found out from Ted Sorensen contradicted everything JFK had just told Bowles and Stevenson. Nitze was to be involved in both the campaign and in transition planning. He would have wide latitude, and JFK would rely implicitly on Nitze's sound thinking. Bowles, Sorensen told Hughes, should welcome the addition of this seasoned pro. In practice, the Nitze appointment led to crossed wires and conflict in the campaign.

Bowles discovered that Nitze had paid a call to Chris Herter and informed Herter that he was now the liaison with the Eisenhower administration. Herter informed Nitze that Chet Bowles had been designated as JFK's official liaison with the Eisenhower administration. This disposed of Nitze's power grab, but Bowles was taken aback by Nitze's chutzpah.

When a crisis developed in the Congo, it was debated whether Kennedy should criticize Ike's inaction. Hughes prepared a memo for Bowles to send to Kennedy. Kennedy would sometimes follow Bowles's advice and sometimes not.

Taking no position on the Congo appealed to Kennedy's inner circle. Kennedy received the Bowles Congo memo and decided it was too aggressive and might embarrass Ike to no good purpose. Ever since the U-2 incident, when JFK had been burned by some press reports that he wanted Ike to apologize to the Soviets, the Kennedy team had been cautious about Kennedy's public statements on foreign policy.

Kennedy was rescued from potential embarrassment by President Eisenhower. Ike spoke out on the Congo and called for exactly what the Bowles memo had recommended. Bowles and Hughes for their part were not certain whether JFK had even seen the Bowles memo. Ever since Bowles became foreign policy adviser, he had sent a stream of memos to JFK. Only intermittently had he gotten any response.

Chet therefore sought to reach Kennedy by phone when he had something important to say. But it was getting harder and harder for Chet to get through to Jack himself. Just before the first televised debate, Bowles telephoned Hughes from Maine with instructions on style for JFK (wear a dark suit, use makeup, and so on). Hughes could not get the tips through to Kennedy, to Bobby, or to Ted Sorensen.

On another occasion, Bowles wrote an article on Senator Kennedy's foreign policy for the magazine *America*. The article had extensive staff input from JFK aides, the speechwriting team under Archibald Cox, and from Hughes. But JFK himself apparently took no interest or saw no need to approve what Bowles would say. As it turned out, Kennedy did not like the end product.

Seeking a role, Bowles attempted to ingratiate himself with LBJ for the Southern campaign. Overcoming his shock at the selection of Johnson as the vice presidential candidate, Bowles wrote an obsequious letter to LBJ, offering his services on foreign policy. Despite Chet's efforts, the idea of a Northern liberal working on the Southern campaign made no sense to Lyndon, who did not reply to Chet's letter.

Discipline in the campaign was getting looser while at the same time the inner circle was trying to tighten its grip on decisions. Hughes had the impression that Kennedy staffers were more interested in their own future roles in the White House than in seeing their man elected. Ted Sorensen, not usually known for his wit, quipped that it was "every man for himself on the New Frontier."

One of the most important of the late moves in the campaign was an unforeseen opportunity to win Black votes, which arose when the family of Martin Luther King Jr. sought help from Harris Wofford after King was jailed in Birmingham, Alabama, for driving without a license. The charge resulted in probation, but then the Reverend King was given a four-month sentence after his arrest at a sit-in. On October 24, Mrs. Coretta Scott King phoned Harris Wofford, who had become close friends with the Kings during his work on the Civil Rights Commission with Father Theodore Hesburgh. Mrs. King told Wofford that she feared for her husband's life if he remained in jail.

Wofford immediately decided that he would have his influential friends call to comfort and reassure Coretta King. Harris called Chet and asked him to call Mrs. King. Bowles promptly called Mrs. King. Adlai Stevenson was with Chet when he received the call from Harris and made the call to Mrs. King. After some conversation with Mrs. King, Chet gestured for Adlai to take the phone. Adlai declined, saying that he did not know and had never even met Mrs. King.[35]

Harris wanted to have JFK call Mrs. King, and Chet encouraged him. But this required some doing since Harris's relationship with Robert Kennedy was strained. Bobby deemed Harris too liberal, too high-principled, and too much like his brother-in-law Sarge Shriver to be a true Kennedy man. Harris got on well with Ted Sorensen and the other Kennedy aides, but Bobby's antipathy blocked easy access to Jack. Harris was also not sure, given Lyndon Johnson's southern campaign, whether a gesture to the Kings would be welcome. Bowles advised him to consult with Sargent Shriver.

Shriver was enthusiastic. He told Harris later how he managed to get through to Kennedy. He went to see Jack but found him surrounded by the Irish mafia. Fearful that they might see a call to Coretta King as gimmicky and at odds with Lyndon's Southern efforts, he waited until he was alone with his brother-in-law. He explained Wofford's idea to Jack. It could be valuable in winning Black votes but was also the right thing to do. No commitments were necessary, just reach out and say you are aware of the situation and want to help. Kennedy sat quietly and said nothing for thirty seconds. Shriver could almost hear the wheels turning.

"That's a very good idea," Kennedy finally said. "Do you have the number?"

Shriver had the number, and Kennedy made the call. The Kennedy campaign was prepared to call for King's release from jail, but this proved to be unnecessary. Knowledge of the Kennedy phone conversation was enough for the Atlanta authorities to release King. Reverend Martin Luther King Sr., who had been a Nixon supporter, announced that he was switching his loyalty to Kennedy.

Meantime, Bowles had continued his efforts to influence JFK's speaking agenda for the critical last month of the campaign. On September 30, he sent a final memo to John F. Kennedy, headlined "Notes on Various Subjects for Speech Materials," identifying topics and volunteering his services for Kennedy speeches. Republican failures were generally a result of their efforts to "freeze existing situations . . . thereby associating us with the despised old order."[36]

Chet criticized Republican indifference to Africa, Herter's policies on Nkrumah and Ghana, the Republican approach to the Middle East, and Nixon's statements on Indochina. On the problem of Castro, the best policy, he suggested, would be "to sit quietly and watch developments."[37] Chet got no response from Kennedy for his late efforts. This period was, as Hughes's diary records in mid-October, a "pathetic situation for Chet. He hasn't talked to Kennedy in over a month."[38]

Bowles spent much of the campaign's final month on a get-out-the-vote tour of the West and Midwest, speaking engagements in Pennsylvania and New Jersey, and TV interviews. Tom accompanied Chet on the midwestern and western tour. Their point of contact with the campaign was the man Bowles privately referred to as "that little s.o.b. Dick Goodwin."

On November 3, Tom had lunch with a reporter friend from the *Minneapolis Star-Tribune*. The two men reviewed the secretary of state sweepstakes and concluded, "Big victory helps Chet & Stevenson. Small one improves chances for an unknown acceptable to the Establishment (Dean Rusk)."[39]

On election day, November 8, Tom and Jean drove to Essex, Connecticut, to join Chet and Steb Bowles and a large group of Bowles's friends and neighbors. The Connecticut returns came in first, showing very heavy voting, with JFK well ahead. Kennedy won the state with a comfortable 94,000-vote margin. But Bill St. Onge was defeated for Chet's House seat by Horace Seely-Brown Jr., the Republican predecessor, whom Chet narrowly had defeated two years earlier.

The national results came in slowly, and most of the party went to bed in the early morning with the result still hanging in the balance. Only on the following morning was it clear that JFK had eked out a thin popular and electoral vote victory.

The key issue was now where Bowles stood in the campaign for secretary of state. Hughes conferred with Abe Chayes and Chet on Chet's appointment:

> We agreed that a relationship with Dean Rusk might be very important and that Chet should have him in mind for Under Secretary in case the question comes up. I am going to contact Andy Biemiller to see how solid the labor people are. Abe is going to work on Kissinger, Cox, (Schlesinger says that Chet would bore JFK as Secy of State. He is for Stevenson.) Jewish groups are actively opposing Fulbright.[40]

The campaign for Chet continued, with Tom working from Washington, Abe sounding out his Cambridge colleagues, and Chet visiting JFK in Palm Beach.

In one of the last entries in his diary, Tom reported that, "Joe Kennedy and Herbert Hoover Jr., have arranged a summit meeting (golf) for Jack and Nixon tomorrow."[41]

The November 14 golf summit was intended to reassure Americans and underscore the nation's tradition of the peaceful transfer of power. The patriarch reasoned that the event would show the president-elect and Vice President Nixon in a friendly match, which would be good for the country and for his son politically.[42]

The foursome consisted of the president-elect, his old carousing buddy from the Senate, George Smathers of Florida, Vice President Richard Nixon, and John Sharon, a Stevenson supporter who was in Florida to deliver a handsome bound volume of Stevenson position papers to Kennedy. Sharon was lobbying for Adlai's appointment as secretary of state.

The day after this golf match, Tom Hughes got a phone call from an excited John Sharon, with a story to tell. John was arriving back in Washington from Palm Beach; could they have lunch?

On the first tee, Sharon told Tom at the lunch, the foursome's atmosphere was rather stiff. There was some forced small talk and an awkwardness. On the second tee, Nixon said to Kennedy,

"Jack, I know you stole the election in Illinois. But I want to assure you that I'm not going to barnstorm around the country complaining about it. I'm not going to put the country through that."

On the third tee, Nixon said,

"Jack, there's one more thing. If you appoint a certain person to your cabinet, I might be strongly tempted to reconsider my decision."

Kennedy was bemused.

"Well, Dick, who has got you so riled up?"

"Chester Bowles. That son-of-a-bitch wants to recognize Red China."[43]

7

The New Frontier

Planning for the new administration would have to take into account the narrowness of the victory. How to account for the slim margin? The Democrats running for Congress received slightly more than 54 percent of the total popular vote, whereas Kennedy's presidential plurality over Nixon amounted to only 49.7 percent of the popular vote. The Kennedy forces had been expecting a more comfortable victory, based on their latest polls. In Joseph Kennedy's retrospect on the election, the villain was Cardinal Francis Spellman of New York City. The cardinal quietly favored Nixon because of the vice president's hard-line anticommunism. Spellman was also disturbed by Kennedy's attempt in his famous Texas speech to separate his political views from his Catholicism. The cardinal saw this as a disparagement of the Church's teaching and a contradiction of Vatican guidelines.

Joseph Kennedy suspected that Cardinal Spellman had been responsible for the failure of American bishops and the Vatican to line up behind Jack. The result, he felt, was a lower-than-expected Catholic vote for JFK, which was directly attributable to the failure of the American Church and the Vatican to support Jack actively. Fortunately, Spellman's betrayal was offset by strong Jewish and Black turnout. The patriarch, however, never forgave Spellman. He cut off all contact with him and halted all funding for the special mental health hospital that he had negotiated with the cardinal and pledged to support.[1] Cardinal Spellman continued to haunt the Kennedys postelection with his self-styled role as the vicar of Vietnam.

BOWLES FOR SECRETARY OF STATE?

For Tom Hughes, the Bowles performance in the campaign had been excellent and, as far as he could tell, Bowles had not permanently offended any of the key Kennedy people. Yet the comment of a reporter friend that a close election would hurt Bowles's chances stuck in his mind. Bowles had another, more immediate problem, though, which demanded Tom's attention. As the campaign for secretary of state entered the most critical phase, a tape shown on British TV falsely claimed that Bowles, in May 1959, advocated U.S. recognition of Communist China. Bowles, in fact, had merely discussed potential future scenarios that might strain relations between Formosa and mainland China but steered clear of any call for recognizing Red China. However, Senator Norris Cotton (R-N.H.), fresh from reelection, picked up the issue and stormed onto the Senate floor to level the charge against Bowles. Nixon believed the charge, too, as evidenced in his remark to Kennedy at their golf encounter in Florida. Hughes was assigned the task of rebutting the accusation against Bowles.

Chet's prolific writing was part of the problem. Senator Cotton contended that a March 1960 Bowles article in *Foreign Affairs* was further proof of Bowles's softness toward mainland China. Hughes, who had drafted that article for Chet, was worried that his handiwork might have sunk Chet's chances of becoming secretary of state.

Hughes issued press releases denying the Cotton charge and met with Cotton's staffers to refute their boss's statements. Hughes phoned the BBC to check on Chet's broadcast and called the AP and UPI to challenge Cotton's allegations. Tom also sought the aid of Sig Harrison, a friendly journalist from the *New Republic,* to view the TV tape and explain the circumstances of the filming. Harrison was satisfied that Bowles had not called for recognition of Communist China.[2]

On November 12, a nervous Chet Bowles phoned Hughes "from Essex 3 times and from New Haven twice."[3] After Senator Cotton backed off, Bowles and Hughes shifted their attention to planning the transition at the State Department. Bowles had been given this assignment early in the campaign from Kennedy, and it was reaffirmed in their phone call the morning after the election. There was a strong chance Bowles would land somewhere in a senior post, but it was not guaranteed that he would get what he wanted. While waiting for the president-elect's decision, he could not hurt but only help his chances by pressing ahead with planning for the transition at State. Hughes was still on the Bowles congressional payroll until January and assumed that he would follow Chet into the government in some capacity. But Tom prepared a résumé just in case and made soundings of his own with his friends in the Kennedy camp.

Tom's most frequent point of contact with the Kennedy team during the campaign for secretary of state was his old friend Harris Wofford. Harris and Abe Chayes continued to push for Chet. Harris agreed that William Fulbright's star was fading, as civil rights groups were beginning to oppose him. Wofford remained adamantly opposed to Stevenson as secretary of state or anything else, but he agreed that Adlai remained a formidable candidate for the secretary post. He saw David Bruce as a strong candidate, too, having the support of Dean Acheson and the Euro-Atlantic national security community. Acheson was also backing his son-in-law Bill Bundy for state, national security adviser, or some high-level post in defense. Acheson fumed at the presumption of McGeorge Bundy, who evidently took pleasure in outdoing his older brother. Harris and Tom surmised that an interview Bowles had with *U.S. News and World Report* had probably hurt Chet's chances. The story, published under the heading "World Peace—The New Approach," featured various quotes from Bowles, such as "Power involves not only missiles but ideas, people," "Faith, not fear, built U.S.," and "On arms control we must be prepared honestly to negotiate."[4] The Kennedy hardliners would view the article as an example of Chet's softness toward communism and his fuzzy, Third World orientation.

On Tom's prospects, Harris believed that Tom was likely to be offered a position on the NSC staff but could stay with Chet, depending on what appointment Chet got. Abe Chayes, their fellow Chet-setter, was firmly locked in as State's legal counsel. The Kennedy crowd was young, but for that reason they had to be careful in filling too many top posts with other young people.

Tom turned thirty-five on December 11, 1960, and Harris was four months younger, so they thought it might be a stretch for either of them to be nominated for anything requiring Senate confirmation. Harris wanted to be assistant attorney general for civil rights, but Bobby Kennedy considered Harris too liberal and vetoed him.[5] Harris then sought and got from Ted Sorensen the authority to begin drafting the civil rights legislation the administration had pledged to submit to Congress. He was assured of an appointment as assistant to the president on civil rights. The Democratic platform was a strong civil rights document, but JFK had made no reference to the platform in the campaign. Sorensen, while difficult to deal with personally, was the liberal in the Kennedy entourage. He, along with Sargent Shriver, pushed Kennedy to the left, while the Irish mafia, brother Bobby, and the patriarch, Joe, pulled Kennedy to the right.

Kennedy's own instincts were difficult to read, even to his closest aides. He was both hawk and dove on defense: he favored a big increase in the defense budget but at the same time wanted nuclear arms control and believed in summit meetings with Soviet leaders. He was willing, pushed by Bowles, to express regret over the U-2 incident, if this would be a sufficient condition for a summit with Khrushchev.

The New Frontier

A focus on the Green Berets, the 1960s version of today's Army Special Forces, appealed to JFK as the way for the nation to repel communist aggression in the Third World. Kennedy ran on a foreign policy platform, largely accepting Bowles's argument that the Democrats had a natural advantage on domestic policy and therefore did not need to dwell on domestic issues in the campaign. The biggest concern, therefore, was to debunk the Republicans' contention that they were the stewards of world peace and national security.

But JFK did not buy into the Bowles worldview that the United States should use "soft power" to win the hearts and minds of the peoples of the Third World. JFK was, in his basic instincts, close to his father's views that the United States should build a fortress America in the Western hemisphere and strengthen noncommunist forces in our backyard. We should negotiate with Soviet leaders to achieve nuclear arms control and to bring about stability in other world trouble spots. More than any ideology, however, JFK's foreign policy views were tactical responses to campaign developments. The Alliance for Progress began as a campaign slogan, but the underlying concept was vague beyond the notion that social and economic development in the Western Hemisphere would prevent the rise of communism. The Peace Corps was similarly inspired by campaign rallies in the Wisconsin primary and in the late stages of the general election in Michigan (though based on ideas originating from Senator Hubert Humphrey and Representative Henry Reuss in the 1950s). Summit diplomacy was embraced in the campaign's reaction to the U-2 incident.

In a postelection meeting with Dick Goodwin, Tom found him "full of self-satisfaction. The election was won almost single-handedly by himself, Ted Sorensen, and JFK. . . . Most of the work had to be done on the plane."[6] Sensing that his attitude denigrated the Bowles role, Goodwin added defensively that, of course, all memos were delivered to and read by Kennedy; nothing, not a single memo, was withheld from JFK. So, Tom wanted to ask, JFK read, and rejected, every single one of Chet's memos? This thought was confided to Tom's diary, however, not to Goodwin. Tom did ask about Goodwin's own future role and was told that Dick had been offered a job on the White House staff.

Ralph Dungan was working on names for President Kennedy's attention. Hughes found him "obviously tense about Sorensen" and his own role with respect to Sorensen. Ted was "pushing hard for Mike Feldman for Budget director," a job Ralph wanted.[7] Roger Hilsman, enthused after meeting with Paul Nitze, wanted Tom to join him and Nitze at the National Security Council (NSC) or in Defense. Hilsman thought he could also land in State. If this happened, would Tom be interested in joining him? Tom had worked with Roger on Capitol Hill, and the two men were good friends.

Kennedy's mandate to Chet, early in the campaign, to have regular liaison meetings with Christian Herter seemed to assure Bowles an important role in the transition. But the confusion in the campaign's late stages carried over into the transition planning. There was one odd incident shortly after Bowles began working on the transition for the State Department in mid-November. Chet received a copy of a three-page letter that JFK had sent to John Sharon at the George Ball–Adlai Stevenson law firm, with a cover letter addressed to Bowles. It asked Bowles to "work with the others immediately in setting up task forces so that we will have specific recommendations in shape by the inauguration."[8]

The letter to Sharon directed him to take the lead in setting up a task force with Bowles, Rostow, and Nitze on Latin America, Africa, food for peace, and arms control. Hughes phoned Sharon to ask him what was the status of the work outlined in Kennedy's letter.

"What letter?" said Sharon. "I haven't received any letter from Kennedy."

Sharon was mystified, though intrigued, suspecting that JFK might have settled on Stevenson for secretary of state. Hughes brought the letter to Sharon's law firm, where he and his partners "thermofaxed it in a frenzy over what it meant."[9] Sharon expressed surprise because he had spoken with Kennedy personally in the period since the letter was apparently written and Kennedy had not mentioned the letter. In fact, the president-elect had specifically asked Sharon not to coordinate with Nitze. The letter bore the traces of hasty draftsmanship and misspelled both Fulbright's and Nitze's names. Sharon would attempt to sort this out, he told Tom. He called Hughes later to say that he had "talked with Jack again and the letter was a mistake."[10]

The Sharon correspondence nevertheless triggered a swift reaction from Bowles. He asked Hughes to draft a letter to JFK suggesting a new approach to take better advantage of the interim period and to plan for announcing major appointments in an orderly fashion. Bowles observed that the current confusion was creating a bad impression. The new administration should not start off in a state of disorganization. The solution, as Chet saw it, was for Kennedy to appoint a "czar" to take charge during the transition, ensuring orderliness in the flow of appointments and public announcements. His candidate for this job was Clark Clifford, a Washington insider who was not identified with any of the current office seekers. Bowles sent Tom Hughes to see Clifford, show him the letter, and get his approval.

Clifford had an elegant office with a spectacular view of the Capitol from the window behind his desk. To impress visitors, Clifford usually had the drapes drawn when the visitor arrived and then would push a button to open the drapes and reveal the view. Clifford read the draft carefully and pronounced it excellent.

"But," he said, "there is a problem."

Clifford explained that he had heard disturbing rumblings about the Southern electors. There may be some kind of revolt brewing, he thought, which did not bode well for Kennedy. Clifford made a persuasive case that Kennedy should take the potential revolt of "faithless electors" in the South seriously. Kennedy should nip any revolt in the bud. Clifford recommended that JFK start out with some prominent conservative appointees to mollify the South, saving the announcement of liberal appointees for later. This might not seem logical, but it made sense politically. Given the closeness of the election, JFK should strive for a moderate and bipartisan-looking cabinet.

In the event of a deadlocked electoral college, the U.S. Constitution specifies that the House of Representatives will choose the president and vice president. In that case, the "one state, one vote" basis would portend an unpredictable outcome. A word to the wise was sufficient for Kennedy. His first personnel move in late November was to reappoint J. Edgar Hoover as FBI director and Allen Dulles as CIA director. Following the announcement, Tom Hughes sent a postcard to his friend Harris Wofford, who had campaigned earlier that year for the Kennedy-Bowles-Stevenson-Humphrey view of the world. Wofford, in his book *Of Kennedys and Kings,* records the card's message: "My old friend Tam Hughes sent me a postcard saying 'I want you to know that I finally voted for your J. Edgar Hoover–Allen Dulles–Kennedy–Bowles–Stevenson–Humphrey view of the world.' "[11]

Kennedy subsequently announced his intention to continue Douglas Dillon, a moderate Republican and Eisenhower appointee, in office as secretary of the treasury and to appoint Robert S. McNamara, recently named president of the Ford Motor Company and another moderate Republican, as secretary of defense. McGeorge Bundy, a Harvard dean and a Republican with an Eastern establishment pedigree, was named special assistant to the president for national security. Later, after a shake-up at the CIA, Kennedy added another prominent Republican, John McCone, as the new director of central intelligence.

THE TRANSITION AT STATE

With some measure of order finally established in the transition process, Bowles began to propose organizational changes and key personnel moves for the State Department. Bowles worked with the president-elect himself, but on a daily basis he worked most closely with Sargent Shriver, JFK's brother-in-law. Shriver had been given the role, the czar role recommended by Bowles, of overseeing the whole transition. Chet's team consisted of himself, Tom Hughes, and William "Butts" Macomber, a holdover from the Eisenhower administration, who had been assistant secretary of state for congressional relations. Chet consulted with Sarge on potential nominees for all ambassadorial posts and other key State Department appointments and did not hesitate to make suggestions for other departments as well.

The Bowles team interviewed many potential office seekers in the course of its work. Tom Hughes described how this worked. "The A team list—the most important people and applicants for major jobs, went to see Chet and Sarge. I was in the office next door and I got the B team, the lesser jobs and everybody else who wanted something."[12] Macomber was very useful to the team and made the work bipartisan in important respects. He was able to give the others thoughtful evaluations of sitting ambassadors, for example, and suggest who among the Eisenhower appointees was doing a good job and should be retained in the post. Macomber's knowledge of the upper ranks of the Foreign Service helped the team decide whom to recommend for promotion to important positions.

A Bowles favorite, and someone whose career he sought to advance, was Richard Bissell from Bowles's home state of Connecticut. Dick Bissell, Bowles told his colleagues, was one of the ablest men of his generation. Bissell had been offered a tenured appointment in the Yale Economics Department but had turned it down to remain in government. Bowles was close to the Bissell family in Connecticut. During the transition, Chet asked Allen Dulles for Bissell's release from his CIA duties. Dulles told Bowles that Bissell could not be spared; he was involved in an important top secret mission. Bowles had no idea at this time of Bissell's commanding role in planning the Bay of Pigs invasion. Chet persisted and finally wrung from Dulles permission to talk to Bissell about a potential job in the State Department and a Dulles pledge not to stand in the way if Bissell were interested in moving to State. Bissell met with Bowles, listened patiently to Chet's sales pitch, and expressed mild interest, but in the end he decided to stay at the CIA. The exercise was probably intended to keep Bowles in the dark about the Bay of Pigs.

A delicate issue for Bowles was how to handle Dean Rusk both before JFK's decision on the secretary of state and after the announcement of Rusk's nomination. Bowles praised Rusk to Shriver as perfectly qualified for a senior management position but added that he was especially well suited for under secretary of state. In a "personal and confidential" memo to Sargent Shriver of November 17, Bowles wrote, "Between you and me, if I am asked to take the responsibilities for the State Department, my first choice for Under Secretary, with direct responsibility for carrying out policy decisions, would be Dean Rusk. . . . Although he is not primarily a policy innovator or experienced in dealing with the press or public, he is extremely intelligent, thorough, balanced, and professional."[13] When the decision was finally made and the roles of the two men were exactly reversed, Hughes had "dinner alone with Rusk and Bowles that night. Rusk said he would not have accepted as Secy unless Under Secy was to be Bowles!"[14]

Since he had been meeting regularly with Secretary of State Christian Herter since March 1960 as JFK's representative, Bowles discussed transition issues with Herter. He reviewed the roster of U.S. ambassadors to check who was doing a good job and which issues should be addressed first by the new administration. Bowles also paid courtesy calls on foreign ambassadors on JFK's behalf.

Meanwhile, Adlai Stevenson's fortunes had seemingly risen by virtue of an impressive report on the whole range of foreign policy issues prepared by a team of experts in New York working under Adlai's direction. Bowles said that he did not want to burden Kennedy by sending him long memos, but he had Hughes draft a new memo for JFK, pointing out which of Adlai's recommendations directly contradicted positions taken by Kennedy in the campaign.

On November 29, Chet had breakfast with JFK in Palm Beach and reported on his conversations with Soviet ambassador Mikhail Menshikov and others. Chet described the JFK meeting to Hughes as "a pleasant noncommittal time with Jack at breakfast."[15] Kennedy "asked all the right questions on policy, seemed pleased over Chet's letter, though perhaps a little reluctant at the Clark Clifford assignment, and asked whether anything could be done with Cuba!"[16] The president-elect announced to the press Chet's role in vetting ambassadors and said that Chet would go to Puerto Rico for three days to meet with Munoz Marin and other Latin American leaders. He also directed Bowles to visit Nelson Rockefeller in New York and make overtures about a role of some sort for him in the new administration. Bowles got no indication of his leaning on the secretary of state position but surmised that the appointment would be announced within a week or so.

While it was generally assumed that Kennedy would play an active role in foreign policy and be in some measure his own secretary of state, Kennedy knew very little about the internal workings of the State Department and had limited contacts with Foreign Service professionals and with foreign leaders. Hence Bowles believed that JFK welcomed his initiatives. Bowles was pleased with his team's work. The list of envoys included a blend of distinguished academics such as Galbraith to India, Reischauer to Japan, and Gordon to Brazil, able and experienced career Foreign Service officers, and the inevitable donors and political appointees who had played roles in the campaign.

There were a few misfires. One such case came from the president-elect's intervention. Earl E. T. Smith, who had previously served as U.S. envoy to the Battista regime in pre-Castro Cuba, was nominated as ambassador to Switzerland. The Swiss ultimately declared Smith persona non grata on the grounds that his previous service would make it difficult for them to represent remaining U.S. interests with the Fidel Castro government, a role the Swiss assumed when the United States severed diplomatic relations with Cuba in December 1960. President Kennedy's admiration evidently was not so much for Mr. Smith as it was for Mrs. Smith. Her company could presumably be enjoyed more fully with her husband posted abroad. The nomination's collapse ensured the triumph of family values. The Smiths were reunited, and the president was saved from himself.[17]

On December 5, Bowles reported in a memo to JFK on his trip to Puerto Rico and his conference with Governor Munoz Marin and former president Figueres of Costa Rica. The matter foremost on the minds of Marin and Figueres, and in their view on the minds of other Latin American leaders, as well, was the threat posed by Castro to the region: "The association of Castro with the Soviets was looked upon as a disaster which might have been avoided."[18] The Latin Americans blamed the United States for mishandling the Castro revolution that might have been turned into an anticommunist reform movement in much of the region. But the most crucial observation by Marin and Figueres was their warning that "an American trained and armed force was now in Guatemala waiting for an opportunity to invade the island [Cuba]" and that "under present circumstances such an operation was bound to fail and would be widely resented in Latin America."[19]

The most interesting point of the San Juan conversation was that Governor Munoz "urged us to take whatever steps we could, overt or otherwise, to change the present government in the Dominican Republic as this would be more likely to succeed and would demonstrate our antagonism to right wing as well as left wing dictators throughout Latin America."[20]

The Kennedy administration took this idea to heart. As one of his first actions in foreign policy, JFK authorized the CIA to give arms and ammunition to a group of conspirators planning to assassinate President Rafael Trujillo of the Dominican Republic.[21] Covert actions had seemingly brought success at relatively low cost in Guatemala, Iran, Berlin, and the Congo during the 1950s and had been a favorite tool of Ike and the Dulles brothers.[22]

THE FOREIGN POLICY TEAM

The important foreign policy personnel appointments began on December 9th when JFK offered the UN ambassadorship to Adlai Stevenson. The relationship between the two old antagonists began badly and got worse. The president-elect, still smarting over Stevenson's performance in the campaign, expected that Adlai would let bygones be bygones and accept at once. Adlai did nothing of the kind. He balked at the prospect of accepting the post without knowing who the secretary of state would be. He would have to think it over, he said, for he could not imagine "working with a

42-year-old Republican like [McGeorge] Bundy."²³ After some consideration, Adlai accepted the appointment when he learned that Rusk would be secretary and his old friend Chet under secretary and that he would have cabinet rank along with Rusk. The announcement of the Rusk, Bowles, and Stevenson appointments was made on December 11, 1960.

Kennedy knew Bowles and Stevenson but did not know Rusk. He had reluctantly given up on his first choice, his fellow Senator J. William Fulbright (D-Ark.), because of Fulbright's support for the Southern Manifesto. Rusk was a Democrat, a Rhodes scholar, a former assistant secretary of state for Far Eastern affairs, and president of the Rockefeller Foundation. Kennedy evidently was attracted by Rusk's meritocratic background and nonideological approach to issues and by a strong endorsement from Robert Lovett. Rusk had no political constituency of his own and would presumably be more malleable and less likely to have an agenda of his own than either Bowles or Stevenson.

Bowles, after his nomination, continued to work on the transition with the added authority of his nomination to the number two spot in the State Department. Hughes continued in his role as Bowles's chief aide while arrangements were made to transfer him to the State Department and process the necessary security clearances for his new job. Dean Rusk joined the Bowles transition team upon his nomination and approved of all of Chet's suggestions, insisting only that U. Alexis Johnson, an old friend, have a high-level post. Johnson, an experienced and respected Foreign Service officer, was named to State's number-four post, at the time called the deputy under secretary. Another Rusk favorite, George McGhee, was considered for State's number-three post, but it went instead to George Ball. Rusk made one negative decision: he vetoed the proposed appointment of Walt Rostow to any significant post.²⁴ Rusk was forced to accept Rostow within the first year of his tenure as secretary when JFK transferred Rostow from the White House staff to State as director of policy planning. Rostow remained there until 1966, when President Johnson named him as his national security adviser to succeed McGeorge Bundy.

Other significant appointees were Abram Chayes as the State Department's legal adviser; Roger Hilsman as assistant secretary for intelligence and research; Averell Harriman as assistant secretary for far eastern affairs; the Harvard professors noted earlier, Lincoln Gordon, Edwin Reischauer, and J. Kenneth Galbraith, as U.S. ambassadors; Edwin Martin, a respected career officer, as assistant secretary of state for inter-American affairs; Governor G. Mennen "Soapy" Williams, of Michigan, as assistant secretary of state for African affairs; and Edward R. Murrow as director of the United States Information Agency. William Macomber was retained from the Eisenhower administration as assistant secretary of state for congressional relations.

Chet Bowles estimated that one-third of his time from January to April 1961 was spent on staffing matters.[25] He was trying to recruit a new generation of U.S. ambassadors, and he saw, as one of his first substantive moves upon taking office, the need to strengthen the ambassador's authority in the embassy. Other agencies were now part of the American embassy, including the CIA, the Defense Department, the aid agencies, the Agriculture Department, and the FBI. As ambassador in India, Bowles had experienced the frustrations of trying to control what was going on in a large embassy with the various agencies pursuing their separate assignments and reporting back to their own headquarters. So Bowles assigned to Hughes the job of drafting a new presidential order to strengthen the ambassador's authority as chief of mission. This involved negotiating with other executive agencies. It took a great deal of time and effort and became, when President Kennedy signed the executive order in May 1961, one of the few clear accomplishments of Bowles's troubled tenure as under secretary.

There was no dearth of ideas in the Bowles office. On the contrary, there was an excess of ideas and a lack of follow-through in the work.[26] The team that ran the State Department worked not as a team but as a collection of individuals working at cross-purposes. The problems started at the top with the relationship between Rusk and Bowles. They had first met in 1951 and had a friendly but not close relationship while Rusk was president of the Rockefeller Foundation and Bowles was a trustee (1953–1960). Now in the State Department, they failed to come to an understanding on how to work together.

Rusk wanted help in running the department and considered Bowles's role to be principally that of management, the equivalent to the role of chief operating officer of a firm. Rusk had an appreciation for order and hierarchy from his service as a military officer and respected State Department traditions from his experience as assistant secretary of state during the Korean War. Policy ideas, in his view, flowed up from the Foreign Service ranks for consideration by the policy-level officials.

Bowles held an opposite view. Policy should be made at the top and the job of top-level officials was to shake up the bureaucracy. In the Bowles view, that was how best to serve the president—not by telling the president what the State Department felt about an issue but to tell the department what the president wanted. Rusk, in short, considered himself in the role of a detached CEO whose mission was to empower the operating units, the State Department's five regional bureaus, to formulate policy based on their expertise and that of the nongeographic bureau of intelligence. Bowles, a politician, considered that experts and bureaucrats always had to be redirected and their comfortable professional grooves brought into line with the deeper expertise and wisdom of elected officials.

When Rusk attended White House meetings with the president, his usual procedure was to make a short explanatory statement on a topic and turn the presentation over to a subordinate to present the department's position. It was not clear whether Rusk backed, had initiated, or was neutral on the proposal. The official making the presentation was uncertain whether he had the secretary's full backing and clearance from other bureaus.[27] This procedure was baffling to Kennedy, who liked the crisp, succinct, and forceful arguments he got from Robert McNamara or from his brilliant national security adviser, McGeorge Bundy. The president's impatience and his frustrations with the State Department began almost from the start and mounted.

Bowles, meanwhile, often allowed paperwork to build up while he pursued new ideas on what he saw as the most critical problems. Brandon Grove, the Foreign Service officer assigned to Bowles, greatly admired him but quickly concluded that Bowles was not an effective manager in the State Department setting. Grove often had to demand an hour's time and bring in a stack of papers for Bowles to sign, patiently explaining what each piece of paper was and why Bowles's signature was necessary.[28]

Bowles's personal style did not help him in his relations with either Rusk or JFK. Chet's didactic manner was not in sync with the way Kennedy liked to operate. Bowles tended to lecture on his latest enthusiasms, which was at odds with JFK's crisp, impatient style. This was evident during the campaign and became more problematical as the new administration took office. John Kenneth Galbraith describes a telling encounter in his memoir: "One day, when he was Undersecretary of State, I went into the Oval Office just after Chet came out. Kennedy said, 'Chet tells me there are six revolutions going on in the world. One is the revolution of rising expectations. I lost track of the other five.'"[29] The New Frontier style, personified by the president, was brisk, laconic, and to the point, not discursive, rambling, and ruminative. Kennedy tolerated Bowles during the campaign because he needed the old New Dealer to reach out to the party's left wing. But he needed Bowles less now, and his impatience was clear in their interactions.

For Hughes, the problem was the lack of an effective connection between Bowles and the career Foreign Service officers. The source was the underlying assumption of a natural antagonism between a stodgy bureaucracy and the dynamism of the New Frontier. As Hughes observed many years later, not sparing himself from the indictment, in an oral history interview,

> I think Bowles and the Kennedy people generally could be faulted for not connecting more successfully with their potential sympathizers in the Foreign Service. The FSOs were not all old fogeys, and many of them could have been of more genuine help than they turned out to be. Most of the assistant secretaries of the geographical bureaus (Europe, East Asia, and Latin America) were Foreign Service officers,

but they were newly appointed to their positions and chosen by the administration. Yet Kennedy himself, privately but frequently, complained about the [lack of] responsiveness at State. I probably should have been more active in bringing Bowles together with promising younger FSOs, and in retrospect I regret not doing so.[30]

PARADOXES OF THE NEW FRONTIER

Being a part of the New Frontier was an exciting time for Tom Hughes. The atmosphere in Washington was electric, and the nation's attention was riveted on the new president and his team. There was a buoyant mood, a sense that youth was displacing tired old age. Movement and action heralded a passing of the *ancien régime*. The new administration's early weeks in office seemed filled with energy and high purpose. The transition also had its mundane aspects, the hours were long, and there was much hard work.

But there were lighter moments as well for Hughes and his colleagues. There were the embassy parties where one constantly encountered one's friends, Georgetown dinner parties where one rubbed shoulders with the rich and powerful, gossip and rumors galore, and all of this in an environment in which public service was respected, learning was celebrated, and the life chances of Americans were improving. The mood seemed to Tom Hughes to resemble the old Student Federalist days.

There were some amusing aspects of his State Department job even though it was very demanding. Hughes had a visit in the transition period from the courtly Claiborne Pell, then a private citizen and later to be an influential U.S. senator and chair of the Senate Foreign Relations Committee. Pell wanted to make an appeal for an ambassadorial appointment. Expecting a request on Pell's own behalf, Hughes was surprised when Pell went on to extol the virtues of his elderly father, Herbert Pell, who had been FDR's ambassador to Portugal. Pell explained that his father did not expect, of course, a major post, such as Paris or London, but it would have to be slightly above Portugal for the sake of his father's dignity, perhaps Stockholm or Rome? Hughes inquired as to the senior Pell's age. Herbert Pell was well into his eighties, the younger Pell said, but he noted that his father was in quite good shape for a man his age.

Hughes observed that the New Frontiersmen made a bit of a fetish about age—youthful vigor, and so on—and the president himself was only forty-three. The senior Pell might thus encounter some resistance, but the president would surely be pleased that the distinguished former ambassador wanted to be part of the New Frontier. Hughes suggested that Pell might take the matter up with the president himself. The former ambassador, Hughes was subsequently informed, had decided upon reflection to remain in retirement.

It was to be expected that Hughes's fellow Rhodes scholars would be among those seeking to join the New Frontier. Eventually, according to an informal canvass conducted by Hughes, there were at least twenty-five Rhodes scholars in various jobs in the new administration (he later revised this number upward, to some thirty-three).

Rusk was a Rhodes scholar, and Hughes surmised that their membership in the select brotherhood was one reason why Rusk seemed to like him. Tom was a regular master of ceremonies and speaker at Rhodes official dinners held in Washington. Rusk admired Tom's witty and urbane after-dinner talks at these events. The presence of Rhodes scholars in its ranks added a touch of prestige to the New Frontiersmen.

Nicholas Katzenbach, a fellow member of the Rhodes class of 1947, paid a call on Hughes seeking a State Department appointment as the department's legal counsel. He had sat out the presidential campaign, remaining in Europe until after the election. The meeting got off on an odd footing when Katzenbach, who had not seen Hughes in years, mistook him for another Rhodes colleague from the class of 1947, kept calling him by the wrong first name, and recalled episodes that Hughes did not recognize. Finally, Katzenbach got to the point and declared that he wanted to be and thought he would be an excellent candidate for the job of legal counsel for the department. Hughes replied that the post was already spoken for.

"Well, can't we do something about that?" said Katzenbach.

Tom said that this was not likely. The person slated for the job was Abe Chayes, a close friend to President Kennedy who had worked hard in the campaign. Hughes suggested that Katzenbach instead should pay a call on Byron "Whizzer" White in the Justice Department, a fellow Rhodes scholar, who was looking for good lawyers. He should say that Shriver and Bowles sent him.

Katzenbach did so and was hired by White. He eventually was appointed U.S. Attorney General, and in 1966 moved to the State Department, replacing George Ball as the number two official in the department.

Another Rhodes scholar and Hughes friend, Phil Kaiser, put in a smoother performance as a job seeker. Kaiser arranged for a U.S. senator and three representatives to speak on his behalf for appointment as U.S. ambassador to one of the new African nations. Hughes decided that a delegation of this heft merited an upgrade, and he immediately brought the group next door to see Chet Bowles and Shriver. Kaiser was an ideal candidate for the new kind of ambassador that Bowles was looking for. He was young but had broad experience as assistant secretary of labor in the Truman administration and had also been a department head for Governor Averell Harriman of New York. He received the post of ambassador for Senegal-Mauritania.[31]

The notes and informal jottings that Hughes recorded from time to time (he no longer kept the daily diary) tell a more complex story than the narrative the Kennedy team sought to convey to friendly journalists. The public face of the New Frontier was one of optimism and self-confidence. Hughes's notes present a more somber assessment. The situation at the State Department was not going well. Part of the problem lay with the department's upper ranks, as noted earlier, but White House expectations and shortcomings were also at work.

Conflicting views about the capabilities of the Foreign Service, Hughes thought, were partly to blame for JFK's frustrations with Rusk and with the State Department. Bowles, Kennedy, the top White House aides, Roger Hilsman at State, and many New Frontiersmen generally were dubious about the Foreign Service's recruitment, training, and promotion practices. The younger officers were gradually hobbled by bureaucratic procedures, which eventually turned them into timid paper shufflers. Roger Hilsman, for example, had insisted on a general service appointment when he became director of the Bureau of Intelligence and Research (INR), because appointment as a Foreign Service officer would have given the impression that he wanted to burrow in as a careerist.[32]

Tom Hughes learned what was happening in the White House through Harris Wofford and other staffers. Because of Southern Democratic and Republican opposition, JFK had decided not to push for civil rights legislation in the near future. Harris, frustrated in his efforts to advance civil rights, shifted his attention to the Peace Corps to work with Sargent Shriver. President Kennedy's chief interest was foreign policy and it was soon evident that Bowles and Rusk did not enjoy high presidential favor.

In preparing his inaugural address, JFK had told Ted Sorensen, "Let's leave the domestic stuff out altogether." For Kennedy, foreign policy was the really important job of the presidency. "After all," as Kennedy remarked to Richard Nixon in April 1961, " . . . who gives a shit whether the minimum wage is $1.15 or $1.25, compared to something like Cuba."[33]

Rusk had made a ringing speech early in his tenure declaring that the president looked to the State Department for leadership.[34] But Kennedy clearly wanted to run his own foreign policy and to leave authority in the hands of a loose circle of White House aides. After the Bay of Pigs debacle, President Kennedy centralized power further in his inner circle. The State Department could not seize the leadership role, but certain presidential favorites, such as Roger Hilsman, continued to enjoy access and influence with the president.

As Hughes sized up the situation, Kennedy had won narrowly and felt obliged to appoint Republicans to some major posts. Kennedy knew that a clash of views was likely and that he would then attempt to manage the conflicting impulses, Hughes recorded in his private notes:

The image through Sorensen is the President as presider over conflicting group interests, pressures; the President as judge—indeed TS says he takes his lead from Cardozo's "The Nature of the Judicial Process." But the important things about a President are all the things that make him more than a judge and different from a judge. If he happens to be judicious as well as a leader determined to achieve things, so much the better. But he must not have that reservation of judgment, that antiseptic distance which judges have—or else he will not be a great President.

The White House [is] . . . all cold, calm, mysterious layers of protective coating—JFK likes this—politically safe, the communicated ambiguities are awesome, non-identification means maximum political pull.[35]

President Kennedy declared in his inaugural address, that "We shall pay any price, bear any burden, meet any hardship, support any friend, oppose any foe to assure the survival and success of liberty."[36] The inaugural's soaring phrases, Hughes thought, promised something more than the president as arbiter of clashing group interests. Kennedy, now that he was actually in office, discovered that the power to accomplish his purposes did not automatically come with the presidency, to be turned off and on like water from the faucet. Exercising power depended on harnessing and aligning the ambitions of other politicians with his own and on building coalitions based on a reciprocity of giving and getting favors. Kennedy had become the nation's youngest president by overturning the normal laws of political gravity, Hughes mused, and now was having to respond to the new order.

Presidents usually honed their political skills and picked up support as they progressed through the stages of a career in elective office. Kennedy had bypassed the usual steps up the ladder—he had short-circuited the process by leapfrogging over his elders.

Kennedy was different from his peers. He was trying to displace, not impress, his elders. He outspent, outsmarted, and outcampaigned his seniors. It was well and good for JFK to declare that the torch had been passed to the New Frontiersmen, to a new generation of Americans, but it was the older generation of Americans that still ran the Congress and filled the ranks of the executive agencies. The older politicians apparently did not get the memo that they were supposed to make way for youth.

The New Frontier's "special appeal and impact was due to the fact that it defied all the tawdry old laws of political propriety," Hughes wrote. "A whole generation of U.S. politicians felt deprived of opportunities. 2/3 of the Senate suddenly was too old [to] be President. In 1961 the Senate, an institution where ambition never dies, watched the ascendancy of its second youngest member and the withering away of the presidential ambitions of everyone between Warren Magnuson and Carl Hayden."[37]

Kennedy was trapped in the mystique he had created. Hughes, reverting to images from the English constitutional history he had studied at Oxford, described the president as lacking "King's men" in the Congress—that is, loyalists whose careers and political fortunes depended on his favor. The tactics that had worked so well in the campaign—glamour, cultivation of the press, youthful energy contrasted with stodginess, JFK's sex appeal with women voters—were not enough to win over the more conventional politicians. A wiser man might have reversed course and played down his differences from the traditional politicians. But Kennedy saw himself, Hughes concluded, as a forerunner of a coming new generation of world leaders.

Thus JFK persuaded Prime Minister Harold Macmillan to name the dashing David Ormsby-Gore, a friend of the president, as the UK ambassador to the United States. Kennedy had the elderly Wilhelm Grew replaced as West Germany's ambassador to the United States. Since he preferred youth over age, JFK liked dealing with Pakistan's Ayub Khan and disliked dealing with India's Nehru. As Kennedy surveyed the ranks of world leaders, he was amazed to discover how many were thirty or more years older than he was, including such diverse figures as Konrad Adenauer, Nehru, Charles de Gaulle, António Salazar, Chairman Mao, Khrushchev, Chiang Kai-shek, Ben Gurion, Harold Wilson, and Tito. These septuagenarians seemed bound to be, in the Kennedy worldview, replaced by the Brandts, Ayub Kahns, Sekou Toures, Ormsby-Gore, and other younger and more sympathetic leaders. Kennedy saw himself as the avatar of this new class of world leaders. Hughes, always disposed to question his own side's operational code as well as the opponent's, considered this cult of youth a flaw that would come to haunt the New Frontier.

THE NEW FRONTIER AND THE MEDIA

The mass media provided oxygen for the New Frontier. The New Frontier relied on friendly journalists to generate the favorable image the Kennedys and their cohorts enjoyed with the American people. Americans fell in love with their new president, who seemed to personify the youthful virtues. Journalists and their readers or viewers, it seemed, could not get enough of Kennedy and the New Frontiersmen, who all, it seemed, had their press contacts and talked freely about their plans. This meant, in practice, that the administration would speak with many voices. So many officials gave so many interviews that different versions were given of what the president said or thought on every topic. "Cuba policy," Tom Hughes observed in his notes, "is what Senator Smathers says it is in Florida, Senator Church says it is in Idaho, Senator Humphrey says it is in Minnesota, and Pierre Salinger says it is in Washington."[38]

The Washington press corps was made up increasingly of young, well-educated professionals who treated the young president almost reverentially. They largely accepted the premise that presidential leadership was the key to effective governance. Dynamic young figures were bringing fresh air and transparency to a formerly closed and lethargic process. It was known that the president was an avid reader of newspapers, often calling a reporter to praise an article he liked. Officials mentioned in a news story might gain favor if the story caught the president's eye. Since the president courted the media, so did other New Frontiersmen.

Tom Hughes, especially after he became the deputy director of State Department's INR, talked frequently with reporters but was circumspect and usually did not allow himself to be quoted. He talked regularly to Joe Alsop, Walter Lippmann, Max Frankel, and a number of friends he had known for years from the Cowles newspaper chain of Minnesota. Hughes recorded eleven private lunches or dinners with Joe Alsop at Alsop's Georgetown home and numerous meetings with Walter Lippmann over a similar period.[39]

Alsop would often claim that he was calling at the president's urging. After Hughes moved to the INR, Dean Rusk called him in one day to discuss a series of leaks apparently occurring in the State Department. Why, Rusk inquired, did anyone at the INR have to have contacts with the press? The bureau was, after all, secret, so why not make it a rule that intelligence analysts should avoid reporters?[40]

Hughes observed that there might be a problem with such a rule. Reporters were sometimes useful in providing information on what was happening in countries they had just visited. The meaning of all-source intelligence included following what was happening in the open press as well as surveying all classified government sources. Hughes wanted his analysts dealing with Southeast Asia, for example, to know what reporters who had visited Saigon and the Vietnam countryside were thinking. He was trying to cultivate an atmosphere of intellectual excitement using all-source information—what was happening in the universities, among media observers, as well as the work of colleagues in the intelligence community.

Furthermore, Hughes said that he had a special problem. He had just received a call from Joe Alsop, the president's friend, who wanted to have lunch to discuss a certain matter. Alsop claimed that he was calling at the president's suggestion. Of course, Alsop might have simply made this up. But maybe not. What should Hughes do? Rusk thereupon "assumed a Buddha-like posture. . . . Finally, he said, 'Well, perhaps, you had better go.'"[41]

As a friend of the president, Alsop went to the movies with the president and Arthur Schlesinger, was a frequent guest at Hyannisport, and befriended nearly every influential figure in the Kennedy administration.

Walter Lippmann was a legendary journalist and public intellectual whose opinions carried great weight with officials and the attentive public. Hughes's conversations with Lippmann were philosophical and intellectual. While the New Frontiersmen's press contacts enhanced their prestige in the elite social circuit, Hughes was circumspect in his dealings with the press because of his intelligence job. Many other officials up and down the ranks were less cautious. The prevailing notion, for the moment, was that all publicity was good publicity.

While President Kennedy loved favorable media attention like most politicians, he bitterly resented critical stories and disliked having to respond to hostile press inquiries. But critical media attention went with a competitive and professionalized press corps. Hughes contrasted "JFK's desire to be liked 100 percent across spectrum to FDR's glory in a 30 percent opposition—JFK wants no enemies. . . . FDR wanted to choose them."[42]

THE FOREIGN POLICY AGENDA

The Eisenhower administration had left JFK a large portfolio of unfinished business in Laos, Indochina, and Cuba, and in negotiations with the Soviet Union over Berlin and nuclear disarmament. The campaign had produced a grab bag of policy options, but these did not form a consistent set of initiatives. One could only tentatively infer what the New Frontier stood for and what its priorities might be. The New Frontier's goals included a military with a special focus on deterrence and successfully fighting, if necessary, the low-intensity conflicts. Such conflicts seemed likely in a context of superpower nuclear parity. There was a need both to maintain nuclear superiority to pursue nuclear disarmament, including as the important first step a ban on nuclear testing.

Kennedy was sold on the concept of flexible response rather than the Eisenhower-Dulles doctrine of massive retaliation. But Kennedy was not averse to—indeed, he welcomed—greater reliance on special forces to deal with low-intensity conflicts. A part of low-intensity conflict might be covert operations that the country might conduct under the concept of plausible deniability.

Though he had attacked the Republicans savagely in the campaign, Kennedy assumed that the country still largely subscribed to the consensus that had prevailed during the 1950s. Some of his campaign attacks on the Republicans were in the nature of Punch and Judy shows for the voters, who viewed politics largely as entertainment anyway. Kennedy had appointed Republicans to important posts, especially in foreign affairs, in recognition of the narrow victory.

The New Frontier did propose changes in foreign policy, the most important of which was the Kennedy team's rejection of Eisenhower's total reliance on nuclear deterrence and the doctrine of massive retaliation. Ike, in JFK's view, depended too heavily on nuclear forces alone to deter aggression. An enemy could wage low-intensity warfare against us—what Khrushchev called "wars of national liberation"—in which our nuclear superiority would be of little use.

A strong interest in the Western Hemisphere seemed to be implicit in Kennedy's views as expressed in the campaign. A strong anticommunism stance, directed especially toward Cuba, coexisted with an impulse to alleviate poverty. The Alliance for Progress was to be Kennedy's vehicle for reducing poverty and promoting social and economic development in the Western Hemisphere.

Kennedy wanted to be a foreign policy president. He would get his wish. The dizzying series of foreign policy crises that characterized the Kennedy presidency was perhaps not exactly what he had in mind.

8

Intelligence and Covert Operations

Tom Hughes faced new challenges when he took up his duties as deputy director of the Bureau of Intelligence and Research (INR) at the end of April 1961. In entering the arcane world of intelligence, he was now working for and with a contemporary, his friend Roger Hilsman, not a distinguished older figure. Tom enjoyed close friendships with both Bowles and Hubert Humphrey and continued to be on good terms with them. There was never a rigid hierarchy or strains in his relationships with them, but they were distinctly senior figures. The Roger Hilsman relationship was different. Tom had an easy relationship with Roger, a man his own age. Roger was direct, forceful, and outspoken to a fault. He was brash, even by the standards of the normally assertive New Frontiersmen.

Roger was an intellectual, but an intellectual of a rather unusual type. He had been in the job as INR director for only four months before bringing Tom in as his deputy. Thus Tom had the opportunity to help shape the bureau's development. The INR, they believed, had declined in stature and needed rebuilding.

Roger was a graduate of West Point and took his Ph.D. at Yale in international relations. He became Hughes's friend and colleague when he ran the Congressional Research Service. In that position, he interacted regularly with senators, representatives, and their staffs. Tom had worked with Roger when he was with Humphrey in the Senate and with Bowles in the House.

Hilsman was the son of a military officer and had the distinction of rescuing his father from a Japanese prison camp in Burma as one of Merrill's

Marauders during World War II. Roger was a war hero and was proud of it, but he aspired to be something more. He wanted to be a mover and shaker in great affairs, and he had experienced something of that feeling in his dealings with John F. Kennedy, as senator and then as president. The problem was to ensure his access to the president, not an easy task given the CIA's continuing efforts to monopolize the intelligence community's channels to the president.

Roger got on well with Kennedy and with Chester Bowles, less well with Dean Rusk, and uneasily with CIA officials, whom he regarded as his natural enemies in seeking presidential attention. His worst relations were with Secretary of Defense Robert McNamara (whose aggressive personality resembled his own) and with the Pentagon military brass.

A key part of Hilsman's mission at the INR, as he saw it, was to get the White House's attention—the president, ideally, and then JFK's key aides, McGeorge Bundy and Michael Forrestal. This would help put the bureau on the map, so to speak, and would motivate the INR's analysts to do their best and to produce their papers in a timely fashion. Timeliness was important to Roger since, in the intelligence business, getting out the first paper often shaped the future policy on an issue.

HUGHES AND THE INR

Roger Hilsman was not necessarily the ideal teacher for Hughes on the subtleties of intelligence. Hilsman was contemptuous of the mystique cultivated by intelligence professionals. Roger was inclined by temperament to upset apple carts and to deflate pretensions, and the pretensions of the intelligence professionals about their craft irritated him. Furthermore, he believed that the CIA had exercised undue influence in U.S. foreign policy during the Eisenhower era. Roger criticized his INR predecessor, Hugh Cumming, for not competing more aggressively with Allen Dulles and the CIA. Roger's view of the appropriate role for an INR director was summed up in an oral history interview he gave for the JFK presidential library in 1970: "You've got to kick the CIA; you've got to tread on their toes; you've got to make them toe the mark. You've got to fight with the Joint Chiefs of Staff. You have to do hard, political things. You have to get out in Congress, and you've got to make some enemies."[1]

Coming from Congress and the world of politics, Hughes and Hilsman were both accustomed to thinking like politicians. They believed in transparency and accountability as overall guiding principles. Generally speaking, Congress provided the natural check on the executive branch. At the same time, it was, of course, the president's responsibility to mobilize the expertise within the executive, formulate policies, and present them to Congress for consideration.

Congress, in discharging its own duties, normally and appropriately relied on the free press to engage the wider attentive public in dialogue. The public dialogue was an important part of the process of governing. Finally, the courts would come into play in the case of disputes between the two other branches. The courts were the referee in ensuring that the rules of fair play were fully observed.

The president, the Congress, the press, the courts, and the public were the important players, and the game was to be played openly, in full view. Of course, this textbook picture was not always completely accurate or fully observed in practice, but it was the norm. The CIA's rise after World War II complicated the picture. Secrecy became a part of government. The CIA's role had to be accounted for and explained. The CIA and the secret world in which it operated had to be accepted, challenged, or amended to fit with democratic norms.

The intelligence community seemed to have turned the normal rules upside down. Transparency was not encouraged but was avoided whenever possible. The executive branch now was adept at keeping secrets, rather than promoting public dialogue. If the CIA had its way, Congress would be kept in the dark except perhaps for a small circle of co-opted senior members. This line of criticism was vigorously disputed by the CIA and its numerous supporters. To outsiders such as Hughes and Hilsman, the criticisms, though perhaps exaggerated, could have had some basis in fact and were in some measure part of their thinking.

In their stewardship of the INR, Hilsman and Hughes blended two quite different styles and perspectives into an effective partnership. Roger was bold, and Tom was circumspect. Roger made waves and enemies; Tom quietly learned the mores of intelligence and made friends. But they agreed on their central task, namely, to transform the INR from a collector of miscellaneous information of doubtful relevance to policymakers into something quite different. Their aim was to make the INR a nimble analytical unit providing timely, policy-relevant papers, using all-source information, to high-level officials in the State Department and the White House.

As one of their first actions, they shed the function of compiling a voluminous databank of economic, political, and cultural statistics on different countries. This data effort, conducted under contract for the CIA, amounted to nearly one-third of the INR's budget and workload. It was a large project, producing information that was of limited use to policymakers. With the reorganization, the INR became a smaller but more focused entity, producing several kinds of papers for decisionmakers on emerging issues.

At no time during the combined Hilsman and Hughes tenure following the reorganization did INR staff exceed 350 employees. Its small size (and the INR never had staff in the field) belied its importance in the intelligence community. The bureau's timely and high-quality studies gained it a high standing among its sister agencies.

The Hilsman-Hughes team recruited an exceptionally high-quality staff. Reaching out to academics and outside experts, talented women, and Foreign Service officers with strong research talents, they built the INR into a highly respected intelligence agency. The bureau's analysts participated in team projects and interacted regularly with their peers in other agencies. The INR experts were also encouraged to keep up with the academic work in their fields and to attend professional conferences.

The experts who helped to build the INR's reputation were Helmut Sonnenfeldt and Allen S. Whiting. Sonnenfeldt was one of the State Department's leading authorities on the Soviet Union. Whiting, a China expert and the author of *China Crosses the Yalu,* had been recruited from the RAND Corporation to head the Asia division. Also on the Asian team were Fred Greene, from Williams College, Evelyn Colbert, and Dorothy Avery. John Plank, from Harvard University, became the INR's Latin American section leader, and Murat Williams, an ambassador with long service in Latin America, joined Allen Evans and George Denney as deputy directors of the INR.

Intelligence notes, typically papers of six to eight pages, became a standard product. They assessed emerging developments and identified policy issues for U.S. policymakers, ideally within six hours of an event, and stimulated the CIA to follow up with its larger resources. Shorter papers and longer studies on larger topics were also part of the INR's analytical repertoire.

The bureau also played an important role, during Hughes's tenure as director, with respect to the interagency United States Intelligence Board (USIB). The USIB issued the national intelligence estimates and special national intelligence estimates. The USIB was the predecessor unit to the national intelligence councils that now, from the White House, purport to coordinate and regulate the government's operating intelligence agencies. The Intelligence Board represented all of the government's intelligence units, including separate military intelligence entities. The most critical intelligence disputes of the Kennedy and Johnson years, especially those involving Vietnam, went to the USIB, where the government struggled, and sometimes failed, to find a consensus on intelligence.

When, in the spring of 1963, Roger moved to the post of assistant secretary of state for the Far East, including Vietnam, Tom succeeded him as assistant secretary of state for intelligence and research and director of the INR. Hughes found the intelligence job well suited for his talents. From the outset he was integrally involved in the INR's management. Tom minded the shop, while Roger pursued one or another pet cause, which often involved Hilsman facing off with McNamara, senior Joint Chiefs of Staff officers, or CIA leaders.

As Hilsman increased his direct dealings with the White House, Secretary Rusk was angered by what he took to be end runs around his office and authority. Hilsman was able to get away with this behavior because President Kennedy was willing to tolerate, within limits, Roger's gadfly role.

Hughes's leadership of the INR won him the admiration of his State Department colleagues. The department nominated him as its candidate for the prestigious Arthur S. Fleming Award for outstanding public service. This award, based on a competition among all federal agencies and departments, was presented to an elect few individuals across the government for their accomplishments and commitment to public service. In February 1965, Tom Hughes was one of three persons honored by the judges for his outstanding public service. The other two were Paul Volcker, of the Federal Reserve System, and Daniel Patrick Moynihan, of the U.S. Department of Labor.

All three men went on to serve the nation further in new roles. Volcker became chair of the Federal Reserve under President Ronald Reagan and adopted tight monetary policies to solve the stagflation problem resulting from the oil shocks of the 1970s. Moynihan later served as domestic policy adviser for President Richard Nixon, U.S. ambassador to India, U.S. ambassador to the United Nations, and U.S. senator from New York. Following his career in government, Hughes became president of the Carnegie Endowment for International Peace, the nation's leading think tank on foreign policy.

A FAILED HILSMAN-HUGHES PLAN

One of Hughes's first practical encounters with the complexities of intelligence came when President Kennedy, in the wake of the Bay of Pigs debacle, asked Roger Hilsman for ideas on reorganizing the nation's intelligence services. The president was so angry with the CIA that he had threatened to break the agency up into little pieces.

As Hilsman and Hughes studied the issue of intelligence reform, they faced a fast-moving situation. Kennedy cooled down and lost his appetite for a major shake-up of the CIA. He had informed Dulles and Bissell, after the failed invasion, that they would have to go. Dulles was to stay through and preside at the opening ceremony for the new CIA building in Langley, Virginia. Bissell would stay somewhat longer, assisting in the transition to the new CIA director (Bissell left in February 1962).

Kennedy had convened a review of the Bay of Pigs operation by a task force under the direction of his brother Bobby and his military adviser, General Maxwell Taylor. Their findings in May 1961 contained no recommendations for major organizational reform of the CIA. The report found that while the operation was a failure, the Castro regime and Fidelismo remained a threat to the hemisphere.

The CIA, in self-defense against the criticism of its Bay of Pigs role, conducted its own review under the direction of long-time career officer Lyman Kirkpatrick. The Kirkpatrick report blamed Allen Dulles and Richard Bissell for what went wrong at the Bay of Pigs. The two men, it said, had overstepped the normal intelligence bounds, had become advocates for their own ideas instead of objective analysts, and thereby had encroached into the domain of the policymaker. The Kirkpatrick remedy was to return to the basics. Specifically, the CIA in the future should adhere strictly to keeping objective analysis separated from the value-laden realm of policymaking.

Hilsman and Hughes concluded that the main problem lay with the CIA's traditional dual role as both analyst and covert operator. If the CIA tried to provide objective advice and at the same time conducted its own covert operations, it seemed to Hughes and Hilsman that the agency would inevitably be caught in a conflict of interest.

The Kirkpatrick analysis was partly right, but the CIA could not look to its own traditions for the right answers. There was an inherent conflict between the roles of the analyst and those of the covert operator. The two functions simply did not mix and should be kept organizationally separate.

The ideal solution, the INR colleagues thought, was for the CIA to get out of covert and paramilitary operations altogether, leaving that function to the Pentagon. The CIA should become solely an analytic agency, providing policy advice to the president just as the INR provided advice to the secretary of state and to the White House.

There was nothing wrong with the CIA and the INR both providing advice to policymakers. Indeed, differing perspectives were valuable. Two sets of advice on a complicated issue would help to guard against the groupthink that was all too common in government and business circles.

Hughes's and Hilsman's reform ideas ran counter to the pet ideas of reformers then, as they did to most modern intelligence reformers. The 9/11 Commission, congressional investigations, and most academic critics have all prescribed centralization as the best means to connect the dots. The solution to intelligence failures, these critics believed, was greater coordination within and between intelligence agencies so as to avoid overlap and to ensure that everybody knew what everybody else was doing.

Back in 1961, Hilsman and Hughes knew that their ideas were bound to seem radical. The president's attention that summer was focused on the Berlin crisis, the summit meeting with Khrushchev, the defense budget, Vietnam, and, secondarily, on the continuing Castro threat. Intelligence reform was apparently no longer an issue on the front burner. Therefore, if they were to propose anything, Hilsman and Hughes decided to propose only modest reform.

They suggested that the INR should assume responsibility for the State

Department's approval or disapproval of the CIA's proposed covert operations. There was an existing State office handling this function, but it was weak and was effectively under the control of the CIA. The office routinely rubberstamped all CIA proposals for covert operations without objection.

If the INR took over the review function, it could gradually squeeze down the number of CIA covert operations. The INR plan was predictably attacked by critics within State and by the CIA as a crude power grab.[2] President Kennedy, his ire at the CIA having meanwhile receded, did not want more trouble and rejected the Hilsman-Hughes proposal.

Hughes drew the lesson that one must be circumspect in proposing policy changes. Hilsman felt that he had been rebuffed. How was he to take the rejection? Moreover, there was a deliberate snub and demeaning of his role when he was excluded from a high-level State Department meeting in early November. Roger sent an indignant memo to U. Alexis Johnson, claiming that this slight "amount[ed] to a public announcement to White House, Defense, and CIA that they need not concern themselves with the head of State Department intelligence."[3]

There was some good news. The president asked for Hilsman's advice on the recommendations of the Maxwell Taylor–Walt Rostow mission to South Vietnam in October–November. The Taylor-Rostow report called for a significant increase of the U.S. presence in Vietnam, the creation of the Military Assistance Command, Vietnam, and sending some 8,000 American combat troops to Saigon.

Hilsman advised the president to reject the Taylor-Rostow recommendations on grounds that the ideas constituted a typical, conventional proposal appropriate for World War II but totally unsuited for the guerrilla war in Vietnam. Kennedy largely followed Hilsman's advice by paring down the request for American troops and making them advisers, not combat forces. This boosted Roger's ego.

Around this time, Roger received an attractive offer from Yale to be the Arnold Wolfers professor and director of the university's international relations programs. Had Roger been a conventional academic, he would have jumped at this opportunity. He was well enough versed in academic mores to know that one normally used such an offer to get a raise. In his present case a pay raise was not the issue. However, the Yale offer would present an opportunity to assess, and potentially to consolidate, Roger's standing in the administration.

This was a delicate card to play. Hilsman arranged a private meeting with JFK in the hope of gaining assurance that the president wanted him to remain in his post. The president praised Hilsman and persuaded him to stay on. Roger attempted to employ the same tactic in February 1964. He paid a call on Secretary Rusk, having in hand a handsome offer from

Columbia University. The move backfired. Rusk could scarcely conceal his glee. He congratulated Roger heartily and asked for the departure date so that he could begin the transition immediately.

Hilsman's ties with the White House after the above-mentioned meeting with Kennedy, however, grew stronger. He began the practice of regular visits to the White House, where he read the *Marine Gazette* and discussed counterinsurgency with the president. Roger forged close ties with Mac Bundy and Mike Forrestal and became, in effect, their partner in recommending policy moves for Kennedy on Vietnam. Roger's visits to the White House angered Secretary Rusk, who saw them as ways for Hilsman to evade State Department protocol and the normal chain of command. Roger had what he wanted: a policymaking role to augment his status as intelligence analyst.

The White House ties enhanced the INR's reputation in the intelligence community. The morale of INR analysts was boosted by knowing their work was read at high policy levels. However, Roger's actions also created some problems for Tom Hughes and the INR. Would Roger's policy enthusiasms distort the bureau's intelligence work? In bringing Hilsman so directly into policymaking, President Kennedy ran the danger of politicizing intelligence. The problem was eventually solved, in May 1963, by shifting Roger to the policy post of assistant secretary for the Far East and moving Tom up to the INR director's position.

Kennedy had created an even bigger problem of this kind when he told John McCone, in recruiting him to be CIA director to replace Allen Dulles, that he wanted McCone's advice on policy as well as management of the CIA and the intelligence community. McCone created a separate staff unit to back up his personal advisory role, causing conflict with other CIA divisions. At United States Intelligence Board (USIB) meetings, McCone sometimes declared his personal policy views as the official CIA position and relegated other CIA views to the status of dissenting footnotes in the final report.

CHESTER BOWLES REASSIGNED

Rumors flew around Washington after the Bay of Pigs that Bowles was about to be sacked. Bowles, however, had his defenders in government and in the press. Hughes, Chayes, and Wofford organized a meeting of "Chet Setters" in Chet's defense. Harris Wofford wrote "the strongest memo I ever wrote in government" to Kennedy, supporting Bowles.[4]

Abe Chayes, Kennedy's legal adviser, also wrote the president a strong memo. He told the president that it would send the wrong signal if the first high-level official to leave was the only one to have opposed the Bay of Pigs invasion. Tom Hughes rallied support for Bowles in the Senate from Humphrey and Fulbright. Influential journalists, including James Reston of the *New York Times,* defended Bowles.

President Kennedy settled the matter himself, temporarily at least, in a press conference. The president opened the press conference with prepared remarks about Berlin and took questions on this subject and on the economy. Finally, there was the question on Chester Bowles:

> *Question:* Mr. President, although the White House has commented on the fact that the Under Secretary of State is remaining in his job at this time, there still remains some doubt as to your own confidence in him, sir . . . ?
>
> *The President:* Well, in the first place, contrary to some reports, I have never asked Mr. Bowles for his resignation, nor has he ever offered it. I have always expected that he would be part of this Administration until it concluded its responsibilities.

The president then launched into a long aside on government reorganization and stated that he was determined to evaluate continuously matters of organization. The press corps, accustomed to crisp answers from the president, was puzzled. Kennedy, sensing that he was creating confusion, returned to the status of Mr. Bowles.

> *The President*: Mr. Bowles has my complete confidence. He is going on the trip which will take him to Africa and Asia, consulting with heads of state and with allies, and I expect that his trip will be most valuable. . . . Mr. Bowles will be, I hope, a valuable part of this Administration as long as it continues, and that he has the confidence of the President and Secretary of State.
>
> *Question*: Mr. President, does your answer mean that there is a possibility that he may be shifted, though, to some other responsibility more in keeping with his talents?
>
> *The President*: We have reached no judgment on how we are going to organize any of these departments. I put the general principle forward that we are going to attempt to maximize the abilities of everyone working in the government. If I came to the conclusion that Mr. Bowles could be more effective in another responsible position, I would not hesitate to ask him to take that position.[5]

Sitting in the State Department auditorium at the press conference, Hughes believed that Bowles had been reprieved but not vindicated. It was only a matter of time, he surmised, until the administration dealt decisively with Bowles. Bowles meanwhile soldiered on, devoting much of his time to the presidential order directing that ambassadors have full authority over all U.S. agencies operating in U.S. embassies overseas.

Three incidents that occurred after the Bay of Pigs permanently ruined the Bowles relationship with Kennedy's brother Bobby, his attorney general. The first took place at a White House meeting following the surrender of the Cuban exile fighters who had survived Castro's attacks. The group of Kennedy officials sat morosely. The president was stone-faced, tapping on his front teeth with a pencil. The attorney general suddenly jumped to his feet and said in a loud voice that he wanted it understood that everybody in the room had favored the president's decision. Nobody was to differ publicly with the president or to leak any details of internal deliberations.

Bobby's explosion took the participants by surprise. There was a strained silence. The president rose and started to leave the room. Bowles rose and followed him, evidently wanting to say something to the president. Bobby Kennedy rushed to block Bowles, and there was evidently shoving between them.

Hughes, who did not attend the meeting but talked to Bowles shortly afterward, was given to understand that the attorney general had rushed over in a fury, struck Bowles in the chest, and cursed at him.[6] Other witnesses said that RFK did not actually punch Bowles but stabbed at him with his forefinger and demanded to know if he had leaked to the press.

Bowles himself in his memoir denied that anything untoward had occurred between himself and the attorney general. He also dismissed as fanciful a *Time* magazine story alleging that he leaked his opposition to the invasion in order to embarrass the President.[7]

The second incident left no doubt that Bowles was in trouble. On April 27, Bowles sat in for Rusk at a NSC meeting and presented two State Department papers on the Cuba situation. The papers, reflecting Bowles's long-standing views of how to deal with Castro, asserted that Castro was now firmly in control and could be dislodged only by a large-scale U.S. military action. Consequently, Bowles, concluded, the best way to deal with Castro was to isolate him. A militant posture toward Cuba would turn a small problem into a big one.[8]

Robert Kennedy denounced the useless paper and the State Department's incompetence. He turned to Bowles and declared, "We'd be better off if you just quit and left foreign policy to somebody else."[9]

The third incident occurred while JFK, Rusk, Bundy, and other top officials were in Vienna for the Kennedy-Khrushchev summit. Kennedy had previously told Rusk that he wanted his brother to gain experience in foreign policy and to that end he should be allowed "to fool around a little" in foreign policy. At the summit, Rusk received word from Bowles saying that the Dominican Republic's dictator, Trujillo, had been assassinated. As a precaution, President Kennedy ordered U.S. naval vessels to be stationed offshore from the Dominican Republic but far enough away to be out of sight.

Robert Kennedy intervened on his own authority and countermanded his brother's order. He ordered Bowles to move the ships closer to shore, in case rapid U.S. action was required to evacuate Americans or to land Marines. Bowles refused and made it clear to the attorney general that he would follow only presidential orders. Bobby Kennedy told Bowles, "You're a gutless wonder."[10]

Something had to be done about Bowles, but President Kennedy had more important immediate concerns. Matters came to a head on Bowles in the fall after the president had decided to launch an ambitious new covert operation to destabilize the Castro regime. This effort, which came to be known as Operation Mongoose (after the animal skilled at killing poisonous snakes), was a top secret project directed by the attorney general and General Taylor.

Bowles had been a thorn in JFK's side for far too long, having opposed the president's stand on Castro during the campaign, objected to the Bay of Pigs, leaked his opposition to the press, and issued papers arguing that Castro did not pose a major threat. If he were still in a policy role, he would be trouble for Operation Mongoose. So it was time to settle the Bowles issue once and for all. But this was a highly sensitive matter from the president's point of view. A noisy or messy Bowles departure could be highly damaging to the administration.

In November, the White House decided it was finally time to move on Bowles. Word was quietly passed to the under secretary that the president had decided to reorganize the management of the State Department. His departure as under secretary was requested, and it was hoped that he might accept new duties. Bowles brushed aside this probe. He was not going to take any hints or indirect orders. He was hired by the president, and he would not go unless the president personally ordered him to go.

Normally, the attorney general would be called in to handle a matter of this sort. However, the incidents between Bobby and Bowles precluded this approach. Instead, the president sent Ted Sorensen to negotiate with Bowles.

In a three-hour meeting, Sorensen persuaded Bowles to accept a new assignment as special Ambassador in charge of policy toward the new nations of the Third World. Thirty-three newly created sovereign states had recently become members of the United Nations. Chet's special touch would help to establish good relations with these new nations. Bowles would have a limo, full diplomatic privileges, a generous travel budget, and the Kennedy's undying gratitude for understanding the president's difficult position. Sorensen declared that the whole problem would have been averted if the president had appointed Chet as secretary of state in the first place. The president had already said as much in a private conversation with Chet. But that was all water under the dam.

When the president learned that Bowles had agreed to go quietly, he told Sorensen that this was his best work since he won over the Michigan delegation at the convention. Bowles was now removed from the policy process by his new special envoy status. He did not bewail his fate and characteristically threw himself into his new assignment. Then in 1963, President Kennedy sent him back to India for a repeat tour as U.S. ambassador. This became necessary when John Kenneth Galbraith gave up the post to return to his teaching duties at Harvard.

Though Chet had loved India the first time, he felt isolated this time around, and his health was worrisome. He sent frequent cables to Hughes asking for updates on the latest developments in Washington. When he returned to Washington on home visits, he usually stayed with Tom and Jean Hughes and avidly caught up on the Washington news.

OPERATION MONGOOSE

Operation Mongoose, which hastened Bowles's transfer, officially began with a White House meeting on November 3, 1961. Only a small group of officials attended: the president, the attorney general, Generals Taylor and Lansdale, the CIA's Richard Bissell, State's U. Alexis Johnson, Defense Secretary Robert McNamara, and White House aides McGeorge Bundy and Richard Goodwin.[11] In memorandums of November 22 and 30, the president spelled out the project's responsibilities and its organizational structure.[12]

Operation Mongoose was the action arm of a new anti-Castro effort led by General Edwin Lansdale. Lansdale was named the chief of operations and charged with coordinating all interagency Operation Mongoose activities. He would report to the Special Group, which was the old NSC special group overseeing the government's covert operations, inaugurated by Eisenhower, but in this case the group would be "augmented" by the addition of General Lansdale, General Taylor, and Attorney General Robert Kennedy.[13]

The November 22 presidential memo, drafted by Mac Bundy, was the first draft of the definitive November 30 memo. The November 22 memo listed the attorney general as the chair of the group. The president reconsidered this move and named General Taylor as head of the augmented group in the November 30 memo. However, it was evident that Robert Kennedy was the point of contact between the president and the group. General Taylor would be the titular and RFK the actual head and the driving force behind the effort.

Operation Mongoose would have the highest classification level. Its existence would be known only to a limited number of officials. The secrecy level, however, quickly became unrealistic, since Mongoose would have to draw on all of the national security agencies to accomplish anything. The Lansdale staff could only coordinate the efforts of the operating departments and agencies. Giving orders to the powerful bureaucracies was not easy. The large departments would usually rather coordinate than be coordinated by somebody else.

Besides Lansdale in the White House, there were 200 CIA employees at Langley assigned to Mongoose and a headquarters in Miami operating out of a large building rented from the University of Miami. Operation Mongoose, in fact, became "the CIA's largest peacetime intelligence operation to date, with some six hundred CIA officers in and around Miami, almost five thousand CIA contractors, and the third largest navy in the Caribbean, including submarines, patrol boats, coast guard cutters, seaplanes, and Guantanamo Bay for a base."[14]

Though uncoordinated, comprising mostly pinprick sabotage actions against bridges, ports, and infrastructure targets, the operation never came close to destabilizing the Castro regime or to building internal opposition to the Cuban dictator. Mongoose did, however, manage to convince Castro that the United States was planning a new invasion.

Operation Mongoose grew surprisingly large even though it never had a clear mission and was opposed by key policymakers and managers of the agencies running the covert operations. Even the man handpicked by the Kennedys to be in charge, General Ed Lansdale, harbored strong doubts about the mission's feasibility. Sitting in Dick Goodwin's White House office one day planning Mongoose actions, Lansdale turned to Goodwin:

"You know, Dick, it's impossible."

"What's impossible?" Goodwin asked.

"There is no way you can overthrow Castro without a strong, indigenous political opposition and there is no such opposition, either in Cuba or outside it."[15]

Although Roger Hilsman and Tom Hughes were not supposed to know about the top secret operation, they soon learned of Mongoose's existence. They considered it an example of the problem of excessive secrecy. Overclassification and compartmentalized knowledge, they believed, hampered the work of intelligence. They could not acknowledge Mongoose's existence or discuss it with their staff. Roger Hilsman feared, and Tom agreed, that Mongoose could be a replay of the Bay of Pigs.

Roger decided to voice his concerns through State Department channels. He sent a memo to Alex Johnson, State's representative on the Special Group, after reading a Lansdale paper. Hilsman said that while he was not familiar with the context of the January 18 paper, he believed that it would be "useful to you to have a few observations on it from a bystander's viewpoint."

While he did not quarrel with the objective, Roger had serious misgivings about the underlying concept. There was no hard intelligence to suggest that a majority of the Cuban people at present could be mobilized against the Castro regime or that the "CIA had assets for bringing into existence in the near future an internal political action organization which would assure the support of a majority of the Cuban people against the Castro regime. . . . Unless a popular uprising is promptly supported by overt U.S. military action, it would probably lead to another Hungary."[16]

The objections Hilsman raised were already troubling many others in the State Department and the CIA. Many analysts believed that Castro was stronger now than he had been at the Bay of Pigs and would be harder to overthrow. Castro's counterespionage forces were much stronger. Castro's army was larger and better equipped than it had been at the time of the Bay of Pigs invasion. Dissidents were now regularly imprisoned and tortured or executed. Any serious planning to overthrow Castro would thus have to include U.S. military intervention. Hilsman concluded his argument by saying that, in Mongoose, "we may be heading for a fiasco worse than the ill-fated operation of last year."[17]

Roger's views may have bolstered the case Alex Johnson was to present at the next Special Group meeting. The Special Group had met on January 17 to consider a planning paper prepared by Lansdale recommending thirty-three sets of potential actions for Operation Mongoose. The attorney general made an eloquent appeal for action, but no decision was reached on Mongoose's next steps.

The Special Group met again on January 24 to discuss three papers: a new memo by Lansdale, a CIA commentary (delivered by the new CIA director John McCone), and a State Department paper. The aim was to focus the Group's thinking and to emerge with a consensus on an action plan. The discussion did not go well for Lansdale. McCone questioned the premise of the whole Mongoose plan, namely, that the U.S. could organize a popular uprising to overthrow the Castro regime with no need for U.S. military intervention.

General Taylor agreed with McCone. Thomas A. Parrott, the Special Group's executive secretary and Lansdale critic, recorded that "General Taylor noted that the CIA paper of the 24th appears to question the basic objective of overthrowing the Castro regime without overt U.S. military intervention."[18]

Taylor stated that if one accepted the CIA assessment, the concept of contingency planning in the Lansdale plan was totally inadequate. The Defense Department role would have to be completely rethought. The military actions could not be a contingency action but would need to be a technically complex operation requiring more planning by the Joint Chiefs.

The State Department paper objected to Lansdale's plan on multiple grounds. Dodging the censor's scissors, it obliquely criticized a Lansdale reference to potential assassinations of Cuban officials (the term *assassination* was removed and never appeared again in any Mongoose paper). The State paper warned that removing leaders was a bad idea, usually creating martyrs rather than destabilizing a regime. The Cuban security apparatus would become even stronger and more oppressive.

State's paper pointed out that groups potentially hostile to the regime—the wealthy, the professionals, and the educated middle classes—had already fled Cuba in large numbers, leaving a population in which it was difficult to find elements hostile to the regime. The State Department issued a warning that a premature or ill-prepared uprising might result in a slaughter of the insurgents followed by greater repression. Finally, State cautioned that many important overt activities, including building the Alliance for Progress, could be harmed by covert actions that made the United States look like a bully and Castro a victim.

The Special Group decided to postpone basic decisions until February 20, when General Lansdale would issue a progress report. But there was not much progress for Lansdale to report. In the absence of better intelligence on Cuba, the thirty-three original tasks proposed by Lansdale were deferred in favor of gaining better intelligence. The focus on intelligence marked phase one of Mongoose. This indecision by the Special Group members illustrated the basic problems of the whole operation and foreshadowed its ultimate failure.

Operation Mongoose featured delays, endless progress reports, assessments and reassessments, new targets and objectives, evaluations, and bureaucratic reviews. The attorney general made inspection trips to Miami. The Special Group met on Mongoose more than once a week, on average—forty meetings in total—from January to October 1962.

Some spectacularly bungled operations occurred in Mongoose's brief bureaucratic lifetime. One such incident brought the INR, along with other parts of the intelligence community, into action to rescue the CIA, the Special Group, and the nation from embarrassment. In June 1962, Ed Lansdale learned that a British ship carrying tons of sugar from Havana to Odessa had broken a propeller and put into a San Juan port for repairs. This seemed to Lansdale a great opportunity for Operation Mongoose, and he convened an urgent meeting of the Special Group.

The president, Rusk, McNamara, and other principals were absent, but the attorney general chaired the meeting. The idea Lansdale proposed was to send a special team to San Juan to poison the sugar shipment—not to kill but to sicken thousands of Soviet citizens. This would cause the Russians to blame the Cubans and potentially to cancel or curtail future sugar purchases. Lansdale had been thinking about ways to curb Cuban sugar exports. The U.S. sugar embargo had proved ineffectual, since Cuban exports had actually increased since the embargo, albeit entirely to Soviet bloc nations. The Special Group approved the plan and sent a CIA team to San Juan to carry it out. The sugar was stored in a warehouse during the repairs, and the CIA team reported success in injecting the nausea-inducing substance into a large number of the sugar sacks.

Tom Hughes first got wind of the operation from sources in San Juan and passed the information on to Roger Hilsman. They verified the report, and Hilsman brought the ill-fated scheme to the attention of Dean Rusk, who alerted President Kennedy.

Rusk, in a rare show of temper, was furious with Alex Johnson for approving the scheme. Kennedy, similarly, was angry with his brother for poor judgment. A round of finger pointing, mixed with frantic efforts to find a way out of the imbroglio, followed as a trickle of rumors circulated around Washington.

John McCone blamed Mac Bundy's deputy, Carl Kaysen, for leaks to the press. This led to a breach between Bundy and Kaysen, his longtime friend and Harvard colleague, when Bundy temporarily suspended Kaysen's access to Operation Mongoose papers. Some suspected that Under Secretary George Ball was the leaker.

The Kennedys were suspicious of McCone because of his close ties with Senate Republicans, who were now beginning to issue reports of Soviet missiles in Cuba and blaming the administration for weakness. Bobby Kennedy, who had originally proposed McCone to his brother and was one of McCone's strongest backers, became disillusioned with McCone. The attorney general's view was that the Special Group members had lost their nerve. The plan would have worked, and nobody would be the wiser if all involved had just shut up.

There remained the problem of what to do about the sugar. The CIA proposed burning down the warehouse and destroying all of the evidence. The FBI objected on the grounds that it might be called in to investigate the fire, which could have spread and engulfed the whole harbor. Somebody suggested that we tell the British that anti-Castro exiles had poisoned the sugar, leaving it to the British to warn the Soviets. Tom Hughes, as an authority on British politics, advised that this would be tantamount to a confession. The Brits would not believe that anti-Castro Cubans could have undertaken the scheme on their own.

The INR assisted in coming up with a solution when it was discovered that the Mongoose team members, trying to keep straight which sacks they had already poisoned, had marked the sacks. The team was thus able to sneak back into the warehouse and remove the poisoned sugar, dumping it into the San Juan harbor. It is not recorded whether the British suffered any penalty for the shortfall in the sugar they finally delivered to Odessa or if the San Juan fish suffered digestive troubles from the poisoned sugar.

Tom Hughes observed in an oral history interview that the episode became a mere footnote of history when it was eclipsed by the Cuban Missile Crisis and the China-India War.

AFTERMATH

Despite Operation Mongoose's poor performance, it was not immediately clear what should be done about it. On the afternoon of October 16, Attorney General Kennedy convened a meeting of the Special Group in his office to discuss Operation Mongoose. The attorney general opened the meeting by noting the "general dissatisfaction of the President" with Operation Mongoose.[19] He ended the meeting after some inconclusive discussion by declaring that in view of the lack of progress, the Group would "hold a meeting at 9:30 the next day with the Mongoose operational representatives of the various agencies."[20] But President Kennedy that evening canceled the meeting and ordered that all covert Mongoose activities be put on hold for the duration of the missile crisis.

After the crisis had passed, President Kennedy made clear to associates that "an assurance covering invasion does not ban covert actions or an economic blockade or tie our hands completely. . . . We do not want to build up Castro by means of a no-invasion guarantee."[21]

On December 6, 1962, McGeorge Bundy sent President Kennedy a memo outlining a new approach to the sabotage campaign against Castro. Bundy reaffirmed that "our ultimate objective is the overthrow of the Castro regime and its replacement by one sharing the aims of the Free World." Given the disappointing performance of Operation Mongoose, however, a reorganization was in order. The special office of Operation Mongoose would be disbanded, General Lansdale would be reassigned to other duties, and a new Office of Coordinator of Cuban Affairs would be created in the State Department.[22]

The new arrangement was not much of an improvement. One of its proposals, vetoed by the president, was to drop 500,000 balloons on Cuba with leaflets containing unflattering depictions of Castro's top lieutenants. Cartoon illustrations of sabotage techniques were to be included for easy use by potential saboteurs.

The new arrangement continued into the fall of 1963 amid growing disillusionment on the part of most participants. In early November, Secretary of State Rusk ended the State Department's involvement at the urging of the INR and other offices. There was concern that the sabotage campaign might lead to more Soviet troops being sent back to Cuba. A meeting was called to reappraise the whole covert operation. The CIA view won out: "Since CIA's sabotage operation is in the main low cost and since it does worry the Castro regime, denies him some essential commodities, stimulates some sabotage inside Cuba, and tends to improve the morale of the Cubans who would like to see Castro removed, CIA should proceed with those operations."[23]

The covert actions against Cuba were finally ended. After Kennedy's death, President Lyndon Johnson created a presidential commission, chaired by Chief Justice Earl Warren of the U.S. Supreme Court, to examine the circumstances surrounding Kennedy's death. Johnson thereupon ordered an immediate end to all covert operations in Cuba. He did not want the Warren Commission's investigation to uncover evidence of U.S. covert actions against Castro.

In the end, Operation Mongoose had little to show for its efforts other than minor damage to Cuba's infrastructure of ports, bridges, roads, and airfields. However, assessing the operation only from how much damage it inflicted on Cuba's infrastructure is too narrow a perspective. Operation Mongoose had a much broader historical significance. Mongoose had the large unintended consequence of pushing Cuba into a military alliance with the Soviet Union.

9

The Cuban Missile Crisis

In July 1962, Fidel Castro gave a speech in Chile that was picked up in U.S. intelligence circles but otherwise went largely unnoticed. The speech had a cocky tone. It hinted at important developments in Cuba's defense posture.[1] The Latin American specialists in the INR and the CIA noted the tone but had no explanation beyond the fact that ship traffic to Cuba was beginning to increase from Soviet bloc nations.

What lay behind the speech was the recent visit to Moscow of Fidel's brother Raul, Cuba's defense minister. Raul had reached agreement on a defense pact with the Soviet Union in June.[2] The agreement strengthened Cuba's defenses generally. Most significant, Soviet nuclear missiles were included in the aid package, ostensibly to deter a U.S. invasion of Cuba. Castro's July speech made no explicit reference either to the defense treaty or to the nuclear missiles.

Fidel Castro believed that public mention of the treaty and of the missiles would be highly desirable. He thought this would halt America's sabotage tactics against his country: the U.S. government would be forced to drop any invasion plans, as the whole question of U.S. aggression would be thrust into the diplomatic arena. Castro drew an analogy between the Soviet deployment and America's similar placement of missiles in Europe, especially in Turkey on Russia's border. Using America's own arguments against them, Castro argued, would give the Soviet Union and Cuba a diplomatic advantage in the United Nations and other international forums. Negotiations were sure to follow the treaty's disclosure. In that arena, the best defense is to go on offense.

Nikita Khrushchev was unmoved. He insisted that both the treaty and the missiles be kept secret until the missiles were operational. He would then make a triumphal visit to Cuba, stopping on the way to inform Kennedy about the missiles. Kennedy would fume but would have no choice but to accept the missiles as a fait accompli. Neither man fully appreciated the fact at the time, but Castro had touched on a critical issue.

CASTRO AND COMMUNISM

Fidel Castro had earlier told world capitalists, his fellow Cubans, and friends in Moscow that he was and would remain a dedicated communist to his dying day. Castro had decided to put behind him any lingering quarrels with Cuba's old-line communists. Fidel had once disdained the urban intellectuals who had not joined him when he was fighting Fulgencio Batista and living in the mountains. He saw them as potential counterrevolutionaries and threats to his regime. Fidel wanted to reassure the Kremlin that he was now totally committed to world communism.

The Kremlin was initially uncertain how fast and how far to push Castro toward an alignment of his July 26 movement with Cuba's old-line communists. Soviet intelligence on Cuba did not provide much useful guidance to Kremlin policymakers.

Both "the KGB [Soviet secret police] and the GRU [Russian armed forces] exhibited little reluctance in forwarding what in retrospect appears as gossipy or second-rate information to the Kremlin."[3] Although the intelligence reports were not always credible, Khrushchev did pay some attention to them. But he did not hesitate to act on his own intelligence sources and rely on his own judgment when he was dissatisfied with the advisers.

In particular, Khrushchev wanted to buttress Soviet intelligence on counterrevolutionaries in Cuba and on Castro's domestic political maneuvers. He decided in 1959 to move Alexander Alekseev, a promising KGB agent, from Argentina to Cuba to fill the need. Alekseev became the best source of reporting on Cuban developments for Kremlin policymakers.

Castro's July speech came, by coincidence, on the anniversary of the day in 1961 that President Kennedy announced the embargo of Cuba's sugar sales to the United States. This U.S. action had delivered a heavy blow to Cuba's one-crop export economy. Castro urgently needed and sought economic assistance from the Soviet Union.

Soviet premier Khrushchev responded by sending Deputy Premier Anastas Mikoyan to Cuba to assess the situation. Mikoyan recommended that Moscow purchase the entire Cuban sugar crop. A complicated barter formula was worked out covering the next five years. Mikoyan's visit also helped to pave the way for the much deeper security relationship with Cuba that was to follow.

Castro also began a campaign in the summer of 1961 to persuade the Russians to enhance their military assistance to Cuba, but he encountered Soviet foot-dragging. Initially, the Czechs and the Poles, at the Kremlin's direction, had taken the lead within the communist bloc to ship weapons to Cuba. Most of what was sent was old, however, and the arrangement did not suit Castro.

The Soviets evidently doubted that the United States would actually invade the island. Moscow did not assign high priority to Cuba's defense needs. Its experts on America considered that Kennedy's choice of Bowles as foreign policy adviser in the 1960 campaign put JFK in the liberal Stevenson wing of the Democratic Party. That Kennedy ran to the right of Nixon on Cuba and on defense generally was attributed to political expediency: Kennedy had to rebut the usual Republican arguments that the Democrats were soft on communism.

The bugbears for the Kremlin's Americanists were the CIA, the Pentagon brass, and the capitalists behind the military-industrial complex. They saw the Republican Party as the tool of the capitalists. It was the Republicans, naturally, who conceived the Bay of Pigs invasion.

That Kennedy did not use military force to support the anti-Castro exiles showed good sense to the Russians but also suggested that he was not a strong leader. Khrushchev got the same impression of Kennedy's weakness from the June 1961 summit meeting.

Yet there were some contrary indications. Kennedy raised the U.S. defense budget 15 percent after the June summit, and he went ahead with the Jupiter ballistic missiles in Turkey despite Soviet protests. But these actions were probably related to the Berlin crisis. Once the Berlin question had been settled, as it was in August 1961, Kennedy's basic instincts would likely reemerge.

Alexseev was called on for an authoritative assessment of American intentions. He considered that the Kennedy administration relied on the Alliance for Progress as its main instrument to curb the spread of Castroism in the region. The United States would use the Alliance for Progress plus economic sanctions to isolate Castro in the Organization of American States. Invading Cuba would defeat the larger policy ends and cost Kennedy the support of Latin American leaders.

The CIA conducted some minor sabotage activity, but this did not amount to much. Its purpose was probably to keep Castro off balance and prevent him from pursuing an active foreign policy.

Nevertheless, Khrushchev agreed to a modest program of military assistance for Cuba. The Kremlin promised an aid package of $133 million, which included some Soviet tanks of World War II vintage, trucks, trailers, and other vehicles, plus artillery and small arms. However, the effort seemed to lack a strong impetus from the top. It fell short of what Castro expected. Fidel and Raul urgently renewed their appeals in 1962 and found, somewhat to their surprise, a more receptive climate.

Several factors had changed Khrushchev's thinking. A December 1961 speech by Roswell Gilpatric, the Defense Department's deputy secretary, showed that there was no missile gap, as the Democrats had argued in the 1960 campaign. Indeed, the United States enjoyed an overwhelming strategic nuclear advantage, estimated at a nine-to-one ratio in nuclear warheads and delivery systems, over the Soviet Union.[4] Moreover, the Soviet Union was having some technical difficulties in producing long-range missiles with heavy payloads. The strategic picture did not look favorable to Khrushchev and other Kremlin leaders.

Furthermore, a private meeting between Kennedy and Khrushchev's son-in-law, Alexei Adzhubei, in late January 1962, was troubling to Khrushchev. Kennedy seemed to Adzhubei to be obsessed with Cuba. Kennedy told him that Cuba would probably be the central issue in the 1964 presidential race and that something had to be done or Kennedy would not be reelected. The president made an analogy to how Premier Khrushchev dealt with Finland. Similarly, he would have to be tough with Castro. Most alarming, JFK went on to compare Cuba to Hungary in 1956 and how the Soviet Union had dealt decisively with the situation. To Khrushchev, his son-in-law's report suggested a shift in Kennedy's thinking on Cuba and called for a reappraisal of Soviet policy. Khrushchev ordered a review of Soviet military assistance plans for Cuba and a reappraisal of the whole Cuban situation.

Then there was an unnerving intelligence report for Soviet leaders in March 1962. A Soviet agent in the United States reported that in June 1961 the Pentagon-CIA complex had planned a preemptive strike against the Soviet Union for the following September.[5] The Soviets believed that the resumption of Soviet nuclear testing in August had deterred the planned strike. Soviet intelligence considered that the Americans were frightened by the unexpectedly powerful bombs that were tested.[6]

But there was ample evidence of hostile American intent toward Cuba as indicated by stepped-up sabotage tactics. There was general agreement in the Kremlin that the nuclear balance of power had swung in America's favor. The danger was that fanatics in the United States might believe that their nuclear superiority gave them the capability to launch a first strike and to destroy the entire Soviet nuclear capacity with impunity (dubbed "the counterforce strategy").

On a bright day in April 1961, while vacationing in the Crimea, Nikita Khrushchev had a visitor. It was his friend and ally, Defense Minister Rodion Malinovsky. In the course of their conversation, Malinovsky gestured toward the south and remarked that the American Jupiter missiles had just become operational. "Why," Khrushchev mused, "should Americans have the right to put missiles on our doorstep and we not have the same right?"⁷

INTELLIGENCE AND POLITICS IN THE UNITED STATES

Tom Hughes's involvement in the Cuban Missile Crisis began in its earliest stages. The sugar fracas had poisoned the CIA's ties with the White House along with the sugar. McCone now took a huge step that compounded his problems. At an August 10 meeting of the Special Group, he announced to RFK's shock that the Soviet Union had deployed nuclear missiles in Cuba, and he sent a separate memo to the president with that message. McCone had thus thrust himself into the middle of the 1962 midterm elections—and on the side of the Republicans. This was much to the embarrassment of the Kennedy administration and seemed to add fuel to a political firestorm gathering strength in the Senate.

The Republicans had accused the Kennedy administration of weakness at the Bay of Pigs. The public, however, was willing to forgive the mistakes of the youthful new president. To attack Kennedy in April 1961 was like kicking a man when he was down. Republican leaders did not even call for an investigation of the failed invasion. Now, in the summer of 1962, as the midterm elections approached, the Republicans made Cuba their central campaign issue.

Homer Capehart, a veteran Republican senator from Indiana, was running for reelection against the promising Democratic newcomer Birch Bayh. Attempting to regain his momentum, Capehart became the first in his party to suggest publicly that Soviet nuclear missiles were in Cuba. Capehart denounced the Kennedy administration for allowing Soviet missiles to be deployed only ninety miles from the U.S. mainland. He called for an immediate invasion of Cuba to remove the threat.

Capehart, however, was not the ideal spokesperson for the Republicans on Cuba. Not only was he in the midst of a tough campaign fight, he was also viewed as too partisan, a publicity seeker, and as somewhat reckless by his own party leaders.

A new and more formidable Republican spokesperson emerged in the person of Senator Kenneth Keating of New York. Keating was a widely respected Republican moderate who was not up for reelection in 1962.⁸ Keating charged in a series of speeches on the Senate floor that Soviet offensive missiles and armaments had been deployed to Cuba and were a serious threat to U.S. national security. He seemed to be well informed and to base his remarks on credible information, but he adamantly refused to reveal his sources.

President Kennedy turned to Roger Hilsman and asked him to find out where Keating was getting his information. Hilsman turned the task over to Tom Hughes. Hughes conducted the first of a number of reviews of possible Keating sources. Tom canvassed his colleagues on the USIB and consulted others he thought might be knowledgeable. Did they have work underway, or did they know of anyone in their agencies who could be supplying Keating with information?

Hughes also conferred with his Senate friends, such as Humphrey and Fulbright, to see if they knew anything. Keating apparently talked only to his Republican colleagues and to only a select few of them. No one on Capitol Hill or in the intelligence agencies could identify Keating's sources.

Hughes studied the kinds of intelligence that could be proof of missile deployments. The main sources of intelligence came from one or more of the following categories: aerial photography from high-flying U-2 flights over Cuba or from low-altitude reconnaissance flights; photographic evidence or visual observation by U.S. naval pilots overflying Soviet transport ships on the high seas or from British and Norwegian pilots observing shipping activity in and near Soviet ports such as Murmansk; observations by CIA (Mongoose) spies in Cuba or refugee reports from the Mongoose refugee center in Miami; and assessments by teams of experienced analysts drawing inferences from data or from long experience with the subject.

Technical interpretations of raw data, photos, or visual descriptions of objects seen by field agents were also possible sources. Experts could infer from photos that crates of this or that size on a ship's deck could carry the parts for this or that fighter or for bombers. Agents in the field would estimate the length of an object on a trailer as either fifty or seventy feet, which could mean it was either a surface-to-air defense missile (SAM) or an intermediate range ballistic missile (IRBM), which could hit the United States.

There was a hierarchy of evidence, from the hard to the soft. Photographic evidence from a U-2 was hard, in comparison with the soft observation by an agent at night under stress describing what a truck carried as it passed by.[9] There were no reports from defectors because there were no defectors from Cuba's military forces. Spies in the Soviet Union had nothing to report. Evidently, what was happening was top secret.

In July–August 1962, there were certainly signs of a military buildup in Cuba. In July, soon after the heavy ship traffic began to appear at Cuban ports, President Kennedy ordered weekly U-2 flights over the island. The U-2s, as well as reports from agents in Cuba, showed increased activity at ports. New construction was evident in the western part of the island. Soviet military shipments increased significantly in August, including trucks, tanks, various other kinds of armored vehicles, and transport planes.

U.S. intelligence picked up much but also missed much of what was taking place in Cuba. Later, it was determined that eighty transport ships made at least 180 trips from ports in Murmansk, Vladivostok, and the Black Sea. It was an impressive feat of transportation. The CIA estimated that as many as 3,000 Soviet technicians and support personnel arrived with the shipments in the summer and fall of 1962.

In fact, the United States greatly underestimated the number of Soviet personnel in Cuba, which had reached a total of 41,900 by the fall of 1962. This number included some 10,000–12,000 Soviet combat troops; forty-one Il-28 light bombers; a squadron of MIG-21 fighters; four submarines, each with three torpedoes with a one-megaton nuclear warhead in addition to regular torpedoes; 100 tactical nuclear weapons with forty-kiloton explosive force; multiple SAM air defense batteries; and forty medium- and intermediate-range missiles (twenty R-12s with a range of 1,050 miles and twenty R-14s with twice that range). Cuban forces in 1962 amounted to about 275,000, counting police, militia, and regular military units.

OFFENSIVE VERSUS DEFENSIVE WEAPONS

Although Washington did not understand the scope and dimensions of the Soviet buildup, the politicians were aware that something significant was happening in Cuba. With the Senate Republicans saying that the buildup included nuclear missiles, the debate increasingly turned to what was actually being deployed. Were the systems defensive or offensive in nature, and what threat was posed to the United States?

John McCone's apparent shift to Senator Keating's side of the debate complicated Hughes's task of discovering Keating's sources. McCone was not backing off from his position. He made a number of trips to Capitol Hill to brief selected, mostly Republican senators, which angered the Kennedys, especially Bobby Kennedy.

Bobby had recommended McCone to his brother as a reliable "silver haired Republican" for the CIA post. Now that McCone was strutting around as a self-proclaimed guru on Cuba, RFK became convinced that McCone was up to something. Bobby told his brother that McCone's frequent visits to Republican senators meant that he could no longer be trusted. In private conversations, JFK began referring to McCone as "a horse's ass" and a "son of a bitch."

The shift from admiration to antipathy on Bobby's part was not a good sign for McCone. As the patriarch of the Kennedy clan, Joseph P. Kennedy Sr., once reportedly said of his son Bobby, "When Bobby hates you, you stay hated."

Hughes could not figure out what McCone was telling the senators when he briefed them in secret. There was no transcript of the testimony, and the director's staff professed not to know, and probably did not know, what McCone was telling them. McCone had made a practice from early in his tenure of making trips abroad to foreign leaders, much to the irritation of the State Department. State officials had no idea what McCone was telling them and were unsure whether the White House had authorized these trips.

Part of the problem lay with the president himself for telling McCone, as one element of the sale's pitch to recruit him, that he was to be a presidential policy adviser as well as an agency head. The dispute over the missiles in Cuba convinced Kennedy that he had made a mistake. After the missile crisis was over in November, JFK sent Bundy to inform McCone that henceforth he should focus on his duties as director of central intelligence.

Tom Hughes determined that the CIA's professionals had concluded that McCone was simply acting as a well-intentioned amateur when expressing his views on Cuba. He should simply be ignored on Cuba. McCone was relying solely on his own intuition and nothing else.

McCone had on several occasions surrendered the chair at the weekly USIB meetings to his deputy, General Marshall "Pat" Carter, so that he could register a personal dissent. Though the CIA's old-timers simply ignored their director on his Cuban missile claims, Hughes found that General Carter and others nonetheless did not discount the threat entirely and continued to insist on the need for regular U-2 and other reconnaissance flights. The agency could not relax in its efforts to detect the presence of Soviet missiles.

Tom passed this assessment on to Roger, who told the president. McCone asked for a personal meeting with Kennedy on August 22 and repeated his belief on the missiles. The CIA director then departed on his honeymoon to the French Riviera, leaving General Carter in charge. Unaccountably, however, McCone proceeded to shower the CIA with a series of what came to be known as "honeymoon cables," giving orders.

The joke at the CIA was that the director was spending so much time on the cables that he had forgotten what he was supposed to do on the honeymoon. It was not a joke to President Kennedy, however, who expected clarity and not confusion from the CIA.

The situation took a dramatic turn on August 29, when photo evidence from a U-2 flight showed the presence of the latest Soviet surface-to-air anti-aircraft missiles near San Cristobal in western Cuba. U.S. naval reconnaissance flights also detected at this time what appeared to be disassembled Soviet light bombers, IL-28s, on the deck of a Soviet transport headed for Cuba.

On August 31, Senator Keating told the Senate that there was evidence of new Soviet missile installations in western Cuba, urged the president to take action, and proposed that the Organization of American States send an investigative team to Cuba.[10] Keating was possibly referring to the SAM sites. But there was now an obvious question: What were the SAMs protecting?

The Kennedy administration had received assurances from Khrushchev via Soviet Ambassador Anatoly Dobrynin that all Soviet systems deployed in Cuba were defensive in character. Bobby Kennedy's Russian friend, Georgi Bolshakov, gave him the same assurances. The Kennedy administration, for its part, had warned Soviet officials that there would be consequences if these assurances were false.

The detection of the SAMs had changed the situation. The missiles were conceivably defensive systems insofar as they were intended to deter American U-2 flights, which were assumed to be part of an imminent invasion. But, as McCone was to argue later, when he returned from his honeymoon, SAMs are not usually deployed to protect fruit orchards. Kennedy decided to issue an unambiguous warning to the Soviet Union in the form of a presidential press release.

The attorney general and the assistant attorney general, Nicholas Katzenbach, drafted the press release. The president's statement was read by Pierre Salinger, the White House press secretary, on September 4 to a group of correspondents and was published the next day in newspapers across the country. For the first time the president had officially warned that the United States would not tolerate offensive weapons in Cuba.

The press release began by noting broad concern in the United States and Latin America over the recent moves of the Soviet Union in Cuba.

> Information has reached this government in the last four days . . . which establishes without doubt that the Soviets have provided the Cuban government with a number of anti-aircraft defense missiles. . . . Along with these missiles the Soviets are apparently providing the extensive radar and other electronic equipment, which is required for their operation. We can also confirm the presence of several Soviet-made torpedo boats carrying ship-to-ship guided missiles having a range of fifteen miles.[11]

The critical paragraph followed:

> There is no evidence of any organized combat force in Cuba . . . ; of a violation of the 1934 Guantanamo Treaty; of the presence of offensive ground-to-ground missiles; or of other significant offensive capabilities. . . . *Were it to be otherwise, the gravest issues would arise.*"[12]

The administration followed up the warning with a U-2 flight over Cuba on September 5, covering parts of the island that had not been recently photographed. Nothing was detected that would trigger the previous day's warning. The White House repeated its warning on September 15. The White House seemed to inch closer to the Republican position in the Senate. More tensions developed, however, in the White House's relations with the CIA.

WHITE HOUSE–STATE–CIA TENSIONS

The intelligence community faced and resolved an internal dispute that developed from the August 29 detection of the SAM sites. An agent recruited by Operation Mongoose reported seeing an object on a trailer bed that was longer than a surface-to-air missile. A SAM should be about forty to fifty feet long. This object, the agent reported, was perhaps seventy feet long and required unusual side actions, such as cutting down trees and telephone poles, to allow the truck to navigate around turns. There were two such reports. The question was whether the two reports were "hard" evidence of medium- or intermediate-range ballistic missiles.

The CIA and the military preferred photographic evidence to eyewitness accounts. But there was no photographic evidence yet. The evaluators at Langley had to assess the circumstances of the two eyewitness reports. The agents in both cases could not help but be afraid of detection. If caught, they would have been shot. Their hearts were pounding. They were under extreme stress.

The evaluators finally decided that the agents were mistaken. What each saw hidden under the tarpaulin was actually a surface-to-air missile, which might have been positioned in such a way on the trailer so as to appear longer than normal.

A special national intelligence estimate (SNIE 85-3-62) was required to get the government's best overall assessment of the situation. On September 19, 1962, the USIB issued the evaluation discounting the eyewitness reports. The SNIE, by all of the government's intelligence agencies (with the Atomic Energy Commission abstaining), reviewed the evidence on the whole Soviet buildup in Cuba and concluded that it was unlikely the Soviet Union had deployed or would deploy surface-to-surface strategic nuclear missiles in Cuba.[13]

The estimators included the State Department's leading Sovietologists Llewelyn Thompson and Charles Bohlen. Tom Hughes represented the INR at the USIB, and the INR's Soviet expert Hal Sonnenfeldt was active in the experts' sessions leading up to the USIB meeting of September 19. The SNIE reaffirmed the long-standing assessment that Soviet leaders, despite their revolutionary backgrounds, were generally cautious in their strategic decisions. Since they had never done so in the past, they were unlikely to deploy strategic missiles in Cuba now.

The buildup to date, the SNIE noted, seemed to focus on strengthening Castro's air and coastal defenses. Twelve SAM sites had been established and were manned by Soviet technicians. Patrol boats of several kinds augmented Castro's weak naval units. Soviet shipping activity stepped up significantly in July 1962, and the number of Soviet technicians and advisers had increased substantially (the SNIE dramatically underestimated the number of Soviet technical personnel and missed the fact that Soviet combat troops were present). Soviet intentions, the SNIE held, were probably political: the military assistance would ensure Castro's hold on power and demonstrate Soviet leadership in the communist bloc.

The SNIE hedged its bets, however, by noting that there were clear strategic advantages for the Soviet Union if it were to deploy strategic missiles or to use Cuba as a submarine base. Tom Hughes argued for this cautionary point. The Soviets had only 36 intercontinental ballistic missiles stationed on their own soil that were capable of reaching the United States. In contrast, the United States had 203 such missiles capable of reaching the Soviet Union, not to speak of the U.S. bomber superiority.

Moreover, the Soviet Union was having some technical difficulties in producing long-range missiles with heavy payloads. By deploying intermediate-range missiles in Cuba, the Soviet Union would significantly improve its strategic posture by increasing the number of missiles that could reach the United States. The SNIE concluded that it was probably more likely that the Soviets would develop a base for its subs to patrol off the nearby U.S. waters. But the SNIE warned that analysts should look carefully for any signs of intermediate range missiles. The USIB's overall judgment was as follows:

> The establishment on Cuban soil of Soviet nuclear striking forces which could be used against the US would be incompatible with Soviet policy as we presently estimate it. It would indicate a far greater willingness to increase the level of risk in US-Soviet relations than the USSR has displayed thus far. . . . However, Soviet military planners have almost certainly considered the contribution which Cuban bases might make to the Soviet strategic posture. . . . Therefore this contingency must be examined carefully, even though it would run counter to current Soviet policy.[14]

The implication, Hughes saw from General Carter's stance at subsequent meetings, was that more U-2 and other reconnaissance equipment was needed. Acting CIA director Carter was so convinced that he began pushing for twice-daily U-2 flights to settle once and for all the issue of offensive missiles. In this conviction, Carter ran head-on into the opposing view of national security adviser Bundy and Secretary of State Rusk.

The State Department for some time had warned of the diplomatic problems resulting from a U-2 shootdown. State's lawyers generally believed that even high-altitude flights violated Cuban airspace and would provoke anti-aircraft fire from the SAM batteries. Bundy believed that since the September 5 U-2 flight had produced no evidence of offensive weapons, there was no immediate need for more flights. Rusk was happy to reinforce Bundy's worries about the reconnaissance flights.

Furthermore, Rusk believed in a new kind of aerial photography, called oblique or slanted because the camera took pictures offshore. The plane could photograph without flying directly over Cuban territory. The new cameras could take pictures without invading sovereign airspace.

A shootdown of a Chinese nationalist U-2 flying over mainland China on the weekend of September 8–9 helped to bring matters to a head. At 10:00 a.m. on Monday, September 10, Bundy telephoned James Reber, chair of the interagency Committee on Overhead Reconnaissance that set surveillance requirements. Within thirty minutes, Bundy wanted answers to three questions:

How important were overflights of Cuba to our national security objectives?

How much would our intelligence suffer if we limited our reconnaissance activity to peripheral flights using oblique rather than overhead photography?

Was there anyone in the planning of these missions who might want to provoke an incident?[15]

The last question stunned Reber. Did the White House really believe the nation's intelligence professionals were in league with the hawks in Congress to provoke a war? He asked for more time to prepare a proper response, and a meeting was set for later in the day. Bundy, Rusk, Carter, Reber, and a Joint Chiefs representative met to review the whole range of reconnaissance issues.

The intelligence officials responded to Bundy's third question by ignoring it. Reber felt intimidated by the disparity in rank represented at the meeting and did not participate as fully or as freely as he was accustomed to doing with his peers. General Carter did most of the talking for the intelligence side. He pressed for more flights as soon as possible and opposed what he saw as the hypercautious approach of Bundy and Rusk.

Bundy and Rusk made clear their worries over U-2s being shot down by the SAMs. They cited the advantages of the new oblique photography. Carter, Reber, and the Joint Chiefs officer noted that oblique photography had limitations; it could not, for example, cover areas far inland.

Bundy had rendered the meeting moot by ruling out further flights over Cuba for the rest of September. He made this decision just an hour before he met with the intelligence officials. He wanted a cooling-off period following the U-2 incident over China. He and Rusk wanted to avoid the risk of a U.S. plane being shot down over Cuba.

General Carter made clear at the meeting that the CIA could not live with Bundy's decision. He expressed his determination to recommend any reconnaissance flights—low-level, mid-level, or the high-flying U-2s—that he felt national security warranted. He would seek a presidential decision if he decided a flight was needed.

The meeting ended on an odd note. Bundy had unilaterally declared an outcome in advance of the negotiations. Carter declared that he would authorize a flight if he deemed it necessary. Bundy decided that Carter was posturing and let the apparent defiance pass.

Notwithstanding the bad blood on display, the White House got what it wanted. The overflights were temporarily suspended. Carter's caveat, however, enabled the administration to say later that it never turned down any specific flight request. Carter had said he would not hesitate to request flights but, in fact, made no such requests. The inference was that additional flights were not actually needed during the rest of September.

Meanwhile, John McCone had returned from his honeymoon and erupted like an active volcano, showering initiatives in every direction. He engaged in furious rounds of negotiations on Capitol Hill, visited Eisenhower for his advice, and pressed his case that SAMs, MIG-21s, IL-28s, and ballistic missiles were in Cuba.

In early October, McCone telephoned McGeorge Bundy and argued forcefully that the MIG-21 fighters now in Cuba were clearly offensive weapons. The MIGs had sufficient range to reach Florida and inflict heavy damage on U.S. military bases. Furthermore, photo evidence of crates indicated that the Soviets were shipping IL-28 light bombers to be assembled in Cuba. He was obliged, McCone told Bundy, to report such findings to the appropriate congressional committees and was giving the White House a heads-up.[16]

BOWLES AND DOBRYNIN

On October 9, Chester Bowles received a phone call from Soviet ambassador Anatoly Dobrynin, asking for a luncheon date. This was mildly surprising to Bowles, who had not lately seen much of the ambassador.[17] Dobrynin told Bowles that he had heard on the grapevine that Bowles was leaving shortly for a long trip and thereafter to take up new duties as U.S. ambassador to India. Dobrynin wanted to say goodbye in a proper fashion. Bowles immediately surmised that the call must have something to do with Cuba.

Bowles called Tom Hughes to arrange for an intelligence briefing on Cuba. Hughes provided Bowles with a thorough grounding in every aspect of the intelligence. The detection of the SAMs, the IL-28s observed by naval reconnaissance flights, the special national intelligence estimate, Walt Rostow's September 3 policy planning paper at State recommending the removal of the Jupiters from Turkey and their replacement by a new multilateral fleet, McCone's antics, and the president's decision to resume U-2 flights over Cuba were covered.

Tom gave his old friend a lesson in "cratology," the specialty of inferences about the contents of the crates on decks of Soviet transports heading for Cuba. He explained how difficult it was to evaluate eyewitness reports on events at night under stressful conditions. Tom agreed with Chet that Dobrynin probably had something more in mind than just saying goodbye.

Chet got just what he needed from Tom. He admired how crisply his former aide summed up the situation. Tom told him about the fight between Bundy-Rusk and McCone-Carter-CIA on U-2 overflights, the Keating problem, and Tom's unsuccessful efforts to track down the source of Keating's information. Chet had enjoyed his work with Third World ambassadors, but it was nice to get an update on the larger policy issues.

The lunch with Dobrynin took place several days later. As Bowles had anticipated, almost immediately after the cordial greetings, Dobrynin turned the conversation to Cuba. Why, Dobrynin asked Bowles, are the Americans so obsessed with a small Caribbean island? Bowles launched into a lecture on the Monroe Doctrine, probably more detailed than Dobrynin expected. When Chet finished, Dobrynin pressed further and asked for an explanation of the administration's thinking on the Cuba problem.

Bowles gave his assessment that the president was determined to resist any offensive weapons in Cuba. For a time, the two men debated the meaning of "offensive." Dobrynin insisted that as far as he knew there were no offensive weapons in Cuba. Furthermore, he knew of no plans for any such weapons in the future.

Bowles countered with the observation that Dobrynin would not be the first ambassador to be misled by his own government. The discussion was so detailed that Bowles had the feeling that Dobrynin was well aware that the Americans were watching Cuba carefully. Bowles had no doubt that Dobrynin would give a detailed report to the Kremlin. His performance left no doubt that U.S. reconnaissance flights and other extensive intelligence efforts were underway.

Dobrynin shifted the topic to diplomatic solutions. What did the Americans want? What would solve the problem? Bowles had given the matter some thought and was ready. His proposal started with the Castro government. Fidel Castro must make a public declaration that Cuba was satisfied with the current defense treaty with the Soviet Union, that he felt confident that Cuba was ready and capable of defending itself, and that he had no need for or interest in seeking offensive weapons from the Soviet Union, or any other communist-bloc nation. Cuba would further declare that it would not engage in subversive activity directed against other governments in the region.

Second, the Soviet Union would similarly declare that it had not placed offensive weapons in Cuba and would remove any such weapons deemed by the United States to be offensive. The Soviet Union would further pledge that it would make no future shipments of offensive weapons and declare that its support of Cuba did not require any such weapons, including, in particular, ballistic missiles.

Finally, the United States would declare for its part that it would never invade Cuba and would pledge not to engage in any subversive activities against Cuba. Left unsaid was any indication that the United States would drop its economic blockade or surrender its treaty rights to the Guantanamo naval base (lifting the economic embargo and surrendering Guantanamo were two of the five points later enunciated in Castro's own peace plan).

Dobrynin took note of the proposal but made no comment on the points. He made one significant observation, however. He stated that U.S. missiles in Turkey should be included in any negotiations. Dobrynin asserted that the U.S. Jupiter missiles in Turkey and Italy directly threatened the Soviet Union.

The Soviet ambassador was aware from Soviet intelligence that a year earlier Kennedy had considered not sending the Jupiters to Turkey but had changed his mind and allowed the deployment. Dobrynin asked Bowles why the U.S. missiles on the Soviet Union's border with Turkey should be considered defensive. Why should Turkey not be discussed along with Cuba? This linkage, said Dobrynin, would be a logical way to resolve disagreements over Cuba.

Bowles had sent a memo to Kennedy a year earlier arguing against deploying the Jupiters in Turkey. He had made then some of the same arguments that Dobrynin was making now. Bowles had told Kennedy that the Jupiters were vulnerable, provocative, and unnecessary because better systems would soon be available.

Bowles now, however, ducked the linkage question and told Dobrynin that introducing NATO issues into the Cuba debate would be an unnecessary complication. The Turkish issue could be taken up later as part of a wider arms control negotiation. Such wider negotiations, Bowles declared, could begin as soon as Cuban issues were satisfactorily resolved.

Bowles, after his meeting with Dobrynin, wrote a lengthy memorandum on the conversation for the president. He discussed at length Dobrynin's views on the Jupiter missiles. He delivered it to the White House on October 14. Bowles departed the next day on his lengthy trip and was away for the entire period of the missile crisis and the China-India border war.

On Bowles's return to Washington in late November, he found another message from Dobrynin, which led to another lunch. This time, Dobrynin had a new idea. In the wake of the warming of relations following the missile crisis, Dobrynin proposed a formula for new U.S.-Soviet talks to focus on a nuclear test ban treaty.

Bowles wrote another memo for the president but decided to seek a personal audience to explain Dobrynin's ideas. To his pleasant surprise, Bowles found the president warmly welcoming. Even more surprising, Kennedy eagerly seized on Dobrynin's ideas and assured Bowles that he would follow up on the test ban.

In 1989, Dobrynin first revealed publicly his role in the resolution of the crisis.[18] He claimed it was he who came up with the Turkish swap idea, or at least that he was the one who introduced the idea to Khrushchev.[19] Very shortly after his original lunch with Bowles in October 1962, Dobrynin found himself in the middle of the very crisis they had discussed at that lunch.

10

Diplomacy

Of all the myths surrounding the Cuban Missile Crisis, none was as carefully crafted, or widely believed, as the idea that John F. Kennedy's toughness alone forced the Soviet Union to capitulate. Nikita Khrushchev supposedly withdrew his missiles from Cuba without the slightest concession by the United States. The mythmaking does the president a disservice. For JFK, against the nearly unanimous advice of his advisers, refused to contemplate any military action that might risk a nuclear war. Kennedy sought a path out of the crisis through diplomacy. For this, not for his toughness, he deserves to be honored.

Another key figure in resolving this gravest crisis of the Cold War, an unlikely one, was the man who started it in the first place, Soviet premier Nikita Khrushchev. Kennedy accepted Khrushchev's proposal for the United States to withdraw its Jupiter missiles from Turkey in exchange for the Soviet Union's withdrawal of its missiles from Cuba. This was the explicit bargain that resolved the crisis.[1]

BOWLES AND DOBRYNIN REDUX

Surprisingly, Kennedy knew where he might end up before he was even aware that he was in the midst of the crisis. Dobrynin had suggested to Bowles what should be done to resolve the crisis that did not yet exist. The Soviet ambassador was not privy to Khrushchev's secret plan, but he was not innocent of the ways of the world or of the Kremlin. He followed the political debate in America carefully, was generally informed about the

Soviet buildup in Cuba, and knew from the cable traffic and the stream of visitors to and from the Soviet embassy that something important was happening.

The lunch with Bowles confirmed his suspicions that the United States was monitoring Cuban developments closely. It was only a matter of time before the United States learned of the Kremlin's plans for Cuba. Dobrynin knew that Bowles had a protégé in the State Department's intelligence service. He was bound to check in and get a briefing before the lunch with Dobrynin. The Soviet ambassador also knew from the cable traffic concerning Foreign Minister Gromyko's October 18 visit to Washington that Gromyko was prepared to discuss the missile issue if President Kennedy raised it.

Dobrynin had done his part by denying any knowledge of offensive weapons in Cuba or acting on instructions from Moscow in the matter. Yet the discussion with Bowles revealed that Dobrynin was well aware of the debate about offensive and defensive weapons. What constituted an offensive system was in the eye of the beholder.

The ambassador's task going forward would be different from what it had been, starting with briefing Gromyko for the October 18 meeting with President Kennedy. Dobrynin was no longer in the dark. He would be actively involved in the next stage of the crisis.

President Kennedy, at the first meeting of the Executive Committee of the National Security Council (ExCom) late Tuesday morning, October 16, after he had been shown the U-2 photos of the Soviet missiles, listened to the experts discuss, inter alia, the idea of a missile swap resolving the situation. Adlai Stevenson raised the missile swap idea, but his colleagues on the ExCom came down hard on him. The heated objections to Adlai's proposal resulted partly from his colleagues' dislike of him. The missile swap was seen as not without merit, however, as even Adlai's critics conceded. The main drawback of the plan was its political unfeasibility, from the standpoint of both NATO and domestic politics.

If a diplomatic path was not clear to Kennedy, the military options were even worse. None of the military options discussed by the committee appealed to him. Even a heavy attack on the known missile sites would only knock out about 80 percent of the missiles. Bombing would probably have to be followed by an invasion, which would cost 18,000 American casualties in the first ten days, the president was told. All bets about casualties would be off if nuclear weapons were used against the invading force.

KENNEDY-GROMYKO MISFIRE

The first significant diplomatic opportunity came at a White House meeting on Thursday afternoon, October 18, 1962, involving the Soviet foreign minister and ambassador, Dobrynin, President Kennedy, and Secretary of

State Rusk. The meeting presented a chance for quiet diplomacy, but neither side seized that opportunity. Gromyko had come to New York for a UN session and used the occasion to visit Washington. Following the meeting with Kennedy and Rusk, he would attend a State Department reception and dinner. At the dinner, Gromyko would have further discussions with Rusk.

The Kremlin, not certain how much Kennedy knew about Cuba, instructed Gromyko to concede that there were a few missiles in Cuba, if Kennedy raised the subject and appeared to have proof of the missiles' presence. However, he was to insist that the missiles were there strictly for defensive purposes. He was to argue, in short, the same line the Americans had always used with their intermediate-range ballistic missiles in Europe. Gromyko would mirror his March conversation with John McCloy, in which the American defended the U.S. Jupiter missiles in Turkey—only this time, the roles would be reversed.[2]

Gromyko had simply to turn this argument on its head. Gromyko should stick to his script. If Kennedy did not raise the missile issue, so much the better. The Americans would be told when the missiles were fully operational. In the meantime, Gromyko would have the chance to assess how much Kennedy knew.

The October 18 meeting began stiffly. After perfunctory formalities, Gromyko took out a prepared text and read from it. Gromyko was evidently as nervous as Kennedy. Years later, Gromyko was to describe this meeting as the most significant and difficult of his entire diplomatic career.

Kennedy and Rusk listened impassively as Gromyko issued his routine denials. Kennedy later told aides that he was tempted to pull out the photos from his drawer and lay them in front of Gromyko. But since Kennedy had not decided on any plan of action at this point, he said nothing until Gromyko finished. Then JFK reciprocated by reading from his own September 5 and 13 statements warning the Soviet Union against placing offensive weapons in Cuba.

There was desultory discussion of NATO weapons and of international law. To Dobrynin, the discussion seemed like a strange kabuki drama. The actors were talking so indirectly and abstractly that no one could make any sense of what was said. The meeting ended stiffly, with no substantive exchange of views on anything important.

Gromyko raised the issue of the NATO missiles in Turkey with Rusk at dinner in an effort to sniff out what the United States did or did not know about Cuba. Rusk played dumb and did not take the bait. His behavior confirmed Gromyko's optimistic surmise that Americans were ignorant about Cuban developments.

Dobrynin observed, in his memoir, that Gromyko misjudged the situation badly. The normally cautious Gromyko, evidently in an effort to curry favor with Khrushchev, sent a cable to the Kremlin telling the Soviet leader that the plan to keep Kennedy in the dark was working perfectly. Kennedy had no idea that the missiles were in place and nearly operational. Indeed, Gromyko said that Kennedy did not seem particularly excited about the Cuba issue. Khrushchev could relax and proceed with his plans in full confidence that there would be no serious reaction from the United States.

Dobrynin urged Gromyko to qualify his assessment and be more cautious. The American reaction could be serious, and the Americans may have been deceiving him. But an overconfident Gromyko refused to heed Dobrynin's warnings.[3]

EXECUTIVE COMMITTEE DELIBERATIONS

The first two meetings of the ExCom, on October 16 and 17, raised most of the key issues that the president and his advisers discussed over the next ten days: How serious was the military threat? Could air strikes against the missile sites and SAM batteries destroy them? What were the pros and cons of the various U.S. military moves?

Aside from the more narrowly focused military issues, the committee members debated the broader questions. What was the political context, and what were the political constraints on diplomatic moves? How would NATO react to various proposals, including a possible swap of Jupiter missiles in Turkey for Soviet missiles in Cuba? What was Khrushchev's game plan? What should be the role, if any, of the UN or the Organization of American States in resolving the crisis? Could the United States gain the initiative in shaping world public opinion, and would this matter?

The limitations of the ExCom as a decisionmaking body were also clearly apparent. The participants changed their positions, argued around in circles, and were difficult to manage. Only the president and the attorney general were aware that the proceedings were being taped. Because the president and his brother knew of the taping, the sessions sometimes had the appearance of being staged, or of being "a charade within a charade."[4]

Kennedy maneuvered between the full ExCom, a smaller subgroup within the committee, and a still smaller subgroup to gain their views, but he never lost sight of his own role as commander in chief. All hands were on deck within the administration. Kennedy gleaned every bit of information and analysis he could while trying to maintain tight control and secrecy. But the ExCom members relied on their subordinates to answer the questions that the president or his committee colleagues raised.

The INR was a player from the start. Even though Roger Hilsman did not attend the ExCom meetings regularly, he contributed papers and opinions on a host of issues. Roger had a cot moved into his office, and he slept there for the duration of the crisis. His strength finally gave out on the last Saturday of the crisis and he went home, exhausted.

The president already knew from Chester Bowles's October 14 memo that the Russians, if worse came to worst, might settle for a missile swap involving the American Jupiters in Turkey. Kennedy assumed that this would be the Soviet fallback position. Khrushchev, he thought, was taking "one hell of a gamble" to improve his strategic position.[5] He believed that Khrushchev would sit tight in Cuba if he could get away with it.

Kennedy did not regard the swap as a bad deal. It would look reasonable to any outside observer. JFK's problem was that he did not see a path to negotiations that would not leave him looking weak and irresolute. A diplomatic initiative at this point might simply allow Khrushchev to stall and finish construction on the missile sites while pretending to negotiate. The U-2 intelligence flights indicated that the Russians were furiously working to finish construction at the sites. If a deal could be made soon, or if talks could be linked to a halt in construction, the prospects for a favorable outcome might be enhanced.

Kennedy's instinct was to rely on a small, loyal group of advisers. But the crisis had so many ramifications he was forced to reach out beyond his inner circle and beyond the ExCom. The ExCom members conferred with their Defense, State, and CIA staffs. Kennedy feared that the tense atmosphere could not be maintained for long without a leak. Some decisive action must be taken, and soon. His military advisers warned that U.S. intervention would be more costly in lives as the Cubans and Russians consolidated their defenses.

It was not that Kennedy lacked proposals or options to consider. From the start, many ideas were on the table, including, as noted earlier, the missile swap.

Walt Rostow, State's policy planning head, had a modernization plan to phase out the Jupiters and replace them with a NATO-wide crew operating a nuclear submarine—the multilateral fleet. Abram Chayes, State's legal counsel, had a proposal, and the Joint Chiefs had elaborate plans ranging from limited air strikes to an invasion of Cuba. There were proposals galore, each based on assumptions about Soviet intentions.

President Kennedy, at the end of the first week of the crisis, settled on a naval blockade, or quarantine, to prevent further arms shipments as the least forceful military response, combined with an ultimatum that the Soviets must immediately withdraw all missiles from Cuba. This message was delivered in a nationally televised address to the American people by President Kennedy on Monday, October 22.

After Kennedy's speech, General Issa Pliyev, Soviet military commander in Cuba, decided that unloading the *Androvsk* under American surveillance would be too risky. He left the ship at anchor with its cargo of nuclear warheads in the harbor at Mariopol. More Soviet ships were approaching Cuban ports or were on their way.

The naval blockade, Kennedy hoped, might provide the time and the opportunity for serious negotiations.[6] While the blockade was the least forceful military course, under international law a blockade was still an act of war. Kennedy decided that the best he could do was to use the term "quarantine" to distinguish U.S. action from a blockade as usually understood. The quarantine would not interdict all Soviet shipments to Cuba. Food, medicine, fuel, supplies, and a wide range of cargos (not specifically defined) would be permitted.

Furthermore, by surprising the Soviet Union with the ultimatum and naval action, the United States would be seizing the diplomatic initiative and defining the Soviets as the aggressors. The Soviets indicted themselves by their secrecy and use of stealth to disguise their actions. They were violating a host of treaties protecting the Western Hemisphere from aggression by outsiders.

THE CRITICAL WEEK

Khrushchev was shocked by the Kennedy speech. He took a pugnacious tone in his initial response to Kennedy, accusing the United States of piracy and violations of international law. He declared that Soviet ship captains would never permit their vessels to be boarded by Americans.

There was resentment inside the Soviet government against Khrushchev over the missile gamble, but the urgency of the situation called for backing the premier. Khrushchev did not call the Presidium into session immediately. The Presidium typically met only when a decision had to be made. After Kennedy's speech, however, there was an immediate need to issue instructions to General Issa Pliyev in Cuba. He must have orders on the potential use of the tactical nuclear and intermediate range nuclear weapons under his command in the event of a U.S. invasion of Cuba.

Khrushchev and the Presidium worked on a draft cable ordering Pliyev to put his forces on alert but not to use any nuclear weapons without specific authorization from Moscow.[7] The more the Soviet leaders thought about this instruction, however, the less they liked it. This would, in effect, doom the 42,000 Soviet soldiers and technicians to be slaughtered in the first few days of an American invasion. The Kremlin modified the order with an ambiguous formulation allowing Pliyev to take any steps he deemed necessary.

Meanwhile, on Tuesday, October 23, Robert Kennedy took advantage of a back channel he had established, at the president's urging, to place a call to Soviet Ambassador Anatoly Dobrynin. RFK angrily rebuked him for lies and deception over the missiles in Cuba. Dobrynin protested that he had been kept in the dark by the Kremlin and had been given no instructions after JFK's speech the previous evening.[8] Robert Kennedy was initially agitated, but he gradually returned to a more businesslike demeanor.

Dobrynin took the offensive as RFK calmed down. He said that if the Americans had learned about the missiles by the time of Gromyko's visit on October 18, why had President Kennedy and Rusk not raised the issue with Gromyko? That was the reason for Gromyko's visit to Washington, Dobrynin told RFK.

Bobby said that Gromyko's stiff demeanor had discouraged his brother from attempting any genuine dialogue. The president was and remained concerned that lengthy diplomatic exchanges might be a stalling tactic. The attorney general told Dobrynin that the Soviet Union had to halt construction on the bases immediately.

Dobrynin was now the Kennedys' only back channel with the Kremlin after the attorney general had broken off his close ties with Georgi Bolshakov of Soviet military intelligence because Bolshakov had given him, unwittingly as it turned out, false assurances on Cuba. Bolshakov returned to Moscow and was relegated to a dead-end assignment where he remained for twenty years, spending his time drinking too much and pursuing young women.

After Kennedy's October 22 speech, Khrushchev had an obvious move that he missed, according to Dobrynin years after the actual events. Khrushchev should have proposed the Turkish missile swap immediately. This would have put diplomatic pressure on Kennedy. The rest of the world would have considered it a fair bargain, and Kennedy would have had to yield.

The news media after the president's speech were full of reports of continuing Soviet construction activity and played up the drama over what would happen on the high seas when Soviet vessels reached the blockade. The U.S. warships were to take up their positions to enforce the blockade by Wednesday, October 24. There was no immediate indication that Soviet ships headed toward Cuba had changed course.

President Kennedy had seized the initiative with his speech on October 22. The Soviet Union was cast as the aggressor for deploying the missiles secretly. In the first paragraphs of his October 22 speech, Kennedy castigated the Soviet Union for violating the Monroe Doctrine, the Rio Pact, Organization of American States dictates, UN conventions, and other international obligations. Stevenson and Rusk were active with the United Nations and engaged Secretary General U Thant in the diplomacy. U Thant called for a halt in the shipment of offensive weapons to Cuba.

Kennedy ordered George Ball and Roger Hilsman to brief ambassadors in Washington on the crisis. Assistant Secretary of State Ed Martin took over the role of keeping Latin American ambassadors informed of developments. While the United States had gained a propaganda edge, there was no obvious resolution to the crisis in sight. Public opinion at home, while overwhelmingly supportive of the president for the moment, could shift dramatically if the crisis dragged on inconclusively. Republican politicians were caught between their desire to support the president in a crisis and their instinct to seek out an advantage in the upcoming congressional elections. The military would continue to hammer away on the need for decisive action, particularly if it seemed that the Soviets were gaining strength in the stalemate.

HUGHES AS PUBLIC BRIEFER

The midterm elections were now less than two weeks away. Kennedy's own political fate was involved, for if he did not resolve the Cuba crisis he would almost certainly not be reelected or perhaps not even be renominated. JFK had told the nation on October 22 that the presence of Soviet missiles in Cuba was an existential threat to national security.

He had frightened every man, woman, and child in America when he raised the danger of nuclear war. At this point, he could hardly declare that perhaps he had overreacted and that it did not matter if the Soviets had a few missiles in Cuba. There was a potential solution in the form of the missile swap and the United States's position was actually strong if he could buy time and if the public understood his policies.

"We will have to make a deal in the end," Bobby explained to Arthur Schlesinger on October 22, "but we must stand firm now. Our concessions must come at the end of negotiations, not at the start."[9] But it was getting to be time for a deal.

Even if an idea was promising in theory, the political obstacles could be formidable. There were other ideas besides the missile swap to be explored. President Kennedy authorized Adlai to work with Secretary General U Thant at the UN on a formula to halt the construction work and disable any operational missiles. A quid pro quo of some sort would be required, and the offered removal of the Jupiters might entice Khrushchev. The nonaligned countries at the UN were buzzing with ideas of the missile swap.

Bruno Kreisky, Austria's foreign minister, opined at a political rally in Vienna on Thursday, October 25, that a missile swap between the great powers would stop the drift to war. The *Manchester Guardian* editorialized, "What's sauce for Cuba is also sauce for Turkey."[10]

Closer to home, Walter Lippmann, dean of American journalists, wrote columns in the *Washington Post* on October 23 and 25 in which he argued that the U.S. missiles in Turkey were a strategic liability and then called for dismantling them in return for the removal of the Soviet missiles from Cuba.[11]

Secretary Rusk and Ed Martin were working on a scheme to approach Castro through a Latin American intermediary, possibly Brazil, in an effort to detach Castro from the Soviets. The U.S. ambassador to Brazil Lincoln Gordon arranged such a visit, but the Brazilians botched it.[12]

President Kennedy, even as his advisers struggled with the diplomatic options, wanted to update U.S. politicians on where matters stood on Cuba. In normal circumstances, the director of central intelligence might be called on to give the intelligence briefing. But JFK did not fully trust John McCone to be nonpolitical. He might, under questioning, bring up his own previous disagreements with the administration. Kennedy needed someone he could trust implicitly, a professional and not a politician, who would represent the administration to the audience that mattered most in shaping public opinion—the political class. He needed a representative who was articulate and well informed, fast on his feet intellectually, with good political sense, who would be respectful but not allow himself to be intimidated. Kennedy knew exactly who he wanted.

He remembered Rusk telling him about attending a Rhodes scholar dinner where Tom Hughes had impressed the audience with his polished performance as master of ceremonies. Kennedy had first met Hughes at the February 1945 United Nations Conference in San Francisco and had seen him off and on in the Senate and as part of the Washington social circuit. He called Tom on Wednesday, October 24.

Hughes had just talked to Mac Bundy when his secretary said the White House was calling again. Kennedy asked Tom to fly to New York on Thursday and brief public officials from the Northeast on the missile crisis. Tom would be the administration's spokesperson on the crisis. The audience would be several hundred representatives, senators, governors, and mayors. The White House would handle the arrangements. Tom should show up at the federal courthouse in Manhattan at 8:00 a.m. for the briefing, which would be at the "secret" level.

After the morning briefing in New York, Hughes was to fly to Chicago and repeat the performance for a similar audience of politicians and public officials, again with the briefing classified at the secret level. The briefing was a comprehensive review of the origins of the crisis, what was happening, and the administration's plans. There would be an opportunity for questions.

Senators and representatives running for election would not be eager to take a day off from campaigning, the president said, but they would appreciate the attention. They would like to tell their constituents that the president had called them in for a special briefing. The public officials, Kennedy told Tom, would feel flattered. They would be pleased that they had been consulted. They could look important when telling constituents what was happening in the crisis. This would help reassure the public.

The White House operators passed out the invitations. Tom was briefed on every angle of the crisis. He felt confident when he arrived in Manhattan Thursday morning. Public debate was something he relished. Upon reading the newspapers, however, he had an uncomfortable feeling. The papers reported much of what he was planning to say. He called Roger Hilsman.

"Roger, I think we may have a problem," Tom said.

"What's that?"

Tom explained that virtually everything in his briefing was all over the papers that morning. These guys were not going to be happy if they were pulled off the campaign trail and given nothing more than what they had already read in the papers. Was there any way he might juice up the presentation and get into something they did not know?

"Well, why not go into this whole *Bucharest* thing? That's highly classified, and the papers got it all wrong. Tell them what happened and how we're handling the blockade," said Roger.

Some 300 senators, governors, and representatives showed up for the briefing. They were asked to sign their names on an improvised form with a heading, "Secret Briefing." The hall was plastered with large signs that read "SECRET." Hughes remembered seeing Nelson Rockefeller, Jacob Javits, and Abraham Ribicoff sitting in the front row as he began. Tom quickly found his footing. This is what Tom did, what he had done all his life: talk, hold an audience, and move smoothly through the argument. No jokes today, though. There were many questions, and he began to worry about making the plane to Chicago. He did not notice someone in the back of the room slipping out early.

That person was Representative James E. van Zandt (R-Pa.), who was running for the Senate and in need of publicity. Van Zandt found himself in a gaggle of reporters and TV cameras and launched into an attack on the Kennedy administration. The administration had no idea what it was doing, he said; the president had not done a thing to remove the missiles, and the blockade was a farce. The United States was not actually stopping any Russian ships, and no one knew what to do when a ship entered Cuban waters, as was clear from the encounter with the Soviet tanker *Bucharest*. This interview was all over the television and was seen by the president and ExCom members. Kennedy was in the middle of a meeting, discussing how to describe the Navy's handling of the *Bucharest*.

Hughes, meanwhile, grabbed a cab and headed for LaGuardia airport. As he hurried along the corridors to the American Airlines counter, he thought he heard his name on the public address system. As he approached the counter, there seemed to be turmoil among the American Airlines personnel. The public address system blared out a message to passenger Thomas Hughes to call the White House operator.

Hughes identified himself to one of the American Airlines attendants, who pointed to the public telephone. Tom inserted a dime and asked the operator to place a collect call to the White House. He asked to be put through to the president or to Mrs. (Evelyn) Lincoln, if the president was not available.

"Mrs. Lincoln, eh?" said the operator. "And I suppose you'd like to speak to General Grant, too."

Tom managed to convince her that he was a State Department official who had been paged and he was put through to the White House. An angry President Kennedy finally came on the line.

"What the hell's going on up there?"

Tom, unaware of van Zandt's television appearance, was taken aback. Kennedy explained the van Zandt incident and added, "Whose damn idea was it to brief all those politicians? Everybody knows they can't keep a secret."

Hughes, deeming discretion to be the better part of valor, observed: "Well, Mr. President, I guess the question is whether you want me to go on to Chicago, where we've got 250 more politicians waiting who have accepted your invitation. We can cancel, but it might be worse if we canceled it."

"Oh, what the hell, Tom," said the president. "You'd better go ahead. But don't let any of them get near a TV camera."[13]

The event in Chicago passed without incident. When Tom was able to make it back to Washington, he learned the rest of the story. Roger Hilsman called JFK and told him that he was the one who had told Tom Hughes to talk about the *Bucharest* and therefore was to blame for the incident involving van Zandt. Hilsman received a severe presidential tongue-lashing. Roger was shaken. Then he got a call from Mac Bundy, a man known for his sharp tongue and brusque manner. But a different side of the national security adviser was on display. Bundy told Hilsman that the president permitted himself such an eruption only with the people he knew and trusted most. Every one of his closest aides had experienced such a display of temper. This would quickly pass, and Roger was not to worry. Hilsman never forgot this act of kindness from a man who was not usually known for kindness.[14]

THE SCALI-FEKLISOV AFFAIR

There was evidence that Russian ships heading toward Cuba had now begun to turn around and head back to Murmansk or other ports. This signaling, however, did not signify that an actual negotiation was underway. This picture was to change shortly. When Tom Hughes returned to the office on Friday, October 26, a tense encounter awaited. John Scali, the moderator of ABC's *Issues and Answers* and a friend of Roger Hilsman, had received an urgent phone call from Aleksandr Feklisov (alias "Foman"), KGB chief at the Soviet embassy, requesting a meeting over lunch. Scali had lunched with Foman in the past and knew he was KGB. He usually received a visit from FBI agents after having met with the Soviet agent.

Nothing of consequence had come up in their past meetings. Foman had been rather bland and uninteresting, in Scali's view. But Foman's manner on the phone seemed different this time, and Scali decided to accept the invitation to lunch.

Scali did not have the time or inclination to inform the FBI of this lunch at the Occidental Restaurant. Foman outlined to Scali a plan, which purportedly came from the top levels of the Soviet government. The Soviet agent was seeking a response from the highest levels of the U.S. government.

In fact, Foman's plan was entirely his own invention. He was not acting on instructions from Moscow but was engaged in a freelance peace effort of his own. He had apparently taken to heart Klaus Fuchs's warnings of the devastating consequences of thermonuclear bombs (Foman had been Fuchs's KGB handler during World War II). Foman was motivated by a combination of high-minded concern for world peace and a highly inflated sense of his own importance.

Foman's plan had these elements: The Soviet Union would withdraw its missiles from Cuba under UN supervision, the UN would carry out on-site inspections to verify compliance, and the United States would immediately halt the blockade of Cuba and withdraw its military presence. The United States would then pledge not to invade Cuba and would also vouchsafe to halt any acts of aggression against Castro from any other Latin American country.

Scali hurried directly from the lunch to the State Department, arriving at approximately 3:30 p.m., and asked to see Hilsman. Hilsman, Hughes, Soviet specialist Helmut Sonnenfeldt, and a small team of INR experts met with Scali and went over the Foman plan. Foman was known to the INR experts. After some discussion, the team determined that the plan was a legitimate sign that the Soviet Union was at last seeking a way out of the crisis.

This seemed to be the first serious indication of a Soviet intent to negotiate. Hilsman drafted a short memo for Rusk, which summarized the Foman plan and the circumstances of the Scali meeting. Rusk contacted several ExCom colleagues and asked for their reactions. At around 6:00 p.m., Rusk sent word to Hilsman that he should bring Scali up to the secretary's office in the private elevator. Rusk told Scali to contact Foman at once and convey that there was interest at the highest levels of the U.S. government but that there was "time urgency" for any discussions.

Scali met again with Foman at 7:45 p.m. in an empty ballroom at the Statler Hilton Hotel near the Soviet embassy. Foman seemed nervous and demanded assurances that Scali's message had reached the highest levels of the U.S. government. Scali gave repeated assurances, and the KGB agent was finally satisfied. However, he then insisted that if the UN was going to inspect Soviet forces, it was only fair that the UN should also inspect American bases in Florida. Scali explained that this would be viewed as a distraction and would doom any negotiations. Foman settled down to a businesslike discussion and said that he would communicate Scali's message at once to the Kremlin's highest levels.

In the meantime, shortly after Scali talked with Rusk, the first installment of a rambling letter from Khrushchev to Kennedy arrived in the State Department. The letter had been sent to the U.S. embassy in Moscow before the Scali-Feklisov lunch but had been delayed in the transmission and in the translation. The letter, evidently written by Khrushchev himself because of its earthy Russian idioms, appeared to confirm much of Foman's proposal to Scali.

The letter struck a conciliatory note and seemed to hint at compromise but contained no specific proposals. It was odd that the more detailed proposal came before the Khrushchev letter, but this was attributed to the delay in transmission. The Khrushchev message was probably meant to come first, to be followed by the specifics of Foman's proposal. It was also unusual that the Kremlin would communicate through the KGB and not through the Soviet ambassador. But INR experts knew that Foman had a direct channel to the Kremlin and that frictions between Dobrynin and the embassy's KGB unit might somehow be involved.

The president, though encouraged by the first serious signs of Soviet willingness to negotiate, was not easy in his mind. The Foman plan, if it was a bona fide proposal, was almost too good to be true. The only things required of the United States were to lift the blockade and to pledge not to invade Cuba.

One could infer an intent to seek a solution, but there was no specific proposal in the Khrushchev letter. Kennedy wanted a new and more careful translation of the Khrushchev letter and a side-by-side examination of it with what Foman was proposing. The side-by-side comparison would help to determine whether the two were clearly coordinated. The president also wanted an options paper analyzing all steps the United States might take in reaction to the recent developments. An ExCom meeting was set for Saturday morning, October 27.

DENOUEMENT

The ExCom meeting was quickly overtaken by a dramatic new development. A new Khrushchev proposal, this one delivered over Moscow radio to minimize delays in transmission, changed the terms of the diplomatic bargain. Kennedy's instinct proved to be correct. What had seemed too good to be true was, in fact, not true. Khrushchev was now proposing that the United States dismantle its missiles in Turkey as a quid pro quo for the Soviet Union's withdrawal from Cuba of "the weapons you consider offensive."

Several ExCom members complained that the second Khrushchev message was so different in tone from the first that it must have been written by hardliners, probably military. Possibly there had been a coup. Kennedy dismissed all such suggestions and insisted that this announcement by Moscow radio was the government's official position. Kennedy was almost alone in declaring that the new proposal was the Kremlin's official position.

"To any man at the United Nations, or any other rational man, it will look like a very fair trade," JFK told the ExCom. "Most people think that if you're allowed an even trade you ought to take advantage of it."[15]

Kennedy had one strong ally among the ExCom colleagues: Lyndon Johnson. Johnson's attendance at ExCom meetings was sporadic, but he was present this day. When Kennedy was temporarily out of the room, Johnson spoke up (LBJ rarely spoke when JFK was present) in strong defense of the president's position. Johnson spoke as a politician, deriding anyone who would risk nuclear war rather than trade obsolete missiles in Turkey for Soviet missiles ninety miles from the United States. The experts were against, and the two politicians were in favor of, the missile trade.

Roger Hilsman, near collapse, arrived at the White House in the afternoon with the options paper prepared by the INR. He had worked all night and had had no sleep for forty-eight hours. He presented the options paper to the president, who had called a break in the ExCom meeting. As Hilsman was leaving the White House, he was stopped by a guard.

"Check in with the operator. There's a call from your office," the guard said.

The call informed Hilsman that a U-2 had been shot down over Cuba, and the pilot, Air Force Major Rudolf Anderson, had been killed. Roger returned to the Oval Office and found the president and Rusk in conference. He gave them the news. A Russian surface-to-air missile (SAM) crew had apparently ignored orders and acted on its own. Kennedy was calm and looked fresh to Hilsman, who later wrote of the encounter in admiring terms. In a *Look* magazine article after Hilsman had left government, he wrote that Kennedy seemed to embody Hemingway's definition of courage as "grace under pressure." When told the U-2 news, Kennedy had coolly remarked, "There's always some s.o.b. that doesn't get the message."[16]

Kennedy's cool demeanor came from something only he knew: the solution to the crisis was at hand. He would accept the Khrushchev offer of a missile trade.

Roger Hilsman went home to get some sleep and left word that Tom Hughes was to be notified if anything came up. Hughes, well before there was any missile crisis, had gotten tickets for a performance of the *Mikado* at the National Theater. He left word at his office where he would be on Saturday afternoon with his wife and two small boys. He had enjoyed act 1 and was seated for the second act when the curtain parted and the Lord High Executioner stepped out.

"Is there a Tom Hughes in the house?" inquired the Lord High Executioner.

Hughes looked around and awkwardly raised his hand.

"Please call the White House operator."

Tom called the White House and was told to go to the State Department, pick up John Scali, and bring him to the White House. Rusk wanted to speak with Scali. The ExCom had just begun a 4:00 o'clock meeting when Hughes arrived with Scali. Rusk left the meeting and asked Scali if he would contact Foman once more. The Soviets had evidently changed their position and now included the dismantling of Jupiter missiles in Turkey as a condition for removing their missiles from Cuba. Could Scali find out anything more about what was going on in the Kremlin?

Scali had another encounter with Foman, an unpleasant one that ended up with Scali shouting at the Russian, "You're a lying double-crosser!" Foman had offered the excuse that there was a delay in the cable traffic and that was why he had not included the Turkish missiles in the original proposal.

Foman, as a cover for his lone-wolf diplomacy, told his associates that Scali had approached him with the proposal, claiming to represent the U.S. government. His colleagues found this story far-fetched, and nobody believed him. Foman, having no alternative, stuck to the story and was lucky to avoid being shot for insubordination. Scali and Foman became bitter enemies and broke off contact. Each insisted that the other was a liar.

Meanwhile, the mood of crisis had deepened after the downing of the U-2. Then came news that two more American planes flying low-level reconnaissance missions—the treetop flights that so incensed Castro—had been slightly damaged by antiaircraft fire. One plane was so peppered with holes that its return to base was a small miracle.

The Joint Chiefs demanded retaliation for the U-2 shootdown and the other Cuban actions. They wanted to hit the SAM site that had shot down Major Anderson. Kennedy refused, saying he wanted to wait for Khrushchev's response to the letter before he attacked the SAM site and killed Russians.

Robert Kennedy, possibly by prearrangement with his brother, observed that there would be no harm in responding only to Khrushchev's first letter. Thus they could avoid referring to the Jupiters. If this did not work, they could then respond to the second letter. Kennedy accepted his brother's idea and directed Ted Sorensen to begin drafting the letter to Khrushchev.

The letter to Khrushchev was finalized and sent by 8:00 p.m. on Saturday evening, eastern standard time. This was some three hours after JFK had adjourned the ExCom meeting. The ExCom did not see the final version or have any role in the letter's drafting. The letter did not ignore Khrushchev's second message.[17]

When Kennedy adjourned the afternoon ExCom meeting, he asked a smaller subgroup—Rusk, Thompson, and Ball, from State, McNamara and Gilpatric from Defense, Ted Sorensen, Mac Bundy, and his brother—to assemble in the Oval Office. The president asked for suggestions from the group on what the attorney general should say to Ambassador Dobrynin that evening. Robert Kennedy was to see Dobrynin on the president's behalf to explain the U.S. response to Khrushchev's proposal.

The subgroup members were sworn to secrecy and specifically asked that the larger ExCom not be informed of anything said at the meeting. Robert Kennedy was given the latitude to try the Trollope ploy (pretending to have misinterpreted an action, to one's advantage) by limiting the agreement to the question of the Cuban missiles only—responding, in effect, to the first letter as if ignorant of the second. But he was later secretly instructed by the president to offer assurances that the United States would remove its Jupiter missiles from Turkey if this were required to reach a settlement.

Dean Rusk was the only member from the small subgroup present for the instructions to RFK. He suggested that, to make this assurance to Khrushchev credible, RFK should tell Dobrynin that it would take the United States "four to five months" to remove the Jupiters.

Robert Kennedy met with Dobrynin at 7:45 p.m. in his Department of Justice office. The most detailed and the most credible account of their meeting is the Dobrynin memoir. Though published in 1995, the account was based on the cable that Dobrynin sent at the time to Khrushchev and on a memorandum for the record he then drafted of the conversation with Robert Kennedy.[18]

The attorney general stressed the urgency of resolving the crisis quickly. There were mounting pressures on the president from his military advisers for retaliatory action. The president, said RFK, wanted an answer within twenty-four hours to its proposal to end the blockade and give a noninvasion pledge in return for the removal of the Soviet missiles. Dobrynin asked about the Turkish missiles. Kennedy replied that the president authorized him to give assurances that the Jupiter missiles would be removed, if necessary to reach agreement. But RFK added a condition: Khrushchev would have to keep the Turkish part of the agreement secret. Kennedy explained at length that American politics made it impossible for the president to acknowledge publicly this part of the settlement.

The smaller subgroup of the ExCom met again at 9:00 p.m. after RFK returned from his meeting with Dobrynin. But critical parts of the Dobrynin meeting were communicated only to Rusk and Llewellyn Thompson, the two ExCom members Kennedy regarded as the most tight lipped.

A further secret agreement was known only to Rusk, JFK, and Andrew Cordier of Columbia University. Not even Robert Kennedy knew about Rusk's proposed final point to the plan. To wit: Andrew Cordier, a close friend of Rusk's and the former number-two official at the United Nations, would be asked to have Secretary General U Thant issue a public call for a Turkey-Cuba missile trade. However, Cordier was not to proceed with this plan unless given a further explicit direction from Rusk or from the president directly.

The Cordier–U Thant maneuver would become necessary only if Khrushchev should turn down the Kennedy offer of the missile swap. If U Thant issued the call, Kennedy would immediately agree to put diplomatic pressure on Khrushchev to follow suit. Rusk revealed this secret Kennedy insurance policy twenty-five years later at a retrospective conference on the missile crisis, held at Hawk's Cay, Florida. This astonished Bundy, McNamara, and other Kennedy aides. It explained to this author the rumors that swirled around Dean (and later president) Andrew Cordier, at Columbia University, about a mystery role in the Cuban Missile Crisis. Most significant, the Cordier plan proves that Kennedy would have embraced the missile swap even if the settlement terms had been publicly known.

Khrushchev accepted the secret missile swap offer, and the crisis ended. The Soviet premier paid heavily for his leadership. The secrecy meant that he could not defend himself from colleagues who, after first denouncing him for adventurism in placing the missiles in Cuba, now attacked him for capitulating so readily and suffering a humiliating defeat.

But Khrushchev did not emerge empty handed. The United States was forced to withdraw its missiles from Italy as part of the modernization policy that removed the missiles from Turkey, and Britain also surrendered its Thor missiles. Khrushchev thus achieved the first major arms control agreement of the Cold War—the removal of an entire class of weapons from Western Europe. The missile crisis marked a critical turning point in the Cold War. The superpowers never again came close to the threat of a nuclear war.

The Cuban Missile Crisis dragged on until finally ending on November 22, when the United States officially lifted the naval quarantine. Fidel Castro, infuriated at his exclusion from the superpower negotiations, refused to allow UN inspectors on his soil to oversee removal of the missiles. There were more tense moments over the Soviet Il-28 bombers, but Khrushchev finally agreed to remove them. He also removed the tactical nuclear weapons (unknown to the Americans) despite Castro's urging that they remain as a deterrent.

SINO-INDIAN WAR

There was no rest, however, for President Kennedy and his foreign policy team. Although largely absent from public attention and overshadowed by the confrontation with the Soviet Union, another crisis of great magnitude confronted the Kennedy administration. The Sino-Indian War, which Bruce Riedel describes as "JFK's Forgotten Crisis," erupted almost simultaneously with the missile crisis at the other side of the world.[19]

The missile crisis pitted the two greatest Western powers, the United States and the Soviet Union, against each other in a dangerous nuclear face-off. The Sino-Indian War pitted the two greatest Asian powers, China and India, against each other, with the threat of Pakistan entering and broadening the conflict into a regional conflagration.

The CIA's covert operations in Tibet played a part in prompting China's two simultaneous attacks at dawn, October 20, some 1,000 kilometers apart, on India's western and northeastern borders. These attacks started the war. The United States could conceivably have been dragged into major wars against the world's two leading communist powers at opposite ends of the earth. The prospects were dizzying and posed the gravest challenges to JFK and America's diplomats. There was never a likelihood of American ground troops becoming involved in the conflict, but Nehru wanted U.S. air attacks to slow Chinese advances if the enemy moved inland against Indian population centers.

U.S. diplomacy was aided by the strong presence of Ambassador John Kenneth Galbraith, who hurried back to India from London to bolster Prime Minister Jawaharlal Nehru's morale and help frame his response to the Chinese attacks.

The United States assisted India by committing military advisers, providing U.S. Air Force transport of arms and materiel to India's poorly equipped forces, and sending a delegation of American advisers headed by Assistant Secretary of State Averell Harriman. The delegation was to assist Nehru and the Indians in their diplomatic and military moves. The Harriman delegation arrived in India, coincidentally, on November 22, the same day the missile crisis officially ended with the lifting of the U.S. blockade.

The Sino-Indian War ended on December 1, following a JFK warning to the Chinese. Kennedy's diplomacy achieved a number of important purposes. The United States bolstered its ties to India and the Nehru government; kept Pakistan neutral while maintaining, and even strengthening, diplomatic and intelligence ties with the Ayub Khan government; and created the balance of power that still prevails in Asia.

The president also scored a minor political victory in the midterm elections. The Democrats gained two Senate seats and lost only four seats in the House of Representatives, an accomplishment of sorts since the party in power usually loses more than that at midterm. Representative James van Zandt, to the satisfaction of Tom Hughes, lost his bid for the U.S. Senate in Pennsylvania and disappeared from the political scene.

Roger Hilsman, Tom Hughes, and the INR did well in the Sino-Indian conflict, as they had in the missile crisis. The INR had only a small Asian section consisting of twelve people, but it was a high-quality group. Allen Whiting, recruited from the RAND Corporation, was the section head, and Fred Greene, of Williams College, was his deputy. Several women, including Dorothy Avery and Evelyn Colbert, were highly respected senior analysts and part of the management team. Tom Hughes recruited Avery from Harvard's East Asian Center and brought Colbert back from the CIA. Colbert was originally with the INR but had transferred to the CIA. She was one of the first women to receive a Ph.D. in Asian history from Columbia University.

INR sent four staff members to be a part of the Harriman delegation to India. The bureau's maps of India's borders proved to be superior to those of the Joint Chiefs of Staff. Dorothy Avery wrote a paper on China's negotiating strategy that forecast accurately what actually happened: China struck first. Then, it unilaterally halted operations. It resumed hostilities once more, surprising Nehru, before finally ending the conflict. China was content to deliver a humiliating defeat to India's forces.

NEW ASSIGNMENTS

John Kennedy was now free to turn his attention elsewhere—to arms control negotiations with the Soviet Union, civil rights in domestic policy, NATO issues, the Alliance for Progress, and the slowly developing issue of Vietnam, a guerrilla war halfway across the globe. Vietnam was not a threat to regional stability in Asia, but it was destined to have a grave impact on America itself.

The president decided to promote Roger Hilsman to the key post of assistant secretary of state for the Far East, partly as a reward and partly to have new energy and intelligence in a key post. Roger had been campaigning hard for the job almost since he had arrived at State. The job would give him full scope to engage in policy and not merely in analysis. Roger had been devoting most of his time to Vietnam anyway. Harriman was getting old, was nearly deaf, and was irascible in meetings. The president moved him up to be deputy under secretary of state for political affairs, where his broad experience would be useful.

Tom Hughes became director of the INR and assistant secretary of state for intelligence and research. This move confirmed the fact that Tom had been de facto running the bureau. President Kennedy told Rusk and the three men of his intentions to move them to their new assignments in the spring. Dean Rusk, modestly impressed with his own wit, declared that the three men would be sworn in together, which would be known in State Department lore as "the Day of the Three Hs"—Harriman, Hilsman, and Hughes.

Baby Tam and his grandfather
Thomas Hughes, 1926.

Tom Hughes at age 9 at one of his youthful piano recitals in Mankato, Minnesota.

The Hughes family gathered for a holiday in 1944. Left to right, father E. Raymond Hughes, sister Marianne Hughes, mother Alice Hughes, and Tom Hughes at their home in Mankato, Minnesota.

Student Federalist leaders, 1945: president Thomas Hughes, founder Harris Wofford, vice president Jerry Miller, board member Mary Ellen Purdy, secretary Clare Lindgren.

Tom and Jean Hughes with Chet Bowles at the Hughes wedding reception, June 1955, New Haven, Connecticut.

Summer 1954. On Chet Bowles's yawl—working in a leisurely setting.

Tom Hughes, Chet Bowles, and Marshal Tito in Brioni, Yugoslavia, during a visit to the Yugoslav leader in 1959.

Secretary of State Dean Rusk (left) and Thomas Hughes at Hughes's appointment as assistant secretary of state for intelligence and research, May 1963.

Tom Hughes, front row second from right, next to CIA Director John McCone, center front, at a meeting of the United States Intelligence Board in 1965.

Tom Hughes's sons, Evan, 10, and Allan, 8, with their father on a visit to Vice President Hubert Humphrey's office, Washington, 1966.

To the Hughes Men – with warm regards from their friend
Hubert H Humphrey

Hughes in front of the U.S. embassy at Grosvenor Square in London during his service as deputy chief of mission, 1969.

Tom Hughes and NBC newsman and trustee John Chancellor at an important 1977 board meeting of the Carnegie Endowment in New York City.

Vice President Walter F. Mondale and Tom Hughes in Mondale's office, Washington, 1977.

Roger Hilsman and Tom Hughes at a celebration dinner honoring their service with the Bureau of Intelligence and Research (INR), circa 1980.

Thomas Hughes visiting with former British Prime Minister Harold Macmillan on a Macmillan visit to Washington in 1980.

Kaiser Wilhelm II in Basle with his second wife, Empress Hermine.

Jane Hughes with a portrait of Charles Frederick Schlaberg, Tom Hughes's great great grandfather, 2010.

Jane and Tom Hughes at Sanssouci Castle, Potsdam, Germany, August 2011, for the wedding of Georg Friedrich, Prince of Prussia, descendant of Kaiser Wilhelm II.

11

The Overthrow of Diem

The American presence in Vietnam when Tom Hughes became INR director included some 17,000 civilian and military advisers, a considerable increase over the limit of 700 Americans allowed under the Geneva Accords.[1] The 1960 Kennedy campaign team told the voters that a Kennedy administration would strengthen U.S. conventional and special military forces to deter communist aggression, particularly in the Third World. President Eisenhower, in his transition talks, had warned the president-elect that a dangerous situation was developing in Laos. The Laotian situation would require the new president's close attention and, Ike warned, possible U.S. military intervention.

President Kennedy had gone along with Ike's advice to a degree by increasing the U.S. presence in Vietnam but chose diplomacy for Laos. He was delighted when Averell Harriman negotiated a truce to resolve the issues, temporarily at least. But the stability of the Indochina region remained a concern of U.S. foreign policy. At the INR, Roger Hilsman was spending most of his time on Asia, and Tom Hughes was drawn into the Asia issues, as well. Tom drove to work with Roger nearly every day and routinely got an earful of Vietnam issues. Tom also dealt regularly with Mike Forrestal, the White House staffer covering Indochina.

As Roger's deputy and then director, Tom had to deal with the assessments of progress or lack of progress made by sister intelligence agencies. The assessment agencies as a whole drove the thinking of policymakers on Vietnam. The U.S. intelligence agencies—MACV's G-2, the CIA, the Defense Intelligence Agency, and the INR—saw the war differently and

151

competed for the attention of the policymakers. The intelligence disputes both shaped and were shaped by the policy conflicts.

Tom Hughes had been working for liberal Democrats, and was skeptical of becoming embroiled in civil wars in the Third World. However, he believed that intelligence analysis, while it should be relevant, was different from political debate. Roger Hilsman saw no clear dividing line between policy and most of what the intelligence analyst did. Roger was at home in his new policymaking role as assistant secretary of state for the Far East.

In the aviary metaphors that were becoming fashionable in Washington, Roger's political views were hard to classify: he was more hawkish than the doves and more dovish than the hawks. He was a kind of hawk-dove, much like President Kennedy himself. In 1961 Roger had advised the president to send a delegation to Saigon to assess the situation. However, when the resulting Taylor-Rostow Report recommended deploying 8,000 American combat troops to Vietnam, Hilsman strongly advised JFK to reject the plan.

The president compromised. He decided to create MACV, a new military assistance command, and to increase military and economic assistance to Saigon, but not to send combat troops. JFK, worried about the Pentagon's choice of commander, at first balked when General Taylor recommended General Paul Harkins as the MACV commander. Harkins seemed to the president to be a conventional officer whose background was mainly in staff positions. Harkins was a regular, a West Pointer whom the president found uninspiring. Kennedy wanted an officer who had some experience with the Army Special Forces and could function in the unusual Vietnam environment. Harkins, it turned out, was a Taylor protégé. General Taylor finally convinced the president that Harkins was the right man for the job.

Harkins formulated a strategy that he enjoyed explaining to visiting dignitaries and journalists. His plan for winning the war, the general said, was based on the "three M's—men, money, and materiel."[2] This slogan meant, in practical terms, the following: organize and finance a bigger South Vietnamese army, equip the troops with modern American weapons, and send them out to find and destroy the backward, poorly equipped enemy.

There was a further requirement for this program to work. Peasants should be placed in secure fortifications in areas where the insurgents were present so as to deny the insurgents new recruits from the peasantry and access to supplies. This was not quite akin to winning the hearts and minds of the peasants or to building support for the central government.

The Harkins plan sounded good to visitors. After all, how could a poorly equipped group of insurgents defeat a larger, modernized army using helicopters, armored vehicles, and effective communication? Harkins buttressed his case with statistics relating to enemy casualties, weapons captured, the number of recruits, and other similar measures.

In May 1962, Secretary of Defense Robert S. McNamara, making the first of his many trips to Vietnam, was impressed with what Harkins had accomplished apparently in a short period. At the conclusion of that trip, McNamara observed to news reporter Neil Sheehan, "Every measure we have shows we are winning this war."[3]

McNamara deemed it the appropriate time to ensure that everyone understood the plan for ultimate victory and their roles in it. In July 1962, McNamara summoned the defense planners and commanding officers to a Honolulu conference to review the Vietnam situation.

The defense secretary led off the conference by posing a direct question to General Harkins: How long would it take Harkins to wrap up the fight against the insurgents and begin bringing Americans home?[4]

Harkins said that it would take a year from the time the South Vietnamese army was fully equipped and armed with modern American weapons. Probably 1,000 Americans could be brought home by the end of 1963. To be on the safe side, McNamara said, given all of the problems that might arise, it would be best to tell the president that the job would take three years. Americans would start coming home at the end of 1965. Harkins had his marching orders. A policy framework for Vietnam had presumably been established.

HUGHES AS INR DIRECTOR

Tom Hughes's analysts, though, kept telling him that Harkins had been hoodwinked by the South Vietnamese. Louis G. Sarris, a senior INR analyst who traveled regularly to Vietnam, warned that the quality of the data cited by Harkins was extremely poor. South Vietnam officials had largely fabricated the data, showing progress to please the Americans.

To fight the war effectively, Hughes believed that the United States had to upgrade its capabilities in the gathering and analysis of data and in forecasting, as well as its understanding of the enemy's intelligence capabilities.[5] It seemed obvious to him that the enemy enjoyed significant advantages in intelligence from the outset. The United States would have to build from scratch and improve its efforts in both strategic and tactical intelligence.

Few American officials understood or spoke Vietnamese, and many had no or only limited command of French. They had to rely on interpreters, whose loyalty they had to take on trust. The data on enemy losses, weapons captured, defections in the ranks, and the rest, which the South Vietnam army (Army of the Republic of Vietnam, or ARVN) passed on to MACV, were questionable. The National Liberation Front (the umbrella term for the political arm of the insurgency), or the Viet Cong, the military arm, were well aware of what the Americans knew because they had agents throughout the Saigon government. The United States had no informants inside the National Liberation Front or Viet Cong ranks in the South or in

Hanoi, whereas Ho Chi Minh had agents everywhere in the South. As the writer Thomas Power has observed in a retrospect,

> It would have been difficult for any important American official who dealt regularly with the Vietnamese to pass even a single day without speaking to a spy for the other side. . . . U.S. military forces could go where they chose, and stay as long as they liked, but when they moved on the NLF [National Liberation Front] always reemerged, leaving the situation as before. The American inability to find, fix, and destroy "the enemy"—a failure of intelligence, not of arms—exhausted American patience in the end.[6]

The INR, to be useful, would have to engage in a dialogue with its sister agencies that would sometimes be contentious. The bureau would play the role of critic of those agencies at times. But Hughes also wanted analysts to participate constructively in the joint intelligence efforts.

The INR's mission under Hughes was to think, write, and disseminate high-quality research products. In 1961, when Hilsman and Hughes took over, one-third to one-half of the INR's work consisted of a voluminous data-gathering operation of little or no use to policymakers. Shedding this function reduced the INR's size for all of its divisions to some 350 employees, which included twenty-three staff members in the Southeast Asia division. The INR has never had field agents or operational responsibilities other than research and writing.

As the State Department's representative on the United States Intelligence Board, Tom Hughes, in theory, spoke for the department on all matters of intelligence. But he was not alone in advising the secretary of state on policy issues that included an intelligence component. Walt Rostow, head of State's policy planning staff from 1961–1966, for example, issued numerous reports on U.S. policy toward Thailand, Laos, Cambodia, Burma, Indonesia, and other regions, in terms that were often sharply opposed to INR. Hughes remained on friendly terms with Rostow, who was a fellow Rhodes scholar and Balliol man.

The INR's China expertise enabled Rusk to caution the Kennedy and Johnson administrations to the dangers of Chinese intervention in the Vietnam War. Even when Johnson escalated the war in 1965, he did so in incremental steps, largely in response to Rusk's cautions on Chinese intervention.[7]

The upshot of what his senior analysts were telling him about Vietnam made Hughes skeptical not only of the reports of progress in the fight against the insurgents. He was also dubious about Harkins's overall victory strategy, which was so heavily dependent on the poor data. The strategy agreed on in Honolulu was put to the test soon enough when the Viet Cong demonstrated the capacity to defeat better equipped ARVN forces in an actual battle.

THE AP BAC BATTLE

On January 2–3, 1963, an important engagement—the first major battle of the war—took place in the Mekong Delta at Ap Bac, a village only fifty miles from Saigon.[8] The South Vietnamese army and civil guard units, assisted by American advisers, artillery, helicopters, and ten M-13 armored vehicles, outnumbered a Viet Cong force by at least a four-to-one ratio. By all odds, this should have been an ARVN victory.

The battle, however, was a resounding defeat for the ARVN troops. The Viet Cong prevailed not only because of their brave fighting but also owing to ARVN's failures and poor communications and the hesitations and reluctance of South Vietnamese commanders to engage the enemy.

U.S. helicopters landed the South Vietnamese troops on an open field near the village on a misty morning that made it difficult for a spotter plane circling overhead to see the action. Almost immediately, the South Vietnamese and American advisers came under fire from guerrillas hidden among the trees on the edge of the field. Despite the desperate urging of American advisers, the ARVN forces took cover and refused to engage the enemy. Two helicopters were destroyed by concentrated enemy fire as they hovered and off-loaded troops, and two more helicopters were lost when they attempted to rescue the crews of the first helicopters.

In the early afternoon, the M-13s finally arrived but were driven back by guerrilla fire that killed any crew member who stood up and attempted to fire the .50-caliber machine gun mounted without an armor shield on the top of the vehicle. The flame thrower on the lead M-113 did not work because of a crew error in loading the propellant.

The American advisers' calls for paratroops were ignored by the South Vietnam generals, who appeared to be anxious to avoid casualties. The Viet Cong killed three Americans (making a total of thirty American military advisers killed up to that point in Vietnam), shot down five American helicopters and damaged nine others, and inflicted heavy casualties on the South Vietnamese forces. The guerrillas then melted away into the jungle under cover of darkness, taking their dead with them.

The Ap Bac battle shocked many in America's national security agencies. The engagement made it clear that the enemy was willing to fight, was capably led, and would be a formidable foe, even when outnumbered. The enemy's tactics of mass fire to shoot down helicopters and the willingness to confront armored vehicles were impressive. General Harkins, in his post-battle assessment, attempted to cast the engagement in a more favorable light. The enemy, he explained, had been driven from the fight and did not resume it on the second day. There had been problems, Harkins admitted, but these were minor and were easily fixed. Harkins took at face value the claims of the ARVN commanders that artillery fire in the afternoon had inflicted heavy casualties on the enemy forces and had probably caused their withdrawal.

Yet the battle gave credence to rumors that President Ngo Dinh Diem had issued an "avoid casualties" order to key ARVN commanders in October 1962.[9] General Harkins, spurred by junior officers, felt obliged to ask President Diem if he had given any order to his commanders to avoid casualties and limit engagement with the enemy. Diem feigned astonishment and declared that he had never given such orders. Harkins took Diem at his word and never raised the subject again.

Ap Bac set the pattern for future policy debates. One group of American strategists concluded that if Ap Bac had been as bad as some claimed, the answer was to send more advisers, more helicopters, and more arms to help South Vietnam. The fight was going to be tougher than anticipated. Others back in Washington drew the exact opposite conclusion. No amount of American aid could assist an army that did not want to fight and was so poorly organized and led. Far-reaching reforms were needed in the whole corrupt Saigon regime, or else the United States should get out. In this context an intelligence assessment of the situation was clearly in order.

THE CONTROVERSY OVER NIE 53-63

Civilian analysts at the INR and the CIA believed that the ARVN forces had performed poorly at Ap Bac. But MACV and the Joint Chiefs of Staff, always sensitive to civilians intruding into military matters, disputed the civilians and found grounds for optimism in the ARVN performance.

General Harkins's weekly report to the Joint Chiefs and Secretary McNamara after the Ap Bac incident was entitled "Headway Report." It cited statistics on artillery rounds fired, casualties, and other data that he imagined indicated success.[10] The proposed national intelligence estimate (NIE) was supposed to be a broad assessment of the entire Vietnam situation, not a battlefield report, but the general progress of the war would have to be considered in any comprehensive review.

The staff unit supporting the USIB was the CIA's Office of National Estimates, headed by Sherman Kent, a highly respected former Yale professor of European history and longtime intelligence professional.[11] First drafts of national intelligence estimates were typically prepared by an interagency working group of career intelligence officers selected by Kent. The working group preparing the draft of NIE 53-63 was chaired by Evelyn Colbert, of the INR, and George Carver, from Kent's Office of National Estimates.

The draft was circulated around to agencies, commented on and sent back and forth, and revised by Colbert and Carver. Then, as was the usual practice, the draft was submitted to the Office of National Estimates. The office toned down slightly the conclusions of the draft, which portrayed the Vietnam situation in dire terms. The draft was presented to the USIB at its February 17, 1963, meeting.

Roger Hilsman saw one early version of the draft and told Colbert that it was too cautious and that she should present her assessment in stronger terms. Central intelligence director John McCone had no prior knowledge of or participation in the draft. McCone had been absent from several USIB meetings when NIE 53-63 was discussed in preliminary terms. As presented to the USIB on February 17, the draft NIE concluded,

> The struggle in South Vietnam at best will be protracted and costly [because] very great weaknesses remain and will be difficult to surmount. Among these are lack of . . . firm leadership at all levels of command, poor morale among the troops, lack of trust between peasant and soldier, poor tactical use of available forces, a very inadequate intelligence system, and obvious Communist penetration of the South Vietnamese military organization.[12]

When he saw the draft, McCone was genuinely surprised. Incensed, he demanded a complete rewrite to reflect the input of "knowledgeable officials."[13] The revised version of the NIE was clearly the result of political pressures on the analysts. Colbert and Carver felt that they had no choice but to submit to McCone's direction. The new version was presented to the USIB and approved in April 1963. The estimate had a markedly different tone and conclusion:

> We believe that Communist progress has been blunted and that the situation is improving. . . . Improvements which have occurred during the [recent] past now indicate that the Viet Cong can be contained and that further progress can be made in expanding the area of government control and in creating greater security in the countryside.[14]

This politically inspired NIE was a blow to the integrity of the intelligence community. The actions by McCone represented the low point of his CIA career. However, Colbert and Carver consoled themselves by persuading the USIB to adopt a plan for improving statistics on the war.

The NIE was soon overtaken and rendered moot by events. The Buddhist crisis erupted in Vietnam on May 8. It shattered the illusion that the Saigon government had made important progress over the past year.

THE BUDDHIST CRISIS

Tom Hughes immediately faced the Buddhist crisis in his new role as INR's director. The crisis brought Vietnam to the center of the foreign policy agenda and brought Hughes attention in the process. The largely secular U.S. intelligence services had ignored or discounted the prospect that religious tensions could undermine the regime in South Vietnam.

The South Vietnam population of some 18 million was mostly ethnic Vietnamese and nominally Buddhist, and the nominal Buddhism suggested that South Vietnam's people were not deeply religious. There were several significant minority groups with different religions and customs, the most significant being Catholics, the Montagnards of the central highlands, and the Chinese of the Cholon district of Saigon. The Catholics were slightly less than 10 percent of the population but had disproportionate influence in the army, civil administration, and commerce.

Roger Hilsman, already becoming disillusioned with the Diem regime, was deeply affected by the Buddhist uprising, which began in the regional capital of Hue. Archbishop Ngo Dinh Thuc, a brother of President Diem, ordered that a Buddhist banner be removed during the celebration of a Catholic holiday, which incensed local Buddhist monks, who launched protests across the city. While the protests were started and led by a small group of activist monks, other groups around the country, especially in the population center of Saigon, rallied to the Buddhist cause. Students, urban intellectuals, and other non-Catholic elites joined the protests and broadened the grievances against the repressive Diem regime.

Hilsman arranged a showdown meeting between Ambassador Nolting and President Diem to take place in the first week of May. Nolting was directed to make an urgent appeal for Diem to curb the corruption in civil administration and in the military. Diem received Nolting courteously and listened politely to his warning that the United States might reconsider its support for the regime unless Diem undertook serious steps toward reform. Nolting reported to Washington that Diem remained completely unmovable.[15]

Nolting thereupon decided to take a week's vacation on the Aegean Sea en route back to the United States on home leave, placing Deputy Chief of Mission William Trueheart in charge at the embassy. This was the last straw for Roger, whose estimate of Nolting's performance as ambassador was unfavorable. He persuaded President Kennedy that it was time to replace Nolting. Roger began a campaign to withdraw U.S. support unless President Diem undertook immediate and serious reforms.

Tom Hughes knew that the INR was already researching religious tensions in Vietnam. The INR's work on the tensions underlying the Catholic Diem government provided an excellent opportunity. The bureau was able to produce the first authoritative intelligence report on the Buddhist crisis. Hughes sent a copy of the report to the White House, as was his usual practice, and made sure that Mike Forrestal got a copy.

Forrestal was impressed with the INR's Buddhist paper and passed it along to Kennedy, who read it with interest. The president declared that the paper should be considered the administration's policy on the Buddhist crisis. Hughes was obviously pleased but was not quite sure what the president meant by this, since the paper did not contain policy recommendations.

It was quite evident, however, that the INR was making a serious statement about the shortcomings of the Ngo Dinh Diem government. The efforts of Hilsman as a policymaker and Hughes as intelligence provider were closely intertwined and, for the moment at least, mutually reinforcing. Their joint efforts helped to sharpen JFK's views on Vietnam.

Anticipating that a religious crisis could undermine the Diem regime, Hughes organized a conference of experts on Vietnam, including Wesley Fichel of Michigan State University and Tom's old Student Federalist friend, Gil Jonas, executive director of the American Friends of Vietnam, to explore potential alternative leaders should the Diem regime fall. This group came up with a slate of candidates, examined their potential strengths and weaknesses, and concluded that alternative leaders were available if the United States for any reason could no longer depend on Diem.

The Buddhist crisis deepened in June when monks across the country set themselves ablaze in protest against the regime. In response, on June 11, the State Department cabled the embassy in Saigon that "if Diem does not take prompt and effective steps to reestablish the Buddhist confidence in him we will have to reexamine our entire relationship with his regime."[16]

Hughes on June 21 circulated a new paper suggesting that, although a coup would pose dangers, there was sufficient alternative leadership available in South Vietnam to "provide reasonably effective leadership for the government and the war effort."[17]

This paper put the INR squarely in the camp of Hilsman and Forrestal, Diem's most vociferous critics in the administration. But intelligence could not resolve the policy differences within the administration. CIA Director McCone and State's Hilsman, for example, drew quite different policy conclusions from the same intelligence.

While McCone and Hilsman agreed that the situation in South Vietnam was fragile, to McCone it was so fragile that under no circumstances could the United States risk a leadership shake-up. To Hilsman, on the other hand, shaking up or changing the corrupt Catholic leadership of a Buddhist country was the only way to avoid disaster. Catholics were less than a tenth of the population but held most of the country's leadership positions. McCone was the most vocal critic of the Diem critics, but the

CIA's leadership ranks generally shared his cautious views about the idea of overthrowing Diem.

THE STATISTICS WAR

As the large policy battles over Vietnam were being fought out in the summer and fall of 1963, a smaller war—a statistics war—was underway over the quality of the data that the military was using to chart military progress in the war.

INR analysts Louis Sarris and Evelyn Colbert were convinced that General Harkins's poor statistics were obscuring the real picture in Vietnam. They went to Hughes to discuss a study on the statistics issue. Hughes suggested that Roger Hilsman be consulted for his views on how to organize such a study.

Hilsman suggested to Sarris, who took the lead on the study, that he simply take the same categories that MACV had used in the past and show the trends from six months. The resulting study, RFE-90, titled "Statistics on the War Effort in South Vietnam Show Unfavorable Trends," was published in October 1963. Defense scholar John Prados hailed it as "one of the most celebrated INR efforts of the period" and said that upon its publication, "a tempest then erupted."[18]

The Joint Chiefs compiled a lengthy list of items in the study where the INR allegedly trespassed in ignorance on military matters. The Joint Chiefs forwarded its critique to Secretary of Defense McNamara for action. McNamara forwarded the critique to Secretary Rusk with a cover note: "Attached is the State memo re the war in Vietnam [with] . . . the comments of the chiefs. If you were to tell me that it is not the policy of the State Department to issue military appraisals without seeking the views of the Defense Department, the matter will die."[19]

The sensitivity of the Joint Chiefs to civilian incursions was heightened by the fact that the INR study came out just at the time when tensions between General Harkins and Ambassador Henry Cabot Lodge in Saigon had reached their peak. At this critical point, the Joint Chiefs were looking for any opportunity to win a bureaucratic battle with the State Department.

The stakes were high for Hughes and the INR. Its independence was at issue. Rusk called Hughes and Sarris to his office. The secretary showed them the McNamara note and the Joint Chiefs memo and asked them how he should respond. The men agreed that there was an implicit threat that McNamara, if he did not get his way, would take the matter to the president. The discussion continued inconclusively for a time. Rusk asked Sarris to leave and came to the point with Hughes.

One way to solve the problem, Rusk said, was for the State Department to agree to the loan of six or seven colonels to "help" the INR staff on military matters. What did Hughes think of that idea? Hughes said that his analysts always consulted military colleagues on military issues. This was always done before the INR reached any conclusions, Hughes told Rusk. He never signed off on any research memorandum unless he was satisfied that it was based on inputs from all available sources, especially from the military when it involved issues with military content.

The Joint Chiefs, Tom noted, were mainly interested in process and not substance in their criticisms of the INR study. They were complaining that the INR was invading their turf, not that the numbers presented in the study were wrong. The solution thus lay in conceding the principle of the Defense Department's primacy in military assessments but defending the accuracy of the study.

In 2011, Hughes insisted that the encounter was not dramatic and showed Rusk's calm demeanor. Rusk was invariably courteous and respectful, even if he was at times inscrutable. Hughes did not have to make any dramatic defense of the INR's independence or of his own leadership. As he explained,

> Rusk never wavered in wanting us to be independent and he always wanted me to give him exactly what I thought, even if it was bad news, and I gave him a lot of bad news in those years. He may have allowed McNamara or McCone to move into his territory at times, but he was never passive on intelligence and insisted that we be independent. He also permitted, and encouraged, George Ball to speak up at White House meetings even if Ball contradicted his own views. He felt the President was entitled to Ball's views. Rusk was admirable in that way.[20]

The most serious threat to the INR's independence in Hughes's tenure thus ended without a bang or a whimper. Rather matter-of-factly, on November 8, 1963, Hughes sent Rusk a memo that carefully reviewed the military's assertions about RFE-90. The memo rebutted the attacks but conceded that "we naturally agree that military assessments are basically the responsibility of the Department of Defense." Rusk then informed McNamara: "I have instructed that any memoranda given interdepartmental circulation which includes military appraisals be coordinated with your Department."[21]

Rusk never took any action to enforce his instruction, and the Joint Chiefs did not complain about any INR reports, even though the reports routinely contained military appraisals. McNamara himself became a convert to the view that the Saigon government had provided false and misleading data to MACV and that General Harkins had allowed himself to be duped by the Saigon government.

THE AUGUST 24 CABLE

In naming Henry Cabot Lodge to be Nolting's successor as U.S. ambassador to South Vietnam, Kennedy had once again picked a Republican for a sensitive national security position. He wanted to appear bipartisan and wanted a Republican to share the blame if another Asian country was lost to the communists. Getting Lodge out of the country meant that JFK was taking out insurance against Lodge entering the race for the Republican presidential nomination in 1964.

Kennedy and Lodge had a respectful relationship in Massachusetts. They had competed in two races, once in 1952 when Kennedy defeated Lodge and took his U.S. Senate seat and again indirectly when Lodge ran as Nixon's vice presidential candidate in 1960. They had one head-to-head debate in the 1952 Senate race. Meeting in a high school auditorium, the two men praised each other's war service and generally were polite and statesmanlike in their demeanor.[22]

Lodge met with President Kennedy in the White House before his departure for a Honolulu conference and then Saigon. The two men met alone and until 2020 there had been no published account of what they discussed. Luke A. Nichter of Texas A&M University discovered a memo of the meeting "hiding in plain sight" in the Lodge papers at the John F. Kennedy Presidential Library in Boston.[23]

Lodge and Kennedy discussed the Buddhist crisis and the possibility that a military coup might remove Diem from power. Kennedy asked his fellow Massachusetts politician if he had any qualms about confronting such an eventuality. Lodge did not. Lodge was well informed about the situation in Saigon, having met earlier with and been briefed by his chosen deputies in the State Department, who would serve with him in Saigon. He had already met with numerous diplomats who were knowledgeable about Vietnam.

Kennedy sincerely but cagily wished Lodge well and said that he looked forward to the advice that Lodge would provide Washington. Lodge promised to do his best for the country and the president. Both men seemed to have a politician's instinct that Diem's days were numbered.

In accepting the appointment from his old foe, Lodge's motives were mixed. He understood that Kennedy was trying to use him, but, of course, he was also seeking to use Kennedy. Neither man wanted to take primary responsibility if things went wrong.

Lodge was more than happy to play a role in history by becoming ambassador, but privately he calculated that he might come across something he could use against Kennedy and the Democrats in the future, particularly if Kennedy showed any weakness on Vietnam. Lodge and Kennedy, however, were both sensible politicians. They knew each other well and understood that they had common as well as potentially conflicting interests. They arranged for top secret and eyes-only communications when they deemed this course necessary.

Lodge was in Honolulu when the Buddhist crisis erupted again on August 21. He took off immediately for Saigon. President Diem had finally decided to employ the iron fist. Diem sent thousands of police and ARVN special forces to arrest monks, students, and other dissidents across the country.[24] Troops clubbed the monks and shot and killed more than a dozen in the process of the mass arrests. President Diem's brother Nhu then inflamed the situation by blaming the military for unnecessary brutality, which infuriated the generals. The brutal attacks on dormitories, pagodas, and schools shocked Americans and respectable middle-class supporters of the regime in Saigon.

At this point Roger Hilsman and NSC staffer Mike Forrestal became critical players. It was important to get clear information on what was happening in Saigon. The normal cable traffic from the embassy was flowing to Roger's office in State. Lodge would be reporting to and also asking for instructions from Washington.

On Saturday, August 24, the president, the attorney general, Mac Bundy, McCone, Rusk, McNamara, and most other Cabinet secretaries, as well as General Taylor, were out of town. What happened in their absence on that day has been hotly disputed. One observer commented that "With breathtaking audacity . . . Forrestal maneuvered beyond the scenes to bring a shift in America's Vietnam policy by sanctioning the removal of Diem and Nhu. . . . Forrestal, abetted by Hilsman and Harriman, [was] simply authorizing Lodge to seek the removal of Nhu, and, if necessary, Diem."[25]

But Andrew Preston's account of that day's events, which cast Forrestal and Hilsman as the chief villains, does not stand up to close scrutiny. Tom Hughes, by coincidence, was having lunch with Mike Forrestal in the White House on Saturday and learned part of the story.

As soon as Lodge had arrived in Saigon he received an urgent request for a meeting with several dissident generals. The generals sought an indication of where the United States stood on a potential move to oust Diem. Lodge asked Washington for instructions. This was a request that demanded a response. Roger drafted a cable instructing Lodge to inform President Diem that he must force his brother out of the government or at least temporarily out of the country.[26] Lodge was to inform the dissident Vietnam generals that the United States would not, however, publicly support or directly assist a coup d'état to remove Diem and his brother from power. The generals must act on their own and, if successful, would receive U.S. recognition and support.

Roger had consulted with Mike about his draft earlier that morning and had shown it to Averell Harriman. Hilsman and Harriman, Forrestal told Hughes, were now trying to track down George Ball to get his sign-off on the draft cable. Ball, as acting secretary of state in Rusk's absence, had to approve the cable.

Hilsman and Harriman finally found Ball playing golf with Alex Johnson, whose later account has Hilsman telling him to stand out of earshot because Alex was not cleared for the matter Hilsman had to discuss with Ball. According to Alex Johnson, Roger did not want him to be involved because, as a stickler for protocol, Alex would have advised delaying the cable until Monday when the principals were back.

In any case, Hilsman and Harriman then drove to Ball's home, where they discussed the cable. Ball read the draft and cut it down by half. He then called the president at Hyannisport to discuss the cable. Kennedy, according to Ball, was somewhat vague but said that if Gilpatric and Rusk agreed, it was all right with him to send the cable.[27]

Ball was able to reach Rusk in New York. Rusk said that if the president and Ros Gilpatric (McNamara's deputy secretary of defense) agreed, then it was okay with him. Clearances were obtained from Gilpatric for Defense and from Richard Helms and General Carter for the CIA. The cable was then sent to Saigon.

However, all hell broke loose when JFK and his senior staff returned to work on Monday morning, August 26. An NSC meeting was hurriedly convened to discuss the August 24 cable.[28] Kennedy, according to George Ball's memoir, "showed some misgivings." This was the mildest interpretation of the president's reaction to the weekend's events. Presidential anger was noted, which increased as McNamara, McCone, Taylor, Bundy, and even Rusk, in turn, criticized the clearance process and the cable's inadequate staff work. McCone singled out and denounced Hilsman's failure to clear the cable adequately with the CIA. He declared that Hilsman had ignored intelligence work and appeared to have acted on impulse.

Of the principals, McNamara was the most critical of Hilsman and extended his criticisms to Rusk.[29] In McNamara's reckoning in his 1995 memoir, Hilsman behaved in a devious and insubordinate fashion on the cable and drove policy in a dangerous direction. McNamara described Rusk as a true patriot but a weak manager who allowed himself to be pushed around by subordinates. Rusk never participated effectively in high-level policy deliberations and was a bitter disappointment to President Kennedy. Rusk was also blamed for failing to rein in Lodge in Saigon, who was taking his cues from Hilsman.

The president's ire at the August 26 meeting fell chiefly on Mike Forrestal. Abashed, Forrestal offered to resign.

"This shit has got to stop," JFK shouted. "You're not worth firing. You owe me something, so you stick around."[30]

The president told Forrestal that he would have to fix the problem. The worst part of the whole episode was that it revealed the policy disarray in his administration.

"My God!" the president exclaimed. "My government is coming apart."[31]

FROM CABLE TO COUP

Hilsman and Forrestal maintained that they had properly cleared the cable. George Ball played down the drama associated with the August 26 NSC meeting. The criticism at the meeting, they all believed, had been directed at procedure, whereas the focus should have been on policy. The cable had at least framed the policy issue squarely.

Riding to work with Tom Hughes on Sunday, August 25, Roger had remarked, "It's time to bite the bullet on Vietnam."[32] Roger had received a reply from Lodge to Saturday's cable. Lodge said that there was no point in his asking Diem to part with his brother. He would not do it and might in fact denounce the Americans for political interference. Instead, Lodge asked permission to go directly to the generals and assess their intentions. Ball and Hilsman gave Lodge the permission he sought.

There was near unanimity of view among Defense and CIA officials that the Hilsman cable had not received the normal staff work beforehand or observed the proper clearance procedures. However, these objections were merely the tip of the iceberg. The Defense Department and the CIA really objected to the policy of abandoning Diem. They believed there was no alternative to a policy of backing Diem.[33] Defense and the CIA should have been pressing for rescinding the Hilsman cable and issuing new instructions to Lodge.

Tom Hughes's discussions with Hilsman led him to surmise that the president was in some measure playacting at the NSC meeting. Since the cabinet members were angry at Forrestal and Hilsman, JFK, too, should show anger. But soon the president's temper cooled and the White House staff patterns had returned to normal.

Hughes's contemporary notes on the last week of August were labeled "the Coup Planning Week,"[34] but little more was recorded that was understandable, given the pace of events. Events moved rapidly in Vietnam. Lodge's and the CIA's contacts with the rebellious South Vietnamese generals went forward but under a cloud of uncertainty. The generals wanted clear signals of U.S. intentions. The United States pledged not to interfere with the generals' actions but wanted to know about their plans. The generals, fearing leaks or betrayal by MACV, would not divulge any specifics.

On August 28, word came to the embassy and was passed on to Washington that a coup could take place as soon as the end of August.[35] Rumors flew around Saigon. Washington braced itself for dramatic action. On

August 29, Ambassador Lodge, seeming to speak for posterity, cabled the following message to Washington: "We have now launched on a course from which there is no respectable turning back: the overthrow of the Diem government.... There is no turning back because there is no possibility, in my view, that the war can be won under a Diem administration."[36]

And then nothing happened. The dissident generals called off the coup. The conspirators had apparently gotten cold feet, because their preparations were inadequate or because the Americans were ambivalent or both.[37] The generals were not satisfied with what the CIA's Colonel Louis Conein had told his friends, General Don and General Min, about U.S. intentions.

In this confused situation, JFK wanted consensus among his advisers and better intelligence on what was happening in Saigon. He got neither. The situation in Saigon was so fluid that the CIA station detected as many as ten different dissident military factions talking about coups.

It was clear, too, that Diem and Nhu were plotting countermoves of their own. The CIA and the INR both warned that Nhu had met with French officials to discuss neutrality and was secretly plotting with the North Vietnamese. Nhu was apparently seeking an agreement with Hanoi to end the war, establish a neutral and unified state, and kick the Americans out.

The nonoccurrence of the coup called for policy reviews in Washington. On August 31, a high-level meeting on Vietnam took place at the State Department. Secretary Rusk, chairing the meeting, opened by saying it was amazing that anyone thought that a coup would be a good idea. Did the group agree with him that we should drop any talk of coups and work on better ways to make our Vietnam policy persuasive to the American people?

Secretary McNamara agreed with Rusk, denounced the coup idea, and urged the need to reestablish communications between Harkins-MACV and the Diem government. Paul Kattenberg, a career Foreign Service officer and head of the interagency working group on Vietnam, said he did not believe the Diem government would survive long. The reason the generals did not act, in his view, was that the United States had not given them clear signals of support.

General Taylor interrupted to ask what evidence existed for this statement. McNamara added that he, too, wanted to see the evidence. Kattenberg replied that Ambassador Lodge remarked last week that a regime was bound to collapse if it required bayonets on every street corner, had rampant corruption through the ranks, and made disloyal contacts with the enemy in North Vietnam.

Kattenberg added that he had known Diem for ten years, had spent much time with him, and was deeply disappointed with Diem's leadership. He further added that General Harkins bore some responsibility for the coup's failure by not following his instructions.

Secretary Rusk defended Harkins, saying that he had acted in a completely appropriate fashion. Frederick Nolting, former ambassador to Vietnam, stated that Kattenberg had exaggerated his point. There was some modest decline in Diem's support by midlevel civil servants and the Saigon intelligentsia. Diem still enjoyed substantial support. McNamara observed that intelligence would have told him if Diem had lost support, and it had not. He was not aware of any such evidence that Diem was losing support.

Only Roger Hilsman came to Kattenberg's defense. It was important to move the discussion to the political level, he felt, because the war could not be won without popular support. Moreover, he said, Kattenberg was clearly correct when he said Nhu was talking with the French about supporting de Gaulle's neutralism. Nhu was also probably in touch with the North Vietnamese.

McNamara demanded to know how Hilsman knew this. Roger replied that a radio intercept had been received that proved the point. Mac Bundy said that he would like to see that intercept. McNamara and Taylor also wanted the same. Hilsman then referred to a study of South Vietnam that showed evidence of corruption.

McNamara interrupted and said that he had never heard of such a study and demanded that he see it. Tension rose between Hilsman and McNamara, and a shouting match ensued. Rusk sat imperturbably and sphinxlike in the chair while voices rose, according to Hilsman's later account to Hughes.

Kattenberg made a sweeping assertion to the effect that, whatever came of Nhu's maneuvers, the American presence was doomed to end within six months in a humiliating withdrawal. It would be far better, he said, for us to withdraw now on our own terms and preserve our honor. After much contentious discussion, Rusk finally ended the meeting with two assertions: First, it was overwhelmingly in the United States' interests to stay the course in Vietnam and help our ally to defeat the communists. Second, it was not the business of the United States to encourage or get involved in any coup.

Kennedy convened a follow-up White House meeting in early September. McNamara took the initiative and suggested that the president send a fact-finding mission to Saigon. He had, by coincidence, just the right man: Major General Victor Krulak, already preparing for a quick trip to Saigon. The secretary explained that there was a plane ready to depart for Saigon that afternoon from Andrews Air Force Base.

Hilsman jumped in with a nominee of his own to accompany Krulak. McNamara countered that it would be impossible to delay the flight. This would be no problem, said Hilsman. His candidate, Joseph Mendenhall, could appear at Andrews on time.

Kennedy compromised and sent both men. The two, Krulak for the Pentagon and Mendenhall for State, made the whirlwind trip to Saigon. They came back with flatly contradictory reports to an NSC meeting on September 10.

"You two did visit the same country, didn't you?" President Kennedy quipped.[38]

The two opposing camps competed for the president's support, but Kennedy remained ambivalent. He finally decided that another, higher-level mission was in order. This would look harder at the issues, would not be a rush job, and would, in particular, help to build a consensus among his advisers. He sent Secretary McNamara and General Taylor, his two best-informed defense experts, with their teams to Saigon to review the situation. The Krulak-Mendenhall mission had been set up to fail. Kennedy was confident that the present mission was set up to succeed—and by this he meant it would bridge the policy conflicts.

The team returned to Washington on October 2 with an unusual report that they had composed on the flight home.[39] The McNamara-Taylor report incongruously combined both the Pentagon-CIA support for the status quo with the State-NSC calls for dramatic change and called it a unified approach. The report's military section declared that the war was going so well in general that the United States could withdraw and send home 1,000 American advisers by the end of 1963. America troops likely would have the mission largely wrapped up by the end of 1965.

This optimistic appraisal ran completely counter to the report's political analysis. The report's political section concluded that it was unlikely the political situation in Saigon would stabilize under Diem and "on the contrary there was a serious prospect that an unreformed Diem would bring on chaos or an unpredictable change of regime."[40]

Nevertheless, at the NSC meeting on October 2 the president declared that he was delighted. He approved a policy of "selective pressures" plus continued support for South Vietnam. He told his staff, "As of tonight, we have policy."[41]

The policy included selective pressure for reform but ruled out U.S. backing for a coup. It did recommend that the United States should keep in touch with a wide circle of Saigon officials and opinion leaders and should reassess the situation again in two to four months. The McNamara-Taylor report was thereupon officially adopted as policy in National Security Action Memorandum 263.

No sooner had the memorandum taken the coup off the table than events in Saigon put it back on. General Minh, one of the conspirators, asked for a meeting with his CIA contact, Colonel Lucien Conein.[42] Minh declared that his team was thinking along three lines: an assassination option, which could take care of Ngo Dinh Nhu and Ngo Dinh Can (another Diem brother, a province head) but would keep President Diem in office. Madame Nhu was conveniently out of the country and could simply be barred reentry.

A second option would be the encirclement of Saigon by various military units at Ben Cat. Diem would thereby be forced to surrender without a shot being fired.

The third option would be direct confrontation between all military units involved in the coup and Diem's 5,000 loyalist troops in Saigon, requiring the Minh forces to defeat the loyalists in heavy fighting.

Conein pressed for more details, observing that the United States would be fearful of any botched coup attempt. Minh would not go any further, giving Conein the impression that Minh was still wary of tipping his hand and also suspicious of Harkins.

Duong Van "Big" Minh's suspicion of Harkins was the main reason why McNamara and Taylor (Harkins's mentor) failed to get a signal from him. The Americans inferred that the absence of a signal meant the absence of support for a coup. The U.S. embassy had arranged a tennis match involving Taylor, McNamara, and General Minh to provide an opportunity for private communication. The two Americans expected that Minh might signal his intentions at one of the breaks in the action.

The Americans were instructed not to take the initiative but to listen and watch for a sign from Minh. But Minh gave no sign. Minh was affable, friendly, fluent in English from his days in America at the U.S. Army War College. However, he said nothing even remotely related to politics at the tennis match. It did not dawn on Taylor that Minh might have been aware of his relationship to Harkins.

Minh had once been a close ally of Diem. He had helped Diem to consolidate power in 1954–1955. However, Diem gradually grew suspicious of the general as a potential rival and relegated him to a meaningless titular position.

But Minh had more than personal reasons for opposing Diem. He believed that repression by Diem and Nhu was what had precipitated the 1957 insurgency in the first place. Diem's patronage system for Catholic supporters had corrupted the Army. Minh's anger at Diem boiled over when Nhu tried to deflect blame from his brother by holding the Army responsible for unnecessary brutality in crushing the Buddhist rebellion. Minh had then mobilized significant support within the army for deposing Diem, but he and his allies were unsure of American intentions.

When the August coup failed to happen, the Kennedy administration was not sure why: Had it narrowly escaped a potential disaster? Or had talk of a coup been overblown all along? General Harkins cabled from Saigon that the conspirators were so hopelessly divided and mutually suspicious that they could never coordinate their efforts.[43] There was a suspicion that Nhu might have spread the rumors of a coup himself in order to flush out the disloyal generals.

The Buddhist crisis meanwhile continued to fester. Diem showed no signs of releasing imprisoned monks and students or of lessening his repression of dissent. Lodge was given authority as part of the "selective pressure" campaign to withhold some U.S. aid at his discretion to incentivize Diem to undertake reforms.

However, Lodge's views about how to deal with Diem were different from Washington's.[44] Lodge remained aloof from dealing with Diem on the grounds that it was hopeless to expect Diem to adopt reforms; it was better to keep Diem guessing about U.S. intentions. Washington pleaded with Lodge to achieve some reaction from Diem that could be portrayed as progress to the U.S. Congress. Washington invariably caved in to Lodge, however, who remained willful and a maverick.

Tom Hughes continued to brief Secretary Rusk daily, but unlike Roger Hilsman or Director McCone, Tom did not see his role as being a policy advocate. Hughes briefed Rusk every morning and his fellow assistant secretaries weekly at the large staff meeting, where he usually talked for ten or fifteen minutes on emerging crises and other significant developments.

Tom's own policy views were close to those of Paul Kattenberg. Tom thought that, given all the reports from his INR analysts and his own work on Nhu's machinations with the French and with Hanoi, it would be a convenient time to review the options for a regional peace agreement. This proposal, he thought, should come from a senior official or from a U.S. senator. The INR data study, by challenging the Pentagon's overly optimistic statistics on the war, was forcing a reappraisal of the policy relying on those data.

After the August 31 meeting, Paul Kattenberg was removed from his post as head of the interdepartmental working group on Vietnam. He was given a series of marginal assignments until he finally resigned from the Foreign Service. He tried to mobilize opposition to the war among midlevel officials. Tom Hughes did not know Paul Kattenberg well at this time. They later became good friends, after both had left the government. In the fall of 1963, Hughes did not see how midlevel opposition to the war could or should prevail against the weight of JFK's principal advisers and of the president himself.

Hilsman, Harriman, Ball, White House staffer Forrestal, and Lodge, in Saigon, favored pressuring or ousting Diem, or both. This was a powerful group but not as powerful as Mac Bundy, Rusk, McNamara, and McCone in the president's inner circle, who favored staying the course with Diem.

The president himself was of two minds, as illustrated in his September television interviews with CBS's Walter Cronkite and NBC's Chet Huntley. Kennedy first declared that the war was South Vietnam's to win or lose.

However, JFK said he did not agree with those who called for the United States to leave Vietnam, and he affirmed his belief in the domino theory. Now, in mid-October, after a false alarm at the end of August and two fact-finding missions in September, the administration was back at the beginning. The United Sates apparently could neither reform nor overthrow the Diem regime. Diem was bad, but a successor could be even worse.

On October 25, Lodge cabled the president that events were now largely out of American hands. A new coup was in the works, no matter what Washington intended.[45] It could only be stopped if the United States intervened to warn Diem. Kennedy attempted to control Lodge by issuing more instructions but shortly gave up the effort. Finally, on October 29, Kennedy authorized Lodge to stop or postpone the coup if Lodge deemed either step necessary. Lodge chose not to interfere.

General Minh and his coconspirators, Generals Don, Kim, and Khiem, were surprisingly well organized this time. They struck on the afternoon of November 1 and quickly overcame the troops loyal to Diem. By nightfall, only the palace guard was holding out. As the fighting went on, Diem was in touch with the generals, who were offering Diem and his brother safe passage out of the country in return for their surrender and recognition of the new government.

Diem and Nhu escaped through a secret passage and made their way to a safe haven in Cholon, the Chinese section of Saigon. Whether a deal had been struck was apparently unclear. Exactly what happened next is still not known. One report was that an agreement had been reached whereby Diem and Nhu would attend a ceremony installing the new government before departing for exile in Thailand. In this version of events, General Minh, resplendent in full-dress uniform, was left feeling like a bride jilted at the altar when Diem and Nhu did not show up.

More prosaically, and probably closer to the truth, the two brothers were reported to be maneuvering from their hideout to rally their forces for a counterattack. Documents captured from the presidential palace revealed the location of the hideout. Minh gave orders for Diem and Nhu to be brought to military headquarters. An armored personnel carrier and two vans were sent to pick up the brothers.[46] Diem and Nhu were found and thrown into an armored vehicle. They were shot multiple times by Minh's bodyguard, who apparently acted on his own. For good measure, Nhu was stabbed five or six times. Pictures of the riddled bodies, with hands tied behind their backs, flashed around the world, making a mockery of the junta's absurd initial claim that the two had committed suicide.

AFTERMATH

President Kennedy and his advisers were appalled by the killings. Nonetheless, they were initially "extremely pleased with the overall result."[47] The U.S. embassy issued a statement declaring that the coup d'état meant an end to the talk of neutralism. Ambassador Lodge sent a self-congratulatory cable to Washington on November 4, extolling the generals' careful planning and execution.[48]

The administration waited a few days before affirming its support for the new government, which would be composed of civilians and a presidential council or junta led by General Duong Van Minh. This coup was an example, McGeorge Bundy told his NSC colleagues, of an acceptable military coup, since it had produced results broadly in the U.S. national interest. The coup would enable the Kennedy administration to proceed without the internal divisions that had marked the government's policies toward the Diem regime over the past six months.

The initial euphoria did not last long. Lodge sent a prophetic cable to Washington reporting on a meeting with Minh and expressing his misgivings about Minh's leadership. Bundy observed, at a policy review conference in Honolulu, that the junta might prove to be unstable. It could be followed by a succession of governments even less popular than the Diem regime.

Scarcely three weeks after the death of Diem, John F. Kennedy was dead. So, in short order, were the hopes for a more harmonious period in U.S. relations with South Vietnam. For Tom Hughes, the territory ahead was uncharted. Dean Rusk could be replaced. Bundy and McNamara were both interested in replacing Rusk if he departed. The White House team could be shaken up. Indeed, the spirit of the New Frontier already seemed like ancient history. The pro-Diem and anti-Diem divisions were now irrelevant, and new political lines of fracture would emerge. Lyndon Johnson, as a novice in foreign policy, might reorder administration priorities in a major way.

Surprisingly, LBJ left intact almost the entire Kennedy foreign policy team and pledged continuity in foreign policy. Aside from the Kennedy intimates, most of the key foreign policy appointees stayed on and stayed in their posts. Harris Wofford departed, but he had been away in the Peace Corps in Africa, so Tom had not seen much of his oldest friend in the past few years. As Tom had feared, Roger Hilsman did not last long in the Johnson administration.

Formerly, Roger had two friends in government: President Kennedy and Tom Hughes. Now he had only Tom Hughes. Lyndon Johnson disliked Hilsman because he considered Hilsman partly to blame for Diem's overthrow and assassination. Rusk disliked Roger because of the many times Roger had ignored protocol and communicated directly with the White

House. McNamara and the Joint Chiefs hated Roger from the start. The CIA was hostile to him because of his well-known contempt for the agency. Although everyone was deeply affected by Kennedy's death, Tom believed that Roger had been affected more by the loss than almost anybody outside of the Kennedy family.

The only foreign policy areas in which President Johnson took a direct and personal interest were Latin America and, to a lesser extent, the Middle East. Johnson dropped the Kennedy obsession with Castro and changed what he thought were ineffectual parts of the Alliance for Progress. He sought to win over the American Jewish community largely for domestic political reasons and did so, in part, by quietly abandoning the American effort to keep the Israelis from acquiring a stockpile of nuclear bombs.

As for Vietnam, President Johnson pledged to maintain the Kennedy policy, which he understood to mean not losing an Asian country to communism. More important, he embraced JFK's goal of keeping Vietnam a limited engagement in a distant land and out of the 1964 presidential campaign. Johnson wanted to demonstrate firm but prudent leadership—just enough firmness to hold together the coalition that would enable him to enact the Great Society. He was the majority leader, and he counted on the votes of southern senators, who would support his domestic legislation only if he backed military assistance for South Vietnam.

Tom Hughes thought that this Johnson approach to Vietnam, though cautious, might permit some innovative steps in the direction of diplomacy. Hughes was not turned off by General Minh, as were Lodge and others in the administration. In refusing to permit U.S. officers to be part of ARVN operations and refusing to authorize new covert operations against North Vietnam, Minh was showing independence from MACV, which was politically important to the junta. Minh was also keeping open the path toward eventual negotiations with Hanoi by limiting the war to the South.

Hughes wrote a memo to Rusk in mid-December 1963 analyzing the reports of diplomatic contacts between Saigon and Hanoi officials.[49] If the United States had been worried about Nhu's efforts to forge some sort of neutralist status for Vietnam, Hughes suggested, the issues of neutralism and war weariness were still strong and may have grown even stronger under the junta. Neutralism would have to be reckoned with in relations with the junta, though Minh himself did not favor neutralism as a realistic option at present.

General Minh, it appeared to Hughes and his INR team, was behaving in a reasonable way for a leader trying to consolidate his position. It was logical for Minh to keep some distance from the United States as a sign of his independence. To rebuff MACV's demands for more-aggressive military measures was sensible. Minh, it seemed, was trying to play down the military side of the conflict and to focus on the war's political dimensions.

In January 1964, the INR undertook a broad study of neutralist sentiment and related issues for Rusk. The bureau confirmed recent CIA findings that neutralist sentiments and war weariness were strong among students and urban professionals in Saigon, among peasants, and in the ARVN ranks. The study also examined Hanoi's willingness to negotiate with the United States and found that Hanoi would respond favorably to a U.S. initiative. However, Hanoi would not take the first step.[50]

The INR study concluded that Hanoi had a strong interest in preventing the Americanization of the war. Nevertheless, Hanoi's leaders felt confident that they could cope with any offensive military steps the Americans were likely to take. Bureau analysts cited statements by Ho's lieutenants, including Premier Pham Van Dong, indicating that a decision had been made to increase Hanoi's assistance to the National Liberation Front. Hanoi would henceforth take a more active role in the insurgency to counter the increased American assistance to Saigon.

To Hughes and his team, the logical policy response for the United States should be to probe Hanoi's intentions regarding negotiations. This approach was unacceptable to virtually all of LBJ's key advisers and most of the intelligence community at this time. To signal a willingness to talk would undermine South Vietnam's morale and embolden de Gaulle's campaign for a neutral Vietnam.

One other issue remained on Tom Hughes's mind. That was the vice presidency. This was a looming question for every Washington insider. For Tom, the obvious choice was Hubert Humphrey. He made a mental note to seek out Max Kampelman and consult on how best to assist the prospective Humphrey campaign for the vice presidential nomination.

12

The Gulf of Tonkin Crisis

On Sunday morning, August 2, 1964, Tom Hughes was awakened by a call from Dean Rusk. Hughes was summoned to Rusk's home for an urgent breakfast meeting. Rusk alluded to "developments in Vietnam." Always cautious, the secretary apparently did not want to say anything too specific on a public line. This was odd. What could be so important that a meeting had to take place at breakfast on a Sunday morning?

The summer of 1964 had been hot and lazy, like every Washington summer Tom could remember. Two big events had dominated everything: the presidential election and Vietnam. But the events were like the Potomac, powerful but slow moving and seemingly going nowhere. That description applied more to the early parts of the summer. In recent weeks, the pace of events seemed to have suddenly quickened. A resolution of sorts, the hint of an outcome, had finally occurred. This was the case both for the election and the U.S. presence in Vietnam.

POST-DIEM AND U.S. PRESIDENTIAL POLITICS

In Vietnam policy, Hughes had expected that President Johnson's administration, while rhetorically adhering to Kennedy's policies, might be more action oriented than his predecessor had been. What had happened under LBJ so far, however, was more the appearance of action than concrete actions. Johnson affirmed Kennedy's last Vietnam policy statement in his own National Security Action Memorandum (NSAM) 273 of November 29, 1963.[1] The two memorandums largely restated the pre-coup policy of support for the Saigon government combined with "selective pressure" to promote reforms.

Johnson permitted General Harkins, MACV's commander, to propose to the junta Oplan (Operation Plan) 34A. The plan called for covert torpedo boat attacks on Hanoi's ports and storage sites located on the Gulf of Tonkin coast, north of Danang. General Minh refused to authorize Oplan 34A and also turned down MACV's request to have Americans accompany ARVN commanders in field operations. Minh had good arguments for his positions. The proposed Oplan 34A attacks were "pin pricks" that made little military sense. Injecting U.S. advisers into the ARVN command structure made even less sense.

The most consequential U.S. action of the Minh period was a nonaction by Ambassador Lodge at the end of January 1964. When he learned that General Nguyen Khanh planned a coup to prevent conspirators favoring neutralism from overthrowing General Minh, Lodge did nothing. He had soured on Minh and believed, on the basis of scant evidence, that General Khanh was a highly competent leader.

Khanh had telephoned Lodge and told him of an alleged plot by conspirators within Minh's own government to overthrow him. Supposedly inspired by the French, the plotters planned to seize power and then declare South Vietnam a neutral sate. General Khanh proposed that he would nip this conspiracy in the bud by preempting the conspirators. He would then reaffirm Saigon's close ties with the United States.

Khanh struck within hours of his call to Lodge. There were no deaths other than the killing of the Minh bodyguard who had shot Diem and his brother. The United States was left unable to influence the course of events except to demand that Minh not be harmed and that he be given a post in the new government to ensure continuity.

Khanh was happy to oblige by kicking Minh upstairs to a meaningless titular post. Khanh also, in one of his first official acts, reversed Minh's decision and allowed the proposed U.S. covert operations of Oplan 34A to go forward.

The U.S. disillusionment with Khanh, Tom Hughes observed, set in even faster than it had with Minh. Hughes and the INR held a more favorable view of Minh than many colleagues in the Department of Defense and the CIA. The military did not like Minh because he seemed to prefer diplomacy to fighting. This was precisely why Tom liked him: Minh recognized that political support was the base for any effective military action. The situation was not getting any better. Khanh kept demanding more U.S. military assistance without demonstrating that he was making good use of his current aid. There was something else, too, that Tom Hughes's staff was telling him. An INR study diagnosed what was happening in Saigon as an eruption of a kind of democratic interest-group politics. Various groups, having been suppressed under Diem, felt liberated and were demanding to be heard. This trend had started under Minh but had now become full blown under Khanh.

Lyndon Johnson would have been happy to let matters in Vietnam stand. Aside from authorizing Oplan 34A and secret electronic reconnaissance, which he assumed no one at home would know about, LBJ resisted appeals to widen the war that were advanced regularly by the Joint Chiefs of Staff, MACV, and CINCPAC. Bombing North Vietnam or Laotian supply routes was becoming a favorite proposal for hawks.

Studies conducted by the INR and CIA debunked this idea, arguing that bombing the North would not work because Hanoi had no industrial infrastructure to destroy. Hanoi's industrial infrastructure was, in effect, Russian supplies by ship and Chinese aid by rail. Bombing might only invite further Chinese and Russian intervention on Hanoi's behalf.

President Johnson's desire to stand pat, however, presumed that matters in Vietnam were not getting totally out of hand. He had managed to keep the Senate hawks in line and the Senate doves for the most part from going public with their opposition to the war. The problem was that six weeks into Khanh's rule, the status quo was no longer tolerable.

Johnson took a page out of the Kennedy playbook and sent his two most trusted aides to Saigon to review the situation in March 1964. This McNamara-Taylor trip was as unusual as any previous fact-finding mission to Saigon. On the team's arrival, McNamara held a press conference in which he announced that the United States was opposed to any regional negotiations to settle the Laotian and Vietnam conflicts. British ambassador Gordon Etherington-Smith cabled London that "it is strange on a fact-finding [mission] to announce decisions on arrival."[2]

The team's interviews with ARVN officials included American military advisers and featured canned briefings by junior American officers. Khanh assured the Americans that he had his hands full in his own country and had no interest in attacking North Vietnam. Soon, however, Khanh shocked his American allies with a newfound enthusiasm for a march to the North.

After McNamara presented the mission's findings and a plan based on those findings to the president at an NSC meeting on March 17, Johnson asked him if this plan would ensure victory in South Vietnam's fight against the insurgents. McNamara said that if all of the recommended steps were energetically carried out, the plan would achieve victory in four to six months. General Taylor, chair of the Joint Chiefs, stated that the Joint Chiefs stood solidly behind the recommendation. Johnson went around the room and asked each man present if he agreed with McNamara's and Taylor's assessment. Everyone agreed.

The McNamara-Taylor memorandum to the president was adopted verbatim as official U.S. policy in NSAM 288 of March 17, 1964, replacing NSAM 273 of the previous November.

The adoption of NSAM 288 has been generally viewed as an important turning point in the Vietnam War in that it "called for considerable enlargement of the U.S. effort . . . and an increased involvement of the United States in the internal affairs of South Vietnam."[3] Max Frankel of the *New York Times* observed on March 21 that "the decision to hold the line lies at the end of a long reasoning process by which the administration has rejected a graceful withdrawal [from Vietnam]."[4]

Yet the memo's details did not support the conclusion that it represented a significant escalation of U.S. involvement. In Tom Hughes's view, NSAM 288 did not produce the hoped-for sense of stability or finality in U.S. policy. The memo's main call was for the institution of a draft in South Vietnam and an upgrade in the paramilitary forces. These reforms were expected to produce an increase of 60,000 troops in Saigon's armed forces, giving the government a great advantage in numbers over the insurgents. However, the ARVN already had a significant advantage in numbers, but this had not defeated the insurgents. The memo did not really spell out the U.S. role. There was no reference in the memo, or even a hint, that U.S. involvement in ground combat and the bombing of Laos or North Vietnam had been ruled out. But there was no increase either in the numbers of U.S. advisers to assist the Saigon government in making effective use of the new aid. What was called for was an upgrade and modernization of helicopters, transport aircraft, armored vehicles, communications equipment, and a special program to increase fertilizer production.

Like other such documents, NSAM 288 was the product of interagency bargaining and compromise, and it dodged or left ambiguous key policy issues. The Senate's Armed Services and Foreign Relations Committees demanded to know what, if anything, the McNamara-Taylor trip had produced. McNamara was to testify in the Senate and to give a speech on March 26. His Senate testimony and his speech were reviewed and edited in an interagency process. However, the McNamara Senate testimony and his speech did not clarify U.S. policy toward Vietnam.

McNamara made another trip to Saigon on April 17–18 and was disappointed to find that Khanh had made no progress in implementing his promises of March. On April 29–30, a delegation headed by Secretary of State Dean Rusk and General Earle Wheeler, vice chair of the Joint Chiefs, held inconclusive discussions with Khanh. On May 1, Khanh complained to Lodge that he needed more American advisers throughout all ARVN ranks and that the Americans should take the fight to Hanoi. McNamara returned to Saigon again on May 17–18 for more discussions with Khanh. When he returned home, he said the situation in Vietnam was worse than it had been in March.

President Johnson demanded from Mac Bundy a definitive review of his military and political options in Vietnam. Four working groups of the government's leading national security experts, including INR analysts, prepared papers for a conference on Southeast Asia policy, to be held in Honolulu June 1–3, 1964.

The Honolulu Conference to advise the president on the next steps in Southeast Asia policy in the broadest terms was the most comprehensive Vietnam policy review to date. The conference was notable not only for what it recommended but also for what it decided not to recommend to President Johnson. The three main points agreed on were that the U.S. advisory effort should be expanded in certain key provinces; that planning for military pressure on North Vietnam should continue, but no stronger military action should be taken at the present time; and that a campaign should be launched to influence U.S. public opinion, and a similar campaign should be undertaken to gain support from our allies.[5] These were modest proposals for a team of advisers dominated by Defense Department personnel.

The conference explicitly rejected U.S. bombing of North Vietnam, whether of the tit-for-tat variety in response to explicit Hanoi actions or in the form of a continuing campaign. There was no reference whatsoever to any role for U.S. ground forces or to any form of joint command with the ARVN. The advisers decided not to recommend that the president seek a congressional resolution giving him authority to take military action in the region.

To Tom Hughes, this seemed to have resolved the Vietnam debate, at least for the near term. Ambassador Lodge was the only remaining wild card. He was a lone voice pressing for bombing the North. Hughes played an unexpected role in ensuring Lodge's departure from Vietnam.

Tom was swimming one afternoon in June at the Chevy Chase Swimming Association when he encountered a journalist friend and neighbor, Max Frankel. As they treaded water, Max casually asked if Tom had any news for the *Times*. Tom replied that he had just seen a cable indicating that Lodge wanted to be relieved of his post. He presumed that Lodge wanted to be home to play some kind of role at the Republican Convention in July.

"Wow!" said Frankel. "Can I use that? Can I mention you?"

"Keep me out of it," said Tom.[6]

Frankel was excited. This was a scoop, his favorite as he later described it, but he could not tip his hand by rushing off to a telephone. He noticed a number of his friends and competitors, such as Marvin Kalb and his wife, Mady, at the pool as well as a number of government officials he knew. So Max lounged around for an hour and then casually left. He telephoned the story in, and the paper ran it on the front page the next day, along with a flat denial by the White House.

For eight days the story ran as a controversy, with the White House continuing to issue denials. A nervous Max Frankel kept his distance from Tom Hughes. An even more nervous Tom Hughes waited as LBJ conducted an investigation to find the leaker. Bundy sent the president a memo proposing himself, Robert Kennedy, and Robert McNamara as candidates to succeed Lodge as ambassador. Lodge in Saigon played his part. Notwithstanding that he had himself cited ill health as a possible reason for his departure, Lodge declared to reporters that he would swim ten laps in the embassy pool at full speed and then they could judge if he was in good health. Johnson finally announced at the end of eight days that Henry Cabot Lodge was returning home (on June 23) and General Maxwell Taylor would replace him (on July 14) as U.S. ambassador in Saigon.

Just as the Vietnam situation was settling down, the domestic political picture became clearer. Senator Barry Goldwater was the Republican nominee. Johnson had moved carefully and on July 30 eased the attorney general out of consideration for the vice presidency. The Kennedy forces had waged a campaign for Bobby Kennedy as the logical heir and standard bearer for his fallen brother. Johnson was never going to put Kennedy on the ticket, but he had to maneuver carefully for the sake of party unity and the good of the country. Hubert had been the floor leader for LBJ's civil rights bill and had successfully brought home this historic measure.

THE FIRST TONKIN INCIDENT

When he got the call from Rusk on the morning of August 2, Tom Hughes was somewhat concerned. He had thought that events had settled into a pattern. The war was under control because the Honolulu Conference had clarified U.S. policy and halted the drift toward escalation. The politics had also settled down.

Present at the meeting, besides Rusk and Hughes, were George Ball from State, Deputy Secretary of Defense Cyrus Vance representing McNamara (who was hiking in Colorado), the new JCS chair, General Earle "Bus" Wheeler, JCS aide Ralph Steakley, and the CIA's Winston Cornelius.

The issue at hand was how the United States should respond to the improbable attack of the previous evening. The powerful U.S. destroyer *Maddox* was attacked in the Gulf of Tonkin by three North Vietnamese torpedo boats. The destroyer easily repulsed the attackers but had to maneuver to dodge several torpedoes.

While Rusk's wife, Virginia, made pancakes for breakfast, the men sat on Rusk's living room floor pouring over maps of the Gulf of Tonkin and trying to establish the three-mile, twelve-mile, and thirty-mile territorial lines. To Hughes, "the scene was reminiscent of Clemenceau and Lloyd George in 1919 at Versailles trying to find Trieste on the map."[7] After breakfast, and collecting their thoughts, the men assembled at the White House to brief LBJ on the incident. As the initial response to the Gulf of Tonkin attack, the White House meeting combined elements of drama, farce, and folksy wisdom from the president.

Johnson quipped, "Where are my Bundys?" He then answered his own question by noting that they were up at Martha's Vineyard enjoying themselves while the rest of them were sweltering in Washington. He asked for an explanation of what brought the group to see him on that hot Sunday morning.

Steakley, the JCS briefer, described the attack on the *Maddox*. Johnson had difficulty understanding why the North Vietnamese, having had success with guerrilla tactics, would suddenly decide to attack a U.S. destroyer. Why would those "little whippersnappers" do that? the president asked.

The Pentagon briefer had no answer. He promised to bring further information as soon as it was available. The group did not know all the details of the attack at that time. This included the fact that each of the three torpedo boats carried two torpedoes, which could have posed a threat to the destroyer. Had they gotten close enough, they might have launched their torpedoes in a coordinated fashion and sunk the destroyer.

Johnson pondered for a moment and then asked, "We weren't up to any monkey business out there, were we?"

The president's instincts were sound. Hughes, as State's intelligence chief, was cleared to know that covert operations (Oplan 34A) were being carried out by the South Vietnam navy under American direction. He also knew that the supersecret DeSoto reconnaissance patrols by U.S. ships were operating in those waters. Hughes wondered, with all of the secrecy, whether the Americans behind the covert operations and those running the DeSoto patrols were aware of each other's moves. There had been a 34A operation against a North Vietnamese coastal base on the night of July 31–August 1, for which Hanoi might have been seeking to retaliate.

The *Maddox*'s crew had no knowledge of the Oplan 34A operations, but Captain John Herrick was cleared to know about them. Captain Herrick was aware that North Vietnamese radar was capable of tracking U.S. vessels (part of his mission was to gain intelligence about the radars).

"Well, you remember, Mr. President," Cyrus Vance responded to LBJ's query. "You signed off on those [Oplan 34A] operations a few months ago—covert operations, deniable of course, performed by the South Vietnamese, no American involvement, lighting up the North Vietnamese radars along the coast, allowing us to get an electronic map of the coast. Some of them may have been occurring in the vicinity about this time."[8]

"And that's all we know?" said Johnson.

"That's all, sir."

"Well," LBJ said. "It all reminds me of going to the movies in Texas.

You're sittin' there next to a pretty girl and you put your hand on her ankle. Nothin' happens. Then you put your hand on her calf. Nothin' happens. Then on her knee. Still nothin' happens. And you're just about to go higher, when suddenly you get slapped. I think we just got slapped."

The president's story was a succinct summary of the facts. At this point, Hughes passed a note to Secretary Rusk with a query: "Knowing what happens at the movies in Texas, do we still want to describe this attack as 'unprovoked'?"

Rusk was not amused but asked Vance, an international lawyer, if the destroyer was in international waters and if he thought the attack was unprovoked.

"Of course it was unprovoked," said Vance. "Our destroyer was in international waters."

Vance's claim stretched the truth. North Vietnam's definition of its territorial waters as extending twelve miles from its shoreline and twelve miles from its offshore islands was disputed by the United States, but the DeSoto patrols normally did not operate closer than eight miles from shore and five miles from the offshore islands. The *Maddox* had specific instructions for the mission of August 2 to patrol closer than its usual limits.

President Johnson was not moved by Vance's comments. Johnson quickly ruled out any retaliatory action by the United States until the circumstances became clearer. He would issue a warning to the North Vietnamese, he said, against future provocative actions against U.S. ships. But for anything more decisive, the president insisted, the aggressive intent must be clearer. Furthermore, he would not make a public appearance around the event but would issue a statement. Nothing else would be changed for now. Patrols and other operations he had authorized would be carried out as usual. Hughes was impressed by Johnson's demeanor and his quick appraisal of the situation,

Johnson suddenly switched the subject from foreign to domestic policy. Hughes noted that the president was immediately more comfortable. Johnson described what he called a real problem—the postal pay bill he had just received from Congress. He went into a description of the dilemma the bill presented for him. He was damned if he signed the bill and damned if he vetoed it.

The president apparently decided to have a little fun with General Wheeler. He turned to Wheeler and demanded to know how, since the general was a strategist, Wheeler would strategize a way out of this dilemma. Johnson developed an elaborate metaphor, likening the postal pay bill to an attacking army that used feints and maneuvers. What would the general recommend?

Wheeler was not sure he was expected to answer. Was it not the case, the president continued, that the postal pay bill was just as complicated and dangerous as any foreign crisis? For some minutes, LBJ confounded the unfortunate Wheeler, who mumbled monosyllabic answers to questions he could not understand. The group sat in stupefaction as the president took off on a riff about the barons of Capitol Hill, union bosses, dim-witted reporters, and so on.

At a conference on Vietnam held in 1991 at the LBJ Presidential library in Austin, Texas, Tom Hughes quipped about the August 2 White House meeting, "We all felt . . . that we had been at one high point of history or another, though we didn't know whether it was the attack in the Gulf of Tonkin or the postal pay bill."[9]

When the White House meeting broke up, Hughes, on instructions from Dean Rusk and George Ball, hurried to the CBS studio to find and brief Hubert Humphrey on the Gulf of Tonkin. Hubert was to appear that morning on *Face the Nation*.

THE SECOND TONKIN INCIDENT AND U.S. RETALIATION

The details of the first Tonkin Gulf incident became clearer the next day. The attack by the three North Vietnamese torpedo boats drew heavy fire from the American destroyer and the launch of jet fighters from the U.S. carrier *Ticonderoga*. The attacking vessels were decisively repelled, though the *Maddox* had to maneuver to avoid two torpedoes that came close. The attacking boats then fled back to their bases. President Johnson issued a warning to North Vietnam against interference with the freedom of navigation in international waters, but otherwise took no further action.

The second incident followed two days later on the evening of August 4, Vietnam time. The second attack was apparently similar to the earlier attack on the U.S. destroyer *Maddox,* only this time there was a companion ship. The U.S.S. *C. Turner Joy* had joined the *Maddox,* and the two American destroyers were much farther out in the Gulf, some sixty miles from Vietnam. Once again, the U.S. warships opened fire on targets picked up on radar and sonar.

From the first reports about the second incident, however, there were doubts about what had happened and, in particular, whether an attack had actually occurred. Why would Hanoi stage an attack on the two American destroyers so far out in the Gulf of Tonkin? The two U.S. destroyers had been on a DeSoto patrol earlier in the evening but had never come closer than sixteen miles from shore—twice as far from the Vietnam coast as the *Maddox*'s August 2 patrol. Patrolling farther out was done under strict orders from the Seventh Fleet.

The *Maddox* and the *C. Turner Joy* had completed their mission and headed out to sea. The initial reports of a second incident, which reached Washington on the morning of August 4, were confusing. Nevertheless, the United States, for complicated reasons, this time decided to retaliate.

The decision to retaliate rested on the theory that Hanoi had deliberately and provocatively ignored President Johnson's warning following the first Tonkin incident. The August 2 attack, as detailed in Edwin E. Moise's authoritative account, was not a total surprise to Captain John Herrick.[10] Under orders, Captain Herrick was patrolling closer to the shore than he had on previous DeSoto missions. He was aware that Hanoi had been improving its radar systems and coastal batteries and that there was always a danger of an incident, given the covert operations against the North's coastal bases. Herrick's orders to patrol closer to the shore than usual worried him.

The radio chatter picked up early in the mission had referred to a pending attack by North Vietnamese forces. Captain Herrick was not entirely confident that his translators' knowledge of the Vietnamese language was of a high order, but he followed their reports closely. Then came more chatter. The translators reported an air of excitement on the part of the radio operators.

The *Maddox* proceeded northward along the coast and finished its mission. The captain was momentarily relieved, but his radar crew reported that three objects, apparently small boats, were approaching at high speeds from the south. The *Maddox* informed the Seventh Fleet that an attack seemed imminent.

Captain Herrick turned his ship around and headed south toward the attackers, giving his forward gunners an unobstructed view and clear firing lanes. He ordered that the *Maddox* open fire if the three attacking boats came closer than 10,000 yards.

At a range of some five and a half miles (9,800 yards), Captain Herrick ordered three or four warning shots to be fired. When the boats kept coming, the *Maddox* began rapid fire at 9,000 yards, using a standard mix of explosive shells. The destroyer's forward five-inch and three-inch guns now had a better firing lane. The time was about 15:05 Greenwich mean time, five hours ahead of U.S. eastern time.[11]

The *Maddox* gun crews had some difficulty in locating their targets because the targets were small and were moving fast, and the automatic radar-controlled firing system had trouble locking onto the targets. An optimum rate of fire for the six big guns was forty rounds per minute, or a shot fired almost every second. A post-incident review showed that the crews registered a respectable rapid-fire rate of twenty-eight rounds per minute, though the gunners were bounced around in their turrets when the destroyer maneuvered to escape the torpedoes. The turrets did not always function properly.

In all, 283 shells were fired at the three attacking boats in the one-sided August 2 battle, which lasted slightly longer than ten minutes. The shells fired were 132 three-inch frag and 68 five-inch frag. The frag shells exploded above the target and sprayed deadly steel shrapnel over a sixty-meter area. Seventy-one five-inch explosives would have completely destroyed the eighty-foot-long attacking vessels, but this would have required a direct hit.[12]

The Navy was never able to resolve clearly how much damage was done by the *Maddox's* guns and how much by the jet fighters from the carrier *Ticonderoga* that arrived on the scene as the destroyer was chasing the fleeing boats. The *Maddox* gun crews scored no direct hits, but the rapid-fire barrage caused the three boats to fire their torpedoes prematurely. The torpedoes passed by several hundred yards from the ship, which maneuvered to dodge them. Two of the boats broke off the attack early and fled. One boat got close enough to hit the destroyer with cannon and heavy-caliber machine gun fire. There was no significant damage, and there were no U.S. casualties. When the third boat also fled, the destroyer broke off the chase. Four F-8E Crusader jet fighters from the *Ticonderoga* attacked the retreating vessels.

All three North Vietnamese vessels made it back to base, though they had suffered varying degrees of damage. Four Vietnamese sailors had been killed and others wounded, but the boats were repaired and remained in service for the duration of the war. U.S. officials disputed whether it had been the destroyer's fire or the planes that had done the damage to the ships, but they were never able to arrive at a firm conclusion.

American officials assumed that Hanoi had been taught a lesson and would heed President Johnson's warning to refrain from attacks on U.S. ships. Hanoi had no vessels comparable to the American destroyers and carriers and had little experience in modern naval warfare. It was generally assumed that the United States had wide latitude to act in naval matters with relatively modest risks.

The intelligence community was asked throughout 1964 to assess enemy reactions to various hypothetical U.S. actions. In particular, the question of bombing North Vietnam was posed under various assumptions. Would bombing or the threat of bombing weaken Hanoi's determination to resist and make its leaders more likely to seek negotiations? Hughes and the INR consistently warned that bombing North Vietnam was not likely to weaken Hanoi's will or to lessen its support for the insurgency in South Vietnam. Rather, bombing might result in Hanoi's moving more men and equipment into Laos and South Vietnam.

Hughes did not think the Oplan 34A operations were useful, but these were so highly classified that they could not be analyzed by his staff. Oplan 34A operations were also highly secret; he could not write papers or have his staff (most of whom were not cleared to know about Oplan 34A operations) analyze them. The early experience under Oplan 34A was not favorable, as the CIA's William Colby had warned McNamara. The South Vietnamese marines were killed or captured almost as soon as they were landed in the North.

As a result, when General Westmoreland took over as MACV commander, he decided to terminate the commando raid. However, he allowed continued attacks on coastal bases and radar installations by speedy PT boats from DaNang.

Admiral Ulysses S. Grant Sharp Jr., the chief of naval operations, and CINCPAC decided after the August 2 incident to continue the DeSoto patrols. It was important, he believed, to demonstrate that the United States could not be intimidated. This went against the recommendation of Captain Herrick, who argued that the *Maddox* crew needed a rest. Herrick was ordered to conduct another DeSoto patrol on August 4. However, as a precaution, he was told to go no closer than eleven miles from the main coast and no closer than eight miles from any of the offshore islands.

Moreover, the *Maddox* would also be reinforced by a sister destroyer, the *C. Turner Joy,* which was a more recently built ship than the *Maddox* and had a fresh crew. The crew was closer to the full complement of 280 sailors for this category of ship (the *Maddox* was undermanned, at around 218 sailors and officers).

On August 4, around 8:00 a.m. Washington time, Secretary of Defense McNamara arrived at the White House. He told President Johnson that a second attack might have occurred on American ships in the Gulf of Tonkin in defiance of his warning. The reports were hazy, McNamara said. Apparently there was some confusion about what had happened. The weather was bad. Waves at six to seven feet were causing unusual radar readings. When the ship turned sharply, its own propellers caused sound waves bouncing off the hull that confused the sonar crew.

Strange blips were appearing and disappearing on the radar. The evening was dark and there was no moon. A kind of surface fog added to the problems of visual sighting. The *Maddox* crew, having experienced an attack two days earlier, was jumpy. It responded hastily to ambiguous radar and sonar signals.

McNamara expected to have more definitive information within an hour. Communications, however, were difficult because the circuits were jammed with so many flash messages. The *Maddox* had no automatic decoding machine and was backed up with incoming coded messages. The captain of the *C. Turner Joy* was not cleared to receive the most secret coded messages, including any information about South Vietnam's covert operations. Washington could not send an authorization via the *Maddox* because the *C. Turner Joy* did not have a classified decoding apparatus that was compatible with the setup of the *Maddox*. It was too late anyway. The Seventh Fleet was reporting that heavy action involving both U.S. destroyers and an undetermined number of attacking vessels was occurring in the Gulf of Tonkin about sixty miles from Vietnam and in the general direction of the Chinese island of Hainan.

The U.S. destroyers were maneuvering furiously to evade torpedoes, firing their heavy guns, and even dropping depth charges. As many as twenty-one torpedoes were supposedly detected on sonar. Visual sightings of the cabin lights of enemy vessels appeared and then disappeared. Captain Herrick could not believe the number of torpedoes supposedly detected on sonar because that number would have required more torpedo boats than existed in the North Vietnam navy. Little was known to the Americans then of the Tonkin radar "ghosts," owing to unique weather features of the Tonkin Gulf that became more fully understood later.

Unknown to the Americans, Chinese observers, hearing the guns of the *Maddox* and the *C. Turner Joy,* had sent a message to Hanoi asking if the North Vietnamese comrades were engaged in a naval battle with the Americans. Almost at the same time that they dispatched their message, the Chinese received a similar inquiry from Hanoi asking if the Chinese comrades were fighting the Americans near the island. The answers were in the negative to both inquiries.

In 1995 General Giap and Secretary McNamara met at a retrospective conference on the war and discussed the Tonkin Gulf incidents. General Giap acknowledged the August 2 attack but told McNamara that the August 4 attack was imaginary. He said no such attack had occurred, and that the North Vietnamese were puzzled over what appeared to be an elaborate charade staged by the Americans as a pretext for escalating the war.

The action of August 4 had apparently taken place beginning in the evening (Vietnam time was twelve hours ahead of U.S. eastern time) shortly before McNamara's first report to President Johnson. The action apparently lasted for some three hours, ending about the time Washington was learning the details. Policymakers in Washington did not, at the time they were making important decisions, have a clear understanding of the timing of events.

Johnson reacted to McNamara's news by directing McNamara to verify the initial report, telling him that in the meantime he was to consult immediately with the Joint Chiefs about possible retaliatory steps. A second attack by Hanoi could not go unpunished.

Johnson's position was extremely difficult. He had refrained from any retaliatory action against North Vietnam after the first attack, in part because the *Maddox* and the carrier planes had so decisively whipped the enemy. Furthermore, from a public relations point of view, the United States had been on the defensive and had reacted to an unprovoked attack. It was unnecessary to retaliate, and world opinion might then cast the United States as an aggressor. The covert South Vietnam operations might be uncovered and traced back to the United States.

But the president had issued a stern warning. Senator Barry Goldwater, now the Republican nominee for president, was castigating the administration for its weakness on Vietnam. Johnson would look foolish if he did not respond more forcefully to a second attack by the communists. He would have to make a statement to the nation. He could not announce to a national television audience that he was not sure whether an attack had occurred and would figure out what happened in the Gulf of Tonkin.

Further word came from McNamara that some sort of engagement involving the two American destroyers was in process. If so, retaliation was a likely response this time.

Bombing North Vietnam was one logical option, though some planners on the Joint Chiefs staff wanted to mine Haiphong's harbor. This was quickly ruled out, but other questions remained. If bombing were the preferred option, what would be the targets? Only the coastal bases where the PT and Swatow torpedo boats were based? Additional industrial targets? An NSC meeting was called for noon on August 4. By the time it convened, the engagement was over, and the meeting focused on the nature of the reprisal.

But the question that LBJ had asked at the August 2 White House meeting about the first attack was still relevant, and even more pressing: Why had Hanoi decided to attack a U.S. destroyer? The president had given a tentative answer with a homely story about behavior in a Texas movie theater. The United States had gotten a slap for patrolling too close to the coast. But the *Maddox* and the *C. Turner Joy* were way out in the Gulf on August 4, so why would Hanoi repeat the same failed tactic?

McGeorge Bundy's handwritten notes from the noon NSC meeting on August 4 suggested that 34A operations must be the explanation, because otherwise, the North Vietnamese action on the evening of August 4 made no sense: "What is 34-A role in all this? Must be *cause;* no other is rational. But sufficient cause?"[13]

Most other officials were simply baffled. They attributed motives of showing toughness or standing up to the Americans—that is, explanations relating to national pride or prestige—to North Vietnam's decisionmakers in the apparent absence of tactical military reasons for the second attack.

The intelligence community had an explanation as soon as radio intercepts were available for study, about forty-eight hours after the alleged incident. Tom Hughes at the INR was convinced that the answer was clear: there was no second attack. There was evidence enough to cast strong doubt as to whether the second attack had actually taken place. Hanoi's torpedo boats were usually deployed to deter or to respond to South Vietnam's covert attacks on North Vietnam's coastal bases and radar stations.

The first North Vietnam attack, on August 2, was probably a response to a South Vietnam commando raid on the night of July 30–31; local commanders must have mistaken the *Maddox* for a support ship for that attack. The radar sightings of August 4 were ambiguous and possibly mistaken, owing to unusual weather conditions on that evening. Some of the claimed sightings by radar operators—for example, twenty-one enemy torpedo wakes—were simply outlandish, because North Vietnam did not have enough torpedo boats to launch that many torpedoes. Sonar readings could not clearly distinguish sounds made by echoes from the *Maddox's* own propellers from alleged enemy vessels maneuvering nearby. A U.S. naval pilot flying overhead apparently reported seeing the wakes of the two destroyers, but not of any enemy vessels.

Hughes could discuss the issues internally only with Allen Whiting, head of the INR's Southeast Asia division, and Whiting's deputy, Fred Greene, because they had the necessary clearances to know about the 34A covert operations and the DeSoto patrols. They could not exchange views with other INR analysts who were not cleared to undertake research on the most sensitive topics. Hughes factored in the most secret information in his briefings to Dean Rusk, George Ball, Bill Bundy, and other policymakers. But he never wrote papers referring to or acknowledging the existence of the 34A operations and the DeSoto patrols. It was assumed that written reports would be seen by people not cleared to know about such matters.

Hughes surmised that some of his staff may have been aware of the covert operations, based on their reading of North Vietnamese newspapers, Radio Hanoi translations from the Foreign Bureau Information Service, prisoner-of-war interviews, and other sources. But they would also have known that their information was incomplete and that they were not supposed to have access to the information. Staff papers might have reflected self-censorship as to covert operations. As Edwin Moise observes, "The problem this posed for analysis of the Tonkin Gulf incident, in which Oplan 34-A was central to DRV [North Vietnam] intentions, is obvious."[14]

Ray Cline, the CIA's deputy director for operations, also doubted that the second attack had occurred. Cline, an expert on naval codes, determined after a quick look at the messages that CINCPAC had probably confused the sequence of the messages sent from the field and made an error as a result. But he could not say for sure without a lengthy investigation. The INR and the CIA interpretations that there was no second attack eventually became the accepted view. "Hell, those damn stupid sailors were just shooting at flying fish," Lyndon Johnson himself concluded a few days after the incident.[15]

But the policymakers at the time, as they struggled to understand what had happened and what to do about it, did not have the luxury of retrospective analysis. In the early afternoon of August 4, Washington time, came a surprise that deeply confused the picture. Captain Herrick sent a cable from the *Maddox* casting doubt on what he had previously reported: "Review of action makes many reported contacts and torpedoes fired appear doubtful. Freak weather effects on radar and overeager sonar men may have accounted for many reports. No actual visual sightings by *Maddox*. Suggest complete evaluation before any further action taken."[16]

The administration was confused by this information. Shortly after his first message, Herrick sent another, which partly contradicted what he had just said. Washington was doubly confused. McNamara telephoned CINCPAC commander Admiral Ulysses S. Grant Sharp and demanded to know whether there had or had not been a North Vietnam attack. Admiral Sharp said that the weight of the evidence indicated that an attack had occurred but that he would definitively review the record. Shortly after that, Herrick sent another cable from the *Maddox*, partially contradicting the prior message. McNamara again telephoned Admiral Sharp, declaring that he would counsel the president to call off the planned U.S. retaliatory strike unless Sharp gave unequivocal assurances that the attack had occurred. Sharp went on record with assurances that there had been an attack.

Late in the afternoon the NSC met again. The council discussed the Joint Chief's Oplan 37-64 ("Military Action to Stabilize the Situation in the Republic of Vietnam"), but decided that the steps envisaged in those plans were too general and directed too much at infrastructure and that a more targeted strike was needed against the torpedo boats and their bases. A compromise included on the target list was an oil refinery near the Laotian border and Planes des Jarres.

CIA Director John McCone backed the more targeted strike because he thought that Hanoi's latest attack was probably in retaliation against the South Vietnam Oplan 34A operations. However, his mention of the covert raid suggested that he could have been referring to the South Vietnam midnight attack of July 30–31 rather than to the incident on the evening of August 3–4. At any rate, the NSC meeting came to a decision that the United States would retaliate and directed the JCS to issue the command for planes from the carriers *Ticonderoga* and *Constellation* to prepare to carry out the strike. At around 6:00 p.m., the president met with a bipartisan group of congressional leaders and told them of his plans for a retaliatory strike against North Vietnam.

When the congressional leaders met with President Johnson, they offered their full support for the president's intended actions. Johnson told them that he proposed to ask Congress to pass a joint resolution supporting his actions. Johnson would speak to the nation on television that evening to announce the retaliatory strike. He would not make the announcement until the U.S. planes were in the air, so as not to give the enemy time to prepare for the attack. The president did not dwell on military specifics but indicated that the strike would be against the torpedo boats and their bases from which the attack on the U.S. destroyers had been launched.

Coordinating the president's announcement with the launching of the planes proved to be a more difficult task than anyone had anticipated. The U.S.S. *Constellation* would supply half the attack force but would have to steam closer to the scene so that its planes could be launched in a coordinated fashion with planes from the *Ticonderoga*. In the meantime, additional planes had to be flown from the Philippines to augment the *Ticonderoga*. There was so much clutter on the *Ticonderoga*'s flight deck that some planes had to be launched to circle overhead to make room for the arriving aircraft. The planes could not leave for their targets right away, lest they arrived ahead of those from the *Constellation*. The plan was to have the planes from both carriers rendezvous at the target for a coordinated attack. Meanwhile, McNamara kept calling CINCPAC, demanding to know if the planes were in the air so that the president could speak to the nation. There was a misunderstanding: CINCPAC replied that planes were circling for the start of the actual attack. But the Secretary of Defense mistook the message and informed the president that the attack had begun. Johnson finally spoke to the nation a few minutes after 11:00 p.m., U.S. eastern time.

Unfortunately, the presidential announcement came in advance of the attack, giving the North Vietnamese full knowledge of the impending strike. Hanoi had already been alerted preliminarily: Senator Barry Goldwater, who had spoken with Johnson, did not get the signals quite straight and prematurely made his own announcement of backing for the president's intended actions at 10:00 p.m. One would have thought that the White House's full attention would be focused on a major escalation in the war. As it happened, however, the FBI sent word early in the evening that the bodies of three slain civil rights workers had been uncovered in a shallow grave in Georgia, a shocking development that sent presidential aides and reporters scrambling.

The U.S. attack finally took place during the lunch hour, Vietnam time, on August 5. North Vietnamese antiaircraft crews had been ready and waiting for several hours, then relaxed slightly and had lunch, at which point the U.S. planes suddenly appeared. Postattack assessments by Hanoi depicted this timing as a particular piece of American trickery: The Americans first announced that an attack was in progress. Then, when nothing happened, they tried to lull the defenders, perhaps by creating the impression that they were bluffing. The U.S. planes then suddenly and cruelly struck, so as to achieve maximum psychological impact. The North Vietnamese would not have believed the truth if their intelligence agents had told them that President Johnson had been given wrong information and made his announcement prematurely, that the U.S. attack had been delayed by a last-minute change to narrow the target list, and that the change was delayed by the need to allow time for the planes from one carrier to catch up with planes from another so that they could coordinate their arrival time at the target. Two U.S. planes from the carrier *Constellation* were shot down. One pilot, Lt. (j.g.) Richard C. Sather, was killed and the other, Lt. (j.g.) Everett Alvarez, ejected and parachuted into the shallow coastal waters of the Gulf and was captured, becoming the first American pilot prisoner of war in Vietnam.[17]

THE CONGRESSIONAL RESOLUTION

Lyndon Johnson had rejected the proposal earlier in the summer that he seek broad congressional authority to act in Vietnam. He was concerned that in seeking such authority, he would look bellicose and create the impression that he intended to escalate the war. He assumed that he had enough authority to act under Article 2 of the Constitution and Article 4 of the Southeast Asia Treaty Organization to act in a crisis.

Now, however, he was faced with a different situation. The United States had been attacked without provocation, despite a warning from the president. The public and the congressional leaders were aroused and wanted retaliation.[18]

On August 5, the president sent a message to Congress asking for a joint resolution to authorize such actions as he might take to protect the peace and to resist communist aggression in Southeast Asia. Johnson gave the impression that the Congress would supply the language of the resolution, but the wording was actually negotiated between presidential aides and congressional leaders, drawing mostly on a draft William Bundy had prepared for a June NSC meeting.

While Johnson seized this opportunity to gain congressional support to neutralize Goldwater's attacks on his Vietnam policy, there was no calculated plan to use the congressional resolution later to escalate the war. Johnson was certainly trying to keep Vietnam quiet before the election. When a third incident occurred in late September involving U.S. destroyers in the Tonkin Gulf, LBJ reacted by suspending all 34A operations and DeSoto patrols. When the insurgents attacked the U.S. air base at Bien Hoa on November 1, killing four Americans and wounding others, the president did not retaliate. Johnson's calculus did not change in the election's aftermath. His commanders and other advisers, many of whom wanted LBJ to signal a willingness to act more forcefully in Vietnam, got from him the same equivocations they had received before the election.

The Joint Chiefs of Staff and the Seventh Fleet commanders were surprised at nearly every turn in the Tonkin fracas. Their actions had been more improvisational than conspiratorial. Right after Congress passed the joint resolution, the Joint Chiefs sent a cable to Ambassador Taylor, asking for his support for a campaign of continuous bombing of North Vietnam, which they wanted to propose to McNamara and the president. It was ironic that Maxwell Taylor, the critic of Eisenhower's New Look strategy and the advocate of conventional infantry and Special Forces whose book, *The Uncertain Trumpet,* had so appealed to John Kennedy, was by 1964 an advocate of strategic air power and bombing.

The Joint Chiefs made the argument that the United States, after flexing its muscles in the Tonkin crisis, should follow up with a bombing campaign and the use of the Navy's big guns on Hanoi's coastal bases. The United States would look weak and vacillating if the Tonkin reprisal were not followed up. Taylor, while agreeing in principle with his former colleagues on the potential usefulness of bombing, cautioned that no bombing campaign could take place until the Khanh government had achieved a more stable position. Once the Saigon government achieved greater stability, he would recommend continuous bombing to the president.

There was a catch-22 in Taylor's position: If the Saigon government were to become stable enough to sustain a bombing campaign, there would be no need for the campaign, since the aim of the bombing was to strengthen the Saigon government. To the consternation of the Joint Chiefs, nothing was done after Tonkin to capitalize on the U.S. show of force and to enhance America's power to deter communist aggression throughout Southeast Asia.

Johnson, McNamara, and Rusk were not candid in explaining to Congress what had happened and why they had responded as they did. McNamara, in testimony before the joint meeting of the Senate Foreign Relations and Armed Services Committees, denied unequivocally (and falsely), in response to a question from Senator Wayne Morse, that there had been any covert South Vietnamese operations at the time in the Gulf of Tonkin that might have led to either the first or the second North Vietnamese attack. After his testimony, McNamara telephoned the president and said that only Morse questioned the explanation. Morse pressed McNamara, asking how we could credibly claim that the United States had nothing to do with South Vietnamese attacks on North Vietnamese bases. McNamara assured the president, "I finally shut him up."[19]

Tom Hughes asked his friend Carl Marcy, the longtime chief clerk of the Senate Foreign Relations Committee, for an assessment of McNamara's testimony. Marcy reported that McNamara read from a prepared statement to begin with and seemed persuasive to most of the senators. However, he lost his footing when the questions began. He did not have a clear grasp of the military ordnance, the radar operations, fire control systems of the destroyers, and other military technicalities. As usually happened with McNamara and other policymakers, Marcy said, career Pentagon officials called to "revise" and "clarify" the testimony. Pentagon officials had called within an hour of McNamara's testimony with a list of revisions. Marcy inferred that some of the Pentagon anxiety might have reflected a desire to protect sensitive classified information. But McNamara could have asked for an executive session if that were a concern, and he had not.

Senator J. William Fulbright, chair of the Foreign Relations Committee, agreed to sponsor the Gulf of Tonkin resolution in the Senate. Joint Resolution 1145, Public Law 88-408, was adopted on August 7 with only two nay votes in the Senate, from Senators Morse (D-Ore.) and Ernest Gruening (R-Alas.). The House of Representatives adopted the resolution unanimously. The resolution declared that "to promote . . . international peace and security in Southeast Asia," the Congress hereby "approves and supports . . . the President, as Commander in Chief, to take all necessary measures to repel any attack against the forces of the United States and to prevent further aggression."

This apparently sweeping authorization was later interpreted by Vietnam hawks to mean that the president did not need to return to Congress to seek approval for future escalatory steps. Johnson joked to associates that the resolution was "like Grandma's nightshirt—it covered everything." But this was certainly not the way the administration sold the idea to the Congress, nor the way the senators and the representatives understood the vote. Senator Fulbright, in introducing the resolution, told his colleagues that everything he had heard indicated that President Johnson did not intend to use the resolution as a blanket authorization for the use of force and that the resolution certainly should not be construed as a declaration of war.

A call-up of the reserves and new appropriations would be required in the event of major action in Vietnam. Thus Congress would have to be consulted and would have to vote specifically to approve those measures. Administration spokespersons made this argument to anyone who feared that the resolution would give the president too much authority.

In the House of Representatives, members explicitly understood that the resolution was not a blanket authorization for all future presidential actions. Thomas Morgan, chair of the House Committee on Foreign Affairs, asserted that the resolution was "definitely not an advance declaration of war. The Committee has been assured by the Secretary of State that the constitutional power of the Congress in this respect will continue to be scrupulously observed."[20]

For LBJ, who had demonstrated firmness and had received Congress's blessing on his retaliatory strike, the outcome of the Tonkin crisis was more favorable than he could have imagined. He could now focus on the campaign. The doves and the hawks were agreed for the moment on the administration's Vietnam policy. The problem was his old friend Hubert. The dammed fool could not keep his mouth shut. He was leaking classified information all over the place.

For Tom Hughes, the outcome of the Tonkin crisis also seemed fortunate, but he had reservations. Intelligence, it seemed, had a hard time catching up to the pace of events. By the time the INR and some voices in CIA had concluded that the second Tonkin incident in all likelihood had not really happened, the president and his top advisers, under pressure from Congress, had already decided to retaliate. That McNamara was handling the response on the second incident, and not Rusk, ensured that military action was more likely. Once the retaliation had been decided, there was no incentive to revisit the issue and to declare that, in retrospect, we had made a mistake.

The fact-finding missions that both Kennedy and Johnson favored were supposed to represent a kind of intelligence. Firsthand information was ostensibly gathered and subsequently weighed in decisionmaking. But to Hughes, the missions were more pageantry than the gathering of facts, and both presidents usually ratified the conclusions that had been reached in advance of the trip.

The Tonkin Gulf mission seemingly resolved, Democrats turned to other business: preparing for the 1964 general election. Tom had no inkling of the trouble he had inadvertently caused Hubert Humphrey by briefing him on the first Gulf of Tonkin incident.

13

The 1964 Vice Presidency

Tom Hughes was convinced that there had not been a second Tonkin attack. The truth would be established sooner or later, but for now the matter would rest without a clear resolution. Events had overtaken the controversy. Hanoi must have been puzzled by the American engagement in an elaborate charade only to bomb a few coastal targets. The Johnson administration, fortunately, was not receptive to the JCS's proposals to extend the bombing.

Hughes naturally also thought about the campaign and especially about Humphrey's chances. When would LBJ choose? Tom, of course, wanted Hubert to be nominated and believed Hubert's chances were good. But what LBJ would do was never certain. Johnson's behavior toward Humphrey had been erratic. At times, he almost seemed bent on torturing his old Senate comrade.

Hughes was in touch regularly with Humphrey and the staff. He had met with Max Kampelman in December 1963 to help launch the campaign. Jim Rowe and others were already canvassing party leaders around the country by January for support for Hubert.

When Dean Rusk asked Tom for his opinion on the respective merits of his fellow Minnesotans, Humphrey and Gene McCarthy, Hughes voiced his strong preference for Humphrey. That was good enough for Rusk, who said he would back Humphrey. Rusk told Tom to brief Humphrey regularly on foreign policy. When Humphrey was nominated, Tom would become the official State Department briefer. Tom would probably have to brief Senator Goldwater, as well. Rusk asked if Hughes was on good terms with Goldwater. Tom said that they were on friendly terms through the Air

Force ROTC unit that the senator commanded. But Tom supposed that the senator would probably want his briefings from his good friend General Curtis LeMay, the commander of the Strategic Air Command.

Hughes had seen the Johnson-Humphrey relationship up close in his old Senate days. Years later, he recorded his impressions of the complex partnership. In the early years, Hubert was one of those who "endured the famous LBJ treatment successfully." Although "Johnson's towering ego and self-pity were already on display . . . Humphrey watched with fascination and even admiration as Lyndon worked his magic. . . . Hubert even acknowledged his own good-humored acquiescence as he watched himself being conned by LBJ."[1]

While there were highs and lows in the partnership, Hughes believed that it had benefited both men. Hubert got key committee assignments and the general support of the majority leader. Johnson got Hubert's contacts with the northern party liberals and his indefatigable work habits.

Humphrey perceived early signals of LBJ's intentions for the vice presidency. Johnson had encouraged Hubert in January to make soundings and to begin rounding up support for the nomination. But Johnson enjoyed the cat-and-mouse game. He dropped hints that a Catholic might be good for the ticket, apparently for no reason other than to worry Hubert.

Humphrey had some understanding of how badly the Kennedy people had treated Lyndon when he was vice president. He attributed Johnson's brusque tactics partly to that painful experience. The delicate question of Bobby Kennedy was a legitimate worry for Humphrey and his supporters. Kennedy was Catholic, but the Kennedy candidacy was, of course, far more complex than the question of his religion.

Lyndon Johnson did not nominate anyone for vice president right after JFK's assassination. The Kennedy forces would have made a strong case for Bobby. Johnson deferred the choice to the convention. The country could live with the remote prospect that the elderly House Speaker John McCormack would be next in line for the presidency in the event of LBJ's death or disability.

Humphrey's supporters knew that LBJ would never go for Bobby Kennedy as his running mate under normal circumstances. But they were not quite sure how Lyndon viewed the matter at any given time. It was not entirely out of the question that LBJ might make Kennedy vice president to torment him or at least to keep an eye on him.

Johnson and Kennedy hated and distrusted each other, but they had to transcend in the country's interest or, at least, to hide their mutual antipathy. Johnson wanted to exclude the attorney general from consideration for the vice presidency but without appearing vindictive. Johnson agonized over how to break the bad news to Kennedy. He consulted with Mac Bundy, Clark Clifford, Bob McNamara, and Kenny O'Donnell before he finally called Kennedy for a White House tête-à-tête on Thursday afternoon, July 30.

Both men were on their best behavior for the meeting. The president reined himself in, told Kennedy of his determination to pass JFK's major domestic bills in this congressional session, and asked RFK to manage the presidential campaign in the fall. The president then politely but firmly told RFK that he would not be the vice presidential nominee. The president said that he would exclude from consideration all members of the cabinet and others in high-level executive branch positions.

Kennedy took the news with apparent calm. He asked if Johnson had made a choice. Johnson said no, he had not (having decided beforehand that he would not reveal his thinking, to prevent Bobby from leaking the news or trying to undermine the choice).

Johnson offered to let Bobby make the announcement of their meeting. Kennedy promised to give the matter some thought and let Johnson know his views. Bobby did not get back to LBJ, who waited until noon the next day. Johnson then called in Kenny O'Donnell to find out RFK's thinking. O'Donnell told Johnson that RFK thought it would be arrogant for him to say anything or to pretend that he had withdrawn his name from consideration. The president should handle the announcement any way he pleased.

Johnson decided that the way to announce his decision was to tell the nation that he would not choose "any member of the cabinet or any of those who meet regularly with the cabinet," specifically mentioning Dean Rusk, Robert McNamara, Robert Kennedy, Secretary of Agriculture Orville Freeman, Adlai Stevenson, and Sargent Shriver.

Before he went on television to make the announcement, Johnson phoned McNamara and Rusk to tell them of his decision. Both men, who had no expectations of being chosen, took the news lightly and in good humor. Rusk, in a witticism that drew laughs from Tom Hughes and other State colleagues, declared that he was "sorry to have taken so many good men down with me."

Johnson placed another call before going on the air, one to Jim Rowe. He wanted Rowe to tell Humphrey that he was leaning toward Hubert but wanted also to express his concerns over loyalty:

> *LBJ*: Now listen, we've got to decide between a good many people yet, but I want to have a good set-to with this good man from Minnesota. . . . I want to be sure that they understand that ain't gonna be nobody running against me for eight years, and gonna be following my platform, and gonna be supporting me and gonna be as loyal to me like I was to Kennedy.
>
> *Rowe*: I don't think you'd have a bit of a problem on Hubert.
>
> *LBJ*: . . . I want him to understand that he is to be loyal to me as long as I'm in that office or running for it. That means no campaigning against me and no disagreeing with me publicly and no going off

and growling like Chester Bowles did on the Bay of Pigs. I'm willing to listen to him and always willing to consider what he's got to say. But when I make up my mind, I don't want to have to kiss the ass of a Vice President. . . . If he don't want to be my wife, he oughtn't to marry me.[2]

Johnson received a call from Humphrey shortly after the broadcast. Humphrey pledged his loyalty in ringing terms: "Now, Mr. President . . . I want to come right to the point. If your judgment leads you to select me, I can assure you—unqualifiedly, personally, and with all the sincerity in my heart—complete loyalty. I just want you to know it. And that goes for everything. All the way. The way you want right to the end of the line."[3]

In those old Senate days, a degree of parity existed between Johnson and Humphrey. Both men were United States senators. Each had one vote in the Senate and a constituency to serve. A degree of reciprocity was always present between members of this revered institution.

Lyndon Johnson was now president. He was not majority leader of a body of lawmakers who enjoyed similar privileges of office. Humphrey would make a grave mistake if he reverted back to the old days and regarded Lyndon as he had then, as a colleague and fellow senator.

There was a hint of trouble in December 1963, when Humphrey opposed LBJ's first State Department appointment. Johnson retained virtually the entire Kennedy foreign policy team when he became president. However, he felt that as a Texan he knew Mexico and thus knew something about Latin America as a whole. Furthermore, Johnson also had views about what was wrong with the Alliance for Progress.[4]

Johnson therefore appointed Thomas C. Mann as assistant secretary of state, as coordinator of the Alliance for Progress, and as presidential adviser on inter-American affairs. This gave Mann powers that John Kennedy had been unwilling to give Adolph Berle at the start of his administration. Mann enjoyed the combined powers of Ted Moscoso as Alliance coordinator, Ed Martin as assistant secretary, and Dick Goodwin as the White House staffer dealing with Latin America.

This alone would have caused resentment in the Kennedy people, but Mann in their eyes was also a dangerous reactionary. He threatened to undermine Kennedy's progressive policies for Latin America. Mann was not an intimate friend of Johnson's but was a fellow Texan and a lawyer with considerable experience representing business clients. He had served during World War II and in the Truman administration in a number of important Foreign Service positions.

Humphrey was persuaded by his staff that Mann would undermine the Alliance for Progress. Hubert made an appointment with his old friend Lyndon to warn him about Tom Mann and persuade him, if possible, to drop the appointment. This was a fool's errand. Johnson would never back off from this appointment, since it was his first independent move in foreign policy.

When Humphrey showed up at the White House, Johnson called in Mann from the next room and seated him on the sofa with Humphrey. As the two men sat in an apparently friendly pose on the sofa, LBJ summoned the White House photographer to record the scene. The White House put out the story that Hubert was Mann's chief sponsor in the Senate. The incident blew over with no apparent damage. Hubert accepted that he had once again been outmaneuvered by his old friend.

Their successful collaboration on the civil rights bill in the summer of 1964 apparently restored Humphrey to LBJ's good graces. Johnson's support for Humphrey as the vice presidential nominee seemed solid. However, the Gulf of Tonkin episode strangely and unpredictably complicated the picture.

Hughes had started briefing Humphrey, since Rusk had encouraged him to do so. On the morning of August 2, Tom hurried from the White House meeting with LBJ to the CBS studio to brief Hubert before his appearance on the *Issues and Answers* Sunday morning talk show. He wanted Humphrey to be informed in case the Tonkin incident came up in the interview. Hubert did field a question from Martin Agronsky on the subject and handled it deftly, in Tom's estimation. Humphrey restricted himself to the bare facts: Reports had come in that a U.S. warship had been attacked in international waters by several North Vietnamese torpedo boats and had repulsed the attack with no American casualties. There was nothing remotely inappropriate or provocative in Humphrey's answer. Yet somehow, in the rush of events at the time, Johnson had got things skewed.

Based on Hubert's highly publicized visit to Moscow in December 1958 and his famous eight-hour conversation with the Soviet premier, LBJ suspected that Humphrey might have secret contacts with Khrushchev. Johnson also became convinced that Humphrey had leaked classified information to Senator Wayne Morse, who had then used it to oppose the administration on the Gulf of Tonkin resolution.

In fact, Humphrey had fought hard to get the resolution passed. Nonetheless, in a telephone call with Jim Rowe, Johnson raged that "our friend Hubert is just destroying himself with his big mouth . . . and he just ought to keep his goddamned big mouth shut on foreign affairs at least until the election is over."[5]

Johnson accused Humphrey of revealing that the United States was conducting covert operations against North Vietnamese coast bases at the time of Hanoi's attacks on the U.S. destroyers. The North Vietnamese were thus probably retaliating against the South's covert operations. The covert operations, the president told Rowe, were exactly what we were doing, but Hubert should never have said so.

Johnson said that Humphrey was blabbing to the media about what the communists were thinking and was contradicting what McNamara and Rusk were telling Congress. Hubert was pretending that ideas he had heard in briefings were really his own. Hubert, said the president, should start saying "I don't know" when asked questions by reporters. Better yet, Hubert should drop the "I" from his vocabulary altogether. Just say, "don't know." Instead, "he just yak yak yak . . . just dancing around. . . . That can ruin a man mighty quick."[6]

The president concluded his conversation with Rowe by warning that he would "have lots of talks before I agree on who I'm going to recommend [for vice president]." He thus appeared to walk back his endorsement of Humphrey.

Hughes was depressed when he learned of Humphrey's new troubles with LBJ. Tom was worried for his friend and appalled by Johnson's paranoia. He felt that Johnson, though a man of incredible force and a political genius, had a dark side. This dark side, perhaps related to LBJ's hardscrabble upbringing, could erupt at any time and lay waste to his surroundings like a volcano.

Johnson had referred to marriage in the loyalty oath he demanded from Hubert. Hubert had made a declaration of loyalty that could not have been stronger. But that evidently was not enough. The Johnson-Humphrey marriage was tumultuous, to be sure. The president calmed down but never quite acknowledged or explained his anger toward Humphrey over Tonkin. As to the convention, LBJ continued to milk all the drama he could out of delaying the vice presidential announcement. Humphrey was in a state of constant torment. He believed that he would be the nominee, but there was nothing he could do to rush the process or to relieve his anxieties.

The process took on a near theatrical aspect when LBJ brought in Humphrey's Minnesota Senate colleague, Eugene McCarthy, as a candidate. McCarthy, though wary of LBJ's tricks, played along with the game for several weeks, evidently half believing or wanting to believe that the president was sincere in dangling the prospect of the vice presidency. McCarthy believed that LBJ had always resented Hubert's gift of gab and that Hubert probably was incapable of restraining his natural ebullience. McCarthy finally recognized he was being played and dropped out almost on the eve of the convention.

Humphrey, meanwhile, was miserable. This was anything but the politics of joy for which the normally upbeat Humphrey was known. Even with McCarthy's withdrawal, the drama was not yet done. President Johnson now persuaded Senator Thomas Dodd of Connecticut that he was in the running for the nomination.

On August 24, the day the convention opened in Atlantic City, LBJ summoned both Dodd and Humphrey to fly back to Washington for final interviews, which would lead to one of them being chosen. Humphrey blew up when he heard about this move. He told Jim Rowe that he would refuse to participate in such a farce. Rowe calmed down the irate Humphrey and told him that this was the last bit of Johnsonian drama. The president had told Rowe that Hubert was not to worry.

When Humphrey and Dodd finally arrived in Washington, they were met by Jack Valenti with a limo. They were told that they would have to drive around Washington for an hour or two until Lady Bird's arrival at the convention had been covered on TV. When they finally arrived at the White House, Dodd was the first to be interviewed. Hubert fell asleep in the limousine and was awakened by a tapping on the window. He was ushered into the Fish Room adjacent to the Oval Office. The president then brought him to the Cabinet Room and told him that he was the nominee.

Johnson secretly taped the conversation. He assured Hubert that he had been the nominee all along and repeated his insistence on loyalty. He repeated that they would be like a married couple, and that there would be no possibility of divorce. Humphrey reaffirmed his loyalty oath. Johnson told Humphrey that he was "goddamned dumb" if he had not realized a month ago that he was the choice. Hubert was told that he could not make the announcement himself. For now, he was to tell only Muriel. Mercifully, Hubert did not have to wait long. The announcement came the next day, just as Hubert was commenting, in a radio interview, that he could neither deny nor confirm having been chosen.

Hughes attended the convention in Atlantic City officially as Humphrey's intelligence briefer. Tom temporarily resumed his old Senate role as Humphrey's chief adviser. Hughes quickly found himself in a replay of the 1957 battle over civil rights that he had fought in the Senate. The convention was torn by a civil rights dispute over the seating of the Mississippi Freedom Party delegation. The Freedom Party was a group of Black activists who demanded to be seated as the official Mississippi delegation instead of the slate of regulars chosen by the Mississippi Democrats. Johnson assigned Hubert, along with labor leader Walter Reuther, to negotiate a solution. This proved to be almost as challenging as passing the civil rights bill had been earlier that summer. Hughes participated in the compromise that seated the regulars but granted concessions to the Freedom Party.

Hughes also helped to write Humphrey's acceptance speech.[7] Humphrey did not like the draft his staff had prepared and asked Tom, his favorite wordsmith during his Senate years, to redraft the speech. Tom wrote a speech that portrayed the election as a contest between "the party of hope and the party of memory," which was how Ralph Waldo Emerson had described America's political parties. The *New York Times* later praised the speech in a year-end editorial as the best speech of the 1964 campaign.[8]

Humphrey had a daunting task when he faced the convention after

Bobby Kennedy's emotional tribute to his brother, which profoundly moved the delegates. Hubert opened with his own tribute to the fallen John Kennedy and praised President Johnson's leadership in rallying the nation after JFK's death. Humphrey cast LBJ as the champion of forward-looking policies such as the nuclear test-ban treaty, tax cuts, civil rights, poverty programs, aid to education, and UN peacekeeping efforts.

Goldwater, in contrast, was "facing backwards against American history." Most Democrats and Republicans supported and voted for progressive policies, "but not Senator Goldwater." The audience quickly picked up the refrain "but not Senator Goldwater" and repeated it in thunderous tones as Humphrey cited each important Senate vote on which Goldwater had voted nay.

Johnson's own acceptance speech, which followed, was anticlimactic. Johnson had asked his speechwriters for an address like Franklin Roosevelt's first inaugural, but the delegates, after the emotional RFK tribute to his brother and Humphrey's stirring ovation, sat listlessly and politely applauded. The president's speech had "neither vitality nor a memorable phrase and left television viewers in their late-night lethargy."[9]

THE 1964 ELECTION

Hubert Humphrey, with his buoyant personality, played an important role in the campaign. He crisscrossed the country and was virtually a nonstop speechmaking machine. In contrast, LBJ followed the model of the president carrying on duties as usual in a manner fitting a political leader. In a major campaign appearance reminiscent of FDR in 1940, President Johnson promised the country that young Americans were not going to be sent abroad to fight the wars that Asian boys should be fighting.

When it came to foreign policy, a subject he touched on sparingly, Hubert Humphrey noted that Senator Goldwater was reckless and a threat to peace, whereas Johnson's steady leadership would keep the peace. As the chances of a big victory grew likely in the late stages of the campaign, the old Johnson-Humphrey partnership reemerged, and the friendship between them seemed to be stronger than ever. The overwhelming triumph of the Johnson-Humphrey ticket in November 1964 created an expectant atmosphere in Washington.

On December 3, 1964, Tom Hughes delivered a speech in which he discussed the astonishing number of fifty new governments in the world, "A New Year of New Governments." "Most of the world," he noted, "lives in Asia, is colored, is poor, is ill-fed, is sick, is illiterate, lacks freedom, is proud, fears war, is neutral."[10] The governments of these countries, and many new governments among the industrialized nations, were struggling to define their identities and roles in the turbulent new world, which seemed to suffer from the loss of fixed principles and values. North-South economic relations, East-West tensions, communism, and ideological conflicts challenged established patterns everywhere. Countries with new governments were looking to the United States for leadership.

"The new administration in Washington with its strong majorities," Hughes concluded, "will not sit idly by. Historic opportunities are there to be seized. Presidential power and public support are there to be used. . . . The time is propitious for review and reconsideration."[11]

Tom used the speech to make the point that the new Johnson government was free to pursue new priorities. Indeed, the administration had a historic opportunity to achieve in foreign policy what the Great Society was achieving at home. It was understood that "review and reconsideration" would include Vietnam policy.

Hubert Humphrey read the speech and liked it, as did many other government officials, politicians, and journalists. The speech caught the spirit of a new beginning. Like Humphrey and Hughes, doves wanted to move toward negotiations in Vietnam. However, they were confronted by hawks calling for a harder line.

The issue of bombing North Vietnam after the Gulf of Tonkin was a principal point of contention. The bombing proposal was the darling of the Joint Chiefs. They pursued it with gusto, seeking to line up supporters all along the policy food chain until the president was finally persuaded. Their first step misfired. They assumed that their former chair, General Maxwell Taylor, ambassador to South Vietnam, would be the ideal supporter.

Taylor surprised them. He agreed with the JCS that bombing was a good idea in theory, but it had a fatal flaw in practice. The Saigon government was too unstable to support a bombing campaign. Once it had become more stable, then bombing the North could be considered. But if the Khanh-led junta or any Saigon government ever became stable, the rationale for the bombing would disappear, since its point was to raise the morale and the stability of whatever Saigon government could be patched together.

The Joint Chiefs were undaunted. They continued their campaign to sell the idea of bombing North Vietnam. Johnson complained to reporters that "every morning the military leaders come to me and say 'bomb, bomb, bomb, and bomb!' and then in the afternoon they come back and say the same thing."[12]

The INR under Hughes produced intelligence that questioned the effectiveness of bombing. The bureau studies pointed to Chinese and Russian suppliers as Hanoi's de facto industrial base. Furthermore, Hanoi had demonstrated the ability to reconstitute bridges and supply routes after bombing raids. It had also received antiaircraft systems from the Soviet Union and from China, along with the trained personnel to operate them.

China was also building a new air base on its North Vietnam border—an indication that Chinese planes might become involved in Hanoi's air war.

Hughes knew that a major Vietnam policy review was underway. The hawks appeared to be in charge and expected the president to be receptive to their proposals for a strengthened military posture in Vietnam. Hughes knew that LBJ did not like to be predictable. He gave the impression of being sympathetic to the importuning of his commanders, but in the end, the president's decisions were guided by political calculations. Johnson had made no commitment to escalate the war after the election.

Johnson's initial decisions on Vietnam merely maintained Kennedy's policies, which were ambiguous. The March NSAM 288 was not a harbinger of an Americanized Vietnam conflict. It called on Saigon to institute a draft and promised only more American equipment. The June Honolulu Conference called for more public relations and ruled out U.S. bombing of North Vietnam or asking Congress for enhanced war powers. Johnson's actions in the Tonkin Gulf crisis were cautious. He authorized the retaliatory strike reluctantly and only after Congress had been told that a second attack had occurred.

In late September, there were two more Tonkin Gulf episodes, but the U.S. Navy by this time was aware of the problem of radar "ghosts" in those waters. Rather than risk new incidents, Johnson called off both the 34A operations and the DeSoto patrols.

Fred Greene, of Tom Hughes's INR staff, told him in October that studying radio broadcasts had convinced him that Hanoi would probably attack U.S. forces at the Bien Hoa air base in the northern part of South Vietnam in retaliation for the August 5 U.S. bombing of North Vietnam's coastal bases. Hughes told Greene to warn the Pentagon of his assessment. Greene did so, but the JCS took no action. They deemed it unnecessary to pass the warning on to the field commander. The field commander was a competent officer, and he knew what he was doing. It would be presumptuous for headquarters (let alone a civilian) to tell a field commander his business.

The retaliatory attack by Hanoi took place on November 1, close to the day that Fred Geene had predicted. The attack killed four Americans and two South Vietnamese and completely destroyed five B-57s and damaged eight others. Johnson authorized the Joint Chiefs to replace the destroyed and damaged planes but refused their request for a U.S. retaliatory strike. Instead, Air Marshall Ky, of the ARVN air force, led a reprisal attack that maintained the notion that the United States was in Vietnam to assist South Vietnam to defend itself against aggression.

Hughes was well aware that President Johnson was in touch with Mike Mansfield, Dick Russell, Frank Church, Bill Fulbright, and other former Senate colleagues who were opposed to deeper American involvement in the war. Johnson wanted to keep them from going public with their opposition before the election but also after the election. Mansfield had sent Johnson more than twenty memos criticizing America's role in Vietnam but never said a word to the press. Senator Wayne Morse's criticisms could be brushed off, since he was the only Democratic senator publicly critical of the war. The Republicans were generally supportive of the war. They would attack him only if there were signs of the administration's weakness.

The outcome of the new policy review, Tom Hughes thought, might include a continuation of Rusk's passive course—that is, neither escalating nor withdrawing from the conflict. Hubert Humphrey's presence as vice president was certainly a positive development. Humphrey's addition to the dove camp could strengthen the position of George Ball, keep Dean Rusk from moving firmly into the escalation camp, and potentially rekindle Bill Bundy's dovish tendencies. It would all depend on the president's thinking. If Johnson moved toward escalation, Rusk would move off his current stance and line up with the president. Contingencies could sway the president either way. The situation was fluid. No outcome was foreordained.

Humphrey's role was bound to be important. Yet Hughes had a certain sense of foreboding. The New Frontier had had its oddities, but so did Johnson's presidency as it took shape. Ever the observer and recordkeeper, Hughes made the following observation in his notes: "Just as Mac Bundy is the one-ups man intellectually, LBJ is the one-ups man politically. He is THE political expert, tolerates no political suggestions from others. He constantly deflects serious conversation and the weighing of serious issues by bringing his advisers up short with lightning and thunder. These are determinative. Decisive. Everything is politics, and no amateur politician is going to question the master professional. Must warn HHH."[13]

But Tom did not warn or express his reservations to Hubert. Humphrey was busy and enthusiastic about his role in the administration. There were hopeful signs, it seemed, or at least Tom hoped, for an active Humphrey vice presidency. This was a time for renewal, using the strong majorities and the strong public support that the election signified.

14

The Humphrey-Hughes Memo

Humphrey's selection as the Democratic vice presidential nominee naturally delighted Tom Hughes. The election and the reconciliation between Humphrey and Johnson were even more pleasing. Aside from how it might affect his own career, the prospect of Hubert as vice president raised Tom's hopes for a shift in Vietnam strategy. Hughes's briefings had kept Humphrey up to date on Vietnam and other foreign policy issues. Humphrey still had been cautious in saying anything on Vietnam or foreign policy generally in the campaign, beyond attacking Goldwater and praising Johnson.

Humphrey attacked Goldwater on farm policy in the South and the Midwest and on civil rights in campaigning with Bobby Kennedy in New York. When Hubert did touch on foreign policy, it was to portray Goldwater as a reckless warmonger. The Republican nominee, Humphrey charged, was an extremist, a man outside the mainstream of America's bipartisan foreign policy. This was a safe position and led naturally to the portrayal of the president as the man who would keep the peace.

Hubert carried the brunt of the campaigning and contributed significantly to the victory in six midwestern states that Kennedy had lost in 1960. He helped Bobby Kennedy eke out a narrow win in the Senate race in New York against the moderate Republican Kenneth Keating. Hubert even performed well in the South, striking a conciliatory tone on civil rights without compromising his principles. He deftly dodged difficult questions on the oil depletion allowance in Texas, telling an audience of oil millionaires that he would defer to the greatest friend of energy of all, his and their great friend, President Lyndon Johnson. One admiring Texan remarked that Hubert handled more tough questions than Pee Wee Reese of the Brooklyn Dodgers handled ground balls.

The magnitude of the victory was overwhelming. The Johnson-Humphrey ticket swept forty-four states and lost only five Deep South states and, by a small margin, Goldwater's home state of Arizona. The ticket captured an overwhelming share of the electoral vote and compiled the largest winning popular vote ever: 41,129,484 to Goldwater's 27,178,188 votes.[1]

Hubert Humphrey had been the Happy Warrior once again. But Tom Hughes wondered how the Tonkin Gulf misunderstanding with Johnson had affected Hubert. Although the president had been in the wrong, Humphrey was careful to avoid any action or statement that could give offense. The lesson was that Hubert had to be extra cautious during the campaign. But the election was now over, and since then, Hubert's working relationship with Lyndon Johnson had been excellent. Personal relations with LBJ were now better than ever. Or so it seemed to Hubert.

As a sign of their renewed friendship, LBJ invited Hubert and Muriel Humphrey to the ranch to celebrate right after the election. The trip proved to be anything but relaxing for Humphrey. Johnson's intensity was such that Hubert thought the plane could probably run on the president's energy alone. At the ranch, LBJ controlled everything from the menus to the conversations to the day's recreation.

Hubert good-naturedly donned an over-sized cowboy hat for photographers and rode a horse, while hanging onto the saddle horn for dear life. To his distress, he was forced to shoot two deer. Johnson insisted that Hubert outdo Bobby Kennedy, who had shot only one during a visit to the ranch. Johnson drove Humphrey on heart-stopping ninety-mile-an-hour rides around the ranch. In the main, however, Hubert was elated and felt that he and Lyndon had returned to the harmonious days of their Senate partnership.

Nevertheless, where Humphrey stood on the Vietnam issue was clear. He was a critic of the war, sharing the views of Fulbright, Church, Russell, Mansfield, and other Democratic senators who thought the United States should negotiate a settlement and get out. Solving Vietnam was perhaps even more important to Humphrey than to his Senate colleagues. He would be running again in 1968 on the ticket with Lyndon or as Lyndon's successor, should Johnson not run again. Hubert wanted Vietnam to be over and forgotten.

Hughes's briefings had only strengthened Hubert's doubts about Vietnam. In December 1964, Hubert sent a congratulatory note to Senator Frank Church for his sharp critique of the administration's Vietnam policy. Although he was obviously unwilling to go public with any criticisms of his own, Humphrey risked writing to Church to show how deeply he shared Church's doubts about the war.[2]

TRANSITION PLANNING

Humphrey and Hughes resumed their regular contacts once Humphrey returned to Washington from the ranch. A small White House task force, chaired by Bill Bundy of State and John McNaughton of Defense, had begun meeting on November 1 to prepare recommendations on Vietnam for the president. The State Department was represented by Bundy and Mike Forrestal of Rusk's office.[3]

George Carver and Harold Ford, of the CIA, represented the intelligence community. Hughes and the INR were not part of the task force. The task force's deliberations and recommendations were tightly held on a need-to-know basis. From what he was able to learn, Hughes was concerned that there was a bias toward escalation in the way the task force was formulating the options.

Hughes recalled that he and Humphrey began meeting regularly in November after the election to discuss the transition at the State Department. They reviewed the roster of current ambassadors, the openings in senior positions, and potential reorganizations. After getting an unenthusiastic report from Hughes on a current political appointee in a somewhat obscure post, Hughes remembered Humphrey saying, "Well, we'll leave him where his is. He can't do any damage there."

Humphrey's knowledge of the State Department was surprising. Hubert had been given the president's blessing to focus his energies on State Department organization and policy in general. The focus of many conversations, however, was the problem of Vietnam.

Tom Hughes met with Mac Bundy about the level of classification for Humphrey's briefings in the period before he was sworn in as vice president. Tom had discussed the issue briefly with Rusk, and Rusk told him to see Mac Bundy. Rusk was concerned that Humphrey might build up a large foreign policy staff, which could cause problems for the State Department. Rusk preferred that Tom continue as Humphrey's main source of information on foreign policy.

Bundy's instructions generally favored Humphrey's being told almost everything, but there were some exceptions. Tom assumed from what Bundy said that the president had given thought to Hubert's interim status and had set some guidelines. Johnson had apparently made suggestions that were generous toward the vice president. He asked Bundy whether Humphrey could be included immediately in NSC meetings. Bundy was inclined to recommend against this on the grounds that Humphrey was not yet sworn in and was still a sitting senator. This would appear to violate the separation of powers. Bundy asked Hughes's legal opinion on this point, and Hughes agreed that NSC attendance should probably wait until the inauguration.

The White House wanted to clear Humphrey's speeches and public statements on administration policy, but LBJ had not defined the boundaries he expected the vice president to observe. There was no sign yet of the humiliations that would be imposed on Humphrey immediately after the February 17 memo. On the contrary, Hughes got the impression that Hubert was talking and meeting with the president constantly and that LBJ was encouraging Hubert to look into personnel and policy changes for the State Department.

Humphrey, still in transition from the Senate, was bemused by some of the changes that came with his new position. The security arrangements were a startling change for Humphrey, who had always done his own shopping, driven himself to work, and enjoyed informal contacts with his neighbors. "Can you imagine, Tom?" he said at a Hughes visit to the Humphrey home. "Lead curtains, and bulletproof curtains in your living room."[4]

One conversation between Hughes and Humphrey in December is noteworthy for the light it sheds on their Vietnam memo to LBJ in February 1965. The conversation turned to the latest developments on Vietnam. Hughes noted that his first contact with Vietnam came when he was working for Chet Bowles in the State Department in January 1961. Tom learned about the problems of coordinating foreign aid policies. So much aid was flowing to Saigon that there was massive confusion. Tom proposed to Chet that a new office of manager or coordinator be created in Chet's office to monitor the situation.

Humphrey mused that Lyndon Johnson was spending too much political capital on the war. You only have so much political capital, Hubert told Tom, and if you use it up on causes that are not the most important, you will not have much left for the really important things. Humphrey said that he had tried to talk to the president about the war, but it was always difficult to talk to Lyndon because he dominated every conversation. No one could get a word in, so it was always a good idea to give him something in writing. That way he had to read it. Hubert went on to say that the present time presented great opportunities. The president's popularity was sky high. Johnson could do almost anything he wanted. Humphrey and Hughes returned to this theme in Georgia a month later.

In preparing for their discussions, Tom reviewed the latest intelligence on Vietnam and what was happening at the White House. Every government in the world knew that nothing was going to be decided about Vietnam during the election. With the election over, the hawks and the doves were pushing hard for their pet solutions. The hawks—McNamara, MACV, CINCPAC, the Joint Chiefs, Mac and Bill Bundy—thought the situation was dire and that escalation was the only viable option. War weariness and neutralist sentiment were growing in South Vietnam. Viet Cong spies had infiltrated the Saigon government. Midlevel functionaries were in contact with National Liberation Front elements in what seemed to be preparation for negotiations. Effective prosecution of the war had been all but abandoned by the unstable Saigon government.

What distressed Hughes, however, was that the White House task force reviewing Vietnam policy seemed to be ignoring altogether the option of negotiations leading to eventual withdrawal from Vietnam. Tom was not quite sure of what was in the White House policy review, but evidently little or no attention at all was being paid to negotiations.

The Canadians had inquired whether the United States would like their envoy, J. Blair Seaborn, to sound out Tran Van Dong again about Hanoi's potential interest in negotiations, or perhaps meet with Ho Chi Minh, as Dong had suggested at his June meeting with Seaborn. The Canadians were flatly rebuffed.

In the State Department, Ball was a strong dove, Rusk was wavering, and Bill Bundy reportedly was showing some dovish tendencies. Tom, however, had not seen any such indication on Bill Bundy's part since he had come from Defense to replace Hilsman in March 1964. Rusk, Hughes told Humphrey, was cautious because he was always worried about China. He did not want another Korea. Rusk always asked about signs of Chinese intervention when Tom briefed him each morning. Tom felt that Rusk would continue to sit on the fence so long as the president had taken no strong position.

Hubert wondered about younger Foreign Service officers and how they could be promoted faster. Then Hubert asked Tom what job he would like. Tom said there was an opening for the deputy under secretary for political affairs position held by Alex Johnson, who had been named deputy chief of mission in Saigon. This was the department's number-four position, traditionally held by a senior career officer. Tom said that he had not raised the matter with Rusk but thought that Rusk would be favorably disposed. Rusk's only reservation might be that Tom was not a career Foreign Service officer and that some eyebrows might be raised over his age (he was only thirty-nine).

Tom was interested and would certainly accept the offer. In the political affairs job, Tom would be Bill Bundy's superior, which could give Bill cover for standing up to his brother and siding with George Ball. Tom's appointment would give George Ball some needed support. Rusk might move to a more dovish position if his top officials dealing with Vietnam (Ball, Hughes, and Bill Bundy) were united in favor of negotiations.

Humphrey spoke with Rusk and found him receptive to the idea. He spoke with Mac Bundy and reported to Tom that if Rusk wanted to promote Tom to the post, the White House would have no objection. A personnel meeting for the State Department was held at the LBJ ranch on December 30. Dean Rusk, White House personnel chief John Macy, Mac Bundy, Bill Moyers, and President Johnson were present. The meeting began with a discussion of the replacement for U. Alexis Johnson. Rusk said that he wanted to promote Tom Hughes to the position. Bundy liked the idea. President Johnson said, "Fine. Let's do it."

The discussion moved on to other matters. Later, as the meeting was about to adjourn for lunch, Rusk suddenly announced that he had changed his mind. He wanted to withdraw the appointment of Tom Hughes for deputy under secretary, saying "He's too valuable right where he is. I need him there."

About a week after the meeting at the ranch, Hughes had lunch in the White House with Bill Moyers.

"Did you hear about the discussion of you at the ranch?" Moyers asked Tom.

"No."

Moyers described the scene, giving his recollection of the dialogue and noting that both Bundy and the president were surprised by Rusk's sudden change of mind.

"Can you figure this one out?" Moyers said.

"No," said Tom. "I can't figure it out."

"I can't either." Moyers shrugged and shook his head.[5]

Hughes never raised the matter with Rusk, and Rusk never mentioned it. The "ephemeral appointment," as Hughes referred to it in his reminiscences, remained one of the war's minor mysteries.

PRESSURES MOUNT FOR ESCALATION

In January 1965, Humphrey and Hughes met less frequently. Humphrey was busy with the inauguration and closing his Senate office. Hughes was occupied with a number of assignments, including several new Special National Intelligence Estimates. The White House, mostly Bundy, wanted answers to questions about enemy reactions to hypothetical U.S. actions. Hughes was often troubled by the artificiality of some of the questions posed, but that the decisionmakers were asking questions indicated that they had not made up their minds.

In December 1964, LBJ had made some limited moves on Vietnam in response to growing pressures for action. He did not approve the big move favored by the hawks of bombing targets in North Vietnam. The president authorized armed reconnaissance flights and bombing raids against supply routes in Laos. The bombing took place in the jungle and did not attract publicity back home.

However, INR and CIA intelligence reports showed that the bombing had not succeeded in halting the flow of men and supplies from North Vietnam to the South. The intelligence assessments left open the question of whether the bombing should be intensified or whether a bombing pause might test Hanoi's willingness to negotiate. The policy debate thus had not changed much as a result of the limited bombing of Laotian supply routes. The hawks wanted more bombing of more targets.

In early January, Tom Hughes helped Clark Clifford to reestablish the President's Foreign Intelligence Advisory Board. The board had become inactive under President Kennedy. Clifford asked for Hughes's advice on the board's role in the overall intelligence picture. Clifford asked Hughes if he would be his "eyes and ears in the State Department." Hughes said that he would be happy to keep Clifford informed on developments in State. Hughes met regularly with Clifford, who served as the board's chair until February 1968, when he joined the Johnson administration as secretary of defense.

Meanwhile, the Vietnam debate began to take on an ominous tone. The disputes over bombing had not primarily involved the issue of political stability. The Joint Chiefs had originally argued that bombing the North would improve the morale of Saigon's leaders, but Ambassador Taylor had debunked the idea. Bombing the North, Taylor insisted, would put a dangerous strain on Saigon's stability. But what if the issue of political stability was even more serious than Taylor imagined? Suddenly, in January, the issue of the Saigon government's stability came front and center. It had been the United States' position since Eisenhower that we could only aid a stable regime. If Saigon no longer had a stable government, what were the implications for U.S. policy?

On January 6, 1965, Bill Bundy sent a memo to Secretary Rusk saying South Vietnam morale had plummeted and the collapse of the regime was likely unless the United States took decisive action.[6] This apparently meant a major increase in U.S. military assistance and a more active role for American advisers in combat operations. Tom Hughes told Rusk that his analysts did not foresee the danger of an imminent collapse. The INR had credibility, since it had been first to foresee the instability resulting from Diem's persecution of the Buddhists and urban intellectuals. The bureau's analysis was that the self-expression by previously suppressed groups was somewhat deceptive, creating the impression of more disorder than was the case. Hughes told Rusk that in his view the intelligence community had been preoccupied with responding to narrowly framed questions from the White House and had not undertaken a general intelligence estimate for some months.

Rusk agreed with Hughes that the Vietnam situation was not as dire as Bill Bundy had said. He believed that drastic new U.S. action was unnecessary. President Johnson was also unmoved. Johnson's thoughts were on his inauguration and his State of the Union address. Mac Bundy agreed with his brother and decided that he would make his move after the inauguration, when he and Robert McNamara would urge the president to act.

On January 27, LBJ's hand was finally forced when Mac Bundy, speaking for himself and McNamara, sent him a memo asking for an urgent meeting on Vietnam. Bundy stated that "both of us are now pretty well convinced that our current policy can lead only to disastrous defeat.... Bob and I ... are both convinced that the time has come for harder choices."[7] Bundy believed that the president was moving in the right policy direction but needed prodding. Hence he took the unusual step of demanding a meeting the same day. This assertion of authority was somewhat akin to the time Bundy told JFK that he was reorganizing the White House staff.

The choice, Bundy now told LBJ in the January 27 memo (which became known as the "fork in the road" memo), came down to either military action to force change in North Vietnam's behavior or disengagement. The latter course meant serious negotiations leading to U.S. withdrawal from Vietnam. He and Bob McNamara, Bundy wrote, strongly endorsed the first option. It was not too late to reverse the course of events by a display of U.S. resolve. Bundy described the negotiations route as unpalatable.

Bundy stated that "Dean Rusk does not agree with us."

> He does not quarrel with our assertion that things are going very badly and that the situation is unraveling. He does not assert that this deterioration can be stopped. What he does say is that ... both escalation and withdrawal are so bad that we simply must find a way of making our present policy work. This would be good if it was possible. Bob and I do not think it is.[8]

Bundy told Rusk in advance that he was sending a memo to the president and described it in general terms. However, he did not tell or show Rusk the specific wording.

The requested meeting took place from 11:00 a.m. to 12:15 p.m. on January 27, with the president, Mac Bundy, McNamara, Rusk, Ball, and possibly Abe Fortas present.[9] The president heard out Rusk and Ball but appeared to side with the Bundy-McNamara analysis. Johnson dropped his previous insistence that helping South Vietnam required a stable government to work with and accepted the likelihood that the United States would be stuck with a military junta as Saigon's government. General Khanh would emerge as the man in charge.

Johnson authorized a resumption of the DeSoto patrols off the North Vietnamese coast (but later postponed the patrols when Soviet Premier Kosygin arrived in Hanoi for a visit). While leaning at the January 27 meeting toward military escalation, the president postponed a final decision on the main Bundy-McNamara request—the call for a bombing campaign. That decision would be made, the president said, after Bundy had completed a previously arranged fact-finding trip to Saigon.

Ambassador Maxwell Taylor threw a monkey wrench into the arrangements for Bundy's trip by insisting that Bundy postpone the trip until the new Saigon government was formed. When told that Washington was not willing to postpone the trip, Taylor demanded that the United States oppose General Khanh as leader. Rebuffed again, Taylor attempted to circumscribe what Bundy could discuss and with whom he could meet.

Bundy and his team arrived in Saigon on February 3. It was unclear what position, if any, he would take on Saigon's governmental succession. Bundy finally clarified his brief by calling his brother. The Bundy brothers decided that Mac would not take a position either for or against anyone for prime minister. He would leave that decision to the Vietnamese. The Bundys presumed that Khanh would emerge as the strong man and would probably renew the call to take the fight to North Vietnam. In this case, Bundy would simply repeat that the U.S. position was to help South Vietnam win the war in the South, not to extend the war into North Vietnam. This was a position not quite in sync with what Bundy was arguing in Washington.

On February 5, Bundy's mission took a sharp turn when the Viet Cong attacked the U.S. Marine bases at Pleiku. The attack killed nine Americans, wounded more than 140 others, and destroyed a large number of helicopters and a smaller number of fixed-wing aircraft.[10] Bundy's visit to the hospital to see the wounded Americans had a profound emotional impact on him. He was already a believer that only strong U.S. military action could save Vietnam, but now his intellect was reinforced by his emotions.

Following the Pleiku attack, Bundy explained what he meant by a policy of sustained reprisal: a gradual campaign of stepped-up U.S. military pressure to persuade Hanoi to drop its support for the insurgency in the South.[11] Bundy portrayed his proposed actions as a logical and measured response to the enemy's actions, not as a dramatic departure from existing policy.

Bundy had not anticipated returning with what became his most important memo as national security adviser. On February 4, Bundy wrote his brother that the mission was proceeding routinely. He and his team would have a field visit to an American base the following day for some local color to add to the report. He would draft the report on the flight back to Washington.

The visit to an American base turned out to be a shattering experience for the normally imperturbable Harvard dean. General Westmoreland, not a man known for wit, remarked that once Bundy "smelled a little gunpowder he developed a field marshal psychosis."[12]

The memo Bundy drafted for the president on the flight home filled out the argument of his "fork in the road" memo of January 27, adding a passionate appeal for action. A technical annex prepared by Assistant Secretary of Defense John McNaughton outlined in detail what became the pattern of U.S. bombing of North Vietnam for the next three years (until

President Johnson's March 31, 1968, speech to the nation). The upshot of the Bundy-McNaughton report was that the United States would "go big" in Vietnam.

Tom Hughes was aghast at the "sustained reprisal" memo, recognizing it as a step toward a full-scale military engagement and one that would be difficult to reverse. He wrote an intelligence memo to George Ball, dismayed that Bundy had paid no attention whatsoever to the likely reactions of Peking and Moscow to U.S. bombing of North Vietnam.[13] Bundy and McNaughton had ignored all of the INR, CIA, and DIA intelligence assessments that any boost to South Vietnamese morale from American bombing would be temporary and that world opinion would come down heavily against the bombing.

At a White House meeting following news of the Pleiku attack, LBJ asked his advisers for their individual views on what action to take against North Vietnam. George Ball recommended that the United States not launch retaliatory airstrikes while Soviet Premier Kosygin was in Hanoi. Vice President Humphrey agreed with Ball. McNamara and Rusk favored immediate retaliation, which the president approved. But Johnson limited the retaliatory attacks to targets that were far from Hanoi. The strikes were interrupted by bad weather and were halted after only two of the targets had been hit. The strikes were intended to "signal" that the United States would retaliate for any attack on American bases or troops.

Humphrey's intervention at a February 7 meeting was deemed a mistake in judgment by his first biographer, Carl Solberg, who observed that "at the first important occasion of their partnership, Humphrey had broken his [loyalty] pledge."[14] Humphrey failed to understand, said Solberg, that he could not interact with Johnson as he had when they were Senate partners. This judgment seems unfair, since Johnson asked for individual views and Humphrey had merely concurred with George Ball. The president gave no sign of outward disapproval of what the vice president said.

On February 8, the president authorized a program of continuing air strikes under the code name Rolling Thunder. However, it would take time to plan the strikes, and good weather, before the attacks could actually get underway. Rolling Thunder did not actually begin until early March 2. The president told congressional leaders that he did not want them to describe this decision as a departure from past policy. The attacks merely continued the existing policy of responding to aggression from Hanoi.

THE HUMPHREY-HUGHES MEMO

A February 10 White House meeting was apparently critical to Humphrey's relationship with the president. Humphrey biographer Solberg again records Humphrey as "popping off" and violating his pledge never to get out of step publicly with the president.[15] The meeting revisited the issue of whether to bomb North Vietnam while Kosygin was still in the country. Humphrey had talked with Rusk and McNamara in advance of the meeting and apparently had misunderstood their intentions. Hubert again spoke up against bombing with Kosygin in Hanoi, but Rusk and McNamara did not, leaving Hubert dangling as the lone dissenting voice.

Nonetheless, officials at this time evidently were still confused over what had actually been decided. At a February 11 cabinet meeting, Adlai Stevenson stirred up the waters by reporting his recent conversations with UN officials. He urged that the United States undertake a diplomatic initiative before embracing military escalation in Vietnam. Secretary General U Thant meanwhile issued public statements suggesting that Hanoi was ready for negotiations, but the United States had been procrastinating for six months. U Thant further implied that the U.S. government was withholding the truth from the American people. Americans, if informed of the facts, would be strongly in favor of negotiating an end to the Vietnam hostilities. The slur angered many American officials, even those who favored negotiations.

Johnson was deeply engaged at this time in urging Congress to pass critical Great Society programs—education reform, voting rights, immigration reform, access to health care for the poor, and fair housing. This required him to trade off votes from different constituencies, regions, parties, and ideological groupings. Resistance to the war from traditional Democratic constituencies was growing. McGeorge Bundy, to LBJ's irritation, began to negotiate with former academic colleagues to make an appearance at a giant national teach-in on the war, to be held in Washington.

On February 13, the president again met with key advisers to discuss the bombing issue. This time, he limited attendance to a small group of his top advisers. Humphrey was away in Georgia but had not been invited. George Ball made a passionate appeal for pursuing negotiations before embarking on the bombing. He was overwhelmed by a McNamara barrage of statistics showing progress in the war. Rusk sided with McNamara. Rusk had moved from opposition to the Bundy-McNamara position into the escalation camp, apparently deciding that the president was moving toward escalation as well.

Although the president had apparently decided to approve the bombing campaign at the February 13 meeting, he resisted appeals to make an announcement of his decision. Since LBJ refused to make a public statement, some officials were not satisfied that the issues had been fully resolved. George Ball, though realizing that his own arguments had not prevailed, believed that the meeting had ended inconclusively. McNamara complained to Bundy later that he did not have a clear sense of what orders he was to give to his military commanders.

Tom Hughes was working hard on two national intelligence estimates, one issued on February 11 and the other to be ready a week later. He hoped that they could have an impact on policy. Hughes was aware that Humphrey had not attended a February 13 meeting and that Hubert was now in Georgia.

During this period, Tom Hughes was recognized as an outstanding public servant. He was awarded the Arthur S. Fleming Prize for Outstanding Public service as the State Department's nominee for this government-wide competition. The two other award winners from across the government were Paul Volcker from the Federal Reserve and Daniel Patrick Moynihan of the Labor Department. Hughes also learned years later, at a 1991 conference at the LBJ School of Public Policy, University of Texas, that McGeorge Bundy had sent a memo to LBJ on February 2, 1965, recommending Tom, along with Bill Moyers and Abe Chayes, State Department legal counsel, as the best qualified candidates to succeed to the national security adviser post when Bundy left government.

The INR continued to put out numerous intelligence notes and short studies on Vietnam. Hughes himself contributed nineteen memos on the Vietnam situation in the first months of 1965.[16] The February 11 National Intelligence Estimate showed different assessments of the likely effects of bombing rendered by the military and by the civilian intelligence agencies. Hughes, as the State Department's representative on the United States Intelligence Board, issued a number of separate dissents on the February 11 and subsequent estimates.[17]

George Ball, as the State Department's leading dove, was an avid consumer of the INR's Vietnam reports. Ball telephoned Hughes on February 13 to tell him what had been decided at the White House meeting that day. Ball told him that he had gotten nowhere with his own argument but that the situation still seemed fluid. Ball told Hughes to call Humphrey and fill him in on the latest intelligence. Hughes said Humphrey was out of town on a visit to Georgia. Ball told him that time was short. Tom should go to Georgia immediately and brief Humphrey.[18]

Ball believed that Humphrey was a valuable ally in the dove camp. Ball's problem was that he had stood mostly alone as the outspoken dove. He was tolerated by LBJ because he never leaked to reporters. The principals—McNamara, Rusk, Bundy, and McCone—were now all hawks. Rusk's recent conversion was probably the result of his seeing which way the wind was blowing. Ball felt that he could not win an argument against his bureaucratic superiors and welcomed the vice president's adding heft to the dovecote.

After talking with Ball, Hughes telephoned Humphrey in Georgia and spoke to him at length on a secure line. Hughes's message was that the situation was dire. Events were moving rapidly toward a major escalation of the war. But LBJ might still be swayed. Ball, said Tom, believed that the president was more flexible than his advisers. There was still time, but not much. He clearly remembered telling Humphrey that "the die was cast," because he seldom spoke in such terms.

Hughes informed Rusk that he planned to visit Humphrey in Georgia to brief him on the latest Vietnam intelligence.

Hughes flew to Thomasville, Georgia, on Sunday morning, February 14, where Humphrey was staying at the lodge of a Minneapolis friend and business tycoon, Ford Bell, for a quail-hunting weekend. Humphrey was aware that he had been excluded from the February 13 White House meeting but believed that the reason was his scheduled absence from Washington. Humphrey and Hughes closeted themselves for most of the day, discussing Vietnam. Humphrey decided that the best course was for him to deliver a memo to Johnson. He asked Hughes to draft the memo.

Hubert gave no indication that he was aware of any strain in his relationship with the president. The memorandum was to be very tightly held and given privately to LBJ as a strictly confidential exchange between the president and Humphrey. The memo, in fact, was one of Washington's best-kept secrets. Only a handful of people in Washington knew of its existence until Humphrey himself published it in his 1976 memoir.[19] Hubert thereby felt that the memo was not in contradiction to his loyalty pledge to the president.

There was reason to believe, based on Ball's assessment of it, that the February 13 meeting had not produced a final presidential decision. Hughes cast the memo not as an expert's assessment of the latest intelligence or as the view of a defense expert or scientist or other expert. Rather, he wrote as a friend and compatriot with whom he had fought many tough political battles. Humphrey was conveying his assessment of the war's effects on the administration's goals. Hubert was speaking as one politician to another, not discussing technical issues, or pretending to be an expert. Hughes, following this formula, produced a masterly draft by the late afternoon of February 14.[20] The two men returned to Washington on the following morning, February 15, and Humphrey made a few minor edits to the draft on the flight.

This memo was, in Fredrik Logevall's estimation, "the most significant effort aimed at stopping and reversing the move to war . . . a tour de force, a memorandum that must rank as one of the most incisive and prescient memos ever written on the prospect of an Americanized war in Vietnam."[21] Michael Cohen's assessment was similar: "The Humphrey memo is a remarkable historical document. It offers a window into the vice president's keen grasp of national politics, but also a glimpse of the path that could have been taken on Vietnam."[22]

The memo began by making clear that Hubert supported whatever the president might decide. Invoking their long partnership, Humphrey declared,

> You do not need me to analyze and interpret the information from Vietnam. You have a whole intelligence community for that purpose . . . [or] for foreign policy advice. . . . I am not a military expert. Plenty of others are. . . . I want to put my comments in the most useful framework . . . because my value to you significantly consists in my ability to relate politics and policy . . . I want to summarize my views on what I call the politics of Vietnam.[23]

Humphrey reminded Johnson that they had just won a remarkable victory. They had won because they had favored a diplomatic solution to the war in the campaign. This was in contrast to the Goldwater approach in favor of a military solution. There was, in short, no reason to switch over to the approach that had been clearly repudiated by the American people.

Humphrey noted that Republicans have often accused Democratic administrations of weakness—for example, losing China, failing to win in Korea, and not supporting the Bay of Pigs invasion of Cuba. The Democrats with responsibility have taken the wiser course. The Truman administration did not want to risk war with China and did not bomb targets across the Yalu River. Military solutions alone are seldom available for complex situations. Progress toward détente and nuclear arms control, making the Sino-Soviet rift permanent, summit meetings with Kosygin, stabilizing defense expenditures, and reordering relations with our European allies could be jeopardized by escalation in Vietnam.

Sustained public support would be necessary for any successful military operations. American leaders had such support in World Wars I and II. In Korea, the United States moved under UN auspices to defend South Korea against aggression. Yet even with those advantages,

> we could not sustain American political support for fighting the Chinese in Korea in 1952. Today in Vietnam we lack the very advantages we had in Korea. The public is worried and confused. Our rationale for action has shifted away from the notion that we are there as advisers on request of a free government to the simple and politically barren argument of our national interest. We have not succeeded in making this national interest interesting enough at home or abroad to generate political support. The arguments are too complicated (or too weak) to be politically useful or effective.

There was something different, the memo pointed out, in the opposition that was beginning to develop over Vietnam. Here, Humphrey showed that his political antennae had picked up something that LBJ, preoccupied with a right-wing backlash, had missed: "Politically, in Washington, beneath the surface, the opposition is more Democratic than Republican. This may be even more true at the grassroots level across the country."

The memo foresaw deeper trends that were about to transform the political landscape. Because LBJ deemed himself the politician in chief, he was angered by Humphrey's presumption in lecturing him about politics. Johnson rejected the solution that followed from Humphrey's analysis: to reduce rather than to increase the American's commitment in Vietnam. Now was an opportune time, said Humphrey, to take a move toward negotiations. Few Americans understood the necessity for U.S. involvement in the conflict in the first place or could grasp the proportionality of massive 150-plane air bombardments against a few guerillas in the jungle.

It was always difficult to cut losses, Humphrey acknowledged, but

> the Johnson administration is in a stronger position to do so now than any administration in this century. 1965 is the year of minimum political risk. Indeed it is the first year when we can face the Vietnam problem without being preoccupied with the political repercussions from the Republican right. . . . Our political problems are likely to come from new and different sources (Democratic liberals, independents, labor) if we pursue an enlarged military policy for very long.

The memo's final paragraphs reviewed the benefits and challenges of moving along the alternative paths to negotiation and escalation. Humphrey referred to President Johnson's unparalleled political skills, which could forge a path to a solution, probably within a year, if he put his mind to the task.

PRESIDENTIAL DECISIONS

Humphrey and Hughes arrived back in Washington late Monday morning, February 15. Tom spent several hours that afternoon typing out a final copy of the memo himself so that no one would see it and delivered it to Humphrey on Tuesday morning. Humphrey decided that the memo should be typed on vice presidential stationery. There was some delay, and the memo was not finally delivered to the president until Wednesday morning, February 17.

Mac Bundy, while Humphrey and Hughes were flying north, was brooding about the loose ends left from the previous NSC meeting. He drafted a memo for the president, urging that another meeting be called to settle all remaining issues. Thus, later on February 15, a small group of LBJ's principal Vietnam advisers (Rusk, McNamara, Ball, McGeorge Bundy, and Ambassador-at-Large Llewellyn Thompson) met to clarify where matters stood on Vietnam.

There were no notes taken of the meeting, but Bundy sent the president a memorandum, "Vietnam Decision," the next day to clarify what had been decided.[24] Bundy said that he had been "brooding about our discussion of yesterday, and I think I am beginning to understand where the problem is. I think that some of us—perhaps mostly me—have been confusing two questions. One is the firmness of your own decision to order continuing action; the other is the wisdom of a public declaration of that policy by you."

The issue, Bundy declared, was whether

> to mount continuing pressure against Hanoi by use of our air and naval superiority. This is not the same . . . as what we did last August [Gulf of Tonkin]. And it is not the same as a policy of episodic retaliation for particular attacks. . . . When you were out of the room yesterday, Bob McNamara repeatedly stated that he simply has to know what the policy is so that he can make his military plans. . . . Thus it seems essential . . . that there be an absolutely firm and clear internal decision of the U.S. government and that this decision be known and understood by enough people to permit its orderly execution.

Johnson apparently received and read the Humphrey memo after he had approved the air campaign. The approval was somewhat ambiguous, and there was no announcement of the decision. On the question of whether the president should make an announcement of his decision to the nation, Bundy reversed himself and now recommended that the president "should avoid a loud public signal of a major change in policy." The public statements, Bundy thought, should come from Rusk and Stevenson and should focus on Hanoi's aggression. U.S. military actions should be referred to only in passing as reactions to Hanoi's aggression.

On February 17, the president had an opportunity to make a public announcement of his new policy if he chose to do so. Instead, he gave a speech to a group of business leaders in which he commented only in general terms about Vietnam. He stopped short of saying anything newsworthy, observing only that the U.S. goal was to defend freedom by helping the government of South Vietnam repel aggression. The president might have felt that Humphrey was attacking a presidential decision that had already been made, in violation of the loyalty pledge. But no announcement had been made, or at least no one outside his small circle of advisers knew about it. Johnson could equally have seen Hubert's input as legitimate and weighed its merits, without feeling that Hubert was betraying him by putting his disapproval on record.

On February 18, the policy of bombing North Vietnam was affirmed at an NSC meeting. The State Department later notified U.S. embassies in Asia of the new U.S. policy on Vietnam consisting of four points: joint naval and air action with South Vietnam against North Vietnam wherever and whenever necessary; intensification of the pacification program in the South; informing world public opinion of documented cases of aggression by Hanoi; and public information programs focusing on Hanoi's aggression rather than on the joint military actions in response (but making clear that military actions will continue as necessary).

Bundy took the unusual step in a February 20 memorandum of specifying, for the record, what steps the president had *not* taken. These two documents—the February 18 cable to U.S. embassies in Asia and the February 20 Bundy memorandum for the record—"appear to be the only policy documents in which the President's decision to wage war on North Vietnam was recorded and explained."

JOHNSON'S REACTION TO HUMPHREY'S MEMO

McGeorge Bundy observed at the LBJ Library Roundtable on Vietnam in 1991,

> I don't want to say it was just that memorandum that did it, but I used to see Hubert quite a lot, especially after he stopped seeing the President, because it seemed important to keep in touch with the Vice President of the United States. But that [the memo] broke it up. That goddamn relationship has been lousy through 200 years of history, but this one went sour faster than most.[25]

Why did Lyndon Johnson react with such rage toward the Humphrey memo? Johnson's anger was manifested in matters small and large. Hubert was excluded from any foreign policy discussions or meetings on Vietnam. The "Tuesday lunch" became the convenient device whereby LBJ could meet with selected aides without the vice president.[26] Humphrey's public statements were monitored closely, with Bundy as chief watcher. Johnson wiretapped Humphrey's staff and complained to Humphrey about the movements and contacts of John Reilly, the longtime Humphrey foreign policy aide with a background as a human rights advocate. A travel ban was put into effect on Humphrey.

While Hubert was in the doghouse, his erstwhile allies abandoned him in droves. George Ball, for example, shunned Humphrey out of concern that his own advocacy would be tarnished if he continued to support Humphrey. This marginalization of Humphrey lasted, according to the reckonings of various observers, to either December 1965, February 1966, or July 1966.[27]

Tom Hughes, who had witnessed Humphrey's relationship with Johnson since their days in the Senate, saw that something drastic had happened. There was a permanent change in the Johnson-Humphrey relationship. The two men were always hard to read and never quite what they appeared to be. Humphrey was never the completely guileless Happy Warrior. Johnson was always the most complicated of men, with sudden emotional outbursts, highs and lows, and periods of brooding. It was never easy to understand him. But with the memo a deep emotional chasm opened between the two men that was different.

Each man had a consuming political ambition beneath the face he presented to the public. Each came to understand that his own path to the presidency could only be through the vice presidency. Vice presidents had to endure much as the price for the grand prize. But with the memo came a level of hostility from Johnson that was incomprehensible to Humphrey, Hughes, and other close friends. There was a breach that would never be fully healed. The two men never trusted each other again. Humphrey feared even after they had seemingly reconciled—and not without reason—that Johnson might torpedo Humphrey's own bid for the highest office.

Tom Hughes commented in his informal notes that LBJ viewed himself as the ultimate politician. His judgments on politics, in his own mind, were unmatched. No amateur, or no lesser politician, could speak more authoritatively than he on a political matter. Now, it appeared, this man who had sat at his feet and learned the ropes was putting himself forward as a better politician than the president himself.

How could a closely held, private communication destroy the relationship between these two who had just won the greatest electoral triumph in American history? Humphrey's vice presidency was, in effect, over before it had even begun. Johnson himself never mentions the memo in his own autobiography. The memo was perhaps a minor episode, but it casts light on what went wrong in Vietnam and with the Johnson presidency.

The delay in the memo's delivery until February 17 instead of the afternoon of February 15 was perhaps important. Had the memo arrived before the final decision on the bombing, it might have seemed less a breach of loyalty. The decision had been reversed several times before it was made final. Johnson, on the other hand, might have felt that he had already made the decision and that Humphrey should not have spoken out on February 10 or should have only spoken out privately.

But something deeper was involved. Humphrey, in directing Hughes to draft the memo as one friend to another, might have offended LBJ by seeming overfamiliar, or might have unwittingly transgressed against LBJ's vanity at its most vulnerable point. Doves like George Ball—as well as the military leaders who wanted stronger action—usually spoke to the president in technical or substantive policy terms. They argued in terms of their subject matter expertise or specialties as scientists in a subject matter. It was not that Johnson never heard dissenting views or refused to tolerate dissent or was free from doubt himself. He tolerated dissent so long as it was addressed to issues on which experts could and did hold differing views. This was familiar ground for the president.

The Humphrey memo was different. Humphrey explicitly disavowed any military or diplomatic expertise. As he told the president, the State Department had a wise secretary of state and a large staff of experienced diplomats with expert knowledge of Southeast Asia. The Pentagon had experienced military leaders who gave him all the advice he could possibly need on military matters. Hubert spoke instead in terms that would be familiar to politicians. He spoke as a partner who had just helped Johnson to win the presidency. His remarks carried an implication of equality of experience and knowledge in the arcane arts of politics.

Tom Hughes pointed out, in an August 2007 e-mail exchange with Janet Lang and James Blight, that "Humphrey had every reason to believe that he had helped LBJ to win the 1964 election and become the first southern president since the Civil War (excluding Wilson who had spent most of his adult life in the North). Hubert's presence on the ticket helped to win over voters in the Mid West, the West, and the Northeast."[28]

In Humphrey's view, LBJ was well aware of the Humphrey contribution to the landslide victory but would never admit it. Moreover, Hughes told Lang and Blight, the election had taken place scarcely three months earlier. The president and vice president had been sworn in on January 20, only three weeks before the memo was written.

Humphrey had just come from the Senate, where he was familiar with the thinking of the Senate leadership (Hubert, as majority whip, had been part of that leadership). Humphrey knew that Senator Mike Mansfield had sent the president twenty-three memos critical of the Vietnam War. He was aware of LBJ's conversation in 1964 with Richard Russell on the war. Hubert believed that he was helping the president by telling him what was happening in the Senate now, knowing full well that Johnson would be dependent on Hubert's former Senate colleagues to enact the remaining Great Society measures. And of course, Humphrey was familiar with where the various senators stood on the war.

"Why do you think Humphrey did it?" Lang asked Hughes. "You say emphatically in your oral history that he understood the price of joining the ticket in 1964; absolute loyalty on all things, of course, but especially on Vietnam?"[29]

Humphrey believed, said Hughes, that LBJ still could be influenced. Johnson knew that his own thinking was not out of step with the reservations held by many leading senators. Hubert had just attended an NSC meeting where he and George Ball had expressed reservations about bombing North Vietnam at that time because Kosygin was in Hanoi. That apparently had not aroused LBJ's wrath.[30]

LBJ'S POLITICAL FAILINGS

In February 1966, Chief Justice Earl Warren told columnist Drew Pearson that a seasoned politician like Lyndon Johnson would surely find his way through the maze of Vietnam. "This is going to last a long time," said Warren, "and the President will go through some rough sailing. But he's used to it.... He's working hard on Vietnam and has been for a long time, and he knows the answers for it.... He will find some way out."[31]

Johnson's reactions to the Humphrey memo show him as less than a master politician. He shared the conventional thinking of the day on containment and displayed his limitations on foreign policy. He also manifested a more fundamental flaw in his broader thinking about politics.

Politics to Lyndon Johnson was personal and was mainly a series of transactions with other politicians and interest group leaders. This view grew out of his long experience as a southern politician and as a master legislative tactician. His dealings were chiefly with key political figures who could deliver votes and with influential lobbyists who could deliver public support. Like many of his fellow southern politicians, once elected and safely ensconced in office, he paid major attention to how to influence other politicians. He did not have to worry much about the voters and electoral competition. The South was, for most of his political career, solidly Democratic, but Lyndon Johnson knew his support for civil rights would change that.

Humphrey's view of politics was different. Whereas Johnson saw politics as transactional, Humphrey, from his early success in merging the Democrats and the Farmer-Laborites of Minnesota into the Democratic Farmer-Labor Party, believed that political parties should stand for something. Humphrey's electrifying speech at the 1948 Democratic National Convention, calling for America and his party to emerge from "the shadow of state's rights into the bright sunlight of civil rights," was a good example. Humphrey showed the way for his party to champion the civil rights movement.

In 1950, persuaded by his friend Evron Kirkpatrick, executive director of the American Political Science Association, Hubert backed a project—"Toward a More Responsible Two-Party System"—that called for transforming America's bland centrist parties into two clear-cut ideological parties. This would give voters a choice between liberals and conservatives.[32]

Humphrey eventually concluded that he could never be nominated by his party and would have to seek the presidency by first becoming vice president. Humphrey began to campaign early in 1964 to persuade Johnson to put him on the ticket as his running mate. Humphrey understood that he would have a constituency of one—Lyndon Johnson. Winning and keeping Johnson's confidence, he knew, would not be easy.

The task proved to be more difficult than Hubert had imagined. Rousing an audience with a brilliant speech was nothing compared with dealing with the psyche of Lyndon Johnson. In his memoir, *The Education of a Public Man,* Humphrey said of Johnson, "Lyndon Johnson had many of the qualities of a true political leader: drive, confidence, great ability, toughness, persistence. But, legend to the contrary notwithstanding, when it came to politics, he was not good."³³ Humphrey was not referring to Johnson's stubbornness, deviousness, or crudity. His insecurities and his bitterness toward Ivy Leaguers, the well-born, and the better-educated were personal vices, but that was not what Humphrey meant. Humphrey knew that these personal vices were parts of the whole package that was Lyndon Johnson. What Humphrey referred to were LBJ's limitations as a politician.

Johnson could not understand how civil rights in the North could so differ from civil rights in the South. Why would activists want to overwhelm the welfare rolls to break the whole welfare system? Why should the poor, once given opportunities to escape from poverty, not be grateful and take advantage of the opportunities instead of rioting and destroying their own communities? It baffled Johnson that the civil rights movement in the North could produce lawlessness, destruction of property, and urban riots.³⁴ The more one did for them, it seemed to Johnson, the more truculent the northern urban poor became.

Civil rights in the South meant removal of legal barriers that blocked progress for people who had been held down for decades. In the North, the civil rights movement pursued a more militant agenda: the equality of results as well as of opportunity. Martin Luther King Jr., LBJ's ally in passing the Civil Rights Act in 1964 and the Voting Rights Act in 1965, broke with him over Vietnam. Militants such as Angela Davis showed up in East Berlin, and Stokely Carmichael in Cuba, to denounce U.S. Vietnam policy. An infuriated Lyndon Johnson instructed J. Edgar Hoover, the FBI director, and then Richard Helms, the new CIA director, to search for communists in the civil rights movement. They could not find any.

Johnson's approach to Vietnam was incomprehensible to a political man like Humphrey. Johnson treated opponents as enemies, equivocated and dodged decisions, and sank into depression, anger, and volatile moods. Worse, in Humphrey's view, President Johnson refused to address the American people candidly and explain his Vietnam policies. Johnson relied on secrecy and deceit instead of speaking frankly about the war.

This was the source of LBJ's anger at the Humphrey memo. It embodied a totally wrong view of politics and how to get anything done. Johnson was being patronized by this yak, yak, yak liberal as someone who did not understand what was happening, as a bumpkin from the South.

Johnson's focus was on what he understood from the past. He feared a right-wing Republican backlash. He dismissed the Humphrey-Hughes argument that the war was tearing apart the Democratic Party coalition.

With Humphrey sidelined, the State Department doves, George Ball and Tom Hughes, embarked on a final, desperate last-ditch effort of their own to create a path toward negotiations on Vietnam.

15

Point of No Return

George Ball and Tom Hughes had been acquainted since Tom began working for Chet Bowles in 1954. Both Ball and Hughes had attended meetings of the Thomas Finletter Group, the informal advisers that Bowles helped to establish for Adlai Stevenson. Hughes was Bowles's aide, and Ball served as Stevenson's liaison with the group. Ball and Hughes worked together on the Platform Committee at the 1960 Democratic convention in Los Angeles.

Ball was a key Stevenson backer in the competition for secretary of state after the election. In a gesture to Stevenson, John Kennedy named Ball to the number-three position at the State Department. When Chet Bowles was reassigned in November 1961, Ball took over his position as Dean Rusk's chief deputy.[1]

At State, Ball had looked to Hughes and the INR for intellectual backup when it suited his purposes. He and Hughes engaged in sharp policy disagreements on various issues. Tom thought that Ball was mistaken, for example, in backing the multilateral fleet plan for a NATO nuclear force. The Atlanticists in the Department, Hughes felt, had concocted the scheme as an ill-conceived solution to a nonproblem (that is, an alleged Berlin effort to acquire nuclear weapons). Despite the policy differences, Hughes came to regard Ball as one of the two ablest officials he worked with in the State Department.[2]

Ball's advocacy of the multilateral fleet plan pitted him against McGeorge Bundy until December 1964, when Bundy, with the aid of Hughes, finally killed the plan. The Ball-Bundy conflict became increasingly sharp edged in late 1964 and into 1965 as Bundy moved toward escalation in the war. Bundy sought to mobilize the principals (himself, his brother Bill, McNamara, Rusk, and McCone) into a coalition to ensure that George Ball would remain an isolated minority voice on Vietnam.

White House staffer Bill Moyers became a convert to George Ball's views on Vietnam. Moyers ensured that Ball's views still reached the president despite Bundy's efforts to limit Ball's access. Strangely, Ball seemed to acquiesce to a ritualistic role as "devil's advocate" on Vietnam, a role sanctioned by Bundy. In this role, Ball would speak out against intervention in Vietnam in front of the president and a small circle of presidential advisers. It was assumed that Ball's views and working papers would never receive wide distribution within the government when he spoke against the war. Ball's loyalty to LBJ was never questioned, and he was a true insider. He did not play the game of leaking to friends in the press.

Ball and Bundy were natural antagonists for reasons beyond their differing policy positions. They both harbored ambitions to be secretary of state if Rusk should step down or be replaced. The issue of Rusk's succession was lively in the Kennedy years and continued into the early Johnson administration. Rusk, however, solidified his position in an ingenious move that proved to be politically deft. He went to see the president and offered to resign if Johnson would be embarrassed by the forthcoming marriage of his daughter to a Black man. There was no way LBJ would now replace his secretary of state.

Johnson and Rusk were both country boys from the South, and they got along well. Each had a grandfather who had fought in the Civil War. LBJ had a routine that he would frequently employ with Rusk. When Rusk entered the room for a meeting, the president would announce that our great secretary of state, a great American, Mr. Dean Rusk, had arrived, and the meeting could now start.

Notwithstanding the president's decision on Rolling Thunder, George Ball still believed that Johnson might pursue negotiations under the right circumstances. That LBJ was unwilling to go public on Rolling Thunder as a major shift in U.S. policy left the door open for a peace overture to Hanoi. Bundy, McNamara, MACV commanders, Ambassador Taylor, and CIA director McCone were pushing hard for more bombing. Some but not all hawks wanted American combat troops as well. Now was the time to stop this push toward escalation before it built up momentum. It was not so easy, however, to figure out how to do this. George Ball had been butting his head against a bureaucratic wall for some time and getting nowhere.

Mac Bundy was George Ball's most formidable opponent in bureaucratic warfare. Bundy held the strategic position as the gatekeeper for the president. He had started out viewing his role as a facilitator and coordinator, but by February 1965 he had become a policy advocate.

The former Harvard dean saw his own role as being at least the equivalent of the cabinet members. Mac Bundy knew a Nathan Pusey when he saw one. He had asserted himself easily with the courtly and deferential Rusk.

Bundy now had the job of monitoring the unfortunate Humphrey. Bundy showed tact in this assignment. Handling McNamara was a different case but was not difficult. McNamara was his close ally. He and Bob were birds of the same analytical feather. All Bundy had to do with McNamara was let him talk. Then he would translate McNamara's analytic-speak for the president.

John McCone was on his way out and was not a threat in any case. McCone was his own worst enemy. He had wearied the president by showing up at the White House unannounced and by talking too much. McCone was too intent on briefing the president himself, a habit that, before long, LBJ found irksome.

With Ball, Bundy had to be more cunning. For some reason that Bundy could not quite fathom, the president seemed to like Ball and to tolerate his excessive talk. Bundy's tactics for isolating Ball ran the gamut, deferring or delaying his memos to the president, limiting the distribution of Ball's memos, not allowing Ball to speak on Vietnam at large meetings, and arranging in advance that Ball would have limited time at meetings. The result was that the president would want to listen carefully to Ball before rejecting what he said.

Meanwhile, Bundy's own standing with LBJ was slipping, as was Bundy's taste for the job. In a casual conversation after the inauguration, Johnson and Bundy were discussing White House staffing. Bundy mentioned that at some future point it would probably be in the president's interests for him, Bundy, to leave the job. Fresh blood was always needed. Johnson then asked Bundy to share his informal thoughts on his own succession, when he had a chance to reflect on the matter.

Johnson, always sensitive to slights real or imagined, was surprised when Bundy came back with a February 2, 1965, memo on the subject. The memo included a list of possible successors. Johnson had not asked for a formal memo.

In the memo, Bundy disclaimed any intentions of leaving his post. He went on to recommend three doves as his possible successor: Bill Moyers, Abe Chayes, and Tom Hughes. The endorsement of Bill Moyers was odd. Johnson was fond of Moyers but had his own reasons for not grooming him to succeed Bundy. If he had wanted to, LBJ would have done so without prompting from Bundy. Moyers, only thirty at the time, was probably too young, and his dovish tendencies were already on display.

As for Chayes, there was an obvious question of loyalty. Chayes was too close to Bobby Kennedy, and Bundy was aware that this would make him unacceptable to Lyndon. Tom Hughes, the third on Bundy's list, seemed to be his preferred candidate but was reputed to be dovish on Vietnam. There was that odd episode in December when Rusk had wanted to promote Hughes but then changed his mind. Did that raise any concerns for Lyndon Johnson? Tom was also close to Humphrey, which might have given LBJ pause. What was Bundy up to, anyway, in presenting such a list of doves for his job when he was not leaving?

Johnson had always admired Bundy's crispness, clarity of mind, and ability to sum up complex issues. Bundy was usually able to state an argument better than the proponents of a proposal. These were qualities that were invaluable in any White House meeting. Bundy's public stature was also an obvious asset for Johnson. The national security adviser could be forgiven the occasional lapse because of his obvious competence.

The bloom, though, was off the rose. In LBJ's view, Bundy was taking much too seriously the academic protests over Vietnam and was letting his ties to the academic community cloud his judgment. In particular, Johnson considered that Bundy was spending too much time in discussions with leaders of the proposed nationally televised teach-in against the war. Apparently Bundy wanted to appear at the event to defend administration policy in a debate with a war critic. LBJ believed that Bundy would defend administration policy but did not fully trust him.

The president's irritation with Bundy was evident in a misunderstanding over Bundy's monitoring of Humphrey. Johnson mistakenly thought that Humphrey had strayed into discussing Vietnam peace negotiations in a New York speech. Bundy tried to explain that Humphrey was referring to a completely different negotiation, namely, a nuclear discussion with the Russians. The president would not listen and rebuked Bundy for failing to monitor Humphrey carefully enough.

Despite his polish and urbanity, McGeorge Bundy was in his own way as stiff-necked as the president. There was a point beyond which Bundy was not going to be pushed. He did not take kindly to bullying unless he was doing the bullying. Bundy was getting tired of the president's crudeness, self-pity, and vindictiveness.

As to the teach-in, Bundy was offended at being kept from participating. The president sent him to San Juan during the Dominican crisis after he had made a commitment to appear at the event. Bundy was not quite at the point of calling Harvard president Nathan Pusey and asking if there was a job for him back at Harvard. He finally did call in August, when he had made up his mind to leave government, but did not get quite the reception he wanted.

Bundy, maneuvering behind Johnson's back, finally did appear at a June 21 televised national debate on Vietnam, where he ran verbal circles around Professor Hans Morgenthau of the University of Chicago, leaving him stammering and flustered.[3] One of the event's sponsors, Professor Stanley Diamond of the University of Michigan, ruefully wrote his colleagues, "I am forced to conclude that we pursued McGeorge Bundy until he caught us."[4]

President Johnson was stunned when he learned what Bundy had done without telling him. He did not mind firing people, but he did not like anyone leaving him voluntarily. He had made a half-hearted attempt to fire Bundy earlier, but this effort failed when Moyers lacked the heart to tell Bundy that LBJ wanted him to go. The president wanted Moyers to pass along the message that if Bundy wanted to leave, there would be no obstacle to him doing so.

Thus the president had to suffer the indignity of not being able to fire Bundy. The wily Bundy had struck a deal to become the president of the Ford Foundation. Bundy left government service in February 1966 with a salary of $75,000, roughly three times his government salary.

A PATH TOWARD NEGOTIATIONS?

In April and May 1965, in a context of palace intrigue, antiwar protests, and U.S. intervention in the Dominican Republic, George Ball and Tom Hughes carved out a path for negotiations on Vietnam, with the assistance of INR analysts and a pair of outside notables providing gravitas. The effort was undertaken at the president's invitation to fill the gap between the Pentagon's military plans and comparable planning on the diplomatic track. As such, it was the first serious attempt of the war to spell out a path toward peace negotiations.

George Ball's calculations at this time were clear.[5] He had been the Johnson administration's most prominent in-house critic of the Vietnam policy since at least May of 1964. Hughes, too, was a voice of dissent, but a midlevel voice. He was bound by professional constraints and needed high-level political support. Ball had gotten a hearing, mostly respectful, from his government peers but had failed to persuade them.

Vice President Humphrey, all too briefly, offered the hope of becoming an ally. But when Humphrey fell out of favor with the president, that hope was gone. There was no telling when, or whether, Hubert could regain presidential favor.

Scholars of the Vietnam tragedy have generally agreed that during 1965 the war was Americanized.[6] But this process did not occur in one big step. It took place incrementally. A series of decisions on the bombing campaign, the American troop deployments, and the nature and scope of American military operations added up to the Americanization of the conflict. By the end of 1965, the number of American troops had increased from some

23,000 to 184,000, with thousands more American combat forces scheduled to arrive in 1966.[7]

The pattern of the Americanized war was set by the end of 1965.[8] The basic decisions included overt intervention, the separation of U.S. from South Vietnam operations (thus negating the advantages of larger-scale actions and demoralizing the ARVN), the fundamental strategies for air and ground war, and the privileging of military over diplomatic activities. As Leslie Gelb and Richard Betts concluded, "The United States had galloped beyond the Rubicon . . . but the road to Rome for the next two years was really a dark and unending tunnel."[9]

At this point, the sheer weight of the American military presence overwhelmed the U.S. civilian agencies and Saigon's own government. It became increasingly difficult for any U.S. diplomatic voice to counterbalance the military's influence: "With the deployment of American combat troops, policy-making took on a new complexion. Up to this point the civilians, whether in the Department of State or Defense, played the leading roles in all policy discussions. Now . . . military participation in virtually every facet of our Vietnam involvement was taken for granted."[10]

Despite the obstacles, there were secret negotiations throughout the 1965–1968 period between the United States and North Vietnam.[11] The conflicting interests of the United States and North Vietnam, however, became sharper and more pronounced as the war wore on. The secret negotiations usually foundered quickly and produced nothing. In the end, the negotiations failed for serious substantive reasons, not because of bungled diplomacy. There was "ample evidence of bungling diplomacy and of misperceptions on both sides," George Herring concludes, "and there were probably lost opportunities along the way. More than anything else, however, the utter irreconcilability of the negotiating positions staked out by both sides made a settlement impossible."[12]

But the peace plan developed by Ball and Hughes in April–May 1965 was different from the negotiations that Herring studied. The Ball-Hughes plan could have slowed or halted the Americanizing of the war. Because it was the first, the most comprehensive, and the most carefully thought out plan, it could have prepared the ground for further promising negotiations. Instead, the Pentagon's alternative plan—the ill-conceived Project Mayflower—poisoned the ground for all future negotiations.

George Ball's initial problem in the spring of 1965 was that he had produced too many anguished and hasty outpourings under stress. He relied too much on past personal experience. His reflections were, in general, too Eurocentric in orientation.

Ball often woke up in the middle of the night, got out of bed to dictate a rush of observations, and then used the dictation to compose his memos.

He recognized that this process was a mistake that put him at a disadvantage with, for example, McNamara. The secretary of defense invariably showed up with a flood of statistics and charts and bombarded everyone with these so-called hard facts.

Most of McNamara's data were rubbish, in Ball's view, but the McNamara presentations went over well with the president. In recent NSC meetings, Ball had tried to argue more on the basis of facts (such as INR papers showing that bombing of Laotian supply routes was ineffective). But when needled by Bundy, Ball got emotional and fell back into his former pattern. He knew he had to try something different.

As the second-ranking official in the State Department, Ball was often the acting secretary of state because Rusk traveled frequently. As the under secretary, he had fewer staff resources than the department's assistant secretaries. The assistant secretaries ran the large geographic and functional bureaus that were the equivalent of the operating divisions of a large corporation. Ball could draw on all departmental resources, of course, but on Vietnam it was Bill Bundy who was in charge of the Far East Asia bureau. Bill was a strong proponent of the war. As Mac Bundy's older brother, he was likely to tell Mac what George was doing.

Walt Rostow, head of State's policy planning staff, was an outspoken hawk and not a likely ally for Ball. George Ball looked to Tom Hughes and the INR for the analytical help he needed. In early 1965, Ball began to use the INR's Allen Whiting extensively in preparing analyses for White House meetings. Tom Hughes was an enthusiastic supporter. Ball saw that he would have to use INR expertise as well to brief any outsiders he might bring in to impress the president.

Events produced an opportunity in mid-April for Ball to employ two prestigious outsiders and the INR's analytical resources to outline a negotiating strategy the president might approve. President Johnson, pushed by Mac Bundy, sent instructions to Ambassador Maxwell Taylor in Saigon to institute a series of changes in how Americans were to assist South Vietnamese army units. Taylor was exasperated by the multiple U.S. agencies he was supposed to supervise. He replied with his own memo, complaining of the many demands being placed on the embassy:

> As a result of the decisions taken in Washington . . . this mission is charged with securing implementation . . . of a 21-point military program, a 41-point non-military program, a 16-Rowan USIS program, and a 12-point CIA program. Now this new cable opens up new vistas of further points as if we can win here somehow on a point score. We are going to stall the machine of government if we do not declare a moratorium on new programs for at least six months. Next,

it [the Bundy memo] shows a far greater willingness to get into the ground war than I had discerned in Washington during my recent trip.[13]

The Saigon government and the U.S. embassy, Taylor insisted, were overwhelmed. With new troop arrivals and with the bombing campaign in need of review, it was time to have a look at the responsibilities of various U.S. agencies. More important, it was time to chart a clear policy course for the future.

Johnson called for a conference to take place in Honolulu, bringing together Ambassador Taylor and the top layer of military commanders. Bill Bundy was sent out from Washington. The conference concluded that the bombing campaign should continue at its present tempo, that more American troops should be sent, and that American forces should assume a direct combat role. This Honolulu Conference, in effect, called for the opposite of what the June 1964 Honolulu Conference had recommended. The new conference favored the Americanization of the war, a course that was well underway already with the Rolling Thunder campaign. Now the key decision was whether to raise troop levels.

The president held a Tuesday lunch meeting on April 20 with Rusk, Ball, Cyrus Vance from Defense, and Mac Bundy to ratify the Honolulu proposals. Ball seized the opportunity to make an appeal to shift policy from the military to the political track. By his own later admission, Ball exaggerated and told the president and the others that there was clear intelligence pointing to Hanoi's willingness to negotiate. The president said, "All right, George, I'll give you until tomorrow morning to get me a settlement plan. If you can pull a rabbit out of the hat, I'm all for it."[14]

THE PEACE PLAN

Ball did not manage to do the trick overnight. However, he did come up with a plan with Tom Hughes for a realistic path to negotiations. The president gave Ball his blessing and apparently his backing. Ball's idea was to bring in Dean Acheson and Lloyd Cutler, two fellow lawyers and well-known Washington insiders. Acheson and Cutler were to work with Tom Hughes and his East Asia experts to develop a concrete negotiating proposal. The proposal would be credible to Hanoi and give Lyndon Johnson a well-thought-out alternative to further military escalation.

The key meetings on the project were held in Hughes's office on April 21, 22, and 26 and a two-hour session in Ball's office on April 27.[15] There were other individual consultations between Acheson and Cutler and INR analysts, notably Allen Whiting, whose help Dean Acheson acknowledged in a White House meeting in May. Five short INR papers were produced to back up the report. By early May, the team of Acheson-Cutler and Ball-Hughes had produced the draft report.[16]

The plan brought together the scattered peace ideas that were floating around the government into a coherent strategy for negotiations. The negotiations would focus first on local government and regional economic development. The talks would eventually provide an opportunity for the Vietnamese people to decide whether they wished to be a unified country or two separate countries.

The report drew on the proposals in LBJ's Johns Hopkins speech of April 7, which called for U.S. economic assistance to Hanoi and Saigon. McGeorge Bundy's ideas for local government were included, along with proposals borrowed from North Vietnam's four-points plan emerging from a program devised by seventeen nonaligned nations. The Acheson-Cutler plan included a provision for a halt in U.S. bombing of North Vietnam so long as fruitful negotiations were underway. The plan also included peace proposals put forward by Canadian prime minister Lester Pearson.

A notable feature was the absence of any call for the withdrawal of all North Vietnamese troops from the South as a prior condition for negotiations. Finally, there was a commitment for the phased withdrawal of U.S. forces if Hanoi observed various step-by-step indicators of compliance with the plan's peace requirements. The key provisions of the thirty-five-page Ball-Acheson-Cutler plan, "The Social and Political Development of Vietnam," were the following:

- an offer of amnesty to all Viet Cong adherents who cease fighting
- a phased schedule for establishing a constitutional government based on an electoral process in which all peaceful citizens, including the National Liberation Front, would take part
- minimum disturbance of existing local administrative arrangements, pending the outcome of local elections
- immediate economic and social aid, including education, medical care, seeds and fertilizers, land reform, debt cancellations or moratoriums
- withdrawal of foreign troops, beginning when the insurgency stops and governmental authority has been established[17]

An officially announced bombing pause would precede the offer to negotiate. The pause would continue in force so long as negotiations were fruitful. The details of who would conduct the negotiations were not fully worked out. However, according to Ball's later account, the mechanics of the negotiating process and the various steps in implementing the plan were included.[18]

The United States was to be represented by a friendly third party, such as the Canadian or British government. How to deal with the Saigon government remained to be settled. Ball wanted to exclude Saigon from having a veto power or any direct role in the negotiations. He was determined that the United States should not be "the puppet of our own puppet." In his retrospective assessment, Ball blamed Saigon (and Ambassador Taylor as spokesperson for and defender of the Saigon government) for the plan's failure: "The episode confirmed an opinion I had not wanted to accept. America had become a prisoner of whatever Saigon military clique was momentarily in power. Like a heroine in an eighteenth-century novel who got her way by fainting if anyone spoke crossly, each clique understood how to exploit its own weakness."[19]

Speed was essential in developing and in selling the plan. Decisions were being made daily to implement the Honolulu strategy. Ball urgently needed to get the president's ear.

Hughes, meanwhile, had written a memorandum to NSC staffer Chester Cooper on Hanoi's negotiating posture, pointing out that Hanoi's position had hardened after the Rolling Thunder campaign was launched. Tom added that Hanoi's position was not likely to become more flexible unless the bombing stopped.[20] This intelligence finding both helped and hurt the prospects for George Ball. Tom's memo helped insofar as the evidence suggested that negotiating sooner rather than later was advisable. Deeper U.S. military involvement would harden Hanoi's position. The memo would not be helpful if it were read as evidence that it was too late for successful negotiations. The hawks took the position that Hanoi was bluffing and would negotiate only when the bombing became unendurable.

BUNDY-BUNDY VERSUS BALL-ACHESON-INR

Bill Bundy's stance on the prospects for negotiations was critically important for the plan's chances. His opposition would not be easy to overcome. Bundy had not been in on the takeoff of the Ball-Hughes effort because he was in Honolulu with the military commanders. But it was hoped that his father-in-law's involvement would make Bill more receptive. So far as Ball and Hughes knew, Dean Acheson and Bill Bundy were on close personal terms. Acheson had lobbied for Bill, not Mac, to be Kennedy's national security adviser.

Allen Whiting, working closely and effectively with Acheson, had suggested to Hughes that Bundy should be kept at arm's length until the plan was ready. Hughes told Whiting that this was not possible. Bill was the department's point man on Vietnam. It could not be kept from him. Bill was Acheson's son-in-law and Mac's elder brother. Bill would have to be brought in. The team would have to persuade him that the plan was a good one or at least to agree that it should be given a try. "Looking back on it," Tom Hughes later said, "if Bill had decided in 1965 to join Ball and oppose the war, it might have made all the difference. Bill's opposition would have caused a problem with many people, including Mac Bundy. It would have been very difficult for Mac to take the line he did if his brother had sided with Ball."[21]

But Bill sided with his brother rather than with Ball and "the moustache" (as Mac privately referred to Acheson). Bill doubled down on his position that it was not the right time to negotiate with Hanoi, not even as an experimental probe. The North Vietnamese, according to Bill, had no incentive to negotiate on any terms that would be remotely acceptable to the United States.

At the first meeting that Bill attended with the Ball-Acheson-INR team, Acheson made a forceful presentation of the plan. Bill launched a harsh attack on his father-in-law's argument that startled Tom Hughes.[22] Bill opposed the idea of a bombing pause of any length, insisting it would be used by Hanoi for military maneuvers. Moreover, a pause would undermine Saigon's morale. To acknowledge any validity to the concept of a bombing pause would totally undermine the U.S. position. Bundy displayed a testiness and rigidity that rarely emerged in his interactions with colleagues.

Hughes was surprised by the vitriol of Bundy's attack on Acheson's plan. Here was Bill declaring in uncivil terms that his father-in-law's plan contradicted everything the United States had been saying for years and would negate everything it was trying to accomplish in Vietnam. Tom remembered an odd thought crossing his mind: he wondered what the atmosphere would be like at the Bundy family's next Thanksgiving dinner. In his informal notes, Hughes wrote that the Bundys' opposition "torpedoes the Ball-Acheson ploy. Bill Bundy did it with full knowledge that it would.... Ball is sick: cuckolded. Bill to Mac to LBJ apparently. Acheson undermined in the family."[23]

A staggering blow came on May 12, when Ball and Hughes learned that their plan had been displaced by an alternative peace plan devised by the Pentagon. Ball, despite having been repeatedly assured that he had full authority to develop the diplomatic track, had been kept in the dark about an alternative to his efforts. Ball told Hughes that he was "stunned" to learn that LBJ had instead opted for an unenticing peace initiative involving Moscow and a temporary bombing pause but with "no carrots or concessions at all."[24]

This alternative was Project Mayflower, a poorly conceived plan featuring a temporary bombing pause set for May 12–18, 1965.[25] The bombing pause was supposed to demonstrate U.S. interest in talks and to test whether Hanoi was willing to reciprocate. The scheme was put together in haste, however, and paid so little attention to details that it was doomed to failure.

Even if Project Mayflower were to fail as a peace initiative, its authors thought, it could have propaganda value abroad and at home. Robert McNamara commented on the eve of a second bombing pause some months later, "Our first pause [May 1965] was a propaganda effort."[26] President Johnson, at a May 16 NSC meeting, declared that domestic political pressures led to the decisions both to start and to stop the first bombing pause: "My judgment is that the public never wanted us to stop the bombing. We have stopped in deference to Mansfield and Fulbright, but we don't want to do it too long else we lose our base of support. . . . I'm afraid if we play along with this group we will end up with no one on our side. We tried out their notions and got no results."[27]

The Mayflower proponents did not pay close attention to how the proposal would be communicated to Hanoi. The proposal, it was decided, would first be communicated to Soviet ambassador Dobrynin by Secretary Rusk in Washington. But when this was done, Dobrynin indicated that his government was not interested in acting as an intermediary between Hanoi and the United States at that time. Rusk was nonetheless confident that the message would be passed on to Hanoi. As insurance, Rusk sent a cable to U.S. ambassador Foy Kohler in Moscow with instructions to deliver the proposal to the North Vietnam ambassador. The North Vietnamese ambassador refused to accept the message from Kohler on the grounds that his country had no diplomatic relations with the United States.

Kohler then sent the proposal by the mail, but the letter was returned unopened, signaling a contemptuous rejection. Though generally confident that Hanoi had full knowledge of what the United States was proposing, Kohler returned to the Soviet Ministry of Foreign Affairs to seek assurances, only to be informed that the Soviet Union was washing its hands of the matter. The Soviet government would have nothing further to do with the so-called U.S. peace initiative. The acting minister repeated the familiar Soviet stance that the United States was the aggressor, since it was intruding into a civil war in Vietnam. The only path to peace was for the United States to cease its aggression and withdraw its forces from South Vietnam.

This chain of events might have been embarrassing had it been generally known. But the United States had made the bombing pause known only to a small number of key Western allies and a tightly limited circle of influential senators. The White House subsequently informed the key allies and U.S. senators that Hanoi had unceremoniously rebuffed President Johnson's peace initiative.

THE FAILURE OF MAYFLOWER

The May bombing pause was adopted without regard for the peace planning then underway in the State Department, and with no serious thought given to how Hanoi might react. It did not occur to Project Mayflower's authors that a bungled initiative might poison the waters for future peace efforts.

Ball and Hughes, though shocked at having been kept in the dark, tried to salvage something from their work and the wreckage of Project Mayflower. Ball arranged a meeting of his team with the president for the afternoon of May 16, before an NSC meeting that evening to consider a resumption of the bombing. Ball gave the floor to Acheson to lay out the plan.[28] The president, according to Ball, showed "qualified interest," and Rusk was somewhat supportive. Rusk suggested that the opinion of Taylor in Saigon should be sought. No decision was made at the afternoon meeting of May 16, but the president gave Ball a weak endorsement by agreeing that more attention should be paid to the Vietnam conflict's political dimensions.

Nevertheless, several hours later, at the 6:00 p.m. NSC meeting, LBJ ordered a resumption of the bombing campaign to begin two days later. Ball was present but made no argument for an extension of the bombing pause. The political dimension, discussed with Ball and Acheson just that afternoon, was scarcely mentioned. The president did declare that Hanoi still had two days in which to "signal" peaceful intent. But since North Vietnam had not yet reciprocated, it probably would not do so.

The White House staff tried its hand at the political track with a minor propaganda initiative. Jack Valenti and Chester Cooper developed a plan to send college students to Vietnam for the summer of 1965 to gain firsthand knowledge of America's assistance to Saigon. The students would then return to their colleges and universities in the fall and give glowing accounts of what they saw. The Bureau of the Budget threw a monkey wrench into the proceedings by ruling that the White House lacked authority to spend public funds on the project. Valenti called Sidney Weinberg, an LBJ supporter, to raise funds for the students. Nineteen students were recruited and sent to Vietnam. Vice President Humphrey was temporarily let out of the presidential doghouse to give a pep talk to the students before they left. Everything went as planned—except that several of the students returned home and joined the antiwar movement.

Chester Cooper developed other peace ideas. On May 25, at his urging, the president called for a high-level working group to study Hanoi leader Pham Van Dong's four-point peace plan, which had been proposed in April.[29] Johnson noted that Mai Van Bo, North Vietnam's ambassador to France, had told the French foreign minister that Pham's four points were not preconditions for negotiations, as the Americans mistakenly imagined. Rather, they were topics for negotiations.

Cooper recommended that the United States once again enlist the services of J. Blair Seaborn, Canada's representative on the International Control Commission, to probe how Hanoi would react to serious new peace overtures. Seaborn was, in short, to repeat the assignment he had undertaken in the first half of 1964, when he made six trips to Hanoi in search of a peace formula. Seaborn met again with North Vietnam's foreign minister but found the discussion marked by evasion and obfuscation. He could not get a straight answer on whether American troops had to be withdrawn before negotiations could take place.

George Ball had a last hurrah in the summer and fall of 1965 in the so-called XYZ affair.[30] This episode involved Hanoi's ambassador to Paris in top secret negotiations with the United States. Ball and the State Department broadly supervised the negotiations, which were conducted on the U.S. side by Edmund Gullion, a retired American diplomat who had been deputy chief of mission in Saigon and was fluent in French. Gullion was designated by the code name of X and Bo as R in the top secret U.S. cables.

There were five scheduled meetings between X and R over the period from July to September 1965. Four of the meetings took place and were serious, efficient sessions that appeared to make surprising progress. The fifth never took place because Ambassador Bo did not show up, indicating that the talks were suddenly broken off. The issue of a new bombing pause, not discussed in the first two meetings, was raised by Bo in the third and especially in the fourth session. In the fourth session, Bo insisted that all U.S. "bombings must stop unilaterally, immediately, totally, and definitively. Then there would be a possibility for negotiations."[31]

Bo complained that in recent weeks American air attacks on the North had increased even as he and X were attempting to negotiate. The tone of the third and especially the fourth session became decidedly more confrontational. R changed his position on the staged withdrawal of troops and several other points that X thought had been settled.

After Bo failed to show up for the fifth scheduled meeting, American officials speculated about Hanoi's motives. Why did progress stall what seemed like a promising beginning? Several of Hughes's INR analysts speculated that China was pressuring Hanoi not to move too quickly. China would gain and the Soviet Union's influence would be undermined if the negotiations and events played out slowly.

Once again the lack of coordination between the military and the diplomatic tracks was important. American air attacks near Hanoi suddenly increased just before the scheduled September 18 meeting between X and R, potentially angering the North Vietnamese. The American military commanders were unaware that talks had been underway. No definitive explanation for the failure of the XYZ affair was ever forthcoming.

THE DOMINICAN REPUBLIC

New complications arose for Lyndon Johnson as he struggled with the Vietnam developments. The proposed nationally televised teach-in, as noted, had received much publicity. A dispute with Senator J. William Fulbright (D-Ark.), chair of the Senate Foreign Relations Committee, changed him from an ally to an enemy of the administration. Johnson's quarrel with Fulbright was a self-inflicted wound. Fulbright blew up when Johnson unnecessarily deployed U.S. marines to the Dominican Republic, beginning on April 28, 1965, to stave off what the president called a new totalitarian dictatorship in the hemisphere.

The Dominican Republic invasion became bound up with President Johnson's appointment of a new, hand-picked director of Central Intelligence, Admiral William F. "Red" Raborn Jr. It also exacerbated State Department frictions between the holdover Kennedy officials and LBJ's new Latin American adviser, Thomas C. Mann. Tom Hughes found himself caught in the middle of the State Department tensions.

When Johnson chose Mann as his Latin American adviser in December 1963, the Kennedy appointees in charge of the Alliance for Progress were appalled. Shortly before Johnson announced his choice of Mann, Hughes was asked to arbitrate a dispute between State's Inter-American bureau head, Edwin Martin, and the U.S. ambassador to Brazil, Lincoln Gordon. The two men clashed over the U.S. stance toward the leftist Brazilian president "Jango" Goulart. Ed Martin supported Goulart against the Brazilian military. Ambassador Gordon, on the other hand, was convinced that Goulart was about to seize power and make himself a dictator. Hughes assessed that Martin had the better of the argument, but events overtook the policy dispute when the military ousted Goulart in a coup.

Mann, in the meantime, had been confirmed and had taken up his duties. The Kennedy liberals blamed Mann, along with Ambassador Gordon, for being too friendly toward the military dictators.

A second dispute arose when Mann decided to bump Murat Williams, the ambassador-designate to the Dominican Republic, in favor of his friend W. Tapley Bennett, then serving as envoy in Greece. This move upset the Kennedyites because Williams, a distinguished career Foreign Service officer and former Rhodes scholar then serving as U.S. ambassador to El Salvador, was regarded as a far better choice for the Dominican assignment. Tom Hughes was distressed because Murat Williams was the first person he and Chet Bowles had recommended to President Kennedy when they were staffing the ambassadorial posts at the start of the new administration. Hughes solved the Williams problem by offering him the job at INR. Tom pleased the Kennedy supporters by bringing Williams over to see

Attorney General Kennedy and introducing him as INR's new, additional deputy director.

Tom also fortuitously made his peace with Tom Mann by helping Mann find the right doctor for his son, then a student at Yale. Mann had lost a daughter to an infection while he was serving in Latin America for the State Department during World War II. Now he was understandably worried when his son's face and neck suddenly swelled up and he had excruciating pain in his lower jaw. Mann, hearing that Hughes had gone to Yale Law School and worked in Connecticut, turned to Tom for help.

The Yale infirmary was unable to solve the young man's problem. Did Tom know a good oral surgeon who could work with his son? Jean Hughes, whose father was a doctor, knew the New Haven medical community well, found the right person, and called to set up an appointment for Mann's son. The son's problem was soon resolved.

Tom Mann was grateful. Hughes and Mann got along well thereafter. Mann told Hughes that he had returned to government service only reluctantly, at LBJ's urging. He finally left the government in 1966 for private law practice, complaining of financial pressures. He also had been battered by the Dominican crisis and its aftermath.

Lyndon Johnson's choice in 1965 of Admiral William Raborn as McCone's successor at the CIA was somewhat odd. Raborn's experience in the Navy was entirely in research and development. He was credited with being the inventor of the Polaris submarine. While visiting the White House to see the president, Raborn was shown the ticker tape machine. Intrigued, the admiral spent some minutes studying the tapes and apparently found some from the U.S. embassy in Santo Domingo. Around this time, the new U.S. ambassador, Mann's friend Tapley Bennett, sent alarmist cables saying that he was under fire at the U.S. embassy. Some windows had been blown out, and Bennett was claiming that an army of Marxist guerrillas was threatening to overrun the embassy.

Raborn alerted the president. Johnson consulted with Mann, who had a misplaced faith in his friend Bennett's judgment. The president told Raborn not to worry. He was not going to permit another Castro on his watch. Within hours, U.S. Marines were on their way to the Dominican Republic.

When Hughes, Murat Williams, and the INR intelligence professionals tried to piece together the Dominican decision, they concluded that it had been made without the benefit of intelligence review or significant staff work. It was rather an example of decisionmakers relying on a morsel of raw intelligence—shots fired at the U.S. embassy—without benefit of a wider analysis and assessment of the regime's stability, what actions the local authorities took, the damage to the embassy, the identity and strength of the guerillas, the opinions of the marines defending the embassy, and other factors.[32]

Sending the Marines to the Dominican Republic brought negative press reactions and repercussions on Capitol Hill. Senator Fulbright withdrew his support for the administration on Vietnam. The administration had to fight hard to push through Congress a $700 million authorization in the first week of May for both the troops in the Dominican Republic and more funds for Vietnam. There was a call for a new congressional resolution on Vietnam. Johnson declared that the Tonkin Gulf Resolution gave him ample authority for whatever steps he wanted to take in Vietnam. His stepped-up effort in Vietnam, LBJ told the Congress, was merely a continuation of existing policy, not a new policy.

The Dominican crisis had the unfortunate impact of diverting the attention of policymakers from other critical issues. As William Gibbons notes, "[T]he Dominican crisis . . . took up the overwhelming attention of the President and all of his senior advisers. Vietnam was handled with the left hand, and whatever chance there might have been for a careful Congressional review went by the board."[33]

Tom Hughes considered the Dominican intervention one of LBJ's worst performances. Hughes believed Johnson had been misled by his incompetent new CIA director, Admiral Raborn. However, LBJ had brought on the crisis, in part, by his own bravado and by his need to outdo Kennedy and avoid Kennedy's Bay of Pigs mistakes. Johnson declared that he was not going to sit by in his rocking chair (Kennedy used a rocking chair to relieve the pain in his bad back) and allow another Castro in the hemisphere. The Dominican crisis was eventually resolved by diplomacy and the engagement of the Organization of American States (OAS). A key element was that the American troops were withdrawn and replaced by a Brazilian army force acting under the OAS's authority.[34]

Tom Hughes had relished the chance to do something on his own and he found the INR job perfect for that purpose. Now something came along that posed a new opportunity. Tom got a call from Dean Rusk, who asked him to come up to see him to discuss something important. This was unusual. He had just briefed Rusk a few hours earlier and would have expected Rusk then to raise anything important.

Hughes had just enjoyed his first decent vacation since joining the State Department. With the Dominican crisis on the way toward a solution and Project Mayflower having fizzled, it seemed opportune to take some time off. Tom, with his wife and sons, went off to San Juan in August, where he and Jean had bought a house. They enjoyed renovating and redecorating it. This was something Tom and Jean could do together—a pleasure, and something Jean badly needed since the pace of Tom's work and the long hours had taken a toll on her.

Renovating that house also brought Tom back into touch with the collections side of his character: his coins, his paintings, lithographs, stamps, antiques, rare objects, everything he had inherited from Grandfather Lowe and all he had added himself. Working with beautiful objects, displaying and arranging, improving and enriching his collections was important to him. It was something he had done since his boyhood. Even today, Tom's home has the feel of a museum.

"They have their eye on you over at the White House," Rusk said.

It was not quite clear who "they" were, but apparently it was Bundy. Ralph Dungan had served as JFK's special assistant to the president and had continued in that role under Johnson. Dungan, an old friend of Tom's and of the Kennedy men who stayed on with LBJ, had left the White House staff to be U.S. ambassador to Chile. His replacement was being sought, and Tom had emerged as the leading candidate. Rusk was instructed to sound out Tom. If Tom was interested, an announcement could be made as early as that same day. Tom was not interested. He told Rusk that he wanted to stay right where he was. He explained that he had worked for two outstanding men, Bowles and Humphrey, and had benefited enormously. Those were demanding but satisfying jobs. But now he was his own man, enjoying what he was doing, and on an even keel in terms of his home life.

Rusk understood Tom's position. He told Tom of the time, while he was in the military, of serving as the personal adjutant to the commanding officer. He was run ragged, he told Tom. Never had a minute to himself and was glad when he moved on to his next assignment. Rusk was pleased that Hughes wanted to stay in the INR post. He also told Tom, in a sly aside, that Hubert Humphrey could suddenly become president, in which case Tom's fortunes would dramatically improve.

An account of a luncheon with Max Kampelman in the Hughes papers, however, suggests that Tom might have discussed the job offer with Max at the time. Max had apparently told Tom back in 1965 that he should take the Dungan job. It would be ideal for Tom, giving him great scope, and potentially even lead to his succeeding Bundy as national security adviser. Tom had apparently said then that no one to his knowledge, with the possible exception of Harry McPherson as speechwriter, ever actually enjoyed working for Johnson. Why had Max not joined the Johnson administration when he was offered a job? Max said that he could not afford to give up his private law practice but wrote a polite letter to Lyndon Johnson expressing his friendship and gratitude to the president, who, according to Max, went around with tears in his eyes saying that he never had a truer friend than Max Kampelman.

Be this as it may, the basic fact was that Tom did not want to work in a staff role directly under the thumb of Lyndon Johnson. His reluctance was so for both personal and professional reasons. Hughes would have to adopt the administration's Vietnam policies and become a public spokesperson for them, as Hubert Humphrey had been forced to do. Or, like George Ball, Tom could become a tame dove in internal debates but still have to be a hawk in public.

Neither of these roles appealed to Tom. The Vietnam situation was getting worse. INR analysts were telling him that the United States, having committed large numbers of combat troops, should have decided to work closely with the ARVN forces. General Westmoreland rejected this INR advice and did the opposite. The MACV commander decided for maximum efficiency to separate American operations from South Vietnam efforts. American troops would undertake all important engagements. The ARVN forces would be left in a backup and subordinate role, guaranteeing that they would never be an effective army.

The Dominican crisis provided another reason why Tom Hughes did not want to join the White House staff. Johnson decided to send Mac Bundy and George Ball on a fact-finding mission to San Juan, Puerto Rico, in the midst of the crisis to speak with Juan Bosch, former president of the Dominican Republic. These were strange bedfellows. The president added his friend Abe Fortas to the team, apparently to keep an eye on Bundy and Ball. This was apparently not enough for the president. Johnson decided to add a small experiment of his own to the mission. He summoned his old friend and former neighbor, FBI director J. Edgar Hoover, to the White House.

Hoover, a bachelor, dined frequently with the Johnsons when they were neighbors in northwest Washington. The Johnson girls called him "Uncle Edgar." Hoover was happy to get a new assignment from his friend, the president. Hoover was to send a team to secretly wiretap the telephone conversations of Bundy and Ball at the Caribe Hilton Hotel, San Juan, and to supply LBJ with transcripts. All went well except that the Bundy transcript went missing. Johnson asked Hoover for an explanation. It turned out that Bundy was speaking Spanish on the phone, and the FBI, lacking translators of its own, had to contract the job out to cleared translators. The president eventually got the transcripts and found that Bundy and Ball had switched their usual roles. Ball, a Vietnam dove, was a Dominican Republic hawk. Bundy, a Vietnam hawk, was an advocate for diplomacy and the withdrawal of American troops from the Dominican Republic.

Hughes decided that ensuring the quality of the INR's analytic work would be more than enough of a challenge for him. Good intelligence could not guarantee good policy or tell policymakers what to do, but well-informed decisions were better than poorly informed decisions. He would strive to make the INR's voice and his own heard.

16

Speaking Out

With LBJ's decision in July 1965 to increase the American troops to 180,000 by year's end, it was clear the United States was "going big" in Vietnam. The war was now an American war. For Tom Hughes, several broad implications followed. The disputes within the civilian intelligence agencies—the INR's and the CIA's differing assessments of the Diem regime and whether to proceed with bombing the North—were now irrelevant. Analysts at the working levels in the CIA and the INR had ironed out their differences on methodologies and assessed Vietnam developments with a high level of agreement on most issues. The risk of Chinese intervention was the chief remaining point of disagreement, with the INR consistently assessing the threat of Chinese intervention to be greater than did their CIA colleagues. Disagreements over the effects of the bombing of North Vietnam continued for a time between the bureau and the CIA, but the analysts were largely united by the end of 1965 and remained so.

The agreement between the civilian intelligence agencies was evident in the process of preparing national intelligence estimates. This was a welcome development from Tom Hughes's point of view. Hughes had feared that disputes between the INR and the CIA confused and annoyed policymakers and diminished their confidence in what they were told. But the changed situation, and the growing consensus on assessments of the enemy's intentions, had a less encouraging dimension as well.

Since the big decisions had now been made, there was less interest in spending the time and energy to produce the interagency national intelligence estimates. With the big decisions made, what was the point of a new national intelligence reassessment? Smaller-scale issues could be handled in short papers, or intelligence notes, or simply by briefings. And since many issues now involved military tactics and logistics, the Pentagon became a bigger player.

Further, President Johnson's appointment of Admiral William A. Raborn to succeed John McCone as CIA director in April 1965 was a blow to the CIA's morale and also affected the entire intelligence community. The strong-minded McCone occasionally rode roughshod over the CIA staff, but his popularity soared after his departure. The agency became nostalgic for McCone almost from the moment Raborn arrived on the scene. The Admiral, as he was known, had made his mark in the Navy in World War II and later as a project manager for the Polaris nuclear submarine. In the Polaris program, he pioneered the PERT-chart management technique, which featured quantitative benchmarks and statistical measures to control costs and ensure quality. Raborn attempted to impose similar quantitative measures to assess the CIA's work, which promptly led to a staff revolt.

Hughes noted that under Raborn's ineffective leadership, attendance at the weekly United States Intelligence Board meetings fell off. Nobody understood what priorities Raborn had in mind for the intelligence community.

The Admiral cut quite a colorful figure on the Washington social scene. Hughes delivered a speech to an audience of aerospace scientists and engineers in colonial Williamsburg in May 1966. He happened to find himself seated later in the evening next to Werner von Braun, the famous rocket engineer. The two were pleasantly chatting when the evening's entertainment began. Onto the stage came a vaguely familiar figure dressed in a minstrel costume.

"Who is that?" said von Braun. "He looks familiar. Is that . . ."

"Yes, it's Admiral Raborn, the CIA director," said Hughes.

The Admiral proceeded to render a respectable version of "Danny Boy." Alas, his performances on the stage did not translate into his on-the-job performance. He lasted barely a year before a staff coup led by Ray Cline and abetted by Clark Clifford, chair of the President's Foreign Intelligence Advisory Board, forced LBJ to retire Raborn. Clark Clifford called Tom Hughes to inquire about Raborn not long after the Admiral's performance in Williamsburg. Clifford said that he was hearing bad reports about Raborn's leadership of the CIA. He asked for Tom's assessment of the situation. Tom told Clifford that he was forced to concur with the critical appraisals and recommended that Clifford suggest that the president ease out the Admiral and replace him with his deputy, Richard Helms.

Helms was an effective manager and a respected intelligence professional. He had a tendency, however, to give his political bosses what they wanted to hear. Within the CIA, Helms pushed decisions down to the working levels whenever he could. He often settled disputes by treating them as mere semantic matters for the "wordsmiths" to resolve. Helms might summon managers engaged in a turf battle and tell them to work out a compromise.

One story that was part of agency folklore was a dispute about the budget for a proposed special project. The disputants were summoned to Helms's office for a fifteen-minute meeting, the standard amount of time that Helms usually allocated for a meeting. Helms proceeded to summarize the strengths and weaknesses of each man's position for nearly the full fifteen minutes and then asked the rival managers if they had any quarrel with his summary of their positions. When they had no objections, Helms rose, thanked them, and adjourned the meeting.

One of the men observed as they left the meeting, "Did you see a decision in there somewhere?"

"No," said the other. "I guess that this means we are supposed to get together and work out a compromise."

Helms and Hughes were good friends, and this contributed to a good working relationship between most CIA units and the INR. As the civilian intelligence agencies strengthened their ties, the disputes that arose within the intelligence community increasingly pitted civilians against the military. Military commanders generally wanted their intelligence officers to demonstrate progress in the war effort. Since the intelligence officers were a part of the chain of command, they did not dispute their superiors.

The civilian-military tensions showed up within the Pentagon itself, as Secretary McNamara became disillusioned with the mindset of the Joint Chiefs and with the performance of the Defense Intelligence Agency. McNamara, in one of his early acts as secretary of defense, had established the agency to get a unified Pentagon view to counter the parochial and sometimes conflicting intelligence assessments of the army, navy, and air force. But the Defense Intelligence Agency, McNamara concluded in 1966, was uncritically reflecting the views of the Joint Chiefs. McNamara thus quietly sought out a civilian perspective by asking Helms for a comprehensive CIA review of Vietnam. The Joint Chiefs, for their part, tried to outflank McNamara by taking cues from Walt Rostow at the White House.

STALEMATE IN THE WAR

Kennedy and Johnson had both tried to keep the Vietnam conflict below the political radar and to focus public attention on other matters. Vietnam was kept off the front pages except when dramatic events like the Buddhist riots, the coup that ousted Diem, and the Tonkin Gulf crisis drew the public's attention. Even then, the Vietnam conflict did not affect most Americans significantly. As the Johnson administration Americanized the war, however, the country was directly engaged. The president tried to make the case that the United States was strong enough to pursue a guns-and-butter strategy of domestic reform and fight communism abroad. But this strategy became less credible as the war widened and dragged on without a clear path toward victory. A change of course, or at least a new rationale, was needed. It became evident to Americans that the war had costs.

When General William Westmoreland replaced General Paul Harkins as MACV commander in 1965, he believed that North Vietnam was winning the war. Harkins's three Ms—men, money, and materiel—were not working. Westmoreland deemed it his job to reverse the war's momentum in 1965 and then to lay the basis for winning in 1966. The Vietnam conflict was not like World War II, when the Nazis overran Europe and Japan attacked Pearl Harbor, or even like Korea, where the North clearly started the war by invading South Korea. Vietnam was a battle for hearts and minds, a civil war in the South but mixed up with infiltration of men and supplies from Hanoi. And Hanoi was aided by the communist powers, China and the USSR, each in its own way and for its own ends.

Showing progress in the war would improve morale in the American public. The tall, handsome General Westmoreland seemed to be the perfect man to take over as commander. He had fought in World War II and in Korea and had been commandant of the U.S. Military Academy at West Point. He was thus something of a military intellectual. He was skilled in dealing with the press and with the public. *Time* magazine was so impressed that it made Westmoreland its man of the year for 1965.

Westmoreland believed that he had reversed the tide of battle in 1965, just as he had planned. In 1966 the groundwork was laid for ultimate success. In 1967 the general was happy to act as the point man for LBJ's "success campaign."[1] LBJ had launched this public relations campaign to sell the war to the American people in April 1967 by the unprecedented step of calling the General home in the middle of a war. President Johnson had arranged for the general to address a joint session of Congress, a rare honor usually reserved for visiting heads of state.

Johnson decided to build up public support for the war because he did not like the alternatives his advisers were proposing. General Westmoreland, with the support of the Joint Chiefs, was asking for either a "minimum essential force" of 80,000 additional troops, beyond the total of 470,000 American troops already scheduled to be in South Vietnam by the end of 1967, or an "optimum force" of 112,000 more men to bring about victory more quickly.[2]

How long would it take to win the war? the president asked. He was told that under the essential-force option, the enemy would be disposed of in five years, and with the optimum force, the victory would take three years. Johnson did not find either of these options appealing. The public was getting tired of the war. The guns-and-butter strategy that Johnson had backed was not doing well. The conflict in Asia was having an effect on, and was hurting, the planning and execution of the Great Society programs at home. The number of leading politicians, both Republicans and Democrats, who opposed the war was growing. The Democratic coalition, as Humphrey and Hughes had predicted, was particularly vulnerable.

Was there a shift in strategy, like MacArthur's invasion at Inchon, that could bring dramatic results without Westmoreland's requested troop increase? National security adviser Walt Rostow had a proposal: remove the limits on bombing and open a second front by invading North Vietnam with a joint U.S.-ARVN force. The Joint Chiefs and Westmoreland nixed this idea on the grounds that it would be too risky. Sending troops to the North might leave key areas in South Vietnam vulnerable.

Johnson also considered the move too risky because he was warned by the INR and others that China had pledged to aid Hanoi in the event of an American invasion. Whether China would honor this commitment to Hanoi was uncertain, since China was then caught up in its cultural revolution. However, this was a risk Johnson was unwilling to take. He would stay with the present course but would make a determined effort to sell the war to the American public and to our allies.

BUREAUCRATIC DEVELOPMENTS

For Tom Hughes, 1965 had been a most difficult year. He had come close to setting policy on a successful footing, but in the end he had fallen short. There was the Humphrey memo followed by Hubert being sidelined. George Ball's effort to lay out a path for negotiations then failed in the midst of a botched bombing pause. The Dominican Republic invasion added confusion to the scene. The San Juan vacation in August had been a welcome respite. He and Jean loved the chance to work on their villa.

The offer to be White House domestic adviser was a surprise, but he did not second-guess his decision to reject it. It was the right decision, given all of the circumstances. The job had gone to Joseph Califano, a Washington lawyer who had done legal work for many government agencies in the national security field. He was apparently getting along well with the president and was becoming one of his most influential advisers on health policy, fair housing, voting rights, and other domestic issues.

Hughes's decision to turn down the White House job had strengthened his family situation. As head of his bureau, he would have more control over his schedule than if he were in the White House. Jean had largely borne the burden of raising their two boys. She wrote an occasional piece for a magazine and did volunteer work. But there was no escaping the fact that her career had largely given way to household burdens. Tom hoped that he would have more time for the family.

But matters did not quite settle down as Tom had hoped. The White House was not quite done with him, and in 1966 there was another shuffle in high-level posts, this time in foreign policy. Mac Bundy resigned in February 1966 to become president of the Ford Foundation. The president chose Walt Rostow as Bundy's successor, ignoring Bundy's advice favoring Hughes on a short list of qualified candidates.

George Ball left the under secretary post in State to practice law but then rejoined the administration as Adlai Stevenson's successor at the United Nations. Adlai had died suddenly of a massive heart attack in London. There were three positions open at State: under secretary, the under secretary for economic affairs, and assistant secretary for Near Eastern affairs. Tom Hughes was curious about who would take over the under secretary post, held first by Chet Bowles and then George Ball, but none of the open positions directly involved him. Or so it seemed.

Hughes got word one morning that Secretary Rusk urgently wished to see him. He hurried to the secretary's office and was surprised to find an old friend, David Ginsburg, about to leave the outer office. The two men exchanged a hurried greeting and made a date to have lunch later that week. Rusk had another surprise for Hughes, this time telling him that the White House had decided to send his name to the Senate as the administration's choice to be assistant secretary of state for Near Eastern affairs.

The White House planned to make an announcement soon, possibly as early as that afternoon, and wanted Hughes to be prepared for press inquiries. Hughes was taken aback. There had been no hint that he was under consideration for this post. He had made no effort to line up political support and had never expressed interest in the position.

Tom had good reason to think that he was not suited for the position. The personal issues that had contributed to his decision not to seek the Ralph Dungan job were still present. The Bureau of Near Eastern Affairs post was an enormously demanding job. It would involve extensive foreign travel, which would strain his family situation. A host of professional considerations also applied. This position almost always went to an old Middle East hand, and Tom did not have that background. He told Rusk he wanted to stay put in his present assignment.

Hughes had a reputation for being strongly pro-Israel. This arose from the fact that he was a former Humphrey aide, a friend of the American Israel Public Affairs Committee's founder, Si Kenan, and a kibbutznik in his student days. However, the reputation as a friend of Israel was undeserved. Tom was turned off by his student experience in the kibbutz, disliked AIPAC's tactics in attacking Fulbright, and felt that Hubert had gone overboard in defending Israel. Moreover, Tom considered that his nomination would incur the wrath of all Arab nations and would make his tenure in office unpleasant.

Furthermore, as a former aide to Chet Bowles (still in India as U.S. envoy), Muslims would deem him to be pro-Indian and hostile to Pakistan's interests. He would thus find built-in enemies in the Near East post. The politics that would confront him in the job would make it difficult to do the job. When Tom told Rusk that the administration should not consider him for this position, it would be the end of the line for him with the White House. There would be no future job offers. But the question of how this offer came about puzzled Hughes.

Tom never arrived at a clear understanding of the White House's motivations. As best Hughes could tell, the move was probably part of a broader LBJ maneuver to appease Israel on the verge of a new war in the Middle East and to burnish his Great Society credentials by appointing an African American to the Supreme Court.

On the Israel front, LBJ thought he would have gained favor by placing three strongly pro-Israel officials in the top ranks of the State Department: Nicholas Katzenbach, as under secretary (whom LBJ mistakenly believed was Jewish); David Ginsburg as under secretary; and Hughes as assistant secretary. Placing three pro-Israel appointees in key positions would please the Israelis and also make for warm relations with the American Jewish community. The latter would be good preparation for LBJ's expected 1968 reelection bid.

Hughes's old Rhodes scholar and Yale friend Nick Katzenbach would become available by resigning as attorney general. Katzenbach had been moved up from assistant attorney general in charge of the office of legal counsel to the post of deputy attorney general in 1962 when JFK nominated Byron "Whizzer" White for an opening on the Supreme Court.

Not long after taking over as Bobby Kennedy's deputy, Katzenbach got into the first of the quarrels with J. Edgar Hoover that marked his tenure at the Justice Department. Hoover was discovered to be spreading rumors that the Reverend Martin Luther King Jr. was a communist and consorted with communist friends. Katzenbach and Robert Kennedy thereupon decided to authorize Hoover to wiretap King to resolve the question in expectation that this move would outflank Hoover by vindicating Dr. King. Hoover subsequently abused his authority by bugging King's hotel rooms and spying more broadly on King's movements, then passing around tapes revealing King's extramarital affairs. That was just round one.

A number of crises later, Katzenbach was named attorney general when Robert Kennedy departed in September 1964 to run for the U.S. Senate from New York against Republican incumbent Kenneth Keating. Katzenbach tangled again with Hoover, and his frustrations grew over the insubordinate FBI director's behavior. Katzenbach's indignation evidently reached a fever pitch in the summer of 1966.

Nick flew to LBJ's Texas ranch to ask the president to bring Hoover under control or to allow Katzenbach to fire him. Johnson would not permit Hoover's removal but agreed to curb Hoover's continuing efforts to undermine King, who was now opposing LBJ on the war. Katzenbach was not sure that even the president could control Hoover. After further brooding, he decided to resign. His resignation cited the unusual rationale that he could no longer function effectively as attorney general because an unruly subordinate had lost confidence in him. This rationale did not seem credible, and indeed it apparently was a smokescreen.

Katzenbach's resignation would enable the president to appoint Ramsey Clark as attorney general and Thurgood Marshall to the Supreme Court to replace Tom Clark. The attorney general was getting tired of fighting with Hoover and would then be available to be named under secretary of state (with a hint that quite possibly he could later be secretary of state).

Katzenbach's resignation as attorney general was one of LBJ's masterstrokes. Johnson had decided, after he had achieved passage of his two great civil rights measures, that his place in history would be assured as a champion of civil rights by naming the first African American to the U.S. Supreme Court. The place he needed on the Supreme Court came from making Ramsey Clark his attorney general, then forcing Tom Clark's resignation as Associate Justice of the U.S. Supreme Court because his son was attorney general. This would create a conflict-of-interest. The problem, though, could be easily solved, the president told Tom Clark, if he were to resign from the Court and take a well-deserved retirement after his distinguished service to the nation.

Hughes later found evidence in the intelligence reports of Israel's preparation for a new Arab-Israeli war. He also noticed that Israel's top spymaster made a quick trip to Washington with only one official on his schedule: James Angleton, the CIA's counterintelligence chief, who was considered Israel's best friend in the U.S. government. The meeting presumably had something to do with the imminent hostilities in the Middle East.

When Hughes lunched with his friend David Ginsburg, he mentioned what had happened at his meeting with Dean Rusk.

"That's very interesting," said Ginsburg. "But my story will top that."

Ginsburg went on to tell Hughes that Rusk had offered him the job as under secretary and stressed the urgency of a quick decision, since the administration wanted to make an announcement imminently. Ginsburg asked Rusk who the White House had in mind for under secretary. It would be important for him to know with whom he would be working. Rusk said that he was not at liberty to disclose the name at this time but that there was no reason to worry. The under secretary nominee was a "loyal American and you would have no problem working with him." Ginsburg pressed Rusk, insisting that he had been around Washington long enough to know that one's immediate superior was a matter of critical importance. Rusk did not budge. The atmosphere became tense. Ginsburg said that under the circumstances he must regretfully decline the offer.

As it turned out, Rusk then turned to Eugene Rostow, dean of the Yale Law School, and offered him the job. Rostow was also a friend of Israel. Rostow asked the same question Ginsburg had asked, and Rusk gave the same answer. But Rostow, eager for a stint in public service, declared his readiness to serve. Unknown to Rusk and to the White House, Rostow, as Yale law school dean, had turned down Nicholas Katzenbach for promotion to tenure at Yale Law School. Like divorces, there is no such thing as an amicable parting when someone is denied tenure. The relationship of Katzenbach and Rostow on opposite ends of State's seventh floor resembled that of two hostile nation states dealing with each other through third parties and as sparingly as official business would allow. It was possible, Hughes surmised, that the White House was aware of this background, which would account for the unusual secrecy in the appointments.

Katzenbach, to Hughes's surprise and discomfort, extended his coolness toward Rostow on a lesser scale to Hughes. There was no open hostility such as marked the Katzenbach-Rostow relationship, but there was a remoteness of manner that Tom found in sharp contrast to their camaraderie and friendship in the Rhodes days.

Nick, one of the few married Rhodes scholars in the class of 1947, frequently had Tom to dinner for a pleasant evening and welcome relief from the horrible dorm food. Now Tom found in Nick a reserve, a frostiness, and rebuffs to any attempt at socializing or familiarity. More serious, Katzenbach went out of his way to avoid relying on Tom and the INR professionally. Nick had no use for the daily intelligence briefings that Ball wanted and Rusk still enjoyed. Katzenbach established relations with the CIA for intelligence appraisals and briefings.

Although reputedly of a dovish disposition on Vietnam, Katzenbach's first action as deputy focused on congressional briefings that argued for the Tonkin Gulf resolution as legal justification for the president's escalation of the war. Katzenbach's contacts with Rusk were similarly strained. Rusk went from having friendly drinks with George Ball at the end of a long day to very formal and distant relations with his new deputy, who had been imposed on him by the White House. Instead of being called and put to use, as was the case with George Ball, Tom and the INR were deliberately ignored by Katzenbach.

Tom Hughes remained on good terms with Rusk, whom he briefed daily when Rusk was not traveling. Rusk's schedule was punishing; he traveled constantly, and when in the office seemed to subsist on a diet of cigarettes and whiskey. Hughes missed having his friend Roger Hilsman in the Asia bureau, who kept him in the policy loop, and the steady presence of George Ball as under secretary.

Bill Bundy, as Hilsman's successor, was a courtly and gentlemanly colleague, in sharp contrast with his uncivil behavior toward his father-in-law in April 1965. In some ways, Bill was more approachable than his hard-driving younger brother. But Tom also found him difficult to understand and disinclined to reach out to the INR for assistance. Bill had his own sources of intelligence from his prior service in the CIA and the Pentagon. Also, Bill had a prep school manner and frequently used locutions that baffled Hughes. For example, a frequent Bundy expression was "Well, I guess we'll have to suck eggs on that one." What did this mean—"to temporize" perhaps? Hughes did not want to seem like a rube from the Midwest by asking this urbane gentleman what, in God's name, he meant to say.

On occasion, Bill did display a knack for the pithy phrase, such as when he described General Ky: "We are really scraping the bottom of the barrel on this one." Bundy memorably summed up the U.S. dilemma in the Vietnam War: "They are more willing to die than we are willing to kill."

Hubert Humphrey, meanwhile, was off on his personal odyssey of clawing his way back into favor by becoming LBJ's most prominent cheerleader for the war. Tom saw Hubert regularly, but their paths did not intersect. Hubert was becoming a believer in the war effort and, as was his wont, an enthusiastic advocate. As Hughes observed years later to an interviewer,

> [Humphrey] wanted to please everyone.... As was once said of Theodore Roosevelt, 'He was not insincere. He believed it at the time he said it.' When Hubert spoke to a labor crowd, he was the best friend a union man could ever hope to have. If he spoke to a business crowd, well, no one stood up for entrepreneurs like Hubert Humphrey. If he talked to those suspicious of and uncomfortable about U.S. policy in Vietnam, then, by gosh, Humphrey would convince them of the rightness of the war.[3]

Hughes, on the other hand, found himself gravitating toward a role as a public advocate for rethinking current policy and seeking a framework for peace. This was a comfortable position for him as a public advocate and debater. But he was on a different track from that of Humphrey. Tom spoke mainly to elite and professional audiences, and his office distributed copies of the address to 300 or so influential friends and colleagues in Congress, to key congressional staffers, leading academics, foundation executives, and editorial writers for major newspapers.

SPEAKING OUT

Tom Hughes delivered thirty-seven formal addresses, with written texts, to professional and elite audiences from December 1965 through the end of the Johnson administration.[4] The texts were elegantly written, carefully researched, and filled with classical allusions that required careful reading to grasp the meaning. The talks could have been published as essays in an elite opinion journal (and some, in fact, later were).

A few of the talks grew out of his normal duties and were simply convenient vehicles for announcing policy. A prominent example was the Root-Jessup lecture delivered on October 2, 1965, at Hamilton College, which laid out the INR's role in reviewing and clearing Pentagon-funded research projects by American scholars in Third World countries.[5]

Some of the talks dealt with process issues, such as the changing role of the professional diplomat, democracy in the Foreign Service, the participation of new professionals and interest groups in foreign policy, and the role of intelligence in decisionmaking.[6] A number dealt with the Vietnam War, either directly or indirectly, and increasingly criticized American policy. The criticisms, though, were couched in such erudite and witty language that the message did not jump out in headline form.

The talks rebutted the domino theory, pointed out the obsolescence of the containment doctrine, described "wars of national liberation" as sometimes anticolonial in origin and not communist inspired, and declared that the split between the Soviet Union and China had shattered the concept of a unified world communist movement. He explained how other nations viewed the emergence of China on the world scene.

Hughes's lectures became more pointed as the Johnson administration's public relations campaign to sell the war became more strident, and especially as General Westmoreland became LBJ's point man for the public relations campaign.

Tom Hughes delivered one of his best talks "The Odyssey of Counter Insurgency," on July 3, 1967, to an audience at the Foreign Service Institute. This was his most direct attack on U.S. Vietnam policy.[7] He repeated the talk for audiences at West Point and the National War College later in the month.

Tom told his audiences that U.S. Vietnam policy was misconceived from the start. He referred to Homer in developing the argument. What started as a small number of covert operations by the United States to help a friendly ally grew into deployment of a large conventional force of Americans fighting a full-scale war. The objectives the United States sought to achieve were indistinct, the enemy unclear, and the ally of uncertain reliability. Hughes concluded his analysis with an ironic reference to an observation made by Mao in 1926 and asked his audiences to apply the lessons to

Vietnam: "Who are our enemies? Who are our friends? This is a question of first importance," said Mao. "The basic reason why previous revolutionary struggles in China achieved so little was their failure to unite with real friends in order to attack real enemies."[8]

In speaking out on the war, Hughes did not cast himself as an antiestablishment critic, like the antiwar students. He was not an antiestablishment figure, even though he saw himself as a "self-conscious liberal . . . with Midwestern populist roots."[9]

He was, in fact, happy to be considered a part of the foreign policy establishment. His complaint was that that the establishment was badly in need of reform. It was a good thing that he, a boy from a small town in Minnesota, could work alongside patricians like the Bundys, legendary figures like Averell Harriman, and leading politicians. Elites from outside the government could bring energy and vision but also needed the input of a professional class of diplomats who worked the foreign policy vineyards.

The Foreign Service, however, was like an island cut off from the mainland. There was not enough real debate, too much conformity, too much timidity, and much unnecessary secrecy. The Foreign Service, and the whole national security policy process in general, should be more open, more diverse, and less dominated by easterners, WASPs, and Ivy Leaguers. Women, minorities, and Jews were rare in the Foreign Service, the CIA, and the upper ranks of the officer corps, as Hughes saw it. As to those who served in the top-level policy positions, they were too conformist, too narrowly based geographically, and not open enough to new ideas and research findings from the growing community of foreign policy scholars in the nation's universities.

Hughes had made it a practice to hire talented women for the INR, to bring in academics, and to seek out Foreign Service officers with unconventional backgrounds and with a strong interest in research. Meritocracy was in the early stages in the Foreign Service. In Hughes's view this was long overdue, and he did his best to encourage it. The goal should be to have an elite—but an open, competitive, and democratic elite—running foreign policy and exchanging views with an attentive public on the increasingly complex issues of the day.

THE FATE OF FACTS

When Tom Hughes finally resigned as assistant secretary of state for intelligence and research in 1969, he delivered on his final two days in office two classic lectures on intelligence to jam-packed audiences in the State Department auditorium. Hughes was well aware that intelligence and open public discussion were related in complex ways and that both were parts of the policy process. He had seen the relationship between intelligence and politics evolve and mutate over eight tumultuous years. The fortunes of the intelligence community as a whole waxed and waned over the period, and the standing of individual agencies, including his own bureau, changed as well. Hughes's own position, and that of the bureau he led, had waned in the final two years. Whereas at the start of his public service he had easy and frequent contacts with White House staff and even with President Kennedy himself, after 1966, when Mac Bundy and Bill Moyers left, he had less ready access. Harry McPherson was still a friend and could be counted on to make sure INR views got a hearing if Tom pushed hard.

Hughes was on cordial terms personally with Walt Rostow. The camaraderie of the Rhodes brotherhood, to a degree, took the edge off personal frictions. But Walt was clearly opposed to Tom's views on Vietnam and made sure that INR recommendations did not easily get to the president, and if they did, they would carry warning caveats. Not that the president needed much warning: he carried a map in his head with everyone placed in the right box, whether it was Fulbright on Capitol Hill, Hughes in the State Department, or Rostow on his own staff. Rostow and the CIA's Special Assistant for Vietnamese Affairs (SAVA) head, George Carver, had grown close, and by 1967 Carver was the dominant link for filtering and interpreting the work of the intelligence community for the White House. Helms had some standing with LBJ since his excellent prognostications on the Six Days War in June 1967, but in the nature of things he had to tread carefully. Helms was well aware that McCone had made himself a pest and had fallen out of favor with Johnson.

Given the pressures on the presidency and Helms's own responsibilities, face-to-face interactions between Johnson and Helms were limited. Helms, by disposition, was inclined to defer to his political bosses and was cautious in pushing any policy position too hard with the volatile Lyndon Johnson. Carver, on the other hand, was in touch with Rostow often and had a frank relationship with him. Between the formal one-hour briefings that Carver delivered weekly to Rostow, there were informal contacts between them. There was nothing evil in Carver's maneuvers, just the boldness and the seizing of one's chances by a cunning courtier.

The year 1968 was one of tumult, filled with events that blotted out bureaucratic trivialities. His last year caused Tom to reflect more deeply on the nature of the intelligence process. In planning his lectures on intelligence and policymaking, he wanted to avoid the impression of settling old scores. He owed his audience a set of observations that might have some staying power.

There was no right for intelligence analysts to be heard—or, if heard, to be heeded. The making of foreign policy was surely permeated with politics, and there was no institutional framework that could guarantee the attention of the elected officials who were the major policymakers. The best and wisest views might never be heard by those in power. One would have to figure out who had power and how to approach them. The founding fathers had guaranteed a system of shared powers that would invite competition for favor and attention from multiple centers of power, which would assuredly have conflicting conceptions of the public good.

Certainly it was a good idea to have decisionmakers consult their experts and intelligence analysts before making decisions. The analyst had to convince the decisionmakers—some of whom needed convincing, whereas others were too credulous—that what they had to say was worth the decisionmaker's attention.

What was called intelligence was not always intelligent. Flawed systems made for poor recommendations, and excessive secrecy masked policy mistakes. The government classified too much, Hughes felt, using classification to dodge public scrutiny. Some great blunders resulted from intelligence failures, which could mean failures by policymakers to heed legitimate warnings or failures by analysts to identify imminent dangers. Or it could mean politicization—the use of intelligence, like a drunk using a lamp post, for support rather than for illumination. But since intelligence and policy were always interwoven, what some would call an intelligence failure was often a policy failure. There would always be intelligence failures because there were always policy failures. What was considered a policy failure depended on one's politics. There were no perfect systems or organizational structures, and no one correct method or model of professionalism. All systems were run by and dependent on human beings.

Hughes had been around long enough to know that good intelligence could not guarantee good policy and that there was no surefire way to produce optimum intelligence products. And what if, for example, Truman and MacArthur had known the Chinese had crossed the Yalu—what would have been the correct policy response? To have halted the U.S. advance and taken up defensive positions to await the Chinese? To have pulled U.S. forces back to the previous border between North and South Korea? What was the definition of "good" policy in complex circumstances?

In the first of his final lectures as INR director, "The Fate of Facts in a World of Men," Hughes focused on the uses of intelligence by the decisionmakers. The lecture dealt with the complexities that affect, and limit, the utility of the analytic product from the policymaker's point of view. The lecture brilliantly explored how "facts"—the raw data underlying the craft of intelligence—are filtered through a network of ideas—the prism of presuppositions, values, and worldviews held by policymakers—and then further interpreted by various persons in the chain of command. These actors bring to bear their perspectives, their institutional roles, and their professional orientations to refine the product for the policymaker, though the policymaker sometimes wants only the raw data. The discussion covered the different institutional roles, the conflicting interests of the various bureaucratic layers and agencies, and the sharpening (or blurring) of issues as they make their way up the chain of command to the ultimate decision-makers.

Hughes debunked the traditional idea that intelligence can and should be kept totally separate from policy for the sake of "objectivity." In the real world, both sets of players—the analysts and the policymakers—want to influence, manipulate, and or blame the other, taking ownership of the successes and shifting responsibility for the failures.

In the second lecture, "Butcher, Baker, and Intelligence Maker," Tom focused on the human side of the analyst's world. He examined the stresses that confront the different kinds of intelligence analysts and the practicalities that encourage or discourage high quality intelligence work. The "butcher," in Hughes's parlance, produces the raw morsels of intelligence that policymakers often love. But infatuation with the tidbits may obscure the larger policy picture, which can get lost in the details. The reports of body counts, sorties flown, supplies interdicted, bridges blown up, or weapons captured or some seemingly dramatic episode from yesterday may crowd out serious thinking, planning, and evaluating on the larger task at hand.

Hughes analyzed the different intelligence roles with wit, learning, and in his distinctive literary style. He again expressed his view that it is the people inside the institutional structures, and not the structures themselves, that matter most. He concluded by returning to his original theme: "The fate of facts in a world of men leads us to conclude, as Webster once said of the Constitution, that we must write our compacts not alone with ink or parchment, but with 'letters of living light' upon our hearts."[10]

The farewell lectures quickly became classics in the intelligence field and received high praise. Characteristic were comments such as the following: "Yours is the best short primer yet written on the uses and the abuses of intelligence" (Sir Peter Ramsbothom, the British ambassador); "Your lively speeches . . . are the best things that I have read on intelligence" (J. C. Hurwitz, director of the Middle East Institute at Columbia University). From his old friend Max Kampelman came a tribute he cherished the most: "Your lectures are to the intelligence process what Cardozo was to the judicial process."[11]

17

The Most Turbulent Year

The most turbulent year of America's postwar history began, in historian James T. Patterson's view, with the lunar holiday in Vietnam.[1] Most Americans had never heard of Tet, as the season was known to Vietnamese, but they were destined never to forget the name. Tet came to symbolize the beginning of the upheavals and dislocations of that tumultuous year for the United States. The enemy offensive at the end of January 1968, according to most observers, caught U.S. and South Vietnam forces totally by surprise.

The Tet offensive, carefully planned by an enemy that was supposedly weakened and capable of only a limited campaign of attrition, suddenly launched coordinated attacks on Saigon and four other of the six largest South Vietnam cities, thirty-nine of forty-four provincial South Vietnam capitals, seventy-one district seats, every ARVN corps headquarters, and several major air bases. Altogether some 166 cities and towns were struck by a combined Viet Cong and North Vietnam force of between 67,000 and 84,000 troops.[2]

For Tom Hughes, Tet seemed to justify the argument he and Humphrey had made in their ill-fated memo to Lyndon Johnson: that the bitterest opposition to the war would come from the traditional Democratic Party coalition. The problems they forecast in their memo to Johnson were slow in coming but had finally arrived with a vengeance.

Previously, there had been a gradual erosion of support for the war as measured in certain polls and surveys.[3] Now change came suddenly. Moreover, domestic discontents became linked with the foreign policy concerns.

Dr. Martin Luther King's conversion to criticism of the war was important in affecting the outlook of Blacks and liberals. Urban riots broke out that exacerbated racial tensions and contributed to a sense of disorder in the country. Yet the racial riots were set off by the local police shooting of a motorist, which did not directly link them to the antiwar protests.

When the Kerner Commission investigating the causes of the riots issued its report early in 1968, it identified white racism as the cause of the civil disorders. The report looked back to the Watts riots of 1965 in Los Angeles and some 130 other disturbances occurring in the United States in addition to Newark and Detroit. Finding white racism as the main cause, the report made its famous declaration that the United States was becoming two separate nations, separate and unequal.

The report was issued almost at the same time the Tet offensive occurred, so that the domestic discontent and setbacks in the war seemed to be linked in the public's mind. The president's overselling of the idea of progress in the war, now seen as political deception, made matters seem worse. And then the campuses began to blow up, and Martin Luther King was assassinated, which led to more riots. Minorities, students, intellectuals, and media pundits all blamed the Johnson administration for the nation's ills.

A HUMPHREY-JOHNSON DIVORCE?

Hughes had a sense before the riots broke out in Newark and Detroit that Hubert was perhaps growing tired of his role as cheerleader for the war. Tom had remained in regular touch with Humphrey and had fed information and intelligence to Humphrey staffers John Reilly and Ted Van Dyck when he could not reach Humphrey.

One morning in spring 1967, Hughes got a call from Humphrey. The vice president was in his limousine and wanted to pick Tom up and give him a ride to the State Department. As they drove through Rock Creek Park, Humphrey asked the driver to pull over. Humphrey wanted to get some fresh air and asked Hughes to accompany him on a walk. Hubert told his former aide that he was being bugged, his office was bugged, and his new condo was too. He was tired of it. He told Tom the story of inviting Lyndon and Lady Bird to a private dinner at the Humphreys' new condominium in Washington.

Muriel and Lady Bird went into the kitchen to prepare the steak dinner, while Lyndon and Hubert conversed in the living room. Johnson wanted to know why Hubert was so successful in making a case for the war. How did he connect with audiences? Johnson noted that when McNamara visited Harvard, he got booed and his car was rocked by angry students, whereas Hubert seemed to have a magic touch with his audiences. LBJ wanted to hear one of Hubert's speeches. He wanted to hear how Hubert did it.

Humphrey started to give a quick summary of his main points. No, said Johnson. He did not want a summary. He wanted to hear the whole speech, word for word. Johnson stretched out his big frame on the couch and waited. Hubert, feeling a flush come over his face, started to recite his speech. Johnson got up and walked to the men's room, calling over his shoulder, "Keep talking, Hubert. I can hear you."[4]

Mercifully, Hubert was rescued when Muriel and Lady Bird announced that the steaks were ready. As appalling as Humphrey found this incident, it came at a time when the Johnson and Humphrey relationship was apparently improving. They talked more frequently and casually. Hubert was optimistic, but Muriel, perhaps shrewder than her husband in such matters, felt that something had happened to Lyndon in 1965 that permanently poisoned the relationship between the two men.

Hubert meanwhile had a health scare in June when he discovered blood in his urine. Benign polyps were found in his bladder (seven years later the symptoms would reappear, and at that time it was cancer).

Events moved swiftly. The Six-Day War occurred in early June and Humphrey steered clear, warned off by Hughes. Hughes had not endeared himself to the White House when the INR issued a classified paper showing that the Israeli attack on the U.S.S. *Liberty*, a reconnaissance ship, was not likely to have been a case of mistaken identity. Israeli planes had made two low passes over the ship, and sailors sunning themselves on deck reported that one of the pilots waved to them. The *Liberty* recognized the planes as Israeli, and took no evasive action. Fifteen minutes after the overflights, the planes returned and bombed, strafed, and torpedoed the *Liberty*, leaving it to sink. However, it did not sink and instead limped its way to port.

Then came the Newark and Detroit riots, which dominated the news and produced the chill in relations between the president and vice president. Before long, Johnson and Humphrey were back in their normal strained but semi-happy relationship. The proximate cause of the return to normalcy was the tease of Gene McCarthy, who began to talk coyly of challenging Johnson for the Democratic nomination. McCarthy's talk became less coy in October, and in November McCarthy formally announced that he would challenge Johnson in the New Hampshire primary of March 12.

It was not part of Hughes's official duties to concern himself with domestic politics, but he could hardly avoid domestic politics entirely. He talked with Humphrey regularly and knew many of the current senators, prominent journalists, and others who constituted the political class. Hughes attended Humphrey's staff meetings occasionally, at Humphrey's invitation, and was aware of where the various staffers stood politically. Once the campaign started in 1968, he attended more regularly.

The splits in the Humphrey camp were evident to Tom. Chief of staff Bill Connell was hawkish on the war, and Ted Van Dyck and John Reilly were dovish, as was press secretary Norman Sherman. Humphrey's kitchen cabinet was also divided, with Max Kampelman as the leader of the hawk faction and Tom Hughes the leader of the doves. All were professionals who viewed the political scene from Humphrey's point of view and in terms of what would benefit Humphrey. Humphrey's view of the Gene McCarthy candidacy was that he was a spoiler and should be removed from the race as soon as possible. Hubert, first on his own initiative, tried to talk his fellow Minnesotan out of the race and then tried again, at LBJ's behest.

Allard Lowenstein, the activist who succeeded Hughes as Humphrey's legislative counsel in the Senate for a short time and later served a term in Congress, took the lead in the Dump Johnson movement within the Democratic Party in the summer of 1967. Lowenstein went to see Robert Kennedy to persuade him to run against LBJ as an antiwar candidate. Kennedy turned him down flat, telling Lowenstein that under no circumstances would he challenge President Johnson and divide the Democratic Party.

Kennedy suggested, however, that Lowenstein seek out George McGovern and probe his intentions. McGovern also turned him down but volunteered that the Minnesota senator Gene McCarthy would be a good prospect as an antiwar candidate. McCarthy, still smarting over being toyed with by Johnson in the 1964 vice presidential sweepstakes, was interested but initially cautious. However, as he told friends, he was determined "to get that son-of-a-bitch."

McCarthy was aware of the risks and did not want to look foolish, but he hated Johnson more than he feared looking foolish. Upon reflection, McCarthy also realized how bored he was with the Senate. A preliminary indication that he might run was, McCarthy thought, well received. After some further negotiations with Lowenstein about what kind of help he could expect, Gene McCarthy announced in November that he would challenge President Johnson in the New Hampshire primary of March 12, 1968.

McCarthy decided that he did not have the resources to campaign across the country and would have to risk everything on New Hampshire. If he made an impact in the New Hampshire primary—admittedly, a longshot—his candidacy might take off from there. Tet was a godsend for McCarthy. An army of youthful antiwar volunteers, the "Clean for Gene" students, knocked on doors for him across the state.

Robert Kennedy, meanwhile, began to have second thoughts about his disavowal of any intention to challenge Johnson. Like Humphrey, Kennedy viewed McCarthy as a spoiler and tried, and failed, to talk McCarthy out of making the race. In January, RFK told reporters at the National Press Club that he had made no firm plans for 1968. Most likely, he said, he would run for reelection to the Senate from New York State in 1970, but the country was in peril and, who knows, duty might summon him in other directions. In fact, he had already begun to plan seriously for a possible entry into the race. He confided to friends that he was pondering ways to persuade McCarthy to withdraw. The Kennedy forces contacted party leaders across the country and tried to dissuade them from endorsing McCarthy or affirming their support for renominating Johnson. Tet convinced Kennedy that Johnson was in serious trouble. Then McCarthy, with the aid of his volunteer army, did well in New Hampshire, winning 42 percent of the vote to President Johnson's 49 percent. Pundits saw this outcome as a remarkable display.

Four days after the New Hampshire primary, Robert Kennedy jumped into the race. On March 16, he announced his candidacy from the same spot in the Senate Caucus Room that his brother had used to announce his own presidential bid in January 1960. Bobby declared that he ran "not to oppose any man" but because of the issues facing the country. He ran initially as an antiwar candidate but quickly moderated his antiwar fervor when his rhetoric sparked a negative reaction among party regulars.

LBJ BOWS OUT, OR DOES HE?

If RFK's sudden entry into the race was surprising, an even more astonishing development was in store. On March 31, President Johnson made his dramatic announcement that he would not seek his party's nomination for president in 1968. He told Americans at the end of a nationally televised address on Vietnam that he wanted to devote his full energies to seeking peace in Vietnam. The war had divided America, and he wanted to unify the country. He did not want to waste a single precious minute on politics. Furthermore, he announced a partial bombing halt: he would not bomb targets north of the twentieth parallel as a sign of good faith and an invitation for Hanoi to begin negotiations toward peace.

Hubert Humphrey had forewarnings of LBJ's shocking announcement on the morning of March 31 but still had trouble understanding what drove the decision to withdraw. Johnson had first talked about not running in February. Lyndon told him that things looked bad, some of his own people were telling him not to run, and labor, minorities, and the poor were against him. Johnson told Humphrey that he should get moving and start building a campaign.

Unknown to Humphrey, LBJ had considered announcing his withdrawal from the 1968 race in December 1967 but dropped the idea. LBJ had a secret poll taken early in 1968 that showed that he would be preferred by Democrats for the nomination and would defeat Nixon in the fall. He thus satisfied himself that he would not be backing out because he feared a humiliating defeat. Johnson, who obsessed about his health, told Humphrey that his father and grandfather had died young and he wanted to live for a while.

Hubert remonstrated with the president, assuring him that he would win the race. Johnson still had strong support, Humphrey said. A majority of the party and of the American people was still with him. He would be renominated and reelected. What he should do, Hubert said, was to announce a complete bombing halt. But, if that was too much he should at least halt the bombing north of the twentieth parallel, as a gesture of goodwill to Hanoi. He should combine the gesture with an offer to begin negotiations on a ceasefire.

Johnson was not willing to take Humphrey's advice. He had decided earlier in the month to ask his new secretary of defense, Clark Clifford, to evaluate the Vietnam situation and recommend a strategy. Clifford was to review the situation "from A to Z" because of the conflicting advice the president had received from the Joint Chiefs and the civilian intelligence community.

At a White House meeting on March 1, Earle Wheeler, chair of the JCS, gave a somber but ultimately upbeat assessment of the effects of the Tet battles. Wheeler first declared that the U.S. and ARVN forces had made a narrow escape in some Tet battles. However, he ended up by asserting that the enemy had suffered heavy losses in the overall Tet campaign. Therefore, it was now possible to deliver a "knockout blow" to the weakened enemy if the president would only approve 206,000 more American troops for Vietnam. The CIA and the INR independently presented assessments that contradicted the Joint Chiefs' conclusions in important respects.

The CIA and the INR agreed that the enemy had suffered heavy losses but differed on the issue of how soon Hanoi's and the Viet Cong's forces could be reconstituted. Following along the lines of the enemy's "will to persist" in the struggle, the CIA and the INR assessed that Hanoi's goals and its faith in ultimate victory remained the same, that enemy forces could be reconstituted through new recruitment in the South Vietnam countryside and increased infiltration from North Vietnam and potentially from China, and that Hanoi had no immediate incentive to negotiate until it had recovered militarily and demonstrated the ability to mount new attacks.[5]

Clifford assembled a working group of experts inside and outside of government to conduct his review, which, necessarily, like the JCS and the intelligence community's reviews, had to be done quickly and without extensive new research. The Clifford team came back with a recommendation for a bombing halt for most of North Vietnam as an inducement for peace negotiations. The shock of the New Hampshire primary results and then of Bobby Kennedy's entry into the race threw the president into an emotional tailspin.

Johnson's close adviser John Connally told him he should not run. His renomination was in jeopardy, Connally said, and a bitterly divided party would lose the general election in November. Lyndon turned again to Humphrey for advice and support after New Hampshire. Humphrey advised him again not to drop out. The pundits were wrong. The president's position, said Humphrey, was still strong. He would prevail, especially if the situation in Vietnam improved. Hubert repeated his proposal for a bombing moratorium and added to that the idea of a ceasefire and the convening of a new Geneva conference. The party and the people would back the president if he chose to run. As for himself, Hubert repeated that he wanted to remain on the ticket as Johnson's vice president, not to be steamrolled by the Kennedys again.

Tom Hughes could offer Humphrey no assurance that Hanoi would negotiate, that a ceasefire would be feasible at present, or that Hanoi and the Viet Cong would not launch new attacks in the near future. The INR had no analysts in the field to report firsthand on developments in Vietnam. The bureau could comment on CIA's or MACV's reports, assess the implications of NSA intercepts, have access to Hanoi's radio broadcasts and newspapers, and infer Hanoi's intentions from past behavior and still do the quick intelligence notes. But it became harder to keep up with fast-moving developments. The loss of one of the INR's best analysts of Vietnam and China, Allen Whiting, in 1966 hurt as well. Whiting, who always had access to the White House through his close working relationship with Bundy, did not have a similar relationship with Bundy's successor, Walt Rostow. Whiting resigned from the INR in 1966 to take a job in Asia, where he could pursue his research on China and North Vietnam.

Events were pushing the president toward a gesture of de-escalation in Vietnam. He was urged to show a willingness to negotiate, but LBJ believed that he had already made a number of such gestures by pausing the bombing of North Vietnam.[6] Hanoi was totally unresponsive to the latest LBJ overture, because in July 1967 they were already planning their Tet offensive. The president now had one more card to play. He summoned his "Wise Men" again on March 21–24, that reliable group of hardliners, chaired by Dean Acheson, who would surely stand fast and buck any dovish moves, as they had done in November.[7]

Astonishingly, the Wise Men turned completely around from what they had told him four months earlier. They now declared that Vietnam was hopeless. Who briefed these people? Johnson asked. The two briefers who had the biggest impact on the Wise Men, Johnson learned, were Phillip Habib and George Carver. Habib was out of town, so LBJ asked to hear Carver's briefing. Though interrupted frequently by phone calls, Johnson sat through Carver's whole presentation. Carver, the courtier, the reliable friend of Walt Rostow who had told the same group in November that the war was going well, now told them that the war was hopeless. He had apparently put his finger in the wind and, always alert to which way the wind was blowing, now had concluded that the winds were blowing toward peace.

Johnson pondered further and made his decision. He decided to address the nation on Vietnam and asked the networks for time to make a televised address on the evening of March 31. This was a Sunday, and most Americans would be in front of their TV sets, watching their favorite shows. The president would thereby capture the nation's attention.

Tom Hughes knew that the Wise Men had met and what they had been told. But he did not fully understand that the silver hairs had reversed themselves so completely from November. There had been numerous briefings by Defense, State, and CIA officials, but three briefings stood out. General Dupuy, trying to press the Pentagon's case, was tripped up by Arthur Goldberg, who showed that the general's numbers on Tet casualties did not add up. It appeared that the Pentagon was claiming that we had killed more enemy troops than the enemy had in the fight.

Goldberg queried that if the enemy had 80,000 troops in Tet and we had killed or wounded more than that, "Who are we fighting?" The dumbfounded general did not make a convincing reply.

Phillip Habib of State, a former deputy to Lodge in Saigon, gave a brilliant account of what was wrong and why we should reverse course in Vietnam. Habib had been consistent in the dim views he had been expressing for some time. Hughes was not surprised that he had made a big impact on the Wise Men.

Hughes was puzzled by George Carver's briefing. Carver had been a close ally of Walt Rostow and had been decidedly hawkish in his recent views on Vietnam. In December, Carver had dismissed the advance warnings of the Tet offensive from the CIA station in Saigon. He had written a recent paper arguing that Tet was a huge defeat for the enemy. Now, surprisingly, he totally reversed course and argued for peace negotiations and ultimate withdrawal, a position that was even stronger than what he had argued after Ap Bac.

Carver's briefing was persuasive with the Wise Men. Hubert told Hughes that he had urged LBJ to announce a full bombing halt and a ceasefire but was not sure how far the president was willing to go. Secretary of Defense Clifford also urged a complete bombing halt as a prelude to a ceasefire and the basis for peace negotiations.

Notwithstanding the case being made for a complete bombing halt, Ambassador Ellsworth Bunker, the Joint Chiefs, and Johnson's close friend Abe Fortas, associate justice of the Supreme Court, persuaded LBJ to settle for a partial bombing halt. The president told Clifford that he could not go for a complete bombing halt but would propose a partial halt. Johnson asked Clifford to prepare two speech drafts, a peace speech and a war speech, for him to review.

Clifford asked Morton H. Halperin, deputy assistant secretary of defense for international security affairs, to prepare the two drafts. Halperin was instructed to find language to allow the president to bomb the North in some circumstances, since the president would not go for a complete bombing halt.[8] The formula that Halperin proposed in the peace draft was to halt all bombing north of the twentieth parallel and most north of the seventeenth parallel, except for the area immediately to the north of the demilitarized zone, where Hanoi had massed troops for infiltration into South Vietnam.

Enemy action in the demilitarized zone would pose an imminent threat to South Vietnamese and American troops. The bombing halt would thus cover most of North Vietnam's territory and 90 percent of its population. The United States would also reserve the right to bomb in Laos to interdict the movement of men and supplies on the Ho Chi Minh trail. The moratorium on bombing would be extended to a complete bombing halt if Hanoi reciprocated the president's move toward de-escalation.

Harry McPherson, the president's speechwriter, took the Pentagon's drafts and was responsible for the final version of the speech, under the president's direction. The president added a final touch: Horace Busby would prepare a highly secret ending in which LBJ, unbeknownst to the other speechwriters, would announce his decision on running again.

The dramatic announcement that LBJ would not seek and would not accept the nomination of his party for the presidency in 1968 shocked the nation. Listening to the president's speech while driving back to Washington on Sunday night, Mort Halperin nearly drove off the road twice. He recognized his words from the peace draft. The president was opting for peace and he gripped the wheel to contain his excitement. But then he was stunned by the surprise ending and nearly drove off the road.

That morning, Sunday, March 31, Lyndon Johnson went to church with his wife, daughter, and son-in-law. After church, he ordered his driver to take them to the Humphrey apartment, where Hubert and Muriel Humphrey were packing for a flight that afternoon to Mexico City. Inside, Johnson drew Hubert aside for a private conversation in the den. The president gave Hubert a copy of the speech to read and asked for Humphrey's reaction. "Wonderful, wonderful," said Hubert, after reading the text. "The best speech you've ever given."

Johnson then handed him a copy of the final paragraph that he had decided to add to the speech.

"No, no, no! You can't do this," said Humphrey, thunderstruck. Hubert repeated his arguments about the strength of Johnson's position, but Johnson's mind was made up. Johnson swore Humphrey to secrecy. He was to tell no one, not even Muriel. As Johnson left the apartment, he told Humphrey, "Hubert, you have got to get moving!"[9]

Johnson's popularity immediately rose after the March 31 speech, but the gain was temporary. His peace overtures were not enough to satisfy the antiwar protesters and did not elicit a response from Hanoi. Nor was his tough talk tough enough for the war's defenders. Humphrey was under pressure to announce his candidacy immediately, but he held back. Humphrey sought out Larry O'Brien, who had managed Johnson's 1964 campaign, as his campaign manager. But O'Brien was committed to the Kennedys. A triumvirate of Max Kampelman, Bill Connell, and Washington lawyer Robert Maguire, representing the "old" politics that favored party bosses and moderate policies on the war, temporarily assumed organizational duties for Humphrey's campaign. Two young senators, Fred Harris of Oklahoma and Walter "Fritz" Mondale of Minnesota, representing the "new" politics and a more dovish position on the war, were also given authority to organize Humphrey's campaign in key Midwestern states.

Tom Hughes began attending Humphrey staff meetings. He played the conciliator in easing some of the clashes, both ideological and organizational, that arose. Under the arrangement Humphrey set up, there was constant friction between the "old" politicians, like Max Kampelman and Robert Maguire, and the "new," like Fritz Mondale and Fred Harris.

Humphrey had a lengthy meeting with President Johnson before announcing his candidacy formally. Following LBJ's withdrawal announcement, Bobby Kennedy paid a call on the president, seeking an endorsement. Johnson told "the little runt" that he would remain neutral in the Democratic nomination contest. Humphrey understood Johnson's public stance of remaining neutral but was disappointed that LBJ was not more supportive and enthusiastic privately. The Johnson-Humphrey conversation on the campaign turned out to be a lecture by Johnson on the need for Humphrey to organize effectively in the Midwest.

Johnson also told Humphrey that raising funds would be a big problem, which Humphrey took as a code message that the President would not help with the fundraising. The meeting left Humphrey with the sense that Johnson would not be of great help in the campaign.

Humphrey made his formal announcement on April 27 at a Washington hotel to an enthusiastic audience of 1,500 supporters. In his speech, he called for a return to normal politics, a politics of happiness instead of anger and protest. He used the phrase "the politics of joy," which his enemies pounced on as a sign of how far out of touch Humphrey was with reality. Richard Nixon had consolidated his front-runner status as the likely Republican nominee. He was challenged on the right by George Wallace of the American Independent Party.[10] Humphrey's announcement immediately catapulted him to the top of the Democratic candidates as the choice of 38 percent of Democratic voters, ahead of both Kennedy and McCarthy. Robert Kennedy's opportunistic entrance into the race had produced bitterness in the McCarthy ranks. Al Lowenstein and many in the antiwar ranks remained loyal to McCarthy.

Hubert was still the Happy Warrior: he genuinely enjoyed politics and most people. He even liked his political opponents. Tom Hughes remembered watching television with Humphrey one day when Gene McCarthy came on the screen.

"You know," said Hubert. "Despite everything, I still can't help liking the guy."

For all his shortcomings as a candidate, McCarthy continued to run strongly, winning six state primaries (Wisconsin, Pennsylvania, Massachusetts, Oregon, New Jersey, and Illinois) to RFK's four (Indiana, Nebraska, South Dakota, and California).[11] However, Kennedy prevailed in three of the four primaries where they had been running head-to-head: Indiana, Nebraska, and California. By the time Humphrey announced, he was too late for the remaining primaries, but this suited his strategy. He did not want to run against McCarthy or Kennedy in the primaries because they would demand a debate. Humphrey was ahead in the polls, had strength in the nonprimary states, and did not want to debate because Vietnam would be the main subject. Also, Humphrey correctly perceived that the competition between Kennedy and McCarthy would damage both candidates.

In the Indiana primary, held on May 7, the result was somewhat confused by Governor Roger Branigan's favorite-son candidacy. He was pledged to President Johnson, even though LBJ was formally out of the race. Johnson was informally back in the race insofar as he was sounding out party leaders across the country for possible support. Johnson was also cooking up plans with Chicago's mayor Richard Daley for a dramatic appearance at the convention, which he hoped would result in a draft. Robert Kennedy won in the Indiana primary, with 42 percent of the vote, Governor Branigan was second with 31 percent for Johnson, and McCarthy third with 27 percent.[12]

Kennedy won handily in Nebraska on May 14 by the lopsided margin of 51 percent of the vote to McCarthy's 21 percent. McCarthy made only one campaign appearance in Nebraska, whereas Kennedy campaigned extensively throughout the state.

In the Oregon primary, McCarthy pulled a stunning upset, defeating Kennedy by 45 percent to 39 percent of the vote. Kennedy did not have a good organization in Oregon, and his message on civil rights and urban poverty did not resonate with voters in a state with few minorities. McCarthy's Oregon victory set the stage for a dramatic showdown in the winner-takes-all California primary of June 4. The Minnesotan had ample funding and was well organized in California. Polls showed a very tight race. On June 1, the two men met in a high-profile TV debate. Kennedy believed that this was his chance to outshine McCarthy and set the stage for a victory in Chicago. Although Kennedy performed badly in the debate, he still managed to eke out a narrow 46 percent to 42 percent win over McCarthy.

A tired and subdued Kennedy addressed his followers around midnight on June 4. He then walked through the kitchen to shake hands with hotel employees. A deranged kitchen worker, Sirhan Sirhan, shot Kennedy in the head at close range with a .22 pistol. Robert Kennedy died on the morning of June 6. He was only 42 years old. Kennedy would most likely not have won the nomination in 1968, for Humphrey had been consolidating his position in the nonprimary states while RFK and McCarthy were battling in the primaries. With RFK's death, Humphrey became the almost certain Democratic nominee.

THE CONVENTION

Tom Hughes by coincidence had visited Humphrey on March 31, the day Hubert and Muriel were preparing for their trip to Mexico City, following the Johnson's after-church visit. Humphrey told Hughes that he had seen the president, who had told him to watch the speech that evening, but Hubert said nothing further. Humphrey seemed unusually quiet for the rest of the day, not his usual ebullient self.

On the plane, the other people in the delegation noticed that Humphrey was uncharacteristically reserved. Muriel had asked Hubert whether the president was ill. He had looked strange to her. Hubert said no, Johnson was merely worrying about the speech. Humphrey was worried and continued to worry about running, how and when to announce, and how to wage the campaign. After his announcement in April, he assumed that Kennedy would be his most formidable opponent. Kennedy was campaigning in Nebraska at the time of Humphrey's announcement. Kennedy welcomed him into the race but criticized Hubert's failure to enter the primaries and his unwillingness to debate.

Hughes remained in almost daily touch with the Humphrey staff. With Kennedy's death, gloom settled over the campaign. Even though it was now increasingly likely that Hubert would be the nominee, Humphrey's campaign faced some unique problems. People were disgusted with politics generally. The assassination of Martin Luther King and then of Robert Kennedy produced an inchoate rage among political activists. Humphrey was a natural target for the fury felt by many voters. Muriel warned Hubert that the bullet that killed Kennedy had wounded him.

Humphrey's candidacy faced a major problem resulting from the large-scale protests against Johnson and the Vietnam War wherever he went. The vice president had to deal delicately with Gene McCarthy and George McGovern, friends but ideological rivals over the war. A fractured party emerging from a chaotic convention would be a disaster for Humphrey and ensure his defeat by Nixon in the fall campaign.

The old New Deal coalition that had elected Democrats for years now lay shattered. And if all the king's horses and all the king's men could not put Humpty Dumpty together again, could Hubert put the Democratic Party together again? Alabama governor George Wallace complicated the picture by picking off conservative southern and border-state Democratic voters attracted to his populist independent candidacy.[13]

There was a further basic problem: What was Humphrey's message on the war? He was running as a moderate on the war to appeal to southern delegates, but did this mean that he was totally committed to Johnson's position on the war? The Vietnam issue divided Humphrey's own staff, party leaders, and the voters. The split in Humphrey's staff was both on policy substance and on campaign strategy. Basic to both policy and process was Hubert's relationship with LBJ: Could Humphrey manage to distance himself from the war without totally alienating the president?

The campaign got a boost when Larry O'Brien, following Robert Kennedy's death, joined as the overall campaign manager. Hughes, along with campaign staffers John Reilly, Norman Sherman, Ted Van Dyck, Senators Mondale and Harris, and others, represented the Left among Humphrey's key supporters. Max Kampelman, Robert Maguire, Evron and Jeane Kirkpatrick, and Bill Connell represented the Right among the staff, donors, and other key supporters. Campaign manager Larry O'Brien was a mediator between them.

As the campaign went on, Professor Zbigniew Brzezinski of Columbia University sent Humphrey several long memos. Brzezinski knew Humphrey from a year he spent with State's policy planning staff. Humphrey was impressed with Zbig's imaginative approach to Eastern Europe and his openness to new problems of the "technotronic" era.[14] At one point Brzezinski was designated as the campaign's foreign policy adviser.[15] However, this was because Connell and Reilly vetoed each other and settled on Brzezinski as a neutral outsider. Brzezinski rarely made an appearance at campaign headquarters or publicly spoke on Humphrey's behalf. The thrust of his most important memo to Humphrey was to caution him against joining the extremists in the party and alienating the mainstream. Brzezinski, though imaginative in his theories of international relations, was very much a traditionalist on matters of academic freedom and proper protocol. He deftly stood his ground against campus radicals who harassed him with various tactics, including an effort by Students for a Democratic Society to bring a pig to his office.[16]

Henry Kissinger was a more regular participant in the Humphrey campaign just as he was with the Nixon forces. Kissinger was playing a double game, using his sources in the Harriman-Vance headquarters to present confidential information to the Nixon and then to the Humphrey people. Henry was seeking to ingratiate himself secretly with both camps to advance his candidacy for becoming either Nixon's or Humphrey's national security adviser.

Kampelman, as leader of the Humphrey conservatives, considered any move away from Lyndon Johnson's position on the war as perilous. As the convention approached, Hughes, Max's old friend and protégé, took up the cause of a "peace plank" for Humphrey to run on. Tom worked with his friend David Ginsburg, who was active on the platform committee, to develop a strong position that would distance Humphrey dramatically from the president's Vietnam policy.

In May, meanwhile, the Humphrey cause had gained significantly when President Johnson announced that negotiations with Hanoi had begun in Paris and that he had sent Averell Harriman and Cyrus Vance to represent the United States. The negotiations, however, quickly deadlocked. The peace plank idea entered into the discussions over how to break the deadlock. Whether a peace plank in the Democratic platform would help or hurt the talks became an issue. Johnson, to ensure control over the platform, installed Representative Hale Boggs of Louisiana as chair of the platform committee and blocked David Ginsburg's efforts.

In 1960 JFK had paid little attention to the platform, which was much more liberal than Kennedy wanted. But it was well received by the delegates and Kennedy was content with the result.

The situation in 1968 was significantly different. Lyndon Johnson was determined to control every aspect of the convention, including the platform. He was already suspicious of Ginsburg over his performance as executive director of the Kerner Commission. Johnson believed that Ginsburg had double-crossed him, by pointing to America's division into "two societies—one black, one white" and blaming white racism and governmental inaction for the lack of civil rights progress instead of applauding the accomplishments of the Great Society programs.[17] With his elephantine memory for slights, Johnson also remembered that Ginsburg had turned down an offer in 1966 to be under secretary for economic affairs.

Hughes worked with Ginsburg in drafting the peace plank and then was given the task of lining up the senior foreign policy players behind the plank. Hughes lined up Rusk, Clark Clifford, and Walt Rostow. All of them could live with the proposed plank. Hughes did not approach the president. When Johnson learned of the platform effort, he ordered his lieutenants to insist on a hardline platform in support of administration policies. Ginsburg urged Humphrey to denounce the Johnson platform in his acceptance speech and to propose a minority report to present to the delegates. Humphrey had had enough and put a stop to the idea of his urging the delegates to adopt the minority plank. A three-hour debate did occur on the convention floor on the minority plank, but in the end the delegates voted to approve the majority plank.

A bolder plan also was taking shape, which Hughes supported, along with a large group of Humphrey supporters and staffers. Governor Harold

Hughes of Iowa and Ambassador Harriman in Paris, among other politicians, supported the plan. This scheme was the brainchild of Herbert McCloskey, a Humphrey friend and former political science professor at the University of Minnesota (who had moved to the University of California at Berkeley). At his home in Minneapolis in 1944, Herb had started a discussion group that included Hubert Humphrey, Evron and Jeane Kirkpatrick, and Max Kampelman, and other political scientists were frequent participants.

The scheme that McCloskey came up with now, aided by Evron and Jeane Kirkpatrick, was backed by Max Kampelman somewhat equivocally, by Robert Nathan, and by Bill Welsh of the vice president's entourage. The plan was for Humphrey to capture the nation's attention by a bold move at the convention. He was to use his acceptance speech to announce that he was resigning as vice president to devote full time to the quest for peace. This would signify his separation from Johnson's war policies. Polls conducted by McCloskey, a pioneer in polling techniques, had shown that Hubert's main drawback as a candidate was that voters did not view him as his own man. The dramatic resignation would capture the public's imagination and settle the problem of voters' viewing Humphrey as lacking independence. Hubert would tell the nation that a new vice president would be quickly chosen under the Twenty-Fifth Amendment. Humphrey would then present himself to the American people not as a puppet-like vice president but as a bold and independent candidate for president.[18]

The plan called for the Humphrey acceptance speech to be distributed in advance to the press in sealed envelopes—and to be opened only when Hubert began his speech. Humphrey would present a copy to Johnson in advance but inform him that the decision was irrevocable and that copies had already been given to the press. After delivering the speech, Hubert would fly directly to Hyannisport and draft Ted Kennedy to run with him as the vice presidential candidate.

McCloskey drafted a speech to this effect for Humphrey. To ensure a full hearing for the plan, McCloskey and his cohorts decided they should vet their ideas and get the support of a small circle of Humphrey allies, including, in particular, Tom Hughes and Averell Harriman. There was an effort to include Ted Kennedy in the package as the vice presidential nominee on the Humphrey ticket. But Kennedy, still in shock over Bobby's death, ruled himself out of any consideration for the vice presidency.

The group supporting the plan agreed on secrecy before the convention. The plan would be presented to Larry O'Brien, the sagacious campaign manager, after Humphrey's nomination was assured. O'Brien was impressed that a politician of Harriman's stature was on board as well as old Humphrey hands such as Hughes and Max Kampelman. O'Brien agreed to broach the plan with Hubert as a concept but not include the draft speech initially. If Hubert liked the idea, they would then hand him the proposed draft speech.

Humphrey listened carefully as O'Brien outlined the plan on the morning of August 28. Hubert was impressed that a powerful figure like Averell Harriman thought resignation was feasible, but he quickly rejected the proposal. "Well," Hubert said, "it would not be like an act based on principle or conviction; it would look like a gimmick. It would seem strange. And it will enrage the President."[19]

No one knew better than Humphrey what Johnson was capable of, and in the months between LBJ's withdrawal and the Democratic convention, the vice president was cautious. He was torn between his staff's advice that he distance himself from the president and his desire to convince Johnson that his views were not so greatly different from the president's basic position. He was in favor of de-escalation, but only if Hanoi reciprocated any gesture on the administration's part or gave indication in advance that they would welcome a move by the United States. Nothing seemed to shake Johnson's belief that Humphrey was "soft" on Vietnam. Humphrey, for his part, was convinced that the president was withholding information from him on the progress of the peace talks in Paris. Humphrey was getting some information from Hughes on what was happening in Paris, but the discussions were being very tightly held.

Matters reached an intense point on July 25, when Hubert sought a meeting with Johnson to show him a draft of a speech he proposed to give on Vietnam.[20] Humphrey told an aide what had happened at the meeting. Johnson told Humphrey that he "would be jeopardizing the lives of his [Johnson's] sons-in-law and endangering the chances of peace. If I announce this, he'd destroy me for the presidency."[21]

Humphrey for his part was convinced that Lyndon was playing some sort of game with Nixon and was deliberately sabotaging any peace efforts Hubert attempted. Johnson had met with Nixon the day before, on July 24. The Republican contender told the president that he would support the administration on Vietnam so long as Johnson did not waver. For his part, Nixon said, he would not advocate a bombing pause, but he would not criticize Johnson for doing so. He would abstain from attacks on the president provided LBJ offered no concessions to Hanoi for domestic political purposes. In effect, this meant that the president, in a phrase that was not yet popular, had just thrown Humphrey under the bus.

Nixon had offered to support Johnson on the war so long as the president did not attempt to help Humphrey in the campaign. Humphrey's supporters were stunned. Nixon, it appeared, had outmaneuvered Johnson. Since Humphrey was wedded to Johnson, Nixon could attack Humphrey on the grounds that he offered no plan to end the war, was weak, or was being mindlessly hawkish—or for all of the above—while at the same time insinuating that he himself had a plan for ending the war and bringing the boys home.

A worse possibility was that Johnson knew exactly what he was doing, and in crippling Humphrey's candidacy he was doing what he thought would be best for the country: electing Nixon instead of the weak Humphrey.

The truth was even more surprising than these dark suspicions. As late as July, LBJ was still toying with the idea of reentering the race himself. In June, presidential aide Tom Johnson had told LBJ that his former NSC staffer Richard Moose had informally canvassed a large number of mostly young voters. The upshot was that LBJ should reconsider his decision to withdraw and should prepare himself to accept a draft at the convention. There was a groundswell of support for the president from young people all over the country. The young voters were convinced that Humphrey could not beat Nixon. Johnson was hearing the same thing from other contacts, or so he wanted to believe.

Johnson's convention team, working with Mayor Richard Daley, hatched a plan whereby Johnson would be issued a special invitation to attend the convention. The plan included the showing of a movie narrated by Gregory Peck extolling the accomplishments of the Great Society. A special award would honor the president as a historic leader and eminent leader of the Democratic Party. Mayor Daley would then call for a draft of the president as the party's nominee. Thus, as Randell B. Woods observes, "Unbeknownst to the media, the delegates, and the American public, the chief challenger to Hubert Humphrey's nomination at Chicago was Lyndon."[22]

The scheme did not stand a chance. The final blow came when John Connally informally sounded out southern governors and found absolutely no support for the president. With that, LBJ gave up the quixotic plan and directed his team to ensure Humphrey's nomination.

Mayor Daley had balked and declared that he could not go through with the scheme to draft Johnson unless the president publicly declared his interest in a draft. Daley was also toying with the idea of drafting Ted Kennedy as the party's nominee. Ted told Daley the same thing he had told Humphrey: He could not run for family reasons but would support the Democratic ticket and campaign hard for it.

The convention itself was a horror show for the luckless Humphrey. Everything that could go wrong did. There were student riots and police riots. Mayor Daley shouted obscenities at Abraham Ribicoff on national television. Gene McCarthy finally returned from his lengthy vacation on the French Riviera and snubbed Humphrey and stirred up his student followers to protest the convention. The timing was off so that Humphrey's acceptance came too late for the best national exposure and, while competent, it lacked Humphrey's usual fire. It was not surprising that Humphrey started out in the fall campaign well behind Nixon, who had enjoyed a smooth convention in Miami.

THE CAMPAIGN

Tom Hughes decided not to attend the Chicago convention. There was nothing he could do for Humphrey in Chicago. Hughes had a heavy workload at the State Department at the time, even if he had wanted to go to Chicago. And he distinctly did not want to go. The failure on the platform, Johnson's constant machinations, the prospects of antiwar riots, and Humphrey's extreme caution convinced Hughes that the Chicago convention was doomed.

Hughes's gloomy outlook was justified by events. The country witnessed massive antiwar demonstrations on television that bespoke a party in disarray. Chicago mayor Richard Daley's police were seen chasing and clubbing the protesters and evidently gave the same treatment to spectators caught up in the melee. Daley himself was involved in one of the convention's many low points when he engaged in the obscenity-laced shouting match with Connecticut governor Abraham Ribicoff. The normally inoffensive Ribicoff was on the dais placing Senator George McGovern's name into nomination when he suddenly departed from his prepared text. He looked directly at Daley and observed that if McGovern were nominated for president, "we wouldn't have Gestapo tactics on the streets of Chicago."[23] Daley jumped up in a fury from his seat on the convention floor and shouted at Ribicoff, "Fuck you, you Jew son of a bitch, you lousy motherfucker, go home!"[24] Ribicoff shot back that the truth hurts. The truth that hurt most of all was that this convention had doomed Hubert Humphrey's candidacy.

Humphrey's staff and outside advisers, including Hughes, urged Humphrey to make a bold acceptance speech even if he could not accept the resignation proposal. It would have required a near miracle, a speech like William Jennings Bryan's "cross of gold" oration at the Democratic convention of 1896, to salvage his candidacy. The speech was a valiant effort but fell short. Humphrey was interrupted by applause seventy-eight times and received three standing ovations. The nominee did not criticize Mayor Daley or his police. But he expressed "my sorrow and my distress" and deplored "the troubles and violence . . . tragically in this great city." He exhorted Americans to "pray for our country . . . each in his own way the prayer of St. Francis of Assisi: where there is hate, let me sow love; where there is injury, pardon; where there is doubt, faith; where there is despair, hope; where there is darkness, light."[25]

Humphrey had nothing new to say on Vietnam. He had accepted Johnson's platform as his own, and only on civil rights did he veer even slightly from a full down-the-line embrace of the president's policies. In the words of biographer Carl Solberg, "Humphrey, for all practical purposes his [Johnson's] surrogate, stood forth as the lame-duck administration's candidate, offering no change."[26]

Humphrey was sixteen points behind in some polls taken in the immediate aftermath of the convention. Humphrey favored a bombing halt without conditions and inclusion of the Viet Cong in the peace talks. Yet he was still unwilling to risk a public break with the president. Hubert Humphrey understood better than any of his advisers what this wounded giant of a man might do in the event of a Humphrey transgression. The situation, however, was growing desperate. A September poll by Gallup gave Nixon 43 percent, Humphrey 28 percent, and Wallace 21 percent of the vote. There was very little time to alter the momentum of the race.

Hughes stayed in touch with Humphrey's staff almost daily. This often meant Ted Van Dyck, who was traveling with Humphrey. Tom knew from his participation in the campaigns of 1960 and 1964 how chaotic campaigns can be. He fed information he could glean on developments in Paris, on progress in the war, the machinations of various personalities, on whatever he thought might be of use. It was ironic. This was as close as he had ever come to reaching the pinnacles of power. He had every reason to believe that if Humphrey won, he would be in line for a major job. He speculated mostly to himself, and sometimes to his wife, that he might be a choice for secretary of state. There were many others, some more senior, who would be candidates. Clark Clifford, for one, would push hard for the job. He would be a logical choice. Politics would drive the decision.

Hughes would certainly have been offered something. Maybe under secretary of state, like Chet Bowles. He would not mind serving under Clark Clifford or as special assistant for national security affairs. Henry Kissinger was campaigning hard for that job. But Hughes had gotten wise to the game Henry was playing as double agent between the Humphrey and Nixon camp, and he warned Hubert. Hubert liked everybody and wanted to hire them all. He did not have quite the eye for judging and cultivating talent that Chet Bowles had, but Hubert was shrewd and had good instincts. He had chosen Ed Muskie over Fred Harris for vice president because he thought that Muskie had a bit more experience and gravitas.

The basic problem was twofold. Humphrey could not break clearly with President Johnson on Vietnam and Johnson continued to undermine Humphrey's campaign. Johnson's undermining consisted of denying Hubert access to LBJ's wealthy donors. Further, he criticized Hubert publicly for suggesting that beginning in 1969 the war might be de-Americanized and some troops brought home. He also cut Humphrey off from information from and attendance at NSC meetings, and refused to campaign for him until the last few days of the campaign.

From Paris came a hint of something big happening. Rumors swirled that a breakthrough in the negotiations was imminent. There was the smell of "caviar and vodka in the air," Rusk's quaint way of referring to Russian intervention in the peace talks. At the behest of Kosygin, Hanoi indicated that it was willing to accept the participation of the Saigon government in the peace talks if the United States unconditionally halted all bombing of North Vietnam. Hughes saw that it was now time for Humphrey to make his move. Speaking as one politician to another, Hughes appealed to Hubert to take advantage of the developments in Paris by announcing his willingness to "take a risk for peace." Hubert would stop the bombing. There would be conditions: Hanoi must respect the demilitarized zone and show signs of moving toward serious negotiations for peace. It was not too late to reverse the momentum of the campaign and regain public attention to it.

Humphrey decided at last that he would break with the president and propose a bombing halt in exchange for a reciprocal gesture for peace on Hanoi's part. He took $100,000 from his rapidly dwindling campaign bank account and bought half an hour's time for an NBC television address to the nation on the evening of September 30. He was in Salt Lake City, and the talk would become known as the Salt Lake City speech.

Humphrey declared that he would take a chance on peace by calling for an immediate and unconditional halt to all bombing of North Vietnam and expressed a willingness to accept the National Liberation Front as a party to the peace talks. Tom was Walter Annenberg's deputy chief of mission in London (1969–1970). Annenberg told him that Nixon blamed Tom for persuading Humphrey to give the Salt Lake City address, which changed the momentum of the race.

Humphrey's Salt Lake City speech still maintained the conditions that Johnson insisted on in the Paris talks. The speech was thus something less than a full break with Johnson's policy. After he had taped the address and just a few minutes before it aired, Humphrey called the president to inform him about the contents. Hubert told LBJ what he was going to say and tried to assure him that the message was not so different from the president's position. Johnson was surprisingly amiable but pointed out that Hubert's conditions did not specifically mention two of Johnson's conditions, namely, that Hanoi would not shell urban centers in the South and would accept the Saigon government at the bargaining table. Johnson noted that Humphrey only specifically mentioned the demilitarized zone as a precondition for halting the bombing. Hubert said that Johnson's other two points were implied by the requirement for Hanoi to make peace gestures. Johnson said "okay" and promised to listen to the speech.

Momentum began to swing in Humphrey's favor. Antiwar protesters, who had been sitting on their hands, began to return to the fold. Wallace's support began to drop off precipitously after he named General Curtis LeMay as his running mate on October 3. Wallace voters began to conclude that a vote for Wallace was a vote wasted. Most important, however, rumors began to spread of the impending breakthrough in the Paris peace talks, and Humphrey's position on the talks began to look like the reasonable middle-ground position. President Johnson's romance with Richard Nixon cooled. Johnson's aides convinced him that the only way his legacy could be secured was by a Humphrey win.

Johnson, who had done little in the way of campaigning for Humphrey, agreed to a number of campaign appearances that helped to energize the campaign. The long and stormy relationship between Hubert and Lyndon swung back toward a reconciliation of sorts. Though Johnson still had reservations about what he considered Hubert's "lack of balls," his growing distrust of Nixon and the Republicans outweighed his reservations about Humphrey.

By October 24, two weeks before the election, the numbers in one poll showed dramatic movement—44 percent for Nixon, 46 percent for Humphrey, and 15 percent for Wallace.[27] Another poll from this period showed Humphrey at 43 percent and Nixon at 40 percent, with Wallace fading but still strong in five southern states. The campaign was now a horse race. Humphrey apparently was pulling even with Nixon or perhaps even nosing ahead slightly, with Wallace faltering.

VIETNAM AND THE CHENNAULT AFFAIR

The surprises in this surprising campaign were not over. Rumors had been swirling for several weeks that a breakthrough in the talks was near. Such rumors had helped to propel Humphrey's rise in the polls. On October 31, the breakthrough arrived. President Johnson announced that he had halted all bombing of North Vietnam and that Hanoi had made important, though unspecified, concessions in the peace talks. Furthermore, the National Liberation Front and the Saigon government would join the talks in Paris, setting the stage for an agreement among all parties to the conflict.

Nixon angrily denounced the move as a political stunt designed to influence the election. There was a surge of excitement in the Humphrey camp, as the election now appeared to be moving toward a miraculous comeback victory for the vice president.

Yet there was soon evidence of dirty tricks of a shocking nature by the Nixon camp. Nixon and his team, it appeared, were trying to sabotage the peace talks by telling the South Vietnamese leaders to stay home, stall, or refuse to participate in the talks. The Nixon team was urging Saigon to wait for a better deal from Nixon. If South Vietnam did not join the talks, Johnson's bombing halt would look like a purely political gesture aimed at getting Humphrey elected. President Thieu, evidently taking the bait, told the people of South Vietnam on November 2 that he would not participate in any peace talks that included the National Liberation Front as a party.

Johnson first learned of Republican interference in the peace talks through a national security intercept of South Vietnam's ambassador to the United States, Ngho Bui Diem.[28] Bui Diem called President Thieu to warn him, after meeting with a Nixon representative named Chennault at Saigon's embassy in Washington, that a bombing halt was imminent. The ambassador advised Thieu that Nixon and the Republicans were recommending that Saigon not participate in the Paris peace talks and to wait for the outcome of the U.S. election.

The trail of Republican involvement leads from the China lobby to Anna Chennault, widow of the late General Claire Chennault of WWII Flying Tigers fame, to her connections to John Mitchell and to Nixon himself. The "smoking gun" was apparently Chennault's call to the South Vietnam ambassador, telling him to "hold firm" on the strategy they had previously discussed.[29] By refusing to participate in any peace talks with the National Liberation Front, South Vietnam would ensure that it got a much better deal from Nixon after the election.

Johnson deemed the episode an act of treason and called Senator Everett Dirksen, his close friend in the Senate and the Republican Party's highest-ranking elected official, to denounce the action. Nixon telephoned LBJ and denied any knowledge of Chennault's actions or any interference in the election. Nixon's public stance thereafter was a disingenuous "defense" of President Johnson. For example, Nixon would assert that some people say that the president did such and such for political reasons, that he failed to consult allies, did not interdict supplies, and so on but then grandly declare, "This I do not believe."[30] But on an NBC election eve telethon he dropped this tactic and all but did accuse LBJ directly of failing to stop the flow of men and supplies on the Ho Chi Minh trail: "I have read news dispatches and an Air Force general said that the North Vietnamese are moving thousands of tons of supplies down the Ho Chi Minh trail and that our bombers are unable to stop them."[31]

The public knew nothing of Chennault's actions. The affair presented agonizing choices for Johnson and Humphrey. The election was only days away. Nixon would deny everything and charge that the whole thing was a last-minute smear concocted by a desperate candidate. Johnson and Nixon, each pretending to be solicitous of the other but each fully aware that the other was lying, played a game of threats, feints, dissembling, and bluffs as the election approached. Humphrey's basic decency and good nature made him wholly unsuited for a contest involving the likes of Nixon and Johnson.

For Johnson, the dilemma was that if he revealed what Nixon was doing, he might or might not succeed in enabling Humphrey to defeat Nixon. If he succeeded, the nation would be even more bitterly divided than at present. He would have to justify his wiretapping. And could Humphrey be trusted to negotiate an honorable peace? If Nixon won the election, he would be sure to punish LBJ at every turn. Johnson's advisers told him to avoid involvement altogether in this difficult episode. But the president was confident that he could still maneuver Nixon into joining him in the peace process in the last two months of LBJ's presidency.

For Humphrey, the prospects of victory were fifty-fifty if he did not raise the Chennault issue and if the affair did not come to light. It would be a complicated scheme to explain to the public. Voters might not understand and would surely be suspicious of a last-minute charge that the other side was engaged in treason. If the incident became public and if Nixon were nevertheless elected, the Nixon administration would be delegitimized and caught up in a frenzy of investigations. This would paralyze the government and hurt the country. If Humphrey won by publicizing the affair, he would himself have to contend with charges of releasing classified information to the press, playing dirty, and being the kind of politician that was alien to his nature and to his image of himself.

Humphrey's staff came up with a plan that would insulate him from direct involvement in the release of wiretapped national security information. Humphrey's press secretary, Norman Sherman, would leak the information about Republican contacts with South Vietnam without Humphrey's knowledge. Humphrey would then condemn the action and fire Sherman. Sherman, in his memoir, reported that Humphrey rejected the plan but later told Sherman that he believed he had made a mistake in not going along with the idea.[32]

Humphrey was inhibited in taking any bold step by the fear that Johnson might undercut him by failing to support him in the clutch. In one of their early conversations on how to respond to the Republican actions, Johnson told Humphrey that he did not have clear proof of Nixon's complicity in the wrongdoing and thus was predisposed to caution. Humphrey knew that this was not true. He inferred that Johnson was really saying that he would not turn over the tapes of the wiretaps to Humphrey.[33] Without strong assurances of Johnson's backing for any charges he might levy against Nixon, Humphrey knew that his options were limited. There was no doubt on the part of Clark Clifford, Tom Hughes, or any of those in the small circle who knew what was happening that Lyndon Johnson, had his name been on the ballot, would have found a way to make the charge against Nixon stick.

Nixon, shedding crocodile tears, said that he did not believe a word of the media reports about the president acting out of purely partisan political motives. No, that was impossible. Furthermore, Nixon assured Americans that he fully supported the president in urging that South Vietnam join the peace talks. But the damage was done. The favorable impact of the bombing halt on Humphrey's prospects was blunted by President Thieu's November 2 announcement that he would not appear at the peace talks. Negotiations suggested that Johnson had acted on his own and was not supported by his South Vietnam ally.

Humphrey, following Thieu's announcement that he would not participate, called for the talks to begin with or without the South Vietnamese. In any case, the prospects of a breakthrough in the negotiations under Johnson were doomed by the Nixon victory. By the time the Nixon-Kissinger team finally succeeded in ending the war four years later, the toll of American troops killed by then had more than doubled and there were many thousands more Vietnamese civilian casualties.

18

London

Expecting to resign at the end of LBJ's term in January 1969, Hughes was pleasantly surprised when he met with Secretary of State-Designate William Rogers and Under Secretary-Designate Elliot Richardson. They asked him to stay on for a time and help with the transition. The bitterness of the 1968 campaign had evidently not destroyed all traces of bipartisanship. Rogers told him, "Dean Rusk says that you are too good a man to lose and we would like you to stay on the job. Would you be willing to do that—for a while at least until we find a successor?"

Well, said Hughes, he was pleased to hear those kind words. Yes, he would be willing to stay for a time. But he had a job offer from the Brookings Institution to manage their foreign policy and defense studies program. He was very interested in the post and urged Rogers to press ahead with the search for his successor. He got on well with both men, but hit it off especially well with Richardson. Richardson had a real appetite for briefings. At the start, Hughes briefed both men together, but it became evident that Rogers wanted a brief overview and became impatient when Richardson pressed Hughes to elaborate on a point. Finally, he told Richardson that perhaps he and Tom should have a separate session to cover the point in more detail. Hughes got the message and henceforth separated the briefings. He gave Rogers a quick summary and then spent an hour or more with Richardson.

Kermit Gordon, the Brookings president, had been director of the Bureau of the Budget but had left the Johnson administration in 1967 to join Brookings. His ideas were appealing to Hughes. Gordon had been appointed Budget director by Kennedy and was retained in that post under Johnson. Gordon wanted to make Brookings more relevant to the policy debates in Washington and less focused on long-range academic-style research. He was looking for someone, and he thought Tom would be ideal for the job he had in mind to shift Brookings toward shorter, timelier studies. Hughes would replicate what he had done at the INR. The new studies would, it was hoped, command the attention of policymakers and the media.[1]

It had not been easy for some of Johnson's people, particularly the Vietnam hawks, to make a smooth transition to the private sector. Hughes was happy to have an offer from Brookings that would enable him to remain in Washington. He would not have to leave the stately home he and Jean had recently purchased in Chevy Chase, Maryland. Hubert Humphrey, not a wealthy man, fortunately was appointed by his friend William Benton to a seat on the Encyclopedia Britannica's board of directors, which carried a salary and an expense account. Humphrey also had a modest vice presidential pension and teaching positions at the University of Minnesota and Macalester College that helped to make the former vice president financially comfortable for the first time in his life.

Dean Rusk, also not a wealthy man, was less fortunate. For a time, he was conspicuously shunned by many prominent potential employers and former friends in high places. Rusk was a diffident man and, unlike many of his peers, did not push himself forward. He had been badmouthed by the Kennedys and disparaged in the press, and he stayed loyal to Lyndon Johnson even as the president became a toxic figure. After much anxiety, Rusk finally found a place to hang his hat at the University of Georgia Law School, though he was not a lawyer.

Walt Rostow was another one who encountered the vitriol of liberals. Although he was a tenured professor of economics at MIT, his former colleagues went out of their way to make it clear that he was not wanted back at the university. Rostow finally found a home at the LBJ School and the LBJ Presidential Library at the University of Texas at Austin. He turned his energies to ghostwriting LBJ's memoirs and defending the stance he took in office. Rostow was aided by the admiration most people felt for his wife, Elspeth. She received a tenure offer to teach history at the LBJ School and the history department at the University of Texas. Hughes considered himself fortunate to have the Brookings offer.

LIFE AT STATE UNDER NIXON

The transition to the Nixon administration was an orderly one at the State Department. With the Nixon team installed in office, Hughes resumed his regular pattern of briefings to the senior leadership in the department.

Nixon and Kissinger did not want any regular intelligence briefings from State and did not pay much attention to the CIA daily briefings, either.[2] Kissinger took the daily CIA briefing himself and passed on what he considered important to the president. Nixon and Kissinger restricted access to the most sensitive White House policy deliberations. Senior CIA and State intelligence officers often did not have a good sense of what Nixon and Kissinger were thinking. This was in sharp contrast to the practice of the Johnson years. The upshot was that senior intelligence officers did not have a good idea of what intelligence would be useful to the president and Kissinger.

As David Priess states, "Nixon grew increasingly detached from the PDB [president's daily briefing] and other analytic products prepared for them. He told his president's Foreign Intelligence Advisory Board . . . in late 1969 that he valued the intelligence he received but considered the CIA's intelligence estimates 'virtually worthless.'"[3]

Hughes learned later from Walter Annenberg that there was a special problem with Nixon. Nixon blamed Hughes for persuading Humphrey to give the Salt Lake City address at the end of September 1968, which Nixon considered gave Humphrey new momentum and nearly cost Nixon the election. Nixon remembered Hughes from the Senate fight over civil rights in 1957, when they were allies, and had a favorable impression of him at the time. Hughes did not know that Nixon was angry with him, but this was irrelevant. He intended to leave government as soon as the new administration took over. It was evident to Hughes that Nixon and Kissinger intended to run foreign policy from the White House and to leave only a minor role to the State Department. Much less did Nixon and his national security adviser want or need the INR. They believed that their own knowledge and experience were superior to what the typical intelligence estimate had to offer.

Elliot Richardson, the incoming deputy of state, sought out Hughes's views on his replacement. Tom suggested that Morton Halperin, a highly respected deputy assistant secretary of defense in the Johnson administration but someone who had been a colleague of Henry Kissinger's at Harvard, would be an excellent candidate. It was rumored that Halperin would join Kissinger on the NSC staff, but if he could be persuaded to take over the INR, the bureau would have the advantage of ensuring good terms with the White House.

The transition gave Hughes more time to spend with his family. Tom and Jean Hughes had a wide circle of friends and enjoyed entertaining. They had the Hubert Humphreys and the Dean Rusks to their home for a dinner party early in the summer of 1969. Although Tom felt some apprehension that there might be strains at this dinner party, Humphrey and Rusk had a fine time and the evening was a success. Humphrey had recovered his spirits and was his usual exuberant self, and Rusk was relaxed and genial.

Both men had reasons to feel let down by the other, but neither displayed any discomfort. Hughes admired the professionalism and the cordiality of both men. Rusk, a gentlemanly fellow, was invariably respectful, even with people who held strongly different views.

At the office, meanwhile, there were some light moments. Hughes received a letter one morning from his grandfather's publisher addressed to "Thomas Hughes." Mistaking him for his grandfather, the publishers inquired if they could bring out a new edition of his book *Indian Chiefs of Southern Minnesota*.[4] Hughes responded that he was not yet born when the book was published, but he was quite confident that his grandfather would like a new edition. Tom further vouchsafed that his grandfather would like him to undertake the assignment, since he had discussed the Indian chiefs often with his grandfather. Tom volunteered to supply an introduction to the new edition, and the publisher cheerfully agreed.

Around the same time, Hughes received a form letter addressed "Dear Fellow Republican," with a questionnaire from Nixon's transition team asking the recipient what post he would like in the new administration. Hughes returned the questionnaire remarking that since he was the editor of a book on Indian chiefs, the post for which he was ideally suited was that of director of the Bureau of Indian Affairs. He did not hear back from the transition team.

Tom had been friends for a long time with Frances Humphrey Howard, Hubert's irrepressible sister, and ran into her frequently at parties. Frances would embarrass him by remarking in her raspy voice (which sounded uncannily like Hubert's), "You see that man over there? That's Tom Hughes. He came very close to being secretary of state. If Hubert had won, Tom would have been secretary. I know because my brother told me."[5]

The early months of 1969 slid by pleasantly enough. Hughes reassured his INR colleagues that the departmental leadership respected their work. He felt comfortable with the Republicans at State and with Richardson especially. The tumultuous year and the bitterness of the 1968 election had ripped apart many old patterns. Yet Hughes felt that a certain bipartisanship had survived at the working levels: "The 1968 election was supposed to represent the breakdown of the old political establishment. But the acutely sharpened partisanship at the presidential level was not the whole story. The mores of the old establishment survived for a while at the sub-Presidential level just below."[6]

His good relationships with Richardson, a Republican, and with George Ball, a Democrat, typified for Hughes the virtues of the foreign policy establishment or what was left of it at the time. Both Ball and Richardson were strong partisans but never approached foreign policy as narrow partisans. Hughes came to regard Richardson and Ball as the two ablest men he served with in his State Department career.[7]

By staying on for a time, Hughes felt that he was reciprocating in some sense the bipartisan assistance he had received from Christian Herter and William "Butts" Macomber at the start of the Kennedy administration. Macomber, a Republican serving as assistant secretary of state for congressional relations under Eisenhower, helped the team of Shriver, Bowles, and Hughes in 1960 choose the ambassadors who served Kennedy. Hughes was now acting in the spirit of professionalism symbolized by the department's Fleming Award, which he received in 1965.

The frustration in the State Department, however, was already becoming evident in the relationship between State and the White House. The growing influence of Henry Kissinger with the president was clear to everyone. Kissinger expanded the National Security Council staff, nearly doubling its size, and aggrandized his own role in the key policy process.

Nixon blessed these changes. Like Kennedy, he was determined to be his own secretary of state, but unlike Kennedy he delegated unusual powers to his national security adviser. Nixon also, like Kennedy, had appointed as secretary someone he could dominate. Rogers had been attorney general in the Eisenhower administration and a Nixon friend, but he was not an assertive personality. Rogers could not stand up to the duo of Nixon and Kissinger. Every assertion of presidential power expanded Kissinger's own power. It is worth noting that few presidents have had as much experience in foreign affairs as had Nixon when he entered the White House. As vice president, he had traveled widely, knew many leading world personalities, and understood the levers of power in Washington. Kissinger's career as a scholar, adviser to Nelson Rockefeller, administrator of the Harvard summer school program for foreign visitors, his émigré status, and his service in the Army and in the occupation of Germany after WWII gave him an unusually broad grounding in foreign affairs.

Hughes watched the State–White House relationship with some detachment. It was not his fight, but he grew anxious to move on to his new role on the outside. On several occasions, Hughes raised the question of his successor with Rogers. Hughes was beginning to grow uneasy because the Brookings opportunity would soon disappear unless he could give Kermit Gordon a date certain for his departure from State. In May 1969, Hughes raised the subject again with Rogers. He observed that Brookings would not wait much longer for a decision.[8]

"Why do you want to go to Brookings?" said Rogers. "You don't want that. We have something much more interesting in mind for you. How would you like to go to London? They have a Labor government and you were once with the Senate Labor Committee."

In further conversations with Richardson the details were spelled out. Hughes's assignment would be to assist Ambassador Walter Annenberg, who had gotten off to a rocky start in London. Annenberg was displaying signs of breaking diplomatic crockery. Annenberg's inaugural speech as U.S. envoy, by tradition a paean to the virtues of the "special relationship," was instead an attack on student demonstrators as a threat to Western civilization. Also, Annenberg did not like the deputy chief of mission he inherited from the State Department and did not take his advice on protocol or anything else.

Annenberg had a severe stuttering problem that he attempted to control by a pattern of helping words he learned from a speech instructor. He resorted to these helping words when he felt a stutter coming on. The result was that his speech was sometimes an odd mixture of words that made him an object of ridicule with the British tabloids. Annenberg's introduction to the Queen was a legendary case of Annenberg's speech problems. The Nixon administration was concerned that Annenberg, one of America's richest men and a prominent philanthropist, was in trouble in this most visible of diplomatic posts. He needed help.

The help that the State Department came up with was to send Tom Hughes to London as Annenberg's deputy chief of mission.

"You might have some trouble from the White House," Hughes told Rogers at their May meeting. "I don't think they will be happy to have an old Humphrey boy in a plum job."

"Don't worry about that," Rogers had said. "We'll take care of that."

Rogers, Richardson, and Macomber did take care of it. The State Department for once outmaneuvered the Nixon White House. The State Department did not need to get White House permission for the appointment. Henry Kissinger, on behalf of president Nixon, attempted to stop the appointment.[9] Kissinger called Elliot Richardson and told him,

"Elliot, the President has instructed me to tell you to stop the appointment of Hughes to London immediately."

"Henry, it's too late. The British government has already welcomed the appointment in a public announcement. Annenberg has met Hughes and has approved. Hughes has agreed to go. Secretary Rogers has the authority to make a deputy chief of mission appointment and he has exercised the authority."

"The President will not sign anything you send over," said Kissinger.

"He doesn't have to sign anything. This is a Secretarial appointment and the Secretary has made the appointment."

"Find some way to stop it. There must be a security problem you could think of."

"No, our security people have vetted Hughes thoroughly and found no problems," said Richardson.

Kissinger was not quite ready to give up. He concluded the conversation by summoning Richardson and Rogers to a White House meeting that afternoon with the president. Hughes never heard the story of what happened at that meeting, but it was evidently a humdinger. Hughes ran into Richard V. Allen, who was briefly with the National Security under Nixon and much later was President Reagan's national security adviser. Kissinger eased Allen out of any significant role under Nixon, and Allen departed. Running into Hughes, Allen told Hughes with a smile that he had attended quite a meeting at the White House dealing with Hughes's London appointment. Hughes asked what had happened. Allen laughed and said he would save the story for his own memoirs.

There was also opposition to the Hughes appointment from the Foreign Service. The London post was a plum normally reserved for a very senior Foreign Service officer, who would retire after this appointment. Hughes was not a Foreign Service officer and had never served abroad. But Annenberg had met with Hughes on a trip to Washington and liked him. He was enthusiastic about the appointment. Rogers and Richardson brushed aside the objections from the Foreign Service officer ranks. They relished having won a small victory over Nixon and Kissinger. Nixon instructed Kissinger to keep an eye on the situation and also told Annenberg to report immediately to Kissinger if he had any complaints about Hughes.

SERVING IN LONDON

The proof of the pudding was in the eating, and the lingering opposition to Hughes evaporated as the situation at the London embassy quickly stabilized. Annenberg and Hughes developed a smooth working relationship and close personal ties. The ambassador was backstopped by his deputy on official matters, and the Annenbergs were free to "look for opportunities to show their affection for Britain. The ambassador found one outlet after another for his charitable impulses."[10]

Annenberg made numerous generous gifts to British charities that made him a popular figure. He became to the British a good-hearted and bumbling eccentric—a personality type beloved in the United Kingdom. He became a popular figure even with the British tabloids, which had once delighted in making fun of him.

Despite his awkward presentation of credentials to the Queen when he first arrived, Annenberg was drawn to British high protocol. He loved the pomp and ceremony of Buckingham Palace and delighted in hobnobbing with royalty and other dignitaries. The ambassador lavishly renovated the U.S. embassy and entertained frequently. Annenberg wanted to be a social ambassador and to lead the high life in glamorous London. He did not aspire to be a force in U.S.-British bilateral diplomacy or to make a mark in American foreign policy. In this, he was perfectly suited for Nixon and Kissinger, who handled most of the significant issues in British-U.S. relations out of Washington through the British ambassador.

When Annenberg had a meeting with a British minister on an issue not already settled by Nixon and Kissinger, he would bring Hughes along for assistance. The British foreign secretary Michael Stewart was Ambassador Annenberg's nemesis. The following tale presents a typical encounter with the secretary. At one meeting, once the conversation had gone past the amenities and headed toward deeper waters, Stewart flipped the switch into his inquisitory tone: "Tell me, are you seriously going to allow the Israelis to have these airplanes? It will upset the whole strategic balance."

Annenberg was ready: "My minister, Mr. Hughes, will now explain that to you."[11]

A more serious issue arose during Hughes's tour in London. This episode was a strange replay of the campaign interference occurring in the late stages of the 1968 U.S. presidential election. The British Labour Party government of Prime Minister Harold Wilson decided that it would adopt a new policy toward Rhodesia. Accordingly, the government sought U.S. backing for their new policy, which reflected a harder line toward the government of Ian Smith and white settlers in Rhodesia. But the Tories, led by Edward Heath, strongly opposed the new policy. They quietly worked out a back channel to Nixon with the aid of the U.S. embassy's political section. Heath and the Tories urged Nixon to stall and resist backing the Labor position on Rhodesia, saying that the Tories, if they won the impending election, would reverse what Labor had done. Had the embassy's role become known, this could have become a highly charged issue. The special British-American relationship did not extend to interference in British domestic politics.

The embassy in London was the largest American embassy, with more than 1,000 employees representing every important executive branch, department, and agency. The Pentagon and the CIA were prominently represented in a massive national security presence. The ambassador was nominally in charge of everything happening in the embassy under the presidential order drafted by Hughes for Bowles early in 1961 (and issued by President Kennedy in May 1961).

As deputy chief of mission, Hughes was charged with managing the embassy. He struggled with a host of administrative issues ranging from assigning parking spaces to the pecking order at diplomatic receptions. On one occasion, he chanced to overhear a conversation between a contractor and a procurement agent for the embassy that suggested a bribe. The episode occurred when a delegation of eight FBI officials arrived to hang the Annenberg art collection in the newly renovated U.S. embassy. Annenberg had insisted on calling his friend J. Edgar Hoover and having the law enforcement officers sent to London to hang the pictures. The head of the FBI group was slightly bored with the assignment. His interest picked up when Hughes called him aside and suggested that he investigate what was going on in the kitchen with a contractor, which Tom suspected might be a felony in process. The FBI agent thereupon caught the suspects in the middle of a corrupt cash transfer of money.

There was constant activity at the embassy as a stream of visitors came to London on official business or stopped by while visiting England. On one such occasion, Senator Gene McCarthy arrived unannounced and asked for a room overnight. Hughes was giving a dinner reception for the visiting Mr. and Mrs. George Romney and invited McCarthy to join the dinner party. Hughes had been friends with McCarthy for years but was still irritated with him over his appalling treatment of Humphrey in the 1968 election. (Romney had been mentioned as an early Republican candidate in 1968 but had withdrawn hastily after criticism of his comment that he had been brainwashed by the administration over Vietnam.) McCarthy, pleading fatigue, asked to be excused.

"Ah, yes, Tom," said McCarthy, speaking of Romney, "I would not have thought that George needed a full brainwashing. For that brain, a light rinse would have done the job."

"Get upstairs, Gene. Your room is on the third floor, second to the right. I'll send up some sandwiches."[12]

Hughes had speaking duties at numerous ceremonial occasions around the country and enjoyed such events. The pace of work in London was in general nothing like the constant crises and stresses of Tom's State Department career in Washington. Tom and Jean Hughes and their two boys, Evan and Allen, now thirteen and eleven, respectively, had a most enjoyable and memorable time in England.

The family's relationship with the Annenbergs was an important part of the whole experience. Hughes summed up the experience in his oral history interview:

> My wife and I were the beneficiaries of life with an American tycoon, and the experience was an enjoyable social grace note to my State Department career. Of course it was a personal pleasure for me to be back in England, and there were opportunities to revisit Oxford and renew acquaintances from 20 years earlier. The Annenbergs themselves could not have been nicer to us. On arrival we were welcomed by an intimate embassy party at Annabelle's, one of London's celebrated nightclubs. Later they organized a glittering reception for us at Claridge's. . . . When the ambassador discovered that my eldest son had slightly crossed eyes, he insisted on arranging for an operation by a leading Harley Street surgeon.[13]

It was a most pleasant year in England, but after the Labour defeat in the elections of 1970, Hughes decided to return home. Many years later, Hughes found himself chatting with Margaret Thatcher at a reception in the UK's embassy in Washington. They fell into reminiscing about the good old days in London, when Hughes was serving as deputy chief of mission at the U.S. embassy. They swapped stories and fond memories of Walter Annenberg. Dame Margaret summed up, "When they made Walter, they threw away the mold."

DEALING WITH THE ESTABLISHMENT

The Hughes family arrived back in the United States in time for the boys to prepare for school and for Tom to do a serious search for a new job. Hughes was assigned temporarily to the policy planning staff. Secretary Rogers had, in the meantime, picked the CIA's Ray Cline over Mort Halperin as Tom's successor at the INR. Hughes had cautioned against the Cline appointment. He cited Cline's long-standing feud with CIA director Richard Helms and expressed concern that it might complicate relations with the CIA. The INR staff also might find it difficult to adjust to the quite different organizational culture of the CIA, as represented by Cline. Henry Kissinger's dislike of Cline was another factor, but Kissinger apparently was unwilling to part with Halperin, whom he had invited to be a key aide at the NSC.

With Cline, the INR's influence and access to the White House was limited. But it also appeared to Hughes that the CIA faced similar problems of gaining access to the White House, given the president's and Kissinger's negative views about the CIA's competence and their belief that the CIA was staffed largely by liberal Democrats from Ivy League universities. Hughes found morale in his old bureau to be low. The whole department seemed to be in a deep funk. President Nixon, Henry Kissinger, and a greatly expanded NSC were firmly in charge of foreign policy.

State's policy planning staff was not planning any policy and the INR under Ray Cline was apparently demoralized. The INR self-study Hughes had commissioned in 1968 the year before was now finished, but efforts to declassify the study were blocked by the CIA. The CIA evidently did not like the prospect of being outshone by an intelligence rival. Cline had made no effort to fight against his old agency to get the self-study declassified. In fact, he forbade INR staff to even mention the existence of the study. It would be thirty-four years before the self-study was finally declassified, through the efforts of the National Security Archive of George Washington University, and posted on the archive's website. Professor Edwin E. Moise, of Clemson University, played an important role, along with Thomas Blanton and John Prados of the National Security Archive, in finally declassifying the self-study.

It was unfortunate that the INR study, which was the State Department's equivalent of the Pentagon Papers, was not declassified in 1971, when excerpts from the Pentagon Papers were published in the *New York Times* and the *Washington Post*. The national debate would have been enhanced, because the Pentagon Papers reported on military issues and paid little or no attention to the State Department's role. No State Department member was among the thirty-five or so authors who wrote the Pentagon Papers, because the Pentagon officials managing the project wanted to keep it a secret from President Johnson. If State were involved, they feared that Rusk would inform President Johnson, who would quite likely halt the project. Consequently, the Pentagon Papers presented a one-sided view of the Vietnam War, as if the commentary on a football game told what the offense did and paid no attention to the story from the point of view of the defense and special teams.

The Brookings job, meanwhile, had been filled. Brookings turned to Henry Owen, an experienced foreign policy hand and former head of policy planning at State, to take over as vice president for foreign and national security policy. To implement Kermit Gordon's call for greater policy relevance in Brookings studies, the institution launched a new series, called "Setting National Priorities," in which a number of senior scholars collaborated on an alternative national budget. The publication of the "Setting National Priorities" volume was timed to appear shortly after the Bureau of the Budget issued the administration's budget for the next fiscal year.

The section on the defense budget, written by William Kaufman and by experienced military officers on leave for a sabbatical year at Brookings, became an instant success and was widely quoted in the media. Significantly, "Setting National Priorities" became an influential critique of the Pentagon's spending priorities and attracted widespread attention.[14]

The foreign policy establishment was still small enough in 1970 that most of the influential figurers knew one another. While there were strained relationships between the rival camps of hawks and doves on Vietnam, the lines of communication were not totally cut between the two camps. Hughes knew his contemporaries inside the government and had a broad acquaintanceship with the academics and with foundation executives. He was leaving the government as a well-known dove but was widely respected for his professional competence and ability to work across party lines.

When it became known that he was planning to leave the government, he began to get calls from friends suggesting that he look into various opportunities. As it happened, the flagship institutions of New York City's foreign policy elite—the Council on Foreign Relations, the leading journal *Foreign Affairs,* and the Carnegie Endowment for International Peace—were in a state of flux and even disarray. The Cold War–era leadership was aging, and the prominent figures were less active than they had been in the glory days of World War II and the postwar era. The Vietnam War was a burning issue among the 700 or so members of the Council on Foreign Relations. New leadership was needed for the council. In the opinion of many of the younger council members, dramatic reform was called for, a new direction and a new mission required. The council, in fact, had operated within the framework of the postwar consensus, which was now in tatters.

Moreover, the policy action was moving away from New York to Washington, from New York bankers and lawyers to the new generation of meritocrats. The establishment was split along ideological and generational lines. The bankers, lawyers, and foundation executives who were once the heart of the nation's foreign policy elite were being elbowed aside by a thrusting new generation of foreign policy professionals who played by different rules.

All of this was confounding to a man like David Rockefeller, who was committed to good works and public service. David and his siblings adopted the "gospel of wealth" doctrines of Andrew Carnegie and their father John D. Rockefeller. The Rockefellers had a division of labor on where to focus their respective charitable energies. For David, Rockefeller University, one of the world's leading medical research institutes, was a special focus. But he also served on the boards of the leading foreign policy entities. He became chair of the Council on Foreign Relations, was on the board of the Carnegie Endowment for International Peace, and was the founder of the Trilateral Commission. As chair of Chase Manhattan Bank, he was familiar with developments around the world and knew most of the world's leading politicians.

In 1970 a set of unusually difficult circumstances arose that were hard for David to contend with, even for a man of his broad experience. Many of his oldest friends had passed from the scene; others were in the process of retiring and phasing down their commitments. The Republican administration of Richard Nixon had strong California roots and operated quite differently from the Eisenhower administration.

David Rockefeller's immediate concern was to find a replacement for Hamilton Fish Armstrong, who was retiring as editor of the flagship journal *Foreign Affairs* after many years of distinguished service. He was also concerned with finding new leaders for the Council on Foreign Relations and the Carnegie Endowment. There were no obvious candidates standing in line and ready to take over and ensure a smooth transition. He could no longer simply look to his old friends, who were not as active as they once were and gave mixed and confusing signals. All agreed that new blood was needed, since the period ahead would be a time of transition.

David Rockefeller was told that Tom Hughes was among those he should consult. Hughes was a younger man, was about to leave the State Department, and was very familiar with the foreign policy scene. He was a Democrat who had worked for Bowles and Humphrey but had many Republican friends. Hughes might even be a candidate himself for the *Foreign Policy* editorship, but it was rumored that he did not want to leave Washington. Rockefeller spoke with Hughes on the telephone, and the two arranged to meet in New York.

Hughes, in the meantime, had talked with Steve Benedict, his old friend from Student Federalist days, who was now on the staff of the Rockefeller Brothers Fund, and with other friends in New York. He formed some tentative conclusions on the basis of these conversations about developments in New York. The Council on Foreign Relations was badly split between hawks and doves in the membership, and the organization was stodgy at the board level. The board interfered in everything, and possibly might not brook significant changes in the council's operations or in the journal's editorial process. Yet a democratizing movement seemed to be underway that might bring significant changes.

The Carnegie Endowment's president, Joseph Johnson, wanted to retire. He had a potential successor on the inside but evidently a health issue disqualified that individual. A new Carnegie president would probably have a freer hand with the board than would be the case with the Council on Foreign Relations. In Carnegie's case, however, the new president would immediately face a host of difficult management problems. Carnegie had overseas operations, a number of obligations and commitments to other organizations, and lacked a clear mission. Carnegie, for example, acted, in part, as a foundation that awarded grants, but it also ran programs of its own. That is, it was both an operating foundation and a grant-giving foundation, an incongruous status under U.S. tax laws. Carnegie was also the landlord for other organizations working in the field of international affairs.

The other organizations and centers were renters in its spacious Carnegie building located at United Nations Plaza, a building that had been the brainchild of David Rockefeller. Carnegie's own research efforts tended to be focused on rather narrow technical issues of international law and organization. Milton Katz, a distinguished Harvard law professor and former Marshall Plan administrator, had recently become chair of the board. Katz would be an imaginative and supportive chairman for any new president. He would be an asset for someone interested in the Carnegie presidency.

At their first meeting, David Rockefeller began the discussion by presenting Hughes with a list of potential candidates for editorship of *Foreign Affairs* and asked for his assessment of each. Rockefeller was impressed by the younger man's answers and demeanor. He had not expected to raise the question of Hughes's own potential interest in the position, but it seemed obvious that he was well qualified. Would Hughes himself be interested in becoming a candidate? Hughes said that he preferred to remain in Washington and thus would not be interested. They discussed a wide range of other appointment issues, the roles of various organizations, and the problems arising in the current political climate. Rockefeller circled back to the Council on Foreign Relations and *Foreign Affairs*. What did Hughes think of Bill Bundy either as council president or as editor of the journal?[15]

"That would be the kind of appointment the Council's critics would expect you to make," Hughes said.

"What do you mean?"

Rockefeller was startled. Hughes explained that Bundy would probably be viewed as one of the "old boys" in the traditional mold, as someone unlikely to bring changes. He would stick to traditional ways, and his appointment would be controversial with the council's membership.

"Controversial? How could that be?" said Rockefeller, taken aback. "I have known Bill and Mac Bundy since they were little boys. Their father, Harvey Bundy, was my very good friend. There was no finer a man. Bill and Mac were always so polite and well behaved. Such intelligent boys. They have had fine careers. I cannot understand how anyone could dislike Bill."

Hughes said that it had to do with the war. Bill and Mac were considered hawks on Vietnam. There was still bitterness from the war.

Rockefeller, if he was troubled by this line of thought, did not show it, nor did it sway his judgment. David Rockefeller went to visit Bill Bundy and offered him the presidency of the council. Bundy politely turned down the offer, saying that his ulcer was acting up and he could not handle the pressures of the job. He did say, however, that he believed he could handle the job of editor of *Foreign Affairs*. He would very much like to be considered for that post. Rockefeller promptly offered him the job, and Bundy accepted.

The normally staid Council on Foreign Relations thereupon experienced a storm of protest from members. This was an unprecedented occurrence for an organization devoted to seminars, research, and decorous meetings with visiting foreign leaders and current officeholders. More than 100 of the council's membership of 700 lawyers, bankers, and leading academics wrote letters or otherwise expressed their opposition to Bundy's appointment. Some attacked Rockefeller's high-handed and unilateral decisionmaking and demanded a plebiscite of the council members. Others challenged Bundy's temperament and qualifications as an editor.

Hamilton Fish Armstrong, the retiring editor of *Foreign Affairs*, boycotted his own farewell party in protest, leaving board chair John J. McCloy, David Rockefeller, and distinguished guests to celebrate his retirement in an awkward and strained atmosphere. The protest eventually simmered down, and Bundy served out his five-year term and retired. Many of those who complained about Bill initially declared that they were wrong and that he had done an excellent job. The Council on Foreign Relations had also found an effective president in the person of Bayless Manning, former dean of the Stanford University Law School.

Rockefeller, meanwhile, in his capacity as a Carnegie trustee, intensified his efforts to find a successor for Carnegie's outgoing president, Joseph Johnson. After his initial meeting with Tom Hughes, Rockefeller had focused his attention on Hughes as one of the leading candidates. The two men had several long telephone conversations and met again in New York.

From Hughes's point of view the Carnegie opportunity was more promising than the Council on Foreign Relations opening for several reasons. The Carnegie board—and Hughes knew half of them—did not have an agenda of its own to impose on an incoming president. Hughes spoke informally with the board members he knew, once his own candidacy became a possibility. He came to the conclusion that he would have the freedom as president to define his own agenda and would not have difficult personalities to deal with. David Rockefeller himself was an ideal board member. He was interested in process and the organization's success. He had no interest in imposing his policy views.

Moreover the problems besetting the Council on Foreign Relations provided an opportunity for Carnegie to enhance its own standing. Carnegie had been a lesser star in the foreign policy firmament since the council's founding in 1921. Now, with the council suffering a reversal of its fortunes, Carnegie could step up and assert a leadership role.

There was something of a vacuum on the foreign policy scene. The leading foundations, such as the Ford Foundation and the Rockefeller Foundation, seemed divided and confused over America's role in the world. They were beginning to turn inward, to be increasingly interested in inner-city problems and racial issues and to lose interest in the problems of world order.

Domestic issues were of more urgent concern to both the political Left and the Right. Isolationist sentiment was strong in the country. The antiwar movement had been a powerful force in the Democratic Party in 1968 and was to help George McGovern sweep the primaries and gain the nomination in 1972. McGovern's campaign theme was "Come Home, America!" The traditional isolationist sentiments among midwestern Republicans were resurgent as disillusionment grew over foreign entanglements. A strong voice was needed again for America's post–World War II leadership in the world. Carnegie was a natural fit for Tom Hughes and for this challenge.

19

Carnegie: The House That Hughes Built

Tom Hughes, as president of the Carnegie Endowment for International Peace from 1971 to 1991, was the rare individual who bridged the old and new worlds of American foreign policy. He rose from the ranks of the older establishment and then helped to reform it by making it more open and democratic. Like many from the older generation, Hughes was deeply involved with the problems of Europe and of East-West relations. But he was also concerned with the rest of the world, which "lives in Asia, is colored, is poor, is ill-fed, is sick, is illiterate, lacks freedom, is proud, fears war, is neutral."[1] Tom acquired this interest in the Third World from his first mentor, Chet Bowles, and from the UN diplomats who frequently visited Bowles.

Like his first mentor, Tom had a good eye for spotting talent and made a priority of promoting the careers of promising younger professionals. The Endowment under his leadership also provided a respite for more senior persons who needed a break from their usual duties. These people were normally committed to public service. The climate of the Endowment during Hughes's tenure was a stimulating blend of the freedom to pursue one's interests combined with high professional standards and expectations. In one jocose characterization, the Endowment was described as unique in Washington, a "kinder and gentler organization, with teeth."[2]

The new professionals, as a class, have tended to be specialists rather than generalists, to be full-time toilers in the foreign policy vineyards, and to seek publicity for themselves and their ideas rather than to avoid it, as did many of the old establishment bankers, lawyers, and foundation executives. The open, tolerant, and competitive intellectual climate that Tom Hughes fostered at Carnegie was congenial to the ambitious new meritocrats. The new foreign policy experts sought the limelight for themselves and their ideas. They wanted to publish their articles in journals like *Foreign Policy* and their op-eds in the papers and to appear on TV to push their pet causes. Tom welcomed offbeat or unfashionable ideas, and the individuals who championed them, so long as the ideas were well argued and were not dogmatic.

Although he was always ready to challenge dogmas, Hughes was close to the old establishment figures in his basic values and outlook. He disliked bureaucracy, excessive rules, bosses, and privileges based on ranks, and he promoted intellectual laissez-faire. In his personal demeanor he was modest and courteous, almost courtly, like a character in a Jane Austen novel, the gentlemanly Mr. Darcy or Mr. Knightly, affable but somewhat reserved. He might have seemed a bit remote, except for his irrepressible wit, which invariably enlivened any occasion.

The mix of younger and of established professionals, led by a man who was adept at bringing out the best in others, proved to be a winning formula. During Hughes's two decades as president, the Carnegie Endowment produced one future foreign minister, one permanent representative to the United Nations, five assistant secretaries, and four ambassadors.[3] At the start of the Carter administration, a whole group of Endowment staffers took up posts in the State Department. Many other public servants and scholars who were already established figures found Carnegie an exceptional place to work.

CARNEGIE ENDOWMENT

Carnegie was the first nonprofit devoted exclusively to world peace. It was originally located in Lafayette Square, near the White House, and had an office in Paris, as well. The original Washington location was an easy stroll from the White House, so that President William Howard Taft could discuss the virtues of international arbitration with his friend Elihu Root, the Endowment's first president.[4] Taft and Root were pillars of the old Eastern establishment and the Republican Party that more or less ran America's foreign affairs and dominated the federal government for most of the post–Civil War period up to the New Deal.

For Andrew Carnegie, who was used to success, the task of achieving world peace did not seem impossible. There were only several dozen sovereign nations in his day, and only a half dozen of them really mattered. Carnegie would rely on his friends, including Taft, Root, Theodore Roosevelt, and Kaiser Wilhelm II of Germany, to supply good ideas, which he would supplement with his own views on arbitration and other matters.

This handful of well-intentioned and well-informed men could be counted on to come up with practical solutions to the world's problems, thereby in due course producing world peace. When Hughes took over the presidency of the Carnegie Endowment in 1971, the world was just short of 200 sovereign countries. The prospects for world peace were perhaps not quite promising in the midst of the Cold War. The hot war in Vietnam had still not wound down. Simple dispute-solving mechanisms such as arbitration were more like quaint and nostalgic remnants from the past than practical solutions to complex contemporary problems of war and peace.

Andrew Carnegie had founded the Endowment in 1910 as the last of his major philanthropic ventures. The Carnegie Endowment for International Peace was to be the capstone of the great philanthropist's campaign to give away the bulk of his vast fortune.[5] In his philanthropy, Carnegie was the embodiment of the doctrine he called "the Gospel of Wealth" that he propounded as a young man.

Under this doctrine, wealthy individuals were to become stewards of the fortunes they gained through thrift, hard work, and modest living. They were supposed to be wise and cautious benefactors, choosing good causes to support and making sure that funds were not wasted. The causes they should champion would be designed to improve the lot of the poor through upward mobility and not be mere handouts that would keep the poor in a dependent status. The causes were to promote an educated citizenry and to diminish social inequalities.

Andrew Carnegie shared the Progressive Era belief in bringing intelligence and expertise to the affairs of government to promote efficiency and improve the design of governmental institutions. Carnegie's aim in the case of the Endowment was to eliminate the curse of war: "I am drawn more to this cause than to any."[6] This would be done through laws and organizations that would mitigate the intensity of conflicts and ultimately remove the source of war. Carnegie first consulted his friend Elihu Root and asked him how much it would cost to set up an organization to ensure world peace. Would $10 million be enough? Root did not know quite how to answer the question. Finally, he said that the sum might be enough. To be sure, however, Root suggested that Carnegie call on President Theodore Roosevelt and ask his opinion.

Carnegie duly called on Roosevelt, who humored him because Carnegie was a substantial donor to the Republican Party. The president gave as his view that Root's assessment of the sum was probably about right. Roosevelt then suggested that Carnegie travel to Germany and call on Kaiser Wilhelm II for a European perspective. Carnegie visited the kaiser in 1909 and asked for his views. The kaiser, though somewhat bemused, agreed with Root and Roosevelt that the $10 million figure was probably appropriate. Carnegie visited the kaiser again in 1913, taking along his friend Robert

Brookings, on the occasion of the kaiser's celebration of the twenty-fifth anniversary of his reign.

Andrew Carnegie thereupon gave $10 million worth of bonds, paying 5 percent interest, to establish the Endowment. He installed Elihu Root as the first president and put his close friends, St. Louis philanthropist Robert Brookings and Columbia University president Nicholas Murray Butler, on the board of trustees, reserving for himself a key role. He would solicit the views of Root, the kaiser, and the trustees but would combine their views into the harmonious whole that would ensure peace. Carnegie himself would handle the United Kingdom.

One of Carnegie's first actions was to gather the signatures of the presidents of leading American universities on a testimonial to honor the kaiser for his contributions to world peace. In presenting the signatures and the plaque to his friend the kaiser, Andrew Carnegie expressed the hope that the kaiser would continue to preserve the peace and that Europe would enjoy peace for years to come. The kaiser said he, too, hoped that Europe would continue to enjoy peace. The Endowment distributed thousands of copies of the Norman Angell's *The Great Illusion*, which argues that economic interdependence between nations would make war all but impossible and that a world court should be established to settle any disputes arising among commercial nations.[7]

Andrew Carnegie became depressed when World War I broke out. His beloved Endowment adopted a new slogan, Peace through Victory, and put itself at the disposal of the Committee on Public Information of the U.S. government, whose mission it was to influence public opinion in support of the Allied war effort. The establishment of the International Court of Justice in the Netherlands helped to revive the Endowment's focus on international law and justice in the 1920s and 1930s. An office in Geneva was established to work with League of Nations' instrumentalities. Carnegie president Nicholas Murray Butler, in the 1930s, typically worked out of the Paris office in the summer months.

After World War II, the Carnegie trustees built a new headquarters on United Nations Plaza, in New York City. The Endowment could interact with the UN and also lease out space to a host of sister entities working on UN concerns. Board chair John Foster Dulles and his fellow trustee, Columbia University president Dwight Eisenhower, sought out and named diplomat Alger Hiss as Carnegie president, to succeed Nicholas Murray Butler in 1947. Hiss's term as president proved to be short lived. Just months after taking office, he was accused, by Whitaker Chambers and the House Un-American Activities Committee, of having been a member of the Communist Party during the 1930s. The Carnegie trustees defended Hiss for a time, but in 1950 they named Joseph Johnson, a professor of international law and politics at Williams College, to replace him as president.[8] Under Johnson, the Endowment continued to focus on problems of international law, the workings of the United Nations and its subsidiaries, and multilateral diplomacy. The trustees were largely Republican and included members of New York's banking, legal, media, and philanthropic establishments.

In 1970, when Joseph Johnson announced his intention to retire, the trustees commissioned a study of the Endowment by Philip Jessup, the venerable Columbia University jurist and legal scholar, who had been closely involved in the Endowment's work in international law. The Jessup effort did not produce a concise conclusion or a clear path forward. Jessup declared that the Endowment was engaged in a great variety of worthy tasks and functions, none of which stood out over the others. The trustees solemnly debated the Endowment's future at a 1970 board meeting. They passed on to their new president, Tom Hughes, this crisp guidance and summary of their recent deliberations:

> There was a generally felt inability to identify one area of concentration which could properly take priority over all others. Some felt on the other hand that it is very important for the Endowment to do something from time to time in line with what it believes. The Chairman then summed up: The Board is not as confused as it sounds and, in fact, is moving in the direction indicated.[9]

The way was open for Tom Hughes to put his own stamp on the Endowment. Tom came across this old message from the trustees as he was looking through his papers and preparing remarks for his retirement dinner twenty years later. Tom declared at the dinner that he was passing on this guidance to his successor.

CARNEGIE PRESIDENT, 1971–1991

Hughes's first decision, worked out with Milton Katz and the board before he took the job, was to refocus the Endowment's efforts on American foreign policy and to return to its original location in the nation's capital. After opening in Washington in 1971, Hughes still had to spend much time in New York during the 1970s. The Endowment operated in both cities until 1980, when affairs were wound up in New York and the Geneva office was closed. Carnegie had a long-standing friendly relationship with the Council on Foreign Relations in New York. Hughes was happy to work with Manning in setting up a Washington office for the council. The new office was located within the Carnegie Endowment's headquarters, and Alton Frye, a Yale political scientist who had worked for the RAND Corporation and as a top aide to Senator Howard Baker of Tennessee, was named its director.

Hughes had a number of natural allies in Washington's busy nonprofit scene. Soon after Hughes's arrival, the Carnegie Endowment, Brookings, and Resources for the Future began a highly popular and successful program on foreign and public affairs for college students and high school seniors. *Face the Nation* used curricular materials developed by the staffs of the three organizations. Hughes, Kermit Gordon of Brookings, and Charles Hitch of Resources for the Future took turns hosting and organizing the programs. The nearby locations of the three organizations facilitated easy access and contacts among their professional staffs. The collegial relationship has continued, and something of an intellectual division of labor has existed in their respective areas of expertise.

The collaboration with his two sister organizations on *Face the Nation* was part of a larger conception that marked the Endowment's initial emphasis under Hughes. Having seen his role in his last years at State as a kind of dissenter-in-residence, it was natural that he would be a policy critic at the Endowment. Hughes wanted to make the Foreign Service more open, democratic, and diverse. To this end, he developed a program with the American Foreign Service Association, a membership organization of some 8,000 retired and active Foreign Service officers, to bridge the gap between the State Department and its external critics. A December 21, 1971, press release of Carnegie and the association announced "a program to break down barriers between American diplomats and the American public."

William Harrop, chair of the association, and Tom Hughes, for the Carnegie Endowment, defined their project as "an attempt by Foreign Service careerists themselves to combat the problem of Foreign Service insularity, [to] spur innovation and new attitudes in the foreign affairs bureaucracy, and to shed light on selected foreign affairs topics, all with the help of private citizens."[10]

Personnel exchanges, study groups, seminars, and conferences would be used to achieve the goals. By the time the program was formally launched, the Endowment had already begun to work with academic concerns such as the Political Science Association to set up regular meetings between leading academics and State Department officials.

The Endowment's work generally tends to be short papers, think pieces, and op-eds, and TV appearances rather than book-length studies. The Endowment's staff members have sought to make their careers in public service and in promoting enlightened public dialogue more than in specialized academic research. This was the rationale for Hughes's hiring practice: to make a bet on the future and provide an opportunity for new leaders to emerge. These individuals would normally view their time at the Endowment as preparation for a new phase of their careers.

As with all aspects of his presidency, however, Tom Hughes put his faith in people rather than in fixed rules or organizational logic. The Endowment's rationale to provide a temporary home for people on their way up in their public service careers was not an ironclad rule. Tom also backed people with strong interests in finishing a book or pursuing a project that might take years to accomplish. He had some colleagues who stayed on for long periods. Tom and his close associate Larry Fabian, who served with him for his entire Carnegie tenure, provided the best kind of administration. They gave staff members the freedom to do their work without bureaucratic distractions but left them confident that all administrative details would be handled fairly, efficiently, and expeditiously.

Carnegie, like Brookings, the American Enterprise Institute, the AEI, Center for Strategic and International Studies, the Peterson Institute, and other leading Washington think tanks, however, tended to be staffed heavily by persons who had served in government, often in Democratic administrations. In consequence, Brookings and Carnegie studies were often critical of the foreign policies of Republican administrations, especially of the Nixon, Ford, and the first Reagan administrations.

Hughes was eager for the Endowment to avoid being predictable. The Heritage Foundation's orientation to the political right or the Cato Institute's consistent libertarianism made their work less interesting, in Tom's estimation. Similarly, Tom considered studies from the Institute of Policy Studies too predictably liberal for the policy dialogue. Hughes observed,

> Paradoxically the fact that most of the other prominent NGOs working on war/peace issues had clear ideological profiles was of great help to the Endowment's own emerging reputation. As the proclivities of Heritage, AEI, and IPS [Institute of Policy Studies] became more and more predictable and their product more typecast, we were reinforced in our determination to build our credibility on the opposing proposition, namely, to be hospitable to contending viewpoints while remaining as institutionally unpredictable as possible.[11]

He sought to have Carnegie staff speak out and to testify at congressional hearings on opposing sides of controversial issues. Tom tried hard to hire people with different views as opportunities arose. In his long tenure, Hughes also incubated or cofounded a number of other centers and assisted in their growth with the intention of contributing to the public dialogue: the Institute of International Economics (now the Peterson Institute), the Economic Strategy Institute, the Trilateral Commission, the Arms Control Association, the German Marshall Fund, the Mid-Atlantic Club, the Women's Foreign Policy Caucus, and the Washington office of the Council on Foreign Relations, to name only the most prominent and successful. Hughes's colleagues liked to joke that for a monogamous man he certainly participated in a large number of marriages.

The relationship between the Endowment and the Washington office of the Council on Foreign Relations was of particular importance. One could have readily imagined the Council and the Endowment as bitter antagonists. The Endowment's revival might have set the stage for the two organizations to struggle for preeminence in the foreign policy field. The Endowment's feisty and upstart journal, *Foreign Policy,* cast itself in part as a competitor to the council's establishmentarian *Foreign Affairs.* In actuality, the two organizations became great partners and enjoyed friendly relations, cohabiting for more than two decades under Carnegie's roof.

Tom Hughes's open-mindedness and skillful leadership helped make this collaborative relationship possible. Hughes's original discussions with David Rockefeller apparently helped to democratize the council. The council moved away from the pattern of having an illustrious member of the board serving as part-time president. Instead, the Board in 1971 named Bayless Manning as fulltime president. The council also democratized its process of naming members to the board of trustees, engaging the 700 or so members of the Council on Foreign Relations in the process of nominating and voting on board membership.

Hughes got on well with Manning, and he formed a close relationship with Alton Frye, the director of the council's Washington office. Frye described Tom's contribution in these terms: "He proved a deft architect in crafting a bond between two proud and fiercely independent institutions. The Council and the Endowment have tilled the same fields, not only without jealousy, but with a cordial commitment. Our communities overlap, but they are not identical. Our missions intersect, but they do not collide. Tom's large spirit and open mind have fostered fruitful collaboration instead of petty rivalry.[12]

In his twenty years at the helm, Hughes undertook a great many initiatives. He changed the Endowment's mission to ensure that it would be an operating foundation—in effect, a think tank—and not a grant-giving institution. Nor would Carnegie be a pass-through funder of activities, like the Bilderberg Group, that it did not control or of other groups that it funded that were operating under its imprimatur.

He moved the headquarters from its location at United Nations Plaza in New York City to Washington and located it on DuPont Circle, with the Overseas Development Council, and near other public policy organizations.

He changed the focus from international law and organization to issues of American foreign policy, emphasizing near-term and midterm policy issues rather than long-range basic research.

He emphasized policy-relevant research that would be of direct use to decisionmakers—in effect, adopting a working rule of "No research without recommendations."

He phased out all tenured professional staff and placed all new professional employment on short-term or annually renewable appointments, to maximize the opportunities for new hires and fresh initiatives in war and peace studies.

He invested in the future rather than the past, recruiting younger professionals with high promise and important recent experience who wanted to write and speak about the issues.

He brought women into Carnegie operations both as members of the board of trustees and as professional staff members—for example, board members Barbara Newell, president of Wellesley College; Shirley Hufstedler, former secretary of the Department of Health, Education, and Welfare; Marion Fremont-Smith, prominent lawyer; Jean Kennedy Smith, later ambassador to Ireland; and professional staffers Jenome Walker, who was an expert on European affairs, Pauline Baker, who founded the Women's Foreign Policy Caucus, and Doris Meissner, who became commissioner of the Immigration and Naturalization Service.

Hughes encouraged and assisted staff members to gain access to radio, TV, newspaper op-eds, and conferences for their views—thus, while enhancing their own reputations, to enhance the Endowment's reputation for hard-hitting, relevant, and objective research.

He entered into a joint venture and eventually acquired full ownership of *Foreign Policy* magazine, a new quarterly deliberately designed, among other things, to bring the Vietnam Era antagonists—the war was still being fought at home and abroad—back into communication again.

He augmented the Endowment's own work on arms control through a joint venture with the Arms Control Association.

By initiating "face to face" dialogue between governmental and nongovernmental participants in off-the-record discussions, he helped to restore the image of foreign policy as a bipartisan and professional endeavor.[13]

While sometimes taking years to implement, most of the major changes he envisioned began early in Hughes's tenure. Some of the important moves were negotiated with board chair Milton Katz and his colleagues before Hughes officially started work. The major directions of change were hammered out as part of the process of discussing and defining the job.

Various New York trustees continued to fight the move to Washington far into Hughes's term but finally relented. A secretary cleaning out a file drawer found an old letter from Andrew Carnegie to Elihu Root referring to the importance of a location in Washington. Hughes circulated the letter to the trustees, a move that won over the holdouts.

The sale of Carnegie's headquarters on United Nations Plaza involved protracted negotiations but was accomplished on favorable terms. New York activities were run out of rented quarters in Rockefeller Center for several years under Daniel O'Flaherty, a former Rhodes scholar whom

Tom hired to handle interactions with the business community. Finally all operations in New York City and the Geneva offices were closed down or relocated to Washington in 1980.

NIXON, KISSINGER, AND BISMARCK

As the Watergate crisis heated up in 1973, Mady Kalb, the wife of journalist Marvin Kalb, was assigned a task by her colleagues at the Washington Woman's National Democratic Club. She was to invite Tom Hughes to speak at the club's December 15, 1973, meeting. The Kalbs were friends of Tom and Jean Hughes. Tom was to give his views on Watergate, the national scene, or some aspect of U.S. foreign policy. Each of these topics, Hughes surmised, boiled down to the same thing: the crisis of the Nixon presidency.

The topic was unsurprising. Watergate was clearly on everyone's mind at the time. The nation's attention was on the fate of President Nixon. One important part of this larger question was whether Nixon would survive by playing the foreign policy card. As president of Carnegie, an experienced diplomat, and old Washington hand, Tom Hughes was just the man, the club's women reasoned, to discuss the question of Nixon's future. Yet Hughes, for whom public speaking was second nature, was not entirely at ease. He hesitated and asked for time to reflect on the invitation.

It was not that he was afraid to speak his mind. He had publicly opposed the Vietnam War and President Johnson's policies, carefully to be sure, while he was still in government. He had been an advocate since he was eighteen when he urged Republican and Democratic Party leaders to adopt world federalist principles. Public speaking was his métier and very much a part of his current job. He recently had given a well-received address at Portland State College and, as usual, distributed copies widely to his friends and associates. So why did he hesitate now?

Tom felt that as president of the Carnegie Endowment, it was helpful to be on reasonably good terms with the current government. The federal government was a potential employer for the Foreign Service officers and others on his staff. The Nixon administration had not been particularly friendly to NGOs in general and to Carnegie in particular. Pat Buchanan, on the White House staff, was on a crusade against foundations and think tanks for harboring leftists and Nixon enemies. Buchanan was calling for a conservative counterpart to the Brookings Institutions of this world. At the same time, he was looking for ways to punish NGOs. Hughes wanted to improve relations with the Nixon administration, if possible, or at least to avoid fueling Buchanan's ire.

The animosity Nixon had shown at the time of Tom's London appointment, however, had evidently dissipated. Henry Kissinger, at least, was always friendly when he called to see if the president could use Annenberg's stately mansion in Southern California. Hughes had sent Henry copies of some of his speeches when he was at the INR and usually got friendly letters in return. Henry had invited Tom to come up to Harvard and speak at Kissinger's Defense Policy Seminar.

It had surprised Hughes when he learned from Annenberg that vice president Nixon had blamed him for Humphrey's Salt Lake City speech. He was amazed that Nixon could brood over such matters. Politicians have long memories, of course. Hughes was well aware of that. There was no telling what Nixon might do if crossed. In 1957, though, Nixon had been pleasant to deal with in the fight over the civil rights bill. Hughes was aware that politics was a contact sport, but he made it a practice to remain on good terms with everybody and to keep in touch if at all possible. Hughes's correspondence shows letters from eighty-three different U.S. senators, ninety-five ambassadors, at least forty-four former intelligence colleagues both civilian and military, and hundreds of other notables.

The senatorial correspondence included eighteen letters from Senator Claiborne Pell alone and multiple letters from other senators. Hughes had evidently visited Pell's father for some reason while working for Chet Bowles in 1954, a kindness the younger Pell never forgot. Tom and Jean Hughes also entertained frequently and received many thank you letters, a custom that has become regrettably rare.

Tom was apparently somewhat worried about the consequences of a furor with the Nixon administration if he spoke out forcefully on Watergate. There was also the question of his relationships with his trustees. The Carnegie Endowment had for many years been a Republican-dominated institution. The board still had many Republican bankers and lawyers from the old Eastern establishment. Hughes had forged good relations with his board and did not want to jeopardize them by appearing partisan. He wanted Carnegie to be provocative and policy relevant, but there was a fine line to be drawn between policy advocacy and partisanship.

It was an unwritten rule that Carnegie staff should not carry policy advocacy to the point of narrow partisanship. Advocacy should aim at policy improvement, not at advancing the fortunes of a party. With his penchant for history, Hughes liked to quip that Andrew Carnegie had once elected Benjamin Harrison as president, and this had not worked out too well. Tom voiced his concerns and reservations about the talk to Jean, who remonstrated with him.

"Don't be silly," Jean told him. "You were not afraid to take on Lyndon Johnson and Vietnam so you can't back off now. You did Nixon a favor anyway when you went to London to help Annenberg."

So Tom took on the Women's Club assignment for December 1973 and did so with relish. As usual, he cast his subject in a large historical context.

He wanted to draw lessons through a complex argument and exercise in logical thinking. Here was Henry Kissinger, a Bismarckian figure, a man of grand strategic designs, a thinker who had done major scholarly research on nineteenth-century European diplomacy and was now seemingly the steadying force in a shaky Nixon administration. Nixon, the former teacher, is now inferior to and dependent on the pupil.

The analogy between Kissinger and Bismarck came readily to Tom's mind. He decided that he would weave the story of Bismarck and his old pen pal, Kaiser Wilhelm II, into his innocuously entitled remarks—"The Meeting of National and World Politics."[14] But he would turn the story into a parable, a cautionary tale for the present discontents. The headstrong kaiser had finally dismissed the wily old Bismarck in the spring of 1890 after two years of tension between the two men, thus leaving the ship of state without its pilot. A better result would have been Bismarck dismissing the kaiser.

The solution to the contemporary drama, Hughes seems to suggest, was that Kissinger, his star on the rise, should force a resignation from the stumbling and irrational Nixon. Once the senior partner, Nixon was now the subordinate. As it was, Kissinger, by adhering to the status quo, was supplying the legitimacy for the Nixon foreign policy and the Nixon presidency.

"Today few doubt," said Hughes to the women, "that Henry Kissinger has increasingly become de facto President of the United States for foreign affairs. He and his former chief partner now face contrasting pools of deference. Nixon's pool is nearly drained. Kissinger's is mostly full."

Without Kissinger, Hughes noted, Nixon's position would be untenable. A fall for the erstwhile master would now appear almost inevitable. Without saying so explicitly, Hughes offered up the solution that Kissinger should give history a hand and Nixon a shove: "There is another tradition, explicitly Bismarckian, which . . . hears the footsteps of God in history, and then, in the best Hegelian tradition, helps history along."[15]

With this history lesson, Hughes enjoyed his greatest success as a commentator on foreign policy. The speech hit a national nerve. It was immediately picked up and quoted in press reports and in television news shows. The *New York Times Sunday Magazine,* the *Washington Post,* the *International Herald Tribune,* and numerous other papers ran the full text of the speech. A favorite headline for editorial writers was, "Will Kissinger Fire Nixon?"

Henry Kissinger was in Paris and first heard of the Hughes talk from French sources. Back in the United States, Kissinger was besieged by reporters for comment. Many asked if Nixon planned to resign. Kissinger felt obliged to hold a press conference in January 1974 in San Clemente to deny reports of any discord or difference of views between the president and himself. The president is fully in charge of foreign policy, said Kissinger, and reports that he and the president disagreed were completely false. Henry was completely in accord with President Nixon, and there was not the slightest difference of views between them.

Whether all the talk of resignation had any bearing on President Nixon's eventual resignation in August 1974 cannot be known. For Hughes, looking back at age ninety-five, of the many talks he gave in his career, he was most proud of this one.

THE CARTER ADMINISTRATION

The Carter period was a somewhat awkward time for Hughes. He had provided the intellectual rationale for Carterism in a 1975 article on liberalism and populism in *Foreign Policy*.[16] Jimmy Carter had read the article and liked it. He sent Hughes a fan letter saying that he was not quite sure whether he was a liberal or a populist in Tom's terms but was probably a mixture of the two.

The Hughes speech on Nixon-Kissinger-Bismarck had resonated with reporters. As the 1976 election approached, occasional articles reported that Carnegie, under Hughes, was training a group of "exiles in waiting" for a new Democratic administration. In the meantime, the Endowment had hosted a new foreign policy entity, the Trilateral Commission, in its New York offices. The Trilateral Commission was the brainchild of David Rockefeller. Its aim was to provide a forum for thinkers and policy makers from the United States, Europe, and Japan to confer on world problems, such as human rights, economic underdevelopment, arms control, and climate change. The commission's executive director was Columbia University's Zbigniew Brzezinski, a distinguished scholar and professor of public law and government. When Brzezinski became Governor Jimmy Carter's foreign policy adviser, the links between the Endowment, the Trilateral Commission, and the Democratic Party seemed to be strengthened.

Tom Hughes was delighted when his old friend Senator Walter F. "Fritz" Mondale of Minnesota was chosen as the vice presidential candidate on the Democratic ticket. Mondale was to run with Governor Jimmy Carter of Georgia against incumbent Republican president Gerald Ford and his vice presidential choice, Senator Robert Dole of Kansas.

Fritz Mondale asked Tom Hughes to assist with the preparations for the nationally televised debate with Senator Bob Dole, scheduled for October 15 in Houston. As the final prep session broke up, Tom told Fritz what he would say if Dole referred to the blood spilled from Democrat wars. Mondale was incredulous. He told Hughes that Dole would never say such a thing. Hughes said that Dole had already used the line several times on the stump. The two men worked out a response, in the event Dole should make such an allusion.

At the debate, Mondale noticed that Dole seemed nervous. About two-thirds of the way through the debate, the moderator, Walter Mears of the Associated Press, asked Dole what he thought of Ford's pardon of Nixon. Dole tried to switch the subject by referring to all the blood spilled from Democrat wars.

"I figured up the other day," said Dole. "If we added up the killed and wounded in Democrat wars, all in this century . . . it'd be about 1.6 million Americans, enough to fill the city of Detroit."

Forewarned, Mondale delivered the response he had worked out with Hughes:

"I think Senator Dole has richly earned his reputation as a hatchet man tonight. Democrat wars! Does he really mean to suggest that there was a partisan difference over our involvement in the war to fight Nazi Germany? I don't think any reasonable American would accept that."[17]

Mondale considered that this exchange was the second of two turning points in the 1976 election. The first was Ford's gaffe in the second presidential debate, when he said that there was no communist domination of Eastern Europe.

As the signs of a Carter victory grew stronger, Hughes received a phone call from Ted Sorensen. Ted wanted Tom to join him and Zbig Brzezinski for a discussion of jobs in a Carter administration. The presumption on Sorensen's part bemused both Tom and Zbig, but they decided to accept the invitation to see what the former Kennedy aide was planning.

The three men met at Sorensen's apartment in New York City. Sorensen came quickly to the point. He was concerned about unnecessary competition for jobs in the new administration and declared his preference for dividing up the key appointments early before the press began to speculate.

"Zbig," said Ted. "What are you interested in?"

Brzezinski explained that his future role was already settled. He was going to be national security adviser. He would simply plan to push the principles of the Trilateral Commission as his agenda. This had already been agreed to by "Jimmy and David" (the president and David Rockefeller, chair of the Trilateral Commission).

"Well, what about you, Tom?" Ted asked.

Hughes explained that some of his friends were pushing him to become director of central intelligence, but he was not interested in the job. It was not at all clear that he would go into the new administration. It appeared that Cy Vance was slated for secretary of state and wanted his own man, Warren Christopher, a Los Angeles lawyer, as deputy secretary. Tom said that he was happy where he was and did not see a role for himself in a Carter administration. He was certainly not interested in the CIA job.

"Good, good," said Ted. "I'll go for the CIA job."

Carter was elected, and Fritz Mondale offered the CIA job to Tom. When Hughes turned the job down, Mondale and Carter decided that a connection to Camelot would be useful and offered the job to Sorensen. Confirmation problems developed, however, and Sorensen was forced to withdraw. The Carter administration once again turned to Hughes. At a Minnesota preinaugural party in Washington in 1977, Vice President–Elect Mondale and Senator Humphrey sandwiched Hughes between them. Tom recalled that "Fritz and Hubert were giving me the one-two, they said, 'Tom, we really need you on this one. The party needs you. The country needs you. You've got to do it.'" It pained him, but Tom again turned down his old friends.

This time, however, an idea occurred to him. He called the woman in charge of Mondale's transition office not long after he turned down his old Minnesota friends.

"Mr. Hughes," she said. "I hope you have reconsidered and are going to take the CIA job."

"No, I'm sorry," he said. "But I have an idea for you."

"Oh? What's that?"

Hughes launched into a short speech he had worked out extolling the virtues of Admiral Stansfield Turner, a friend and fellow Rhodes scholar from the class of 1947. He rhapsodized over Turner's virtues. Brilliant. Learned. A Rhodes scholar from the first post–World War II class of Rhodes scholars. Outstanding record in the Navy. Then Hughes added what he thought might be a clincher. Admiral Turner had been the president's classmate at the Naval Academy.[18]

This was not quite the selling point it seemed. Turner had no recollection at all that Carter had been in his Naval Academy class, and Carter, for his part, had only distantly heard of Turner. Nevertheless, the suggestion was welcomed by the Carter people. Turner became the CIA director, but his tenure was not a success.

Turner suffered through four tumultuous years at the helm of the nation's intelligence services. He never once met one-on-one with President Carter. Brzezinski, as national security adviser, insisted on receiving all CIA briefings himself and deciding what he should pass on to the president. Admiral Turner, on his side, generated many of his own problems. He was thoroughly disliked within the CIA from the start for giving the impression that he had inherited a mess and had to clean house. Early in his tenure, Turner fired many covert operators and analysts. Much like Admiral Raborn, Turner put a heavy emphasis on the use of new technologies for intelligence collection and adopted the PERT-style of management that CIA old-timers found distasteful. Turner, moreover, arrived with a host of Navy cronies and never shed the impression that he had inherited a wreck of an agency that was badly in need of reform.[19]

The Carnegie Endowment had been a congenial home for young Foreign Service officers who in due course would return to government service.

A number of these people joined the Carter administration and became important figures. These included Bill Maynes (assistant secretary of state for international organization affairs), Don McHenry (U.S. ambassador to the United Nations), Anthony Lake (head of policy planning at State), and Richard Holbrooke (assistant secretary of state for Far Eastern affairs). Warren Manshel, affiliated with the Endowment through the journal, *Foreign Policy,* became the U.S. ambassador to Denmark.

Occasionally, Hughes was drawn into an assignment for the Carter administration. In early 1978, Hughes was part of a group of American educators who planned to visit Cuba. Tom received a call from national security adviser Zbig Brzezinski. Zbig wanted Tom to carry a message to Fidel Castro regarding the Ogaden conflict between Ethiopia and Somalia. Castro had sent 16,000 Cuban troops to the region to assist Soviet and Ethiopian forces against the U.S.-backed Somalis. Would Tom please carry a warning from the Carter administration that Castro should show caution and not risk starting World War III in the sands of the Ogaden.

On his arrival to the hotel in Havana, he heard his name being called. It was Castro's close aide, Carlos Raphael Rodriguez, on the line. Hughes was told that Fidel was anxious to see him but was in Santiago. He would be back in Havana later in the evening. Rodriguez invited Tom to dinner at party headquarters. After dinner, they would watch the U.S. Senate vote on ratification of the Panama Canal Treaty on television and wait for Castro's arrival.

Rodriguez chided Hughes at dinner for dropping the Spanish-language publication of Carnegie papers. "I was one of your readers," said Carlos. Hughes confessed that he was unaware Carnegie had a Spanish-language series and said he would give thought to a possible revival.

For the Senate vote, Rodriguez took out a set of papers with the names of U.S. senators and their likely vote on the Panama treaties. His projections of the results turned out to be correct except for Dennis de Concini (R-Ariz.).

"Damn that de Concini!" said Rodriguez. "Fidel will notice this. He likes telling me I'm incompetent and never get anything quite right."

Shortly after 11:00 p.m. Fidel arrived—"fresh as a daisy," in Hughes's recollection. Fidel inquired about the Senate vote, and Rodriguez said he got them all correct except for this strange character de Concini. Castro smiled but did not comment. The Cuban leader seemed to Hughes to be in an upbeat mood. After a few minutes of verbal sparring with Hughes over the Cuban Missile Crisis, Castro said:

"Well, Tom, I understand you have a message for me from my friend Zbig."

Hughes gave the Cuban leader the gist of Brzezinski's warning on the Ogaden War and a letter from the national security adviser.

Castro could not resist a gibe about who had been responsible for almost precipitating a world war a few years earlier, but he directly addressed the issue.

"Don't worry, you can assure Zbig that I'm not going to start World War III in the sands of the Ogaden."

That was the end of the business side of Hughes's meeting with the Cuban leader. For another two hours Castro carried on with commentary, jokes, and observations about world issues. Finally, as it was approaching two o'clock in the morning, Castro noticed that his American visitor was beginning to droop. Castro gave instructions in rapid Spanish to a bodyguard, who returned shortly with two boxes.

"Our finest cigars, Tom," Fidel explained. "One for Zbig and one for you. As an old intelligence man, I'm sure that you will know how to smuggle these through your Customs."

The Carter administration survived the Ogaden crisis, but its troubles mounted. The Shah's fall in Iran and the imprisonment of American hostages, economic stagflation, and a challenge for renomination by Senator Ted Kennedy all but doomed President Carter's chances for reelection. Tom Hughes meanwhile found his voice as a friendly critic of the Carter administration. Tom expressed his concerns in two carefully crafted articles in *Foreign Policy:* "Carter and the Management of Contradictions" and "The Crack-Up: The Price of Collective Irresponsibility."[20]

The first article pointed out that foreign policy inevitably involved the management of contradictions and argued that the administration had not coped well with this task. Carter read the article and directed White House staffer Douglas Bennett to send Hughes a letter saying that the president had taken the cautions to heart. The second article was a devastating critique of how foreign policy reflected an abdication of responsibility by all parties in the foreign policy process. No recorded response came from the administration.

Over the period 1973–1995, Hughes contributed nine articles to *Foreign Policy,* which became his favored vehicle for expressing foreign policy views. He also wrote many op-eds and other short pieces for the *Washington Post,* the *New Republic, The Atlantic,* and other publications. Although he spoke out critically at times, Hughes remained in contact with his old friends and with the Carnegie alumni now back in government. One of his favorite former Endowment staff members, Bill Maynes, came back after serving in the Carter administration to serve as the editor of *Foreign Policy.*[21]

THE 1980S

By the 1980s, one of the ambitions Hughes envisioned for Carnegie—restoring a respectful dialogue among the warring Vietnam factions—was no longer a worry. The Vietnam War was like a fog that had lifted only to reveal a startling and strange new terrain. The new partisan outlook from the western states posed a different but grave challenge for foreign policy. The Republican Party was no longer run by a coalition of northeasterners and moderate midwesterners committed to America's leadership role in the world. The populism that had helped to produce the Carter presidency was now pushing politics in a different direction. Protectionism, isolationism, nativism, and other unsavory views were gaining strength.

The Republicans were now the party of Ronald Reagan, a midwesterner turned Californian, but one not in the mold of Richard Nixon. The Reagan Republicans distrusted the East, big government, the Ivy League, the labor movement, foreign aid, the media, intellectuals, and elites in general. What this portended for foreign policy was not entirely clear, but to Tom Hughes the outlook was disturbing.

In former days, Andrew Carnegie extolled the virtues of what he called the "representative men." By this, he meant the better-educated, the broad-minded, the wise and experienced people he expected would run the Carnegie Endowment. They would, he thought, direct their energies to strengthen America's peaceful intercourse with other nations. Domestic political wrangles were to be compartmentalized from the nation's larger aspirations and its responsibilities in foreign affairs. Where were the representative men and women now? Andrew Carnegie might have asked why internationalism was suddenly out of favor with the leadership classes.

Tom Hughes was thinking about this problem from the start of the Reagan presidency.[22] He defined the problem most fully on the occasion of the seventy-fifth anniversary of the founding of the Carnegie Endowment. "[Andrew Carnegie's] 'Endowment for International Peace' was preordained to orbit around the internationalist sun. The fact that it was a rising sun in Carnegie's day and a setting sun today makes the topic more nearly one of necessity than one of choice," Tom wrote in 1985.[23] That internationalism was no longer a rising sun was the predicament for political idealism in America. There were still millions of Americans working or stationed overseas, but they now lacked anchorage in a set of supportive beliefs back home and thus lacked confidence in their own futures.

Ronald Reagan ran in 1980 on a platform to cut wasteful domestic spending and to rebuild America's military strength. Reagan's foreign policy team included Hughes's old friends Max Kampelman and Jeane Kirkpatrick. They had made the transition from Humphrey liberals to neoconservatives to Reagan supporters. Democrats like Paul Nitze and Eugene Rostow, who had been passed over by the Carter administration, knew Reagan from the Committee on the Present Danger, a group calling for a stronger defense posture. They joined with the western libertarians to back Reagan and became key defense strategists for him.

Hughes took a dim view of the Reagan administration's foreign policy in the first term. He sized up the foreign policy challenge in 1981, in one of his incisive articles in *Foreign Policy*, as having to overcome Reaganism, that is, antigovernment, anti-Establishment, anti–New Deal, and nativist rhetoric that had percolated into foreign policy.[24] Reaganism made the United States appear illiberal, unilateralist, and self-absorbed.

The Reagan budget cutters and domestic policy advisers intervened opportunistically into foreign affairs, Hughes believed, and made life difficult for the foreign policy professionals. Reagan's foreign policy officials, meanwhile, were struggling to establish some kind of pecking order in their ranks and their foreign policy agenda. The United States was presenting the wrong face to the world—a blend of arrogance and indifference, with foreign policy taking a back seat to domestic feuds. In 1981, however, Hughes held out the hope that the web of military alliances and memberships in multilateral organizations would produce interagency cooperation. Eventually, he surmised, a working order in policy making would emerge. The new team might in time find its footing, and the foreign policy professionals would come into their own.

Hughes's analysis of the foreign policy process recognized that the "vertical" elites—that is, the traditional State Department officials—were increasingly forced to share power with the "horizontal" players from other departments and from the private sector.[25] The NGOs, universities, business groups, and the media all participated in a highly complex policy process. The explosive growth of the think tank industry itself in the 1970s and 1980s added to the din of voices clamoring for attention. Many of the new think tanks fostered the ideological style of politics to which Hughes and the Endowment were opposed. The Carnegie brand was to foster a dialogue that was apart from and above the trench warfare of normal partisan politics. To Tom Hughes, the NGOs were approaching something like the problem of the intelligence community in his days of government. Different advice from the various intelligence agencies was useful, but policymakers could lose faith in the whole process if the intelligence was too discordant or was merely parochial.

That was one problem. But there were other broader concerns affecting foreign policy. Many Americans did not understand why the government should support so many activities abroad. They no longer took on faith the assurances of their leaders that America's interests were thereby well served. Average Americans now saw a conflict between protecting their own privileges, on the one hand, and nation building and providing security for the rest of the world, on the other. America had gone over to playing defense, protecting our standard of living rather than moving forward for humankind. "The traditional internationalist themes," Hughes lamented in 1985, "are no longer significant outlets for political idealism in the United States."[26]

Reagan's crushing defeat of Tom's friend Fritz Mondale in 1984 did not help Hughes's morale. His outlook began to improve, however, almost as soon as he had published his bleak assessment of the twilight of internationalism. Mikhail Gorbachev became the Soviet premier in 1985 and ushered in the era of glasnost and perestroika in the Soviet Union. The Reagan administration, under the leadership of Secretary of State George Schulz, showed strong interest in arms control and embarked on diplomacy that was to help pave the way for the end to the Cold War.[27]

Hughes, in his first address to the Carnegie trustees in 1971, had invoked Andrew Carnegie's faith in the peaceful resolution of conflicts. Hughes had told his Carnegie trustees that, "The service of peace in the 1970s lies, at least in part, in arresting the flight from foreign policy."[28] Tom had wondered since then if he had done enough to arrest the flight from internationalism. Had he merely stood by and watched the internationalist consensus disintegrate? The favorable turn of events in Reagan's second term lifted Hughes's spirits and improved his relations with the administration. The Endowment's own nonideological brand stood up well against its more ideologically predictable competitors.[29]

A minidrama of détente was playing out within the Endowment itself. Hughes hired a Soviet émigré academic, Dmitri Simes, to head the Russian studies effort at the Endowment. Simes was an energetic man with a reputation for hardline anticommunist views. He had become a close friend of Richard Nixon's, accompanying the former president on a number of trips to the Soviet Union and acting as Nixon's interpreter and adviser on Soviet affairs. He later became the executor of Nixon's will. Nixon was best man at Simes's wedding, which took place while Simes was on the Carnegie staff. Simes eventually left Carnegie to become the head of the Nixon Center, taking three other Carnegie staff members with him.[30]

While Simes was with the Endowment, he was determined to aid Nixon's rehabilitation by inviting him to speak at the institution, which figured so importantly in Nixon's rise to national prominence. Nixon's career in national politics had received the first big boost when he, as a freshman member of the House of Representatives, attacked Alger Hiss for having been a communist spy in the 1930s. It became important for Nixon's rehabilitation that he speak at the Endowment, where Hiss had once been president. However, Hughes always found some excuse each time Simes proposed that the former president be invited to speak.

Simes decided to take matters into his own hands. When Tom was away on an extended overseas trip, Dmitri organized a meeting at which his friend Nixon was the featured speaker. The speech by Nixon attracted wide publicity and played a part in restoring Nixon's reputation as an eminent political leader.

The Nixon talk at Carnegie led to another encounter, which was something of an icebreaker in the process of reconciliation between the two men.

Dmitri Simes invited Tom and Jean Hughes to his wedding. The wedding guests were instructed to appear at a precise time for reasons of security. As the guests assembled, the mystery guest was revealed to be Richard Nixon, Dmitri's best man. Jean Hughes whispered to Tom as the guests lined up to shake Nixon's hand, "Well, you have thirty seconds to think of what you're going to say to him."

Tom's need to choose his words was preempted by the former president, who grasped his hand firmly and said, "Tom, the Endowment has never been in better hands."[31]

The reconciliation went a step further when Nixon proposed to Simes that Hughes be appointed to the Nixon Center's board. Hughes politely declined the invitation, telling his new-found friend, the former president, that he would be happy to help informally in making the Nixon Center a success but did not feel that he would mix well with some of the president's friends and associates.

In the second Reagan term, the foreign policy professionals had evidently regained the upper hand in foreign policy. There were lapses, such as the moment when Reagan and Soviet premier Gorbachev were left without aides, causing a prospective nuclear deal to fall apart at the last minute. Agreements, however, were subsequently negotiated with the Soviet Union.

The election of George H. W. Bush as president in 1988 meant a harmonious relationship between the Endowment and the White House. Hughes knew Bush well from the days when Bush was U.S. ambassador to the United Nations and when both men were active with the Trilateral Commission. Hughes was invited to the White House on several occasions, along with other major foundation heads. The foreign policy scene was undergoing remarkable changes. Gorbachev decided not to prop up the East German regime of Honecker and Krenz. The Berlin Wall came down in November 1989. By mid-December, the East German regime had, for all practical purposes, ceased to exist. The Cold War was over. The Soviet Union itself dissolved the following year, replaced by a new Russia under a noncommunist reformist leadership.

RETIREMENT

Tom Hughes's retirement as Carnegie president, though announced the week after the fall of the Berlin Wall, was not directly linked to the end of the Cold War. Although George Bush's "new world order" could provide a convenient point for Tom's retirement, more humdrum reasons were the motivating factors. In December 1990, he would turn sixty-five, the Endowment's retirement age. He owed it to the trustees to give them adequate notice so they could plan for an orderly succession. He felt that he had

had a good run and was proud of what he had accomplished. He and Jean looked forward to a more relaxed period of life.

When Hughes addressed the Carnegie trustees for the last time on November 18, 1990, he drew on the original Carnegie motto, *Pro patria per orbis concordiam*—"For country through world peace"—to set forth the challenges that lay ahead and the potentially bright prospects he saw for the new world. As he spoke to the trustees, some 400,000 American troops were gathered to liberate Kuwait in the first of what was to be two Gulf Wars. At first glance, Tom told his trustees and guests, this action might seem to fulfill the Endowment's age-old goal of a world consensus for peace. Nearly the entire world was united behind the goal of punishing the last remaining aggressor nation, en route to world peace. "Never before," he said, "has American policy had such explicit and nearly universal support. Never before has such a high-profile American military deployment been sent halfway around the world in peacetime to implement an international consensus."[32]

But the impression that one bold stroke could dispose of the remaining threats to world peace was deceptive. Hughes went on to describe how the old Soviet empire had been a perfect enemy. It had united the West and kept intact the old order based on nation-states. Ancient animosities were submerged under the discipline imposed by the bipolar world order.

Now, two sets of conflicts were likely to emerge full-blown by the end of the twentieth century. One threat was the revival of the ethnic, sectarian, and political rivalries between nations that had been held in check by the division of the world into the communist bloc and the West. The other was the new and potentially more disruptive set of rivalries and conflicts within the nation-states. The first threat to world order was that of traditional conflicts between nation-states. The second stemmed from the weakness of nation-states themselves in the face of what Hughes called the "new pluralism." By this, he meant the new constituencies, generation gaps, disruptive instant communications, and new social networks and the inability of national governments to keep up with burgeoning demands of subnational groups. The traditional nation-states were increasingly paralyzed by their own internal divisions. The world scene thus will face new instabilities, he predicted, that would have astounded Andrew Carnegie and the other Endowment founders.

But Hughes did not want to sound downbeat in his parting words to his colleagues. He affirmed his faith in the original Endowment motto. The end of communism, he told his colleagues, made the mission of the Endowment all the more important. If "we still want active membership in the human race—the good old human race, so largely poor, so largely sick ... so largely non-white.... those who work here will often need to find the confidence of unwarranted optimism."

If we live "in the street called Now and the house named Here," we will not have to convince ourselves of the need for timely action, nor for the politics that rises above politics. . . . In the process, perhaps we shall find—who knows?—not only a new chapter in the life of this old Endowment . . . but a new glimpse, as well, into the . . . secret of peace. If we manage that, our discarded old motto, "Pro Patria Per Orbis Concordiam," will come to life again. And we will have reason at this and future Thanksgiving seasons to say once more in Lincoln's words: "Thanks to all—for the Great Republic, for the principles it lives by and keeps alive, for Man's vast future— Thanks to all."[33]

President George H. W. Bush's new international order did not mean an end to history but the beginning of a new era of human struggle for America and the West. The world, frozen into superpower blocs for nearly half a century, now faced new challenges. But this was no longer Hughes's fight. This was a job to hand over to his successor and to a new generation of thinkers and analysts.

A lighter farewell came in June 1991, when his immediate Endowment colleagues and associates, past and present, threw a surprise party for him. The party, a mixture of a roast with light moments and emotional tributes, was not really a surprise. His colleagues could not totally disguise their extensive preparations for the gathering, which included many old friends and Hughes family members flying in from different cities.

The evening began with Sanford Ungar, master of ceremonies, observing that Tom, upon seeing that Sandy was one of the conspirators planning the gathering, remarked "Et tu, Brute?" Ungar proceeded to read from congratulatory fictitious telegrams. One was from Kim Il Sung, president of the People's Republic of Korea, praising Hughes for being an inspiration to all great leaders clinging to power. Tom's tenacity in remaining in power for twenty years had been an inspiration to Kim. The North Korean signed off, "From one great leader to another."

Kitty Kelly, the leading gossip columnist of the day, declared that she was looking forward to Tom's help in her new tell-all book about the secret lives in the think tanks devoted to peace.

Bill Maynes praised Tom for his vision in converting Carnegie from a grant-giving to an operating foundation. You all know, Bill explained, the difference between the two types. In the grant-giving foundation, you give money to others. In the operating foundation, you give the money to yourself. Maynes also thanked Hughes for introducing the MMDBB metric (the Minnesota mean distance between two bodies) to diplomacy. The metric, derived from Minnesota practice, posited that any contact between two bodies closer than four feet, whether the people were clothed or not, was considered intimate. This measure had proved invaluable to diplomacy in weighing the warmth of diplomatic contacts.

Jane Lowenthal, a librarian, mentioned the following examples of Tom's requests for information that would not get either of them into trouble: submarine names based on sea animals, colleges with names like Washington and Lee and Franklin and Marshall, requests to Great Britain for casualty rates of the Crimean War, and the names of American notables who visited Germany in June 1912 with Andrew Carnegie to celebrate Kaiser Wilhelm II's silver jubilee. She willed her old manual typewriter to Tom as a backup when his own was in the shop for repairs.

Larry Fabian was witty and eloquent. A trustee once asked him whether, since Larry had written a history of the Endowment's early days, he would now produce a sequel explaining how Tom actually ran the place. Fat chance, thought Larry, since Tom had no bureaucratic model for the Endowment, no vice presidents, staff meetings, annual reports, tenure, performance appraisals, or organization charts. Tom believed in people, not institutions, in civility and competition, and in thought that was substantive but not dogmatic. Fabian fell back on history and explained that Tom was a Balliol man. Balliol College was created in 1216 when the Bishop of Durham sent a landowner named John DeBallios to Oxford to repent and to seek truth, relying on his own wits and the sixteen impoverished scholars he was to support. Larry was on to something. There was something of an earlier aristocratic age in the worldliness, refined tastes, and gentlemanly demeanor of their retiring president.

Tom Hughes was an active president emeritus, introducing visiting foreign leaders at meetings and serving on the boards of many institutions and academic centers, but he gradually shifted his interests to his music, collections, and genealogical studies.

Hughes was not a religious man. He had stopped going to church some years before his retirement. He had a sense, though, of having put his hand to the plough and not looking back. His Uncle Burton told him that his grandparents and his parents would have been proud of what he had accomplished. He would cherish the institutions and leaders he had worked with, the causes he had fought for, and all those who had been part of his life.

He was by no means through with life. He would enjoy his family, friends, and collections, rare coins, antique maps, his genealogical studies of his German, Welsh, and American ancestors. His life was woven into the life of America. His was an American pilgrimage from small-town truths to cosmopolitan complexities, from family efforts to build peace with the Indians in Minnesota to his own efforts for peace in the world, from contemplation to engagement in public affairs.

History was his friend. He would now dwell more in the land of Then and less in a street called Now. He would resume his work on his ancestors and follow their journeys through life by history's markers. He would reflect on the twentieth century and his own place in it. In the old days, events had beginnings and endings and lessons one could ponder. His cup was full. His was a life of energy, curiosity, and steadfastness. He was not a man of faith, but he was faithful. There was still much to do, miles to go before he slept, his collections to be put in order, and essays to write. And when it came time to cross over the river and rest under the tree, he would be ready.

Epilogue

The connection between knowledge and politics was always important to Tom Hughes. He began his career early as an intellectual, public crusader, and organizer on the national political stage. His self-appointed task was to rescue his home state of Minnesota and the entire Midwest from isolationism. The adults were impressed with his realistic idealism, and they almost believed him when he declared that he spoke on behalf of America's youth.

Tom had a sense that his temperament did not suit him for public office. But he wanted to be in or near politics as an adviser, applying his expertise to some important cause. World peace was always his greatest cause.

Tom confronted the issues of secrecy, covert actions, and the conflicts between military and civilian intelligence agencies in his work with Humphrey. This set of issues became the major concern of his subsequent government career. Hughes found his work as the State Department's intelligence chief stimulating and well suited for his wide-ranging intellectual interests. The bureaucratic aspects of the job, though, were at times stifling. In Tom's view, there was too much secrecy in the federal government. There was too much self-importance by those on the inside. Tom insisted that his INR analysts should rely on all-source intelligence. That is, they should pay close attention to outside sources and, in particular, follow the work of academic experts in the open literature. Hughes and his peers believed that competition among the intelligence agencies was a good thing, not a problem. Overlap of function provided an opportunity for analysts to learn from one another and gain a fuller understanding of complex problems.

Hughes's belief in rationality was a matter of simple faith that was widely shared within both the analytic and policy communities. Faith in rationality went along with faith in democracy and the virtues of a civilized life. Secrecy fit uneasily with these values, but it was necessary to fight evils like Nazism and communism. In the end, though, Tom Hughes always felt more comfortable with the world of open politics.

Tom summed up his views on the role of presidential power and foreign policy in a classic essay, "The Power to Speak and the Power to Listen," sparked by obiter dictum in Justice Arthur Sutherland's opinion in the U.S. Supreme Court's *Curtiss-Wright* case.[1] Given the speed, complexity, and wide ramifications of foreign policy events, Sutherland had opined that decisions must become increasingly and necessarily centralized. Information flows and power thus gravitate to the president. Sutherland asserted that the president thus had the "plenary and exclusive power [and is] the sole organ of the federal government in the field of foreign affairs."

On the contrary, Hughes argued, who speaks to whom and who listens to whom and when were the major questions. Influencing the president was the ultimate aim of all policy advisers, but there was an almost endless chain of steps in the process of influencing a presidential decision. The president listens to many voices, including those of the intelligence community, the career officials in the line agencies, his political appointees, the media, congressional leaders, and his circle of close friends outside government.

Hughes lent his voice only rarely to the future debates on reforming intelligence. This was partly because he felt that he had already spoken out on the subject but also because he thought the reformers were on the wrong track. In the case of Iran in 1978–1979 and in the aftermath of the 9/11 terrorist attacks in 2001, for example, reformers called for more centralization to improve coordination among the intelligence agencies. To Hughes, one virtue of the 1960s intelligence system was a healthy competition among the different agencies. The problem was not that the intelligence analysts failed to connect the dots. The problem was that policymakers often did not heed the warnings from intelligence and there were always too many dots to connect.

Tom did not believe in structural solutions to the problems of intelligence or other failings of government. Even if intelligence estimates were well sourced, carefully footnoted, and objective, this would not guarantee that policymakers would find the ideas relevant to the particular issues at hand. In addition, the more centralization, the greater would be the likelihood of analysts tailoring their findings to fit prevailing official views.

Nevertheless, the problem of politicization of intelligence can never be entirely solved. Intelligence is part of the policy process, which is part of the political process. Intelligence failures are thus inevitable because policy failures are inevitable, and policy failures are often blamed on faulty intelligence. Intelligence matters because it helps explain a complex reality to policymakers, but it can never fully provide answers for all the decisions that policymakers face.

Intelligence to Hughes was thus part of the warp and woof of politics. Politics would always complicate the work and the life of the intelligence analyst. This formulation was more than a figure of speech. Tom Hughes's friend, CIA director Dick Helms, discovered the perils of coming too close to politicians in his dealings with President Nixon and congressional investigators. Helms had tried to ingratiate himself with Nixon by cooperating in clandestine efforts to block the election of Salvador Allende to Chile's presidency. Helms was rewarded for his pains by being fired and sent off to Iran as U.S. ambassador to keep him away from congressional investigators, a maneuver that in the end did not work.

Tom was proud of his record but aware that he had failed on the central issue of shifting U.S. policy toward negotiations on Vietnam. He did not attempt to vindicate himself or to discredit others for this result. Attacking political opponents by retrospective accounts of events was not his way. He knew that he had been a good director of the INR. He had been the State nominee for, and had won, the Arthur S. Fleming award for outstanding public service. He left government with many friends and admirers, even among those who disagreed with him on the issues.

He fought hard for the declassification of the State Department's version of the Pentagon Papers, which he had commissioned in 1968. He resented the fact that his successor at the INR, Ray Cline, had given the study the highest classification, which kept it out of the public domain for years. The INR performance on many issues had outshone that of the CIA. This was finally revealed thanks to the tireless efforts of Thomas Blanton and John Prados of the National Security Archive of the George Washington University and Professor Edwin Moise of Vanderbilt University to force the declassification in 2004 of the *Top Secret State Department Study* of intelligence in the Vietnam War and to post the document to the archive's website.

Although he did not prevail on Vietnam, Hughes's efforts put him in good company. The February 1965 memo with Humphrey became one of the most prescient documents of the Vietnam War. When Lyndon Johnson escalated the war in the spring of 1965 instead of heeding the memo's warnings, he splintered the political alignments that had held the country together. Johnson thereby destroyed the prospects for a bipartisan foreign policy and for a domestic consensus on the Great Society.

LBJ escalated the war despite the fact that by this time the analysts in the CIA and the INR now largely agreed on a range of issues from the efficacy of bombing to the prospects for negotiations. When the CIA had an operational role, it became an advocate for its own programs and not an analyst. The weight of the military effort after spring and summer of 1965 made it hard for civilian advisers to make their voices heard.

Tom had several chances to work directly for LBJ in the White House, including one that might have evolved into a role as Mac Bundy's successor as special assistant for national security affairs. Hughes was an ambitious man, but he had both personal and professional reasons not to work directly for LBJ. The policy and the temperamental differences between himself and the president were simply too great. Thereafter his access to the White House was limited.

After government, Hughes declined an offer to head the prestigious Council on Foreign Relations in favor of becoming president of the Carnegie Endowment for International Peace. He believed the Carnegie board would be easier to work with, and he was particularly impressed by the board chairman, Milton Katz, a Harvard law professor and former Marshall Plan administrator. The Endowment offered the ideal opportunity, Tom considered, for him to chart his own path. Yet he would also benefit from association with a venerable institution—one whose mission was close to his heart.

The foundation giants such as Ford and Rockefeller in 1971 were pulling back from foreign affairs. The Endowment under Hughes moved aggressively to fill the void. Throwing off "the image of prestigious noncontroversiality," as one critic had described philanthropy at the time, the Endowment under Hughes focused renewed attention on the major issues of American foreign policy.[2] Hughes established a program of exchanges between the Foreign Service and its outside critics, sponsored projects on emerging issues such as arms control, and published provocative articles through a sprightly new journal, *Foreign Policy*. He sought to bring the warring factions of the Vietnam debate back into a fruitful dialogue.

Hughes steered the Endowment successfully through two decades of the increasingly cluttered Washington think tank scene. He spoke out and wrote as a critic of Republican and Democratic administrations. He sent many talented members of the Carnegie staff into government service and into responsible positions in the nonprofit world. Tom stepped down as Carnegie president in 1991 as the American Century was at its end. The nation stood on the brink of President George H. W. Bush's "new world order."

Tom stayed active as the Endowment's president emeritus for several years, functioning as, among other things, introducer-in-chief for the many foreign dignitaries who visited the Endowment and the Council on Foreign Relations in Washington. He served on a large number of boards of many nonprofit organizations and academic centers. But he gradually shifted his attention to his personal artistic and intellectual interests.

In 1993 Hughes's life changed when his wife of thirty-eight years, Jean H.

Reiman, died suddenly of a massive stroke. Two years later, he met and fell in love with, as he told friends, "a very lively woman." He met Jane Casey Kucinski at a social function at the Chevy Chase Club in Maryland.[3] He had drifted away from the group he was with and was standing alone in front of a large tree on the club's grounds. Jane approached him and asked, "How old are you, and what do you do?" He replied that he was sixty-nine and was president emeritus of the Carnegie Endowment for International Peace.

She was won over completely when he beautifully played her favorite ballade by Chopin. They were married in the summer of 1995. At the time of this writing, they have been happily married for twenty-six years.

A gifted raconteur, Hughes enjoys telling stories about his ancestors to entertain friends. Tom admits cheerfully to ancestor worship. He especially likes talking about his grandfathers, who had such an impact on his life. The fathers of both of Hughes's grandfathers were foreign born. His two grandfathers married upper-class women with New England roots, and settled down to live the American Dream as pillars of the community in their respective small towns of Minnesota. But Tom's stories also go back to the distant past. Many have a humorous side. For example, Ezra Stiles, president of Yale in colonial days and a distant relation, rallied a group of undergraduates to repel a British landing during the Revolutionary War, only to discover that he had the wrong landing place. The British in any event had decided to bypass New Haven and to shoot up instead the picturesque settlements on the Chesapeake Bay.

A favorite Hughes story is his visit to the Vatican Library in Rome to research the life of his ancestor, Sigismund of Brandenburg, who aspired to succeed his maternal grandfather, King Sigismund I of Poland. To achieve his goal, Sigismund in the 1560s had first to be named the Archbishop of Magdeburg. Tom wrote to the Vatican seeking permission to access papers on Sigismund's term as archbishop. The Vatican, evidently deeming this project harmless, granted Tom permission to see the papers.

When he arrived at the Vatican, Tom was given a translator-assistant to help with the documents, which were all in Latin. When Hughes and his assistant arrived in the inner chamber, there seemed to be a hum of excitement in the air. The room was a rotunda with a balcony, which was lined with priests.

The assistant disappeared and returned with several large boxes of what looked to be very ancient documents covered with dust.

"Perhaps the documents have not been viewed for quite some time?" said Hughes.

"You are an *ab initio* reader."

"What does that mean—that I am the first reader this year?"

"No, the first ever. No one has asked to see these documents in four hundred years."

Sigismund, as it turned out, did not succeed in becoming King of Poland. He died at the age of twenty-eight from the plague, leaving behind his common law wife, twin sons, and one daughter. The papal papers had other items of interest. There was a strong letter of recommendation that accounted for how the sixteen-year-old Sigismund was appointed archbishop.

"Dear Brothers in Christ," the letter began, as was customary since the pope's circle of advisers would see the letter. The letter explained that young Sigismund's relative inexperience in theology would be remediated by the fact that Sigismund, then only sixteen, had a very bright tutor. The tutor would quickly bring him up to speed theologically. Furthermore, Sigismund's father, the Elector Joachim II in Berlin, had an army of 10,000 men, which would come in handy for the pope in any number of circumstances. This argument evidently carried the day, and Sigismund was appointed archbishop.

There was also a letter in the files from the pope to Sigismund, which was dated a few years after Sigismund became the archbishop. The pope congratulated Sigismund on his outstanding work as archbishop, and then came what seemed to be almost an afterthought. The pope had heard rumors, no doubt merely malicious gossip, that Sigismund had a woman and several children living with him. Could Sigismund for the record please be so kind as to put those idle rumors to rest.

The wily Sigismund promptly relocated his wife and children to the Green Court about a mile away from the archbishop's official residence. He then wrote to the pope and flatly denied having a woman or children living with him.

While his genealogical studies continued to interest him, as he approached his eightieth birthday Hughes began to pay closer attention to the disposition of his various collections and to finding a permanent home for his papers. Tom had the collection inventoried and appraised by a New York law firm specializing in such matters. The collection was appraised at $1 million. He then arranged for a public showing of the collection at his home for friends, neighbors, and members of the Institute for Contemporary German Studies.

In 2011, Tom donated to Yale University his large collection of German portraits, books, maps, official documents, sculptures, artifacts, objets d'art, letters from Kaiser Wilhelm II and his second wife, and other memorabilia. He had inherited much of this from his maternal grandfather and had added to the collection himself. Jane Hughes said, "Tom's heart is easy. His art treasures are someplace where they will be well taken care of. That delights us."[4]

Yale President Richard Levin penned a thank you note to Hughes assuring him that the collection "will strengthen the magnificent holdings in a meaningful way."[5] The next year Hughes added a collection of rare coins to the Yale donation, which the museum director wrote Tom was one of the finest of its kind in the world. In 2018, he arranged for his voluminous papers, correspondence, drafts of speeches, and notes to have a permanent home at the Library of Congress, the processing of which has been interrupted by the COVID-19 pandemic.

At ninety-five, Tom is one of the last surviving New Frontiersmen and Johnson administration officials. Visitors come to see Hughes regularly, students doing dissertations, and professors writing books, journalists seeking insights about Vietnam and other events, and others interested in the JFK, LBJ, Nixon, or Carter administrations. Foreign visitors are numerous, especially from England and Germany.

He has been blessed with good health, but in 2015 he fell and broke his hip at a Cosmos Club seminar. As a result, he no longer travels abroad and has limited his domestic travel. But Tom and Jane continued to entertain friends, to participate in Washington social functions, and to enjoy the company of a wide circle of friends until the pandemic of 2020 confined them, like most of us, to exile at home.

Hughes's story is an American story. As noted, both of his grandfathers were sons of immigrants. Both men married well, and became leaders in their small towns. Tom rose from his small boyhood town in the state of Minnesota to national prominence by virtue of his own hard work and good fortune. He worked his way into the top ranks of the foreign policy establishment, then dominated by the privileged families of the Northeast. Tom hired women and minorities and helped to democratize the Foreign Service.

Hughes did not profess but rather embodied the spirit and the virtues of public service. His dedication to public service, and to the cause of world peace, came as naturally to him as defending the rights of Minnesota's Indians had come to his paternal grandfather and namesake. The obligation to serve the public interest was natural, a simple fact of life for him as much as the hot summers and cold winter winds of southern Minnesota.

On a sunny but crisp afternoon before the pandemic, I paid a call to Tom and Jane Hughes. Tom was drowsing and enjoying the sun on his back deck. I imagined that Tom in his mind's eye was thinking of the great, the near great, and others he had known over his long life and career, and was perhaps exchanging a joke with some of those he knew best. There were so many dedicated men and women with whom he served over his long career, most of whom served their country well but with little public recognition or reward. I had read George Packer's biography of Richard Holbrooke, and I gave Tom an account of a few key episodes.

Tom responded with a Holbrooke story of his own. Holbrooke, then a Carnegie Endowment associate, showed up in Hughes's office one afternoon and announced that he had arranged a dinner party to be held the following Thursday evening at the Hughes home. Holbrooke told Hughes that he had only one requirement. Holbrooke's new wife was coming down from New York for the occasion and had to be seated between Senators Ted Kennedy and Frank Church. Other than that detail, Jean Hughes should seat the guests as she chooses and serve whatever she likes. The dinner party in the end, Tom explained, proved to be a great success. Richard Holbrooke and Warren Manshel got the jobs they wanted in the Carter administration, and Carnegie no longer had to contend with them.

At the time of my visit Tom had recently lost his oldest friend, Harris Wofford, and had eulogized him at a Cosmos Club service as "a cultivated man," the highest praise in the Hughesian view of life.

They were almost all gone now, his old friends and the others who had run the country in the last century. The country was no longer the same. It was bigger, more disorderly, and more complicated, something beyond and different from the noisy but stable democracy he knew.

Tom mentioned that Bob Caro had called and that they had talked for an hour about why, in Tom's opinion, LBJ had chosen to escalate the Vietnam War in 1965 when he could have moved to disengage from the conflict. Caro, Tom mused, was having trouble dealing with LBJ's dark side.

This was not my problem with Hughes, because as far as I could see he did not have a dark side. But he was a very complicated uncomplicated man. What was the common thread that ran through his long life, the theme that knitted together and guided his actions? Jane Hughes came out to the deck to say that she was off to deliver a lecture on Montaigne, her favorite author. She asked Tom if he was warm enough outside. It was growing cooler. She thought he might catch a cold. Tom said that he should go back in and review his notes in case Bob Caro called again. I rose to take my leave. Tom walked slowly back into the house. The thought came to me that he was a man from a different age, the last gentleman, the likes of whom we would not soon see again.

Notes

Prologue

1. Thomas L. Hughes, "Experiencing McNamara," *Foreign Policy* 100 (Autumn 1995), p. 156.
2. Quoted in Ted Gittinger, ed., *The Johnson Years: A Vietnam Roundtable* (University of Texas at Austin, LBJ Library, LBJ School of Public Affairs), p. 53.
3. Dean Acheson, *Present at the Creation: My Years in the State Department* (W. W. Norton, 1987).
4. Thomas L. Hughes, "INR'S Vietnam Study in Context: A Retrospective Preface, Thirty-Five Years Later," in *Intelligence and Vietnam: The Top Secret 1969 State Department Study*, National Security Archives Electronic Briefing Book 121 (National Security Archives, May 2, 2004).
5. Harris Wofford, e-mail to Jane Casey Hughes, October 4, 2006, 15:25 p.m.

Chapter 1

1. New Ulm was first attacked on August 19, but suffered great damage from fires when the Indians attacked again on August 23.
2. Grandfather Hughes's research methods featured close collaboration with his wife and his associates. He and his wife collected records, books of photos, letters, and paintings; the materials were gradually divided into categories, the categories into shelves, boxes, and trunks. Over time, the materials shaped up gradually into comprehensive studies, papers, speeches, and finally books. I have mentioned only the most prominent of Hughes's books. For a more comprehensive list, see Thomas L. Hughes, introduction to *Indian Chiefs*, 1969 edition, pp. 13, 15.
3. The Dakota comprised four tribes: the Mewakantons, Wahpekutes, Wahpetons, and Sissetons. These tribes were contacted by the French in about 1650 and were known as the Eastern Sioux to distinguish them from the plains-dwelling Western Sioux. The Western Sioux were the Nakota and Lakota, who had migrated west decades earlier. The Dakota customarily divided themselves into two groups, often referred to as the Lower Sioux and the Upper Sioux, based on the traditional village

location along the Mississippi River. See Gary Clayton Anderson, *Kinsmen of Another Kind: Dakota-White Relations in the Upper Mississippi Valley, 1650–1862* (Minnesota Historical Society Press, 1997).

4. Thomas Hughes describes this dramatic incident in *Indian Chiefs of Southern Minnesota*, pp. 73–80. John Other Day, an Indian who had been converted to Christianity four years before, was one of the heroes of the uprising, saving sixty-five settlers by his bravery and aiding the army in the fighting.

5. Dee Brown, *Bury My Heart at Wounded Knee* (Henry Holt, 1971).

6. Thomas Hughes to Adelaide Stillman, Feb 13, 1928, TLH papers.

7. TLH papers.

8. TLH papers.

Chapter 2

1. Thomas L. Hughes, *Perilous Encounters: The Cold War Collisions of Domestic and World Politic: Oral History Interviews with Thomas L. Hughes* (Association of Diplomatic Studies and Training, 2011), p. 12.

2. Ibid.

3. Autobiography, TLH papers.

4. TLH papers.

5. "Master Tam Hughes Presents Piano Recital at Home," *Mankato Free Press*, copy in TLH papers, dated April 1933.

6. "Prairie physician" is the description used in Hughes's 2011 oral history.

7. The collection was appraised at $1 million prior to the time of his gift to Yale. The collection is known as the Hohenzollern-Schlaberg-Hughes Collection and is distributed over several museums at Yale. Hughes held a number of going-away parties at his home in Chevy Chase, Maryland, around the time the collection was packed up and shipped to New Haven, and he commemorated the occasion with a speech to his guests.

8. There is a set of twenty notebooks with only one year missing, owing to a theft of the contents of his car one year. Hughes supplied me with six pages of notes, filling in from memory what he thought were the highlights of the missing year. The diaries were an invaluable source for this biography.

9. Gilbert Jonas, *One Shining Moment: A History of the Student Federalist Movement in the United States, 1942–1953* (iUniverse Books, 2001).

Chapter 3

1. The ranks of the Minnesota internationalists included Governor Harold Stassen; Representative Walter Judd; Senator (and later vice president) Hubert Humphrey; Governor (and Senator) Ed Thye; Senator Joseph Ball; newspaper magnate John Cowles; Carleton College president Lawrence Gould; Minnesota Attorney General (and later senator and vice president) Walter Mondale; political adviser and later Chief Justice of the United States Warren Burger; journalist Eric Sevareid; pollster Richard Scammon; political scientists Evron and Jeane Kirkpatrick; transplanted Minnesotan Max Kampelman; Governor (and later secretary of agriculture) Orville Freeman; Senator Eugene McCarthy; businessman and philanthropist Dwayne Andreas; the wheat-flour queen and philanthropist Adelaide Enright; and Ambassador Eugenie Anderson.

2. Stassen, in May 1943, published two articles in the nation's most popular magazine, outlining his vision of world government. See Harold E. Stassen, "Wanted: A Forthright Republican Party," *Saturday Evening Post*, May 15, 1943, and "We Need a World Government," May 22, 1943.

3. Harris Wofford to Thomas L. Hughes, letter of January 23, 1944, quoted in Hughes e-mail to author, May 15, 2020, TLH papers.

4. TLH papers, 1945.

5. Gilbert Jonas, *One Shining Moment: A History of the Student Federalist Movement in the United States, 1942–1953* (iUniverse Books, 2001).
6. Clarence K. Streit, *Union Now* (Harper & Brothers, New York, 1939).
7. Wofford to Hughes, June 7, 1943, TLH papers.
8. Thomas L. Hughes diary, November 11, 1943, TLH papers.
9. Thomas L. Hughes, "Liberals, Populists, and Foreign Policy," *Foreign Policy* 20 (Autumn 1975), p. 99.
10. Student Federalist Travel 1943–47: Harris Wofford and Emmy Lou Lindgren (Clare), n.d., TLH papers.
11. *American Forum of the Air,* July 4, 1944, Theodore Granik, host, transcript in TLH papers.
12. Student Federalists, press release, Washington office, November 11, 1944, TLH papers.
13. See Jonas, *One Shining Moment*, pp. 81–82, for specific data on the Student Federalists' successor organization, the National Student Association. As of March 1950, the association had 4,934 members, a figure that included the remnants of the Student Federalists and several other organizations. The Cold War began to cause a big falloff in any student organization pushing for world federalism.
14. Tam Hughes, "Idealists at San Francisco," *Student Federalist*, July 1945.
15. Hughes describes this encounter in his inimitable style in Thomas L. Hughes, *Anecdotage: Some Authentic Retrievals* (Createspace Independent Publishing Platform, 2014), pp. 207–08.
16. TLH papers.
17. The National Student Association later did acquire a role as part of the CIA's covert effort to combat the Soviet takeover of international student bodies. Cord Meyer, who had moved from the United World Federalists to the CIA, spearheaded this operation as the CIA's director of international cultural activities. See Cord Meyer Jr., *Facing Reality: From World Federalism to the CIA* (Roman & Littlefield, 1982).
18. Clare Lindgren to Harris Wofford, November 19, 1946, TLH papers.
19. Thomas L. Hughes, "Seven Eulogies," self-published, 2010.

Chapter 4

1. Thomas L. Hughes, *Perilous Encounters: The Cold War Collisions of Domestic and World Politics; Oral History with Thomas L. Hughes* (Association for Diplomatic Studies and Training, 2011), pp. 30–31.
2. TLH interview, fall 2016.
3. Chester Bowles, *The New Dimensions of Peace* (Harper and Row, 1955).
4. Kampelman, *The Memoirs of a Private Man in Public Life* (HarperColllins, 1991), p. 120.
5. The Carroll Arms was the favorite hangout in the 1950s for many senators. The hotel's second floor Quorum Club room was the headquarters for Bobby Baker, installed by Lyndon Johnson as secretary to the Democratic majority in the Senate and as his "enforcer" on close votes. Baker ran a brothel from the Carroll Arms, where he would line up liaisons for senators and keep close tabs for Johnson.
6. TLH papers.
7. Re: Appropriations, February 15, 1956, memorandum, TLH papers.
8. "People, Peace, and Progress," speech delivered at Boston University, May 5, 1958, reprinted in the *Cong. Rec.* 85 Cong. Rec. 10976, June 12, 1958.
9. Winthrop Griffith, *Humphrey: A Candid Biography* (William Morrow and Company, 1965), p. 276.

Chapter 5

1. Thomas Hughes, "Assignment: MacArthur," in *Anecdotage: Some Authentic Retrievals* (Scotts Valley, CA: Createspace Independent Publishing Platform, 2014), pp. 16–17; Thomas Hughes, *Perilous Encounters: The Cold War Collisions of Domestic and World Politics; Oral History Interviews with Thomas L. Hughes* (Association for Diplomatic Studies and Training, 2011), p. 35.
2. Chester Bowles, *Promises to Keep: My Years in Public Life* (New York: Harper & Row, 1971), p. 272.
3. TLH papers, excerpted in Hughes, *Anecdotage*, p. 4.
4. TLH diary, January 3, 1956, TLH papers.
5. This was the first of two major Kennedy speeches on foreign policy. The second was on Poland and the implications of the 1956 "Polish spring."
6. The ambassador's wife was reputed to be one of Kennedy's numerous liaisons.
7. Thomas L. Hughes, "LBJ Over–Manages a Change," in *Anecdotage*, pp. 29–32.
8. TLH to HHH, November 7, 1958, TLH papers.
9. TLH diary, November 7, 1958, TLH papers.
10. TLH diary, November 17, 1958, TLH papers.
11. TLH diary, November 27, 1958, TLH papers.
12. TLH diary, November 29, 1958, TLH papers.
13. Thomas L. Hughes, interview with author, December 7, 2015.
14. TLH diary, November 29, 1958, TLH papers.
15. Hughes, *Anecdotage*, p. 18.
16. Ibid., p. 19.
17. TLH diary, 1960, TLH papers.
18. Thomas L. Hughes, "Congress and Foreign Policy," *The Reporter*, April 30, 1959. See also Hughes, *Perilous Encounters*, p. 69, for a discussion of how Hughes used this publication to launch his series of mailings to a list of prominent public figures for the rest of his career.
19. Hughes, *Anecdotage*, p. 19.
20. Quoted in Howard B. Schaffer, *Chester Bowles: New Dealer in the Cold War* (Harvard University Press, 1993), p. 165.
21. Hughes's diary entry for November 7, 1958, was one of his longest entries, giving a detailed account of what Kampelman told him about Humphrey's presidential calculations.
22. McLuhan's major work was *Understanding Mediate Extension of Man* (MIT Press, 1994), with an introduction by Lewis Lapham.
23. "Bowles Discounts 1960 Presidential Talk," press release, Madison, Wisconsin, and Washington, D.C., October 11, 1959.

Chapter 6

1. Thomas L. Hughes oral history given in 1977 describing his time with Chet Bowles for the Chester Bowles Papers, Yale University Library.
2. Chester Bowles to JFK, TLH papers.
3. TLH diary, January 23, 1960, TLH papers.
4. Ibid.
5. TLH papers.
6. TLH diary, January 26, 1960, TLH papers.
7. TLH diary, February 6, 1960, TLH papers.
8. TLH papers.
9. JFK to Chester Bowles, February 17, 1960, TLH papers.
10. TLH diary, February 23, 1960, TLH papers.
11. In fact, Kennedy had 741 delegates as the convention opened, Johnson 409, and Symington about 100. Symington switched Missouri's votes to Kennedy on the first day, which put JFK over the top.

12. Theodore H. White, *The Making of the President, 1960* (Harper Perennial, 1960), p. 174.
13. TLH papers.
14. Theodore White, *The Making of the President 1960* (HarperPerennial, 1960), p. 101.
15. When asked about this directly, by moderator Tom Oliphant at a fifty-year anniversary celebration of the West Virginia primary held at the JFK Presidential Library in Boston, Kennedy aides Dick Donoghue and Ted Sorensen acknowledged that luring Humphrey into running in West Virginia had been discussed, but they issued weak denials, saying, "We were not that smart." Oliphant made an oblique reference to an internal memo that talked of "luring Humphrey into a trap."
16. TLH diary, April 18, 1960, TLH papers.
17. A Wikipedia post from in December 2015 claimed that Humphrey spent only $25,000 compared with Kennedy's $125,000. These figures lacked documentation, but they are perhaps not totally out of line regarding the relative expenditures of the two camps.
18. TLH diary, April 16, 1960, TLH papers.
19. TLH diary, July 10, 1960, TLH papers.
20. TLH diary, July 11, 1960, TLH papers.
21. The title appears prominently on the cover of the pamphlet, which was distributed to the delegates on July 12, 1960.
22. TLH diary, July 14, 1960, TLH papers.
23. TLH diary, January 21, 1960, TLH papers.
24. TLH diary, May 16, 1960, TLH papers.
25. TLH diary, May 17, 1960, TLH papers.
26. TLH diary, May 17, 1960, TLH papers.
27. TLH diary, May 25, 1960, TLH papers.
28. TLH diary, May 23, 1960, TLH papers, records that "Chet offered to put together a shadow government for Jack after the nomination and Jack agreed it was 'essential' and that Chet was 'just the right man to do it.' So Chet came back to the office extremely pleased with himself."
29. TLH diary, August 2, 1960, TLH papers.
30. Chester Bowles, *The Coming Political Breakthrough* (Harper and Brothers, 1961).
31. TLH diary, June 24, 1960, TLH papers. Chet "tried to have lunch w. K but was constantly interrupted. Dirksen accused K of appeasement for suggesting that Ike might have expressed regret. . . . Jack was alarmed over his attack . . . and rushed to floor. . . . Tempest in a teapot. Chet was left in Kennedy office to eat lunch alone." TLH diary, May 23, 1960.
32. Dorothy Stebbins Bowles, Chester Bowles's second wife and mother of Sally and Sam Bowles. Bowles had two children by his first wife.
33. TLH diary, August 30, 1960, TLH papers.
34. TLH diary, August 31, 1960, TLH papers.
35. TLH's diary, October 25, 1960, reads: "Stevenson and Chet spent evening together last night. HW interrupted them to seek phone call to Mrs. Martin Luther King. MLK himself had been arrested—four months in jail for no driver's license. Chet phoned her. Kennedy did also. Stevenson declined on grounds that Mrs. K and he had never been introduced! Adlai also refused to make a joint stmt. with Chet on King's arrest."
36. Chester Bowles, memorandum, TLH papers.
37. Ibid.
38. TLH diary, October 11, 1960, TLH papers.
39. TLH diary, November 3, 1960, TLH papers.
40. TLH diary, November 9, 1960, TLH papers.

41. TLH diary, November 13, 1960, TLH papers.

42. David Nassaw, *The Patriarch: The Remarkable Life and Turbulent Times of Joseph P. Kennedy* (Penguin Books, 2013), pp. 752–53. Nassaw does not record exactly what was said at the match but reports, on page 753, that Chris Matthews wrote, "The meeting accomplished just what the Kennedys intended: providing a photo op to showcase the image of loser meeting winner. . . . The result has been validated by the face-to-face meeting on Nixon's own turf." Chris Matthews, *Jack Kennedy: Elusive Hero* (Simon and Shuster, 2011), pp. 318–19.

43. This story also appears in Matthews, *Jack Kennedy*.

Chapter 7

1. David Nassaw, *The Patriarch: The Remarkable Life and Turbulent Times of Joseph P. Kennedy* (Penguin Books, 2013), pp. 753–55.

2. The issue was defused for the moment but was to emerge again during Bowles's Senate confirmation hearing for the job of under secretary of state. See "Nomination of Chester Bowles Undersecretary of State-Designate," Hearings before the Committee on Foreign Relations, U.S. Senate, 87th Congress, 1st sess. (GPO, 1961), pp. 1–56.

3. TLH diary, November 12, 1960.

4. "Interview with Chester Bowles: A Top Foreign-Policy Adviser to President-Elect Kennedy," *U.S. News and World Report*, November 21, 1960, pp. 100–107.

5. *Robert Kennedy in His Own Words* (Bantam Books, 1988), pp. 78–79. "I didn't want to have someone in the Civil Rights division who was dealing not from fact but . . . from emotion and who wasn't going to give what was in the interest of President Kennedy but advice which the particular individual felt was in the interest of a Negro or group of Negroes or a group of those who were interested in civil rights. I wanted advice and ideas from somebody who has the same interest and motivation that I did. That was the reason I looked outside of Harris Wofford. . . . It really came down to Burke Marshall or Harris Wofford and I decided on Burke."

6. TLH diary, November 22, 1960.

7. TLH diary, November 23, 1960. Neither man got the job, which went instead to David Bell, a Harvard economist.

8. JFK to Chester Bowles, November 17, 1960, original and copy in TLH papers.

9. TLH diary, November 24, 1960.

10. TLH diary, November 24, 1960.

11. Harris Wofford, *Of Kennedys and Kings: Making Sense of the Sixties* (University of Pittsburgh Press, 1992).

12. Thomas L. Hughes, *Perilous Encounters: The Cold War Collisions of Domestic and World Politics: Oral History Interviews with Thomas L. Hughes* (Association of Diplomatic Studies and Training, 2011), pp. 64–66.

13. Chester Bowles to Sargent Shriver, November 17, 1960, copy in TLH papers.

14. TLH informal notes, n.d., TLH papers.

15. TLH diary, November 29, 1960.

16. TLH diary, November 29, 1960.

17. Thomas L. Hughes, *Anecdotage: Some Authentic Retrievals* (Createspace Independent Publishing Platform, 2014), p. 58.

18. Memorandum to John F. Kennedy from Chester Bowles, December 5, 1960, TLH papers.

19. Ibid.

20. Ibid.

21. Tim Weiner, *Legacy of Ashes: The History of the CIA* (Anchor Books, 2007), pp. 197–99. Weiner concludes, "The assassination was as close as the CIA had ever come to carrying out a murder at the command of the White House" (p. 199).

22. Gregory F. Treverton, *Covert Action: The Limits of Intervention in the Post-*

war World (Basic Books, 1987); John Prados, *The Presidents' Secret Wars: CIA and Pentagon Covert Operations from World War II through the Persian Gulf* (Elephant Paperbacks, 1996); Stephen Kinzer, *The Dulles Brothers: John Foster Dulles, Allen Dulles, and Their Secret World War* (Times Books, Henry Holt and Company, 2013).

23. Informal TLH notes of a conversation with Stevenson aide Mike Rashish, December 9, 1960, TLH papers.

24. Rusk, in the fall of 1961, did name Rostow to be head of the policy planning staff as part of the shake-up that resulted in Bowles's leaving his post as under secretary. See Chester Bowles, *Promises to Keep* (Harper and Row, 1971), pp. 362–63.

25. Ibid., p. 317.

26. Bowles's own conception of his official duties is laid out in *Promises to Keep*, pp. 307–14. He stressed the importance of new ideas to differentiate the Kennedy from the Eisenhower administration. But see Brandon Grove, *Behind Embassy Walls: The Life and Times of an American Diplomat* (University of Missouri Press, 2005), pp. 71–88, and Hughes, *Perilous Encounters*, pp. 64–68, for rather different views of how the office functioned.

27. The process was well suited to Roger Hilsman, who simply took it upon himself to deal directly with the White House and to inform Rusk later of what he was doing. To get away with this, one had to be unusually skilled in personal relations. Roger was not, and he earned Rusk's enmity from the start of the administration.

28. Grove, *Behind Embassy Walls*, p. 81.

29. John Kenneth Galbraith, *A Life in Our Times* (Houghton Mifflin, 1981), p. 373.

30. Hughes, *Perilous Encounters*, pp. 79–80.

31. Phil Kaiser served in several other important ambassadorial posts; his last and most important was to Austria. He was a regular at the Brookings Institution Friday lunches after his retirement from the diplomatic service. He wrote an engaging memoir, *Journeying Far and Wide: A Political and Diplomatic Memoir* (Charles Scribner's Sons, 1993). He suffered in his later years from a debilitating lung disease contracted in his years in Africa and finally succumbed to the disease. He lived to see his elder son, Robert, become the managing editor of the *Washington Post*.

32. Hilsman and Dean Acheson, conversation, June 1961, transcript, TLH papers, copy of Roger Hilsman papers in box 5, John F. Kennedy Presidential Library.

33. James T. Patterson, *Grand Expectations: The United States, 1945–1974* (Oxford University Press, 1996), p. 465.

34. Hughes, *Perilous Encounters*, p. 64, notes that Rusk wrote a strategically timed article "The President and Foreign Policy" during the 1960 campaign that recognized an important role for the president in foreign affairs but also for the State Department.

35. Miscellaneous notes, no heading, dated 1962, TLH papers; emphasis in original.

36. JFK Inaugural Address, John F. Kennedy Presidential Library, Boston, Massachusetts.

37. Informal notes, TLH papers, n.d. These notes were presumably written sometime in 1962.

38. Informal notes, TLH papers, n.d.

39. TLH papers. The lunches or dinners with Alsop were from March 1963 to December 1965, and those with Lippmann from March 1963 to May 165. Hughes referred to other meetings with Alsop from time to time in his notes. He had regular social contacts with Max Frankel of the *New York Times* and a number of journalists from the *Minneapolis Tribune*, who were personal friends.

40. Thomas Hughes, "Meeting the Press," in *Anecdotage*, pp. 64–65.

41. Ibid.

42. TLH notes, TLH papers, n.d.

Chapter 8

1. Roger Hilsman, oral history interview with Dennis J. O'Brien, John F. Kennedy Library, Digital Collections, August 14, 1970.
2. Thomas Power, *The Man Who Kept the Secrets* (Knopf, 1979).
3. Hilsman to U. Alexis Johnson, memorandum, November 4, 1961, Roger Hilsman papers, box 5, JFK Library; quoted in Thomas A. Reinstein, "The Way a Drunk Uses a Lamp Post: Intelligence Analysis and Policy during the Vietnam War, 1962–1968," Ph.D. diss., Temple University, December 2018, p. 52.
4. Harris Wofford, interview with author, Washington, D.C., December 1, 2015.
5. President John F. Kennedy, State Department Auditorium, Washington, D.C., July 18, 1961, JFK Press Conferences, no. 14 (http://jfk-press-conferences.blogspot.com/).
6. Thomas L. Hughes, *Anecdotage: Some Authentic Retrievals* (Createspace Independent Publishing Platform, 2014), pp. 54–55, has RFK punching Bowles in the chest.
7. Chester Bowles, *Promises to Keep* (Harper and Row, 1971), p. 332.
8. Thomas L. Hughes, *Perilous Encounters: The Cold War Collisions of Domestic and World Politics: Oral History Interviews with Thomas L. Hughes* (Association of Diplomatic Studies and Training, 2011), pp. 50–57.
9. Richard Reeves, *President Kennedy* (Simon & Schuster, 1993), p. 105.
10. Ibid., pp. 50, 57.
11. Robert Kennedy's handwritten notes on the meeting stated, "My idea is to stir things up on [the] island with espionage, sabotage, general disorder, run & operated by Cubans themselves with every group but Batistaites & communists. Do not know if we will be successful in overthrowing Castro but we have nothing to lose in my estimate." Quoted in *Foreign Relations of the United States, 1961–1963*, vol. 10, pt. 1, *Cuba, January 1961–1962*, Edward C. Keefer and John P. Glennon, eds. (U.S. Government Printing Office, 1997), pp. 666–67.
12. Ibid., pp. 688–89.
13. President Kennedy further spelled out the project in a November 30, 1961, memorandum to the secretary of state, the secretary of defense, the attorney general, the director of the CIA, General Taylor, General Lansdale, and Richard Goodwin. The project would "help Cuba overthrow the communist regime" and "be conducted under the general guidance of General Lansdale, acting as Chief of Operations." Ibid., pp. 688–89.
14. Tim Weiner, *A Legacy of Ashes: The History of the CIA* (Anchor Books, 2007), p. 214.
15. Max Boot, *The Road Not Taken* (W.W. Norton & Company, 2018), p. 383.
16. Roger Hilsman to Alex Johnson, memorandum, January 1962. Quoted in Boot, *The Road Not Taken*, p. 748.
17. Hilsman memo to Hojmson, January 1962.
18. *Foreign Relations of the United States, 1961–1963*, vol. 10, January 25, 1962, document 296, Memorandum for the Record, pp. 780–82, and quote on p. 782.
19. U.S. Central Intelligence Agency, *CIA Documents on the Cuban Missile Crisis, 1962* (1992), p. 435; quoted in Jorge I. Dominguez, "The @#$%& Missile Crisis (or What Was 'Cuban' about U.S. Decisions during the Cuban Missile Crisis?)" *Diplomatic History* 24, no. 2 (2000), p. 310.
20. *CIA Documents on the Cuban Missile Crisis, 1962*.
21. Ibid., p. 509.
22. Ibid., p. 435; quoted in Dominguez, p. 310.
23. *CIA Documents on the Cuban Missile Crisis, 1962*, interdepartmental memo, November 1963; quoted in Dominguez, pp. 311–12; ibid., p. 435, quoted in Dominguez, p. 310; Dominguez, "The @#$%& Missile Crisis," p. 312.

Chapter 9

1. See Herbert S. Dinerstein, *The Making of a Missile Crisis: October 1962* (Johns Hopkins University Press, 1976), pp. 175–77.
2. National Security Archive, George Washington University, *The Cuban Missile Crisis, 1962: A Chronology of Events*, pt. 1, July 1962, p. 353.
3. Aleksandr Fursenko and Timothy Naftali, *One Hell of a Gamble: Khrushchev, Castro, and Kennedy 1958–1964* (Norton Paperback, 1998), p. 71.
4. Raymond L. Garthoff, "The Cuban Missile Crisis: An Overview," in *The Cuban Missile Crisis Revisited*, edited by James A. Nathan (St. Martin's Press, 1992), pp. 41–42; Benjamin Schwartz, "The Real Cuban Missile Crisis," review Sheldon Stern's *The Cuban Missile Crisis on American Memory*, *The Atlantic*, January–February 2013.
5. A normally reliable GRU informant in the United States evidently reported to the Kremlin on March 9 and 11, 1962, that sometime between June 6 and June 12, 1961, the United States had intended to launch a preemptive nuclear strike on the Soviet Union in September 1961; Fursenko and Naftali, *One Hell of a Gamble*, p. 155. Eric Schlosser, *Command and Control: Nuclear Weapons, The Damascus Accident, and the Illusion of Safety* (Penguin Books, 2014), p. 153, says that a proposal was made to President Kennedy for a preemptive strike. It was perhaps this proposal that the Kremlin's source in the United States heard about and mistook for an actual decision to launch a preemptive attack.
6. Fursenko and Naftali, *One Hell of a Gamble*, p. 155.
7. Quoted in Raymond L. Garthoff, "The Cuban Missile Crisis: An Overview," p. 41.
8. Keating ran against, and was defeated by, Robert F. Kennedy in 1964 in the U.S. Senate race in New York.
9. This point is discussed in Thomas L. Hughes, "Butcher, Baker, and Intelligence Maker," in *Speaking Up and Speaking Out*, edited by Jane Casey Hughes (Xlibris, 2013), pp. 259–60.
10. James G. Blight and David A. Welch, *On the Brink: Americans and Russians Reexamine the Cuban Missile Crisis* (Hill and Wang, 1989), p. 408.
11. "Statement of President John F. Kennedy on Cuba," September 4, 1962, read to correspondents at the White House by Pierre Salinger. The statement was widely printed in leading newspapers on September 5. U.S. Department of State, *Bulletin* 47, no. 1213 (September 21, 1962).
12. Ibid., italics added.
13. "The Military Build-Up in Cuba," September 19, 1962, SNIE 85-3-62, *FRUS, 1961–1963*, Vol. X, Cuba, January 1961–September 1962. pp. 1071–80.
14. Ibid., p. 1076.
15. David M. Barnett and Max Holland, *Blind over Cuba: The Photo Gap and the Missile Crisis* (Texas A&M University Press, 2012), pp. 5–21.
16. U.S. Central Intelligence Agency, *CIA Documents Relating to the Cuban Missile Crisis*, (1992).
17. My reconstruction here is based on notes in the TLH papers and interviews with Thomas Hughes. Bowles's *Promises to Keep* (Harper and Row, 1971) offers a slightly different version of the October 13 Dobrynin meeting. He claimed it at a much later date and said he had forgotten about it until the last minute. In either case, Bowles called his protégé Thomas Hughes on October 9 soon after the phone call and made an appointment to be briefed on Cuba. In the memo Bowles sent to President Kennedy after the October 13 lunch with the Soviet ambassador, Bowles said that he was surprised by the Dobrynin invitation.
18. Dobrynin made the revelation in a 1989 retrospective conference on the missile crisis that was held in Moscow. Theodore Sorensen, supporting Dobrynin, acknowledged his own role in selectively editing Robert Kennedy's memoir *Thirteen Days* to disguise the explicit missile swap as part of the Cuban settlement. Barton

J. Bernstein, "Reconsidering the Cuban Missiles: Dealing with the Problems of the American Jupiters in Turkey," in Nathan, *The Cuban Missile Crisis Revisited*, pp. 98–99.

19. Anatoly F. Dobrynin, *In Confidence: Moscow's Ambassador to America's Six Cold War Presidents* (Random House, 1995), pp. 79, 84, 86–87; Fursenko and Naftali, *One Hell of a Gamble*, p. 275; Philip Nash, *The Other Missiles of October: Eisenhower, Kennedy, and the Jupiters, 1957–1963* (University of North Carolina Press, 1997), pp. 142–43.

Chapter 10

1. Barton J. Bernstein, "Reconsidering the Missile Crisis: Dealing with the Problems of the American Jupiters in Turkey," in *The Cuban Missile Crisis Revisited*, edited by James A. Nathan (St. Martin's, 1992), pp. 55–129; Sheldon M. Stern, *The Cuban Missile Crisis in Historical Memory* (Stanford University Press, 2012); Fursenko and Naftali, *One Hell of a Gamble: Khrushchev, Castro, and Kennedy, 1958–1964: The Secret History of the Cuban Missile Crisis* (W.W. Norton & Company), pp. 257–89.

2. Ibid., Fursenko and Naftali, *One Hell of a Gamble*, p. 129. The October 18 late afternoon meeting of Gromyko, Kennedy, Dobrynin, and Rusk was stiff and produced no serious discussion of issues or negotiations. Gromyko raised the Jupiter missiles issue with Rusk at dinner later that evening. On the 5:00 p.m. Kennedy-Gromyko meeting in the White House, see Michael R. Beschloss, *The Crisis Year: Kennedy and Khrushchev, 1960–1963* (HarperCollins, 1991), pp. 455–57; Anatoly F. Dobrynin, *In Confidence: Moscow's Ambassador to America's Six Cold War Presidents* (Random House, 1995), pp. 76–78.

3. Ibid., pp. 76–78.

4. Quoted in Philip Nash, *The Other Missiles of October* (University of North Carolina Press, 1997), and p. 142.

5. Fursenko and Naftali, *One Hell of a Gamble*.

6. The term *quarantine* was used at the suggestion of Abram Chayes, State Department counsel, in an effort to soften what was clearly a blockade but was not considered an act of war under international law. The ExCom debated whether the United States had to declare war on Cuba to impose the blockade but decided against it. "Our legal problem," as Abe Chayes declared at the Hawk's Cay Conference in March 1987, "was that the Soviet actions were not illegal."

7. Fursenko and Naftali, *One Hell of a Gamble*, pp. 241–42.

8. Dobrynin, in his memoir, *In Confidence,* recounts that he was given almost no instructions during the entire Cuban Missile Crisis and attributes this to the general disorder in the Kremlin and the paralysis that gripped Khrushchev in the days following the Kennedy speech.

9. Nash, *The Other Missiles of October*, p. 123.

10. Quoted ibid., p. 132.

11. Walter Lippmann, *Washington Post,* October 23, 1962, p. A10, and October 25, 1962, p. A17.

12. Bruce L. R. Smith, *Lincoln Gordon: Architect of Cold War Foreign Policy* (University Press of Kentucky, 2015).

13. Hughes tells this story in his oral history, *Perilous Encounters: The Cold War Collisions of Domestic and World Politics: Oral History Interviews with Thomas L. Hughes* (Association of Diplomatic Studies and Training, 2011), pp. 113–14. I add a few more details based on interviews with Hughes.

14. Hilsman, *To Move a Nation: The Politics of Foreign Policy in the Administration of John F. Kennedy* (Doubleday), p. 45.

15. Quoted in Schwartz, "The Real Cuban Missile Crisis."

16. Roger Hilsman, "The Cuban Crisis: How Close We Came to War," *Look* 28, no. 17 (August 25, 1964).

17. Nash, *The Other Missiles of October*, pp. 136–37.

18. Anatoly F. Dobrynin, *In Confidence*, pp. 85–89. Robert Kennedy's own account in *Thirteen Days* contains the false statement that there was no "quid pro quo" from the United States regarding the Jupiters for the Soviet decision to withdraw its missiles from Cuba. Ted Sorensen admitted in 1989 that RFK's original notes conceded that an explicit missile trade was part of the agreement but that he (Sorensen) had edited RFK's notes so as to conceal this fact and that the Jupiter trade was indeed an explicit, not merely an implied, commitment. See Nash, *The Other Missiles of October*, pp. 144–45.

19. Bruce Riedel, *JFK's Forgotten Crisis: Tibet, the CIA, and the Sino-Indian War* (Brookings Institution Press, 2015).

Chapter 11

1. Fredrik Logevall, *Choosing War: The Lost Chance for Peace and the Escalation of War in Vietnam* (University of California Press, 1999), p. 69; James T. Patterson, *Grand Expectations: The United States, 1945–1974* (Oxford University Press, 1996), p. 595.

2. Neil Sheehan, *A Bright Shining Lie: John Paul Vann and America in Vietnam* (Vintage Books, 1989), pp. 288–89.

3. Ibid., p. 290.

4. Ibid., pp. 290–92.

5. For a well-informed description of how the INR operated, see Allan Evans, *Research in Action: The Department of State's Bureau of Intelligence and Research*, Department of State Publication 7964, Department and Foreign Service Series 133 (September 1966).

6. Thomas Powers, *Intelligence Wars: American Secret History from Hitler to Al-Qaeda* (New York Review of Books, 2004), p. xxxvii.

7. John Prados, "The Mouse That Roared," introduction to *Intelligence and Vietnam: The Top Secret 1969 State Department Study* (National Security Archive, George Washington University, 2004) discusses the INR's role regarding the dangers of Chinese intervention.

8. Harold P. Ford, *CIA and the Vietnam Policymakers: Three Episodes, 1962–1963*, "Episode 1, 1962–1963: Distortions of Intelligence" (U.S. Government Printing Office, 1998), pp. 22–23; Chester L. Cooper, *The Lost Crusade: America in Vietnam* (Dodd, Mead, 1972), pp. 199, 490. The name of the village is "Bac," Americans added "Ap," meaning "village."

9. ARVN Colonel Huynh Van Cao, who met with President Diem in October 1962, was one recipient of this order. In December, Cao issued a statement distributed to his forces in which he applauded his own tactics of caution and criticized the tactics of General Giap at Dien Bien Phu for the needless and wanton sacrifice of troops by careless and overly aggressive attacks on French fortifications. See Sheehan, *A Bright Shining Lie*, p. 122, on Diem's order to his commanders not to conduct offensive operations that would result in serious casualties, particularly to the regular army.

10. Ibid., pp. 287–90.

11. Kent left Yale to join the Office of Strategic Services during World War II, where he provided intelligence for Operation Torch. He returned to Yale after the war but was called back to government service in 1950, during the Korean War. Together with Professor William Langer, with whom he worked at the Office of Strategic Services, he created the Office of National Estimates at the CIA in 1950 and served as its director for the next seventeen years. The agency had a staff of about twenty-five professionals and was much like a small INR within the CIA.

12. *Prospects in South Vietnam*, NIE 53-63, draft; quoted in Ford, *CIA and the Vietnam Policymakers*, p. 1.

13. Ford, *CIA and the Vietnam Policymakers*, pp. 2–3.

14. *Prospects in South Vietnam*, NIE 53-63, final version, April 17, 1963, quoted in *Estimative Products on Vietnam, 1948–1975*, edited by John K. Allen Jr., John Carver, and Tom Elmore (U.S. Government Printing Office, May 27, 2005), pp. 183–98.

15. Ford, *CIA and the Vietnam Policymakers*, p. 27.

16. Quoted ibid., p. 28. See also John M. Newman, *JFK and Vietnam: Deception, Intrigue, and the Struggle for Power* (Warner Books, 1992), p. 335.

17. Ford, *CIA and the Vietnam Policymakers*, p. 29.

18. Prados, "The Mouse That Roared," quoted ibid., pp. 11–12.

19. Ford, *CIA and the Vietnam Policymakers*, pp. 11–12. For Thomas Hughes's own account of the statistics war with McNamara, see Hughes, "Experiencing McNamara," *Foreign Policy* 100 (Autumn 1995), pp. 154–71.

20. Thomas L. Hughes, interview with, Chevy Chase, Maryland, February 29, 2016.

21. Prados, "The Mouse That Roared," p. 13.

22. See Luke A. Nichter, *The Last Brahmin: Henry Cabot Lodge and the Making of the Cold War* (Yale University Press, 2020), pp. 120–29 on the 1952 Senate campaign.

23. Nichter described his finding the memo "hiding in plain sight" during a podcast after the publication of his book. Nichter's finding confirms the secondhand account Hughes gave me of the meeting, which he got from Mike Forrestal, who discussed the meeting with Kennedy shortly after it occurred.

24. A vivid description is found in Sheehan, *A Bright Shining Lie*, pp. 354–83.

25. Andrew Preston, *The War Council: McGeorge Bundy, the NSC, and Vietnam* (Harvard University Press, 2006), p. 122.

26. New York Times, *The Pentagon Papers*, no. 35, "Washington Message to Lodge on Need to Remove Nhu," pp. 194–95.

27. George W. Ball, *The Past Has Another Pattern* (W.W. Norton & Company, 1982), pp. 373–74.

28. George Ball's account of the meeting refers to the president as "showing some misgivings." Others described Kennedy as "furious." See Ball, *The Past Has Another Pattern*, pp. 371–72; Preston, *The War Council*, p. 123.

29. See Robert S. McNamara, *In Retrospect: The Tragedy and Lessons of Vietnam*, with Brian VanDeMark (Vintage Books, 1996), pp. 68–87.

30. Preston, *The War Council*, p. 123.

31. Ibid., p. 123.

32. Hilsman, August 1963, TLH notes, TLH personal papers.

33. Ford, *CIA and the Vietnam Policymakers* (p. 30) asserts that "virtually all of Washington's top officials were critical of the manner in which Hilsman, Harriman, and Forrestal had acted." William Colby, the CIA's Far East Division chief, recorded that the president and the attorney general "were apparently appalled at the speed with which the State decision was reached on Saturday afternoon, 24 August, and felt that more thought, analysis, and preparation should have preceded the instruction to Lodge."

34. TLH papers. The notes were undated but referred to the August 24 meeting with Mike Forrestal and a meeting with Roger Hilsman on August 25, so were probably written at the end of August 1963.

35. New York Times, *The Pentagon Papers*, no. 38, "C.I.A. Station Chief's Cable on Coup Prospects in Saigon," Richardson to McCone, Aug. 28, 1963, pp. 196–97.

36. Ambassador Henry Cabot Lodge Jr. to Secretary Dean Rusk, August 29, 1963, EmbTel 375. *Foreign Relations of the United States (FRUS), 1961–1963*, vol. 4, *Vietnam, August–December 1963*, p. 211; quoted in Ford, *CIA and the Vietnam Policymakers*, p. 26.

37. New York Times, *The Pentagon Papers*, pp. 160–61; no. 43, Cable by U.S. General in Saigon to Taylor on End of August Plot.
38. *The Pentagon Papers: The Senator Gravel Edition*, 4 vols. (Beacon Press, 1971), vol. 2, Chronology, "NSC meeting, Sept. 10, 1963," p. 214.
39. New York Times, *The Pentagon Papers*, no. 47, pp. 210–11. For a useful narrative account of the coup and its background plus excerpts from key cables and memoranda, *Pentagon Papers: Gravel Edition*, vol. 2, chap. 4, "The Overthrow of Ngo Dinh Diem, May–November 1963," pp. 201–74. This is more detailed and comprehensive and includes a day-by-day and hour-by-hour chronology of events surrounding the coup. The full text of the McNamara-Taylor Report is at pp. 751–66. For a penetrating critique of the McNamara-Taylor Report, see Logevall, *Choosing War*, pp. 54–59. McNamara's own account is in his memoir, *In Retrospect*, pp. 68–79.
40. Logevall, *Choosing War*, p. 55.
41. Ibid., p. 56.
42. New York Times, *The Pentagon Papers*, no. 48, "Lodge Message on Meeting of C.I.A. Agent with Gen. Minh," October 5, 1963, pp. 213–14.
43. New York Times, *The Pentagon Papers*, no. 43, p. 202.
44. New York Times, *The Pentagon Papers*, no. 46.
45. New York Times, *The Pentagon Papers*, no. 52.
46. Luke Nichter, *The Last Brahmin*.
47. Logevall, *Choosing War*, p. 127.
48. New York Times, *The Pentagon Papers*, no. 46.
49. Logevall, *Choosing War*, pp. 50–51. See Hughes's retrospective thoughts as recorded in his introduction to the INR self-survey in 2004 and his oral history interview in Thomas Hughes, *Perilous Encounters: The Cold War Collisions of Domestic and World Politics: Oral History Interviews with Thomas L. Hughes* (Association of Diplomatic Studies and Training, 2011), esp. pp. 153–57, and James G. Blight, Janet T. Lang, and David A. Welch, *Virtual JFK: Vietnam If Kennedy Had Lived* (Rowman and Littlefield, 2009), pp. 108–10.
50. Logevall, *Choosing War*, pp. 95–96.

Chapter 12

1. The Kennedy statement is contained in NSAM 263 of November 20, 1963.
2. Fredrik Logevall, *Choosing War: The Lost Chance for Peace and the Escalation of War in Vietnam* (University of California Press, 1999) pp. 1–28.
3. *The Pentagon Papers, The Senator Gravel Edition*, 4 vols. (Beacon Press, 1971), vol. 3, p. 50. See also William C. Gibbons, *The U.S. Government and the Vietnam War*, pt. 2, (Princeton University Press, 2016), pp. 238–44.
4. *New York Times*, March 21, 1964, in *Pentagon Papers, Gravel Edition*, vol. 3, p. 50.
5. Gibbons, *The U.S. Government and the Vietnam War*, part 2, pp. 263–64.
6. Max Frankel, *The Times of My Life and My Life at The Times* (Random House, 1999).
7. TLH papers.
8. In this speculation, Vance was mistaken. There was no Oplan 34A operation that evening. The Military Assistance Command Vietnam had sent the Pentagon a schedule of the full 34A operations scheduled for August, but the details were not known or communicated to Secretary McNamara or Deputy Secretary Vance until after Vance had testified to the Senate Foreign Relations Committee on the morning of August 6.
9. Quoted in Robert Dallek, *Flawed Giant: Lyndon Johnson and His Times, 1961–1973* (Oxford University Press, 1999), p. 149.
10. Edwin E. Moise, *Tonkin Gulf and the Escalation of the Vietnam War* (University of North Carolina Press, 1996).

11. Keeping the time difference straight was a complication in the cable traffic. Hanoi is generally eleven hours ahead of Washington (U.S. eastern time) and seven hours ahead of Greenwich mean time.

12. Moise, *Tonkin Gulf*, p. 78.

13. Handwritten notes, lunch, August 4, 1964, Papers of McGeorge Bundy, Lyndon B. Johnson Presidential Library; quoted in Moise, *Tonkin Gulf*, p. 240.

14. Moise, *Tonkin Gulf*, p. 89.

15. Quoted in Max Boot, *The Road Not Taken: Edward Landsdale and the American Tragedy in Vietnam* (Liveright Publishing, 2018), p. 431.

16. Moise, *Tonkin Gulf*, p. 143.

17. Sather's body was returned to the United States at the end of the war. Alvarez survived his imprisonment.

18. A Harris poll found overwhelming public support for President Johnson's handling of the crisis: 85 percent approval to only 3 percent disapproval, a major shift from pre-Tonkin polls showing disapproval of Johnson's handling of the war in general by a margin of 58 percent to 42 percent. See Moise, *Tonkin Gulf*, pp. 225–26.

19. McNamara, phone call to LBJ, late morning of August 6, 1964, Presidential recordings, Miller Center, University of Virginia.

20. 100 Cong. Rec. 18402–403, August 6, 1964.

Chapter 13

1. TLH papers, n.d.

2. Michael Beschloss, ed., *Taking Charge: The Johnson White House Tapes, 1963–1964* (Simon and Schuster, 1997), p. 499. Beschloss mistakenly dates this conversation as taking place on Tuesday, August 4, 1964. Hughes states in an interview with the author that the correct date was Thursday, August 6, at 1:35 p.m.

3. Ibid., p. 486.

4. Thomas Tunstall Allcock, *Thomas C. Mann: President Johnson, the Cold War, and the Restructuring of Latin American Foreign Policy* (University Press of Kentucky, 2018).

5. "Lyndon Johnson, James Rowe, and Jack Valenti on 6 August 1964," Conversation WH6407-09-4777, 4778, Presidential Recordings Digital Edition (University of Virginia, Miller Center); *Lyndon B. Johnson: Civil Rights, Vietnam, and the War on Poverty*, edited by David G. Coleman and others (University of Virginia Press, 2014), p. 2 of 5.

6. Ibid., p. 4 of 5.

7. Transcript of acceptance by Johnson and Humphrey at Atlantic City, *New York Times*, August 28, 1964.

8. For the text of the address, see "Hubert H. Humphrey Vice Presidential Nomination Acceptance Address," American Rhetoric Online Speech Bank, www.americanrhetoric.com/speeches/huberthumphrey1964dnc.htm.

9. Arnold A. Offner, *Hubert Humphrey: The Conscience of the Country* (Yale University Press, 2018), pp. 207, 208.

10. Thomas L. Hughes, "A New Year of New Governments," in *Speaking Up and Speaking Out* (Xlibris, 2013), p. 33.

11. Ibid., p. 57.

12. Robert Dallek, *Flawed Giant: Lyndon B. Johnson and His Times, 1961–1973* (Oxford University Press, 1999), p. 244.

13. TLH papers, n.d., probably December 1964.

Chapter 14

1. Arnold A. Offner, *Hubert. Humphrey: The Conscience of the Country* (Yale University Press, 2018), p. 214.

2. Fredrik Logevall, *Choosing War: The Lost Chance for Peace and the Escalation of War in Vietnam* (University of California Press, 1999), p. 287.

3. Johnson had moved Forrestal from the White House staff to the State Department, ostensibly to improve relations between the State Department and the White House. Forrestal believed that he was being punished for his role in the cable that set the Diem coup into motion. The move did not work out well, and Forrestal left government.

4. Informal notes, TLH papers.

5. Hughes recounts the episode in Thomas L. Hughes, *Perilous Encounters: The Cold War Collisions of Domestic and World Politics: Oral History Interviews with Thomas L. Hughes* (Association of Diplomatic Studies and Training, 2011), p. 156, and Thomas L. Hughes, *Anecdotage: Some Authentic Retrievals* (Createspace Independent Publishing Platform, 2014), p. 117. The dialogue varies slightly in the two accounts. I used the *Perilous Encounters* version.

6. New York Times, *The Pentagon Papers*, p. 642, no. 94; *The Pentagon Papers: Senator Mike Gravel Edition* (Beacon Press, 1971), p. 684, no. 248.

7. Memorandum for the President, Re: "Basic Policy in Vietnam," from McG. B., January 27, 1965, in William C. Gibbons, *The U.S. Government and the Vietnam War: Executive and Legislative Roles and Relationships* (Government Printing Office, 1988), pp. 47–48. The Gibbons studies, under the author's name and with the same title and pagination, have been published in three parts by Princeton University Press.

8. William C. Gibbons, *The U.S. Government and the Vietnam War*, pt. 3 (Princeton University Press, 1989), pp. 47–51.

9. Ibid.

10. Andrew Preston, *The War Council: McGeorge Bundy, the NSC, and Vietnam* (Harvard University Press, 2006).

11. Ibid., pp. 176–81.

12. Ibid., p. 175.

13. "Incomprehensibly to me," Hughes wrote Ball, Bundy's conclusions had not seriously dealt with the potential responses from China and the Soviet Union; quoted ibid., p. 180.

14. Carl Solberg, *Hubert Humphrey: A Biography* (W.W. Norton, 1984), p. 271.

15. Ibid. Though Solberg says that Humphrey "popped off," it is not clear whether this is a reference to the February 6 or February 10 meeting. Humphrey was in attendance at both.

16. Logevall, *Choosing War*, pp. 444–91.

17. See the Hughes commentary in Ted Gittinger, ed., *The Johnson Years: A Vietnam Roundtable* (LBJ Library, Lyndon B. Johnson School of Public Affairs, University of Texas at Austin, 1993), p. 52.

18. Hughes gave a slightly different version of the events at the 1991 Vietnam Roundtable at the LBJ School, suggesting that Humphrey called Rusk on his own and that Rusk then ordered Hughes to go to Georgia to brief Humphrey (ibid., pp. 51–52). Hughes's memory played a trick here, as White House phone logs show Hughes initiating the call to Humphrey.

19. Humphrey, *The Education of a Public Man: My Life and Politics* (Doubleday, 1976). The memo is reprinted in full, pp. 320–24.

20. Humphrey made only minor edits on Hughes's draft on the plane. The original handwritten memo is in TLH's papers, with the few Humphrey edits penciled in red.

21. Logevall, *Choosing War*, pp. 31, 37.

22. Michael A. Cohen, *American Maelstrom: The 1968 Election and the Politics of Division* (Oxford University Press, 2016), p. 69.

23. Memorandum to the President, reprinted in Humphrey, *The Education of a Public Man*, pp. 320–24.

24. The account and all quotations in this section are taken from Gibbons, *The U.S. Government and the Vietnam War*, pt. 3; quotations from pp. 104, 105, and 109.

25. Gittinger, *The Johnson Years*, p. 53.

26. Henry F. Graf, *The Tuesday Cabinet: Decisions and Deliberations on War and Peace under Lyndon B. Johnson* (Prentice Hall, 1970).

27. Solberg's assessment was that by December 1965, when Humphrey made a strong speech in defense of administration policy on Vietnam, Humphrey had largely regained LBJ's favor. Solberg, *Humphrey: A Biography*, pp. 285–300.

Professor Paul Stone, Humphrey School of Public Affairs, University of Minnesota, who has studied Humphrey's career closely, believes that the presidential disfavor was symbolically ended in February 1966, when Johnson sent Humphrey to speak at a New York conference of religious leaders organized by Reinhold Niebuhr to discuss the war. Johnson reasoned that Humphrey, who knew Niebuhr from their days as founders of Americans for Democratic Action, would ideally represent the administration at the conference. The organization, which had been formed to demonstrate the Left's anticommunist orientation, had in the meantime publicly attacked the Johnson administration's policies on Vietnam. Johnson was pleased with Humphrey's performance at the conference. Telephone conversations with Professor Paul Stone.

28. TLH, e-mail to Janet Lang and James Blight, August 22, 2007, responding to their e-mail of August 20, asking why he thought Humphrey sent his February 1965 memo to LBJ; copies of the e-mails in TLH private papers. Lang and Blight were writing a book on the Vietnam War. James E. Blight, Janet M. Lang, and David A. Welch, *Virtual JFK: If Kennedy Had Lived* (Rowan and Littlefield, 2009). The book was a companion to the film of the same title by Koji Masutani.

29. Janet Lang, e-mail to TLH, August 20, 2007, TLH private papers.

30. Hughes was apparently referring to the February 6 NSC meeting at which Pleiku was discussed. Humphrey had conceivably missed the signs that LBJ was upset. According to informal notes Hughes took on February 6, George Ball had mentioned to him that at a meeting with LBJ that day on ambassadorial appointments, the president had directed that Eugenie Anderson's name be struck off the list. This had occurred when someone had mentioned that Anderson had been nominated by Humphrey. Ball apparently missed the sign, too, because he continued to work closely with Humphrey until sometime after the memo had obviously wrecked the relations between Johnson and Humphrey.

31. Quoted in Robert Dallek, *Flawed Giant: Lyndon Johnson and His Times* (Oxford University Press, 1999), p. 443.

32. "Toward a More Responsible Two-Party System," Report of the Committee on Political Parties of the American Political Science Association, reprinted in *American Political Science Review* 44, no. 3 (suppl., September 1950).

33. Humphrey, *Education of a Public Man*, quotation from the book jacket. For Humphrey's account of the memo, see pp. 317–19. Kenny O'Donnell, a JFK lieutenant who stayed on to serve Johnson longer than any of the other Kennedy men, once said that Lyndon Johnson "was one of the world's worst politicians." So said Randall B. Woods, LBJ's biographer, in response to a question from the audience at a Smithsonian Institution conference in Washington, D.C., on May 10, 2016, which I attended.

34. Randall B. Woods, *Prisoners of Hope* (Basic Books, 2016), pp. 270–71.

Chapter 15

1. Bowles was officially reassigned to a new position as roving ambassador for Third World affairs, which removed him from the policy process.

2. The other highly respected figure was Elliot Richardson, the deputy secretary of state for President Nixon, with whom Hughes served from 1969 to 1970.

3. For a discussion, see Beschloss, *Taking Charge: The Johnson White House Tapes, 1963–1964* (Simon & Schuster, 1997), pp. 319–23.

4. Ibid., p. 321.

5. George Ball, *The Past Has Another Pattern: Memoirs* (W.W. Norton, 1982), pp. 392–95, outlines Ball's efforts with Dean Acheson, Lloyd Cutler, and the INR on a peace proposal in April–May 1965. Ball's efforts were designed to deal with the failure of Rolling Thunder.

6. This view is shared by Fredrik Logevall, *Choosing War: The Lost Chance for Peace and the Escalation of War in Vietnam* (University of California Press, 1999); Leslie H. Gelb and Richard K. Betts, *The Irony of Vietnam: The System Worked* (Brookings Institution, 1979); William C. Gibbons, *The U.S. Government and the Vietnam War,* pt. 3 (Princeton University Press, 1989).

7. According to Richard Helms; see Ted Gittinger, ed., *The Johnson Years: A Vietnam Roundtable* (LBJ Library, Lyndon B. Johnson School of Public Affairs, University of Texas at Austin, 1993), pp. 51–52.

8. Gelb and Betts, *The Irony of Vietnam,* pp. 142–43.

9. Ibid.

10. Chester Cooper, *The Lost Crusade: America in Vietnam* (Dodd, Mead, 1970), p. 275.

11. George C. Herring, ed., *The Secret Diplomacy of the Vietnam War: The Negotiating Volumes of the Pentagon Papers* (University of Texas Press, 1983).

12. Ibid., p. xvi.

13. Gibbons, *The U.S. Government and the Vietnam War,* pt. 3, p. 229.

14. Ibid., p. 232.

15. There were two further sessions in Hughes's office, on May 12 and May 13. Hughes showed his notes of these meetings to Kai Bird in 1998, for Bird's book *The Color of Truth* (Simon & Schuster, 2000), p. 328. I surmise that the two-hour April 27 meeting in Ball's office was probably the critical meeting.

16. David L. DiLeo, *George Ball, Vietnam, and the Rethinking of Containment* (University of North Carolina, 1991), pp. 89–92.

17. Gibbons, *The U.S. Government and the Vietnam War,* pt. 3, p. 260, and DiLeo, *George Ball,* p. 90. I have paraphrased slightly the points since DiLeo's and Gibbons's wordings are slightly different. For the full context, see Gibbons, *The U.S. Government and the Vietnam War,* pt. 3, pp. 259–65.

18. George Ball, *The Past Has Another Pattern: Memoirs* (W.W. Norton, 1982), p. 394.

19. Ibid., p. 395.

20. Thomas L. Hughes, "Negotiating under Pressure—Hanoi's Position," memorandum for Chester Bowles, April 23, 1965, TLH papers.

21. Bird, *The Color of Truth,* p. 359.

22. Ibid., p. 328. I discussed the Bundy-Bundy versus Ball events with Hughes some years after Bird did. Bill Bundy's opposition to his father-in-law's plan was perhaps depicted in even stronger terms. Bill Bundy was testy, rigid, and dogmatic, unusual for a man who was normally courtly and who was on close terms with his father-in-law.

23. TLH notes, quoted in Bird, *The Color of Truth,* p. 328.

24. Ibid.

25. Herring, *The Secret Diplomacy of the Vietnam War,* pp. vii–xxvi, 49–73.

26. Gibbons, *The U.S. Government and the Vietnam War*, pt. 3, p. 255. Ball was also forced to argue for a potential propaganda benefit in his own memorandum in order to sell the Ball-Acheson-Cutler plan. "By shifting the struggle from the military to the political arena," he argued, his plan would have "substantial propaganda both in South Vietnam and throughout the world," whether or not it was put seriously into effect. See Gibbons, pp. 260–61.

27. Ibid., p. 256.

28. Ibid., p. 261. Rusk suggested, and the president agreed, that Taylor should be consulted. Even though bombing was resumed, the Ball-Acheson plan could be worked out in detail if Taylor agreed. Ball's assistant Thomas Ehrlich was sent to Saigon to get Taylor's reaction and returned on May 20 saying that Taylor and Deputy Chief of Mission Alex Johnson opposed the plan. Though Gibbons discusses the meeting, there apparently are no records, but it may be presumed that Ball and Acheson made the case that their plan could still be pursued. It is not known whether they argued for an extension of the bombing pause. Rusk was present, but apparently neither Mac nor Bill Bundy was at the meeting.

29. Gibbons, *The U.S. Government and the Vietnam War*, pt. 3, pp. 257–59; Herring, *The Secret Diplomacy of the Vietnam War*, pp. 71–72.

30. Herring, *The Secret Diplomacy of the Vietnam War*, pp. 74–115.

31. Ibid., p. 81. Again, on January 29, 1966, after the second or the Christmas bombing pause, R (Bo) indicated that "the pause in bombing is not negotiable. . . . We have always demanded that these bombings stop as a prerequisite of any negotiations." U.S. officials interpreted Bo's statement as indicating that a temporary pause was not enough for Hanoi. A temporary bombing pause was, to Hanoi, inevitably coercive in intent and directed at pressuring North Vietnam. Agreeing to negotiate during a temporary pause would be a sign of weakness.

32. For an assessment of raw data versus analysis, see Hughes, "Butcher, Baker, and Intelligence Maker," in David Priess, *The President's Book of Secrets: The Untold Story of Intelligence Briefings to America's Presidents* (Perseus Books, 2016).

33. Gibbons, *The U.S. Government and the Vietnam War*, pt. 3, p. 238.

34. Ambassador Lincoln Gordon adroitly secured the cooperation of the Brazilians and earned the gratitude of the president, who rewarded him by naming Gordon the successor to Mann as assistant secretary of state for inter-American affairs. See Bruce L. R. Smith, *Lincoln Gordon: Architect of Cold War Foreign Policy* (University Press of Kentucky, 2015), pp. 285–86.

Chapter 16

1. Don Oberdorfer, *TeT! The Turning Point in the Vietnam War* (Johns Hopkins University Press, 1991), pp. 78–84. The Johns Hopkins edition is a reissue of the original book, which appeared in 1971.

2. Ibid., p. 79.

3. Quoted in Michael A. Cohen, *American Maelstrom: The 1968 Election and the Politics of Division* (Oxford University Press, 2016), p. 77.

4. An edited collection of some of these speeches, with an introduction by Jane Casey Hughes, is Thomas L. Hughes, *Speaking Up and Speaking Out* (Xilibris, 2013).

5. "Scholars and Foreign Policy: Varieties of Research Experience," in Hughes, *Speaking Up and Speaking Out*, pp. 59–80.

6. "Democracy, Diversity, and the Future Foreign Service," in Hughes, *Speaking Up and Speaking Out*, pp. 180–94; "The World Looks at China," pp. 80–103; "Relativity in Foreign Policy: The Storage and Retrieval of Conviction," pp. 122–41.

7. "The Odyssey of Counter Insurgency," in Hughes, *Speaking Up and Speaking Out*, pp. 157–89.

8. Quoted ibid., p. 178.

9. Thomas L. Hughes, "Liberals, Populists, and Foreign Policy," *Foreign Policy* 20 (Autumn 1975), p. 99.
10. "Butcher, Baker, and Intelligence Maker," in Hughes, *Speaking Up and Speaking Out*, p. 275.
11. Ibid., pp. 178–79.

Chapter 17

1. James T. Patterson, *Grand Expectations: The United States, 1945–1974* (Oxford University Press, 2006), p. 678.
2. John Prados, *The Hidden History of the Vietnam War* (Ivan R. Dee, 1995), p. 142. See also Max Hastings, *Vietnam: An Epic Tragedy, 1945–1975* (HarperCollins, 2019), pp. 434–60, and Don Oberdorfer, *Tet! The Turning Point in the Vietnam War* (Johns Hopkins University Press, 2001) (originally published in 1971) for detailed accounts of Tet.
3. Jacob Hillesheim, "How the Media Shapes Public Opinion of War," *Rewire*, August 4, 2017, www.rewire.org/vietnam-war-media-shapes-public-opinion/.
4. Carl Solberg, *Hubert Humphrey: A Biography* (W.W. Norton, 1984), pp. 302–03. This story has been cited frequently by, among other authors, Robert Dallek, Robert Caro, Arnold Offner, and Kai Bird.
5. "Questions Concerning the Situation in Vietnam," memo, March 1, 1968, in *Estimative Products on Vietnam, 1948–1975*, edited by John K. Allen Jr., John Carver, and Tom Elmore (available only on the CD); "Vietnamese Communists' Will to Persist—Summary and Principal Findings Only," memo, August 26, 1966, ibid., pp. 351–76. See also Harold P. Ford, *CIA and the Vietnam Policymakers: Three Episodes, 1962–1968* (University of Michigan Library, 1998), pp. 127–28; Thomas A. Reinstein, "The Way a Drunk Uses a Lamp Post: Intelligence Analysis and Policy during the Vietnam War, 1962–1968," Ph.D. diss., Temple University, December 2018, pp. 323–25.
6. The bombing pauses included those of May 1965 (Operation Mayflower), December 1965–January 1966 (Christmas bombing halt), December 1966 (Marigold), and again July 1967.
7. The group included such hard-liners as McGeorge Bundy and Dean Acheson.
8. Morton Halperin, interview with author, Washington, D.C., March 19, 2019.
9. Quoted in Arnold A. Offner, *Hubert Humphrey: The Conscience of the Country* (Yale University Press, 2018), p. 273.
10. See Michael A. Cohen, *American Maelstrom: The 1968 Election and the Politics of Division* (Oxford University Press, 2016), "The Democrats," chaps. 3–8.
11. Ibid., pp. 79–91.
12. Ibid.
13. Cohen, *American Maelstrom*, pp. 219–39.
14. Zbigniew Brzezinski, *Between Two Ages: America in the Technotronic Era* (Viking Press, 1970).
15. Justin Vaisse, *Zbigniew Brzezinski: America's Grand Strategist* (Harvard University Press, 2018), pp. 79, 99–100.
16. Ibid., pp. 109–10. The logic of this caper was never entirely clear. It was either an effort to label Brzezinski as part of the "pigs"—the law and order forces—or a play (a rhyme) on Brzezinski's nickname, "Zbig." In any event, the caper misfired when police were called and intercepted the students as they were leading the animal up Amsterdam Avenue to the school of International Affairs.
17. The Otto Kerner Commission (National Advisory Commission on Civil Disorders), with David Ginsburg as executive director, specifically criticized the lack of effective action by the federal government and made no reference to LBJ's accomplishments. For a discussion, see Patterson, *Grand Expectations*, pp. 664–65.
18. For excerpts from the speech McCloskey prepared for Humphrey, see Carl Solberg, *Hubert Humphrey: A Biography* (W.W. Norton, 1984), pp. 361–62.

19. Ibid., pp. 361–62.
20. Robert Dallek, *Flawed Giant: Lyndon Johnson and His Times, 1961–1973* (Oxford University Press, 1998), pp. 571–72.
21. Ibid.
22. Randall B. Woods, *Prisoners of Hope: Lyndon B. Johnson, the Great Society, and the Limits of Liberalism* (Basic Books), p. 384.
23. Cohen, *American Maelstrom*, p. 281.
24. Ibid.
25. Solberg, *Humphrey: A Biography*, pp. 168–69.
26. Ibid., p. 362.
27. Patterson, *Grand Expectations*, p. 703.
28. Ken Hughes, *Chasing Shadows: The Nixon Tapes, the Chennault Affair, and the Origins of Watergate* (University of Virginia Press, 2014), pp. 6–10.
29. This was the gist of the CIA intercept of the conversation. By holding firm, she evidently meant to suggest that South Vietnam would get a better deal from Nixon if he won the election. Luke Nichter, an historian at Texas A&M University, recently wrote in a *Wall Street Journal* op-ed that the charge against Chennault is a fiction. But he cites no evidence other than the fact that he was the last scholar to interview Chennault and that she denied the charge. Nixon aide Robert Haldeman's memoir seems to confirm Chennault's and Nixon's complicity.
30. Hughes, *Chasing Shadows*, p. 40.
31. Ibid., pp. 55–56.
32. Norman Sherman, *From Nowhere to Somewhere: My Political Journey* (First Avenue Editions, 2016), p. 196.
33. Offner, *Hubert Humphrey*, p. 328.

Chapter 18

1. I. M. Destler, Leslie H. Gelb, and Anthony Lake, *Our Own Worst Enemy: The Unmaking of American Foreign Policy* (Simon and Schuster, 1984), pp. 89–126.
2. David Priess, *The President's Book of Secrets* (Hachette Book Group, 2016), pp. 65–70. The CIA went out of its way to give President Nixon special copies of the President's Daily Brief during the transition. Agency officials were shocked when Nixon returned the packet of briefings unopened. The arrangement settled down to Kissinger getting briefings from the CIA and deciding to pass along to the president any matters he felt were important enough for the president to know. Nixon and Haig made their disdain for the CIA's analyses known in a President's Foreign Intelligence Advisory Board meeting in December 1970, where they lamented receiving intelligence estimates they saw as "flavored by policy considerations so that factual data are distorted or omitted in favor of policy preconceptions." Priess, *President's Book of Secrets*, p. 67.
3. Ibid., p. 67.
4. Thomas Hughes, *Indian Chiefs of Southern Minnesota: 1854–1934* (Ross and Haines, 1969).
5. Tom told me this story a number of times in our interviews. He has in his *Anecdotage* a story about Frances: Just as the preacher had risen and the crowd hushed at the start of his wedding to Jane Casey in 1995, a side door squeaked and slowly opened. Frances entered and slowly took a seat in the front row while the rector, groom, bride, and well wishers watched. Tom was very fond of Frances and eulogized her at a memorial service for her in the Cosmos Club, published in Hughes, "Seven Eulogies," self-published, 2010.
6. TLH, memo to Bruce L. R. Smith, summer 2016, in author's possession.
7. Thomas L. Hughes, *Perilous Encounters: The Cold War Collisions of Domestic and World Politics: Oral History Interviews with Thomas L. Hughes* (Association of Diplomatic Studies and Training, 2011), p. 192.

8. The story below is told in Hughes's oral history, *Perilous Encounters*, pp. 161–63. I have added a bit to the dialogue based on interviews with TLH, June–July 2016.
9. Ibid., p. 191.
10. Ibid., p. 193.
11. Ibid., p. 194.
12. Tom Hughes interviews with author.
13. Hughes, *Perilous Encounters*, p. 193.
14. Destler, Gelb, and Lake, *Our Own Worst Enemy*, pp. 111–12.
15. Dialogue here based on several interviews in June 2016.

Chapter 19

1. From "A New Year of New Governments" of December 3, 1964, in Jane Hughes, ed., *Speaking Up and Speaking Out* (Xilibris, 2013), p. 33.
2. Observation attributed to professor Richard Ullman of Princeton University by Sanford Ungar on June 7, 1991, at the retirement dinner for Tom Hughes in the transcript of the program for the dinner.
3. Remarks of Bill Maynes at retirement dinner for Tom Hughes, June 7, 1991, Carnegie International Center, Washington, D.C.
4. Larry L. Fabian, *Andrew Carnegie's Peace Endowment: The Tycoon, the President, and Their Bargain of 1910* (Carnegie Endowment for International Peace, 1985), pp. 12–14. See also David Adesnik, *100 Years of Impact: Essays on the Carnegie Endowment of International Peace* (Carnegie Endowment for International Peace, 2011).
5. Fabian, *Andrew Carnegie's Peace Endowment* pp. 5–6, 7–8.
6. In 1900 he first sought to reduce international disputes by promoting the cause of arbitration and importuned Theodore Roosevelt and William Howard Taft to become arbitration champions.
7. Norman Angell, *The Great Illusion* (CreateSpace Independent Publishing, 2015).
8. Most of the Carnegie trustees continued to support Hiss even during his trial for perjury. They regarded his conviction for perjury as the result of a poor job by his lawyers and the sentence of five years as outrageously severe.
9. Tom Hughes's remarks at his June 7, 1991, retirement dinner, quoting from the minutes of a 1970 trustees' meeting.
10. Carnegie Endowment for International Peace, "Carnegie and AFSA Announce a New Joint Venture to Improve Communication in the Field of Foreign Affairs," press release, December 22, 1972.
11. Thomas L. Hughes, "Two Decades in the Front Office: Reflections on How the Carnegie Endowment for International Peace Operated in Cold War Washington," in *Beyond Governance: Expanding the Public Policy Debate in Emerging Democracies*, edited by Craufurd D. Goodwin and Michael Nacht (Westview Press, 1995), pp. 61–104.
12. Alton Frye, remarks at the June 7, 1991, retirement dinner for Tom Hughes.
13. Hughes, "Two Decades in the Front Office," pp. 64–65.
14. An early draft of the speech included only this title, but when he delivered the talk he added a subtitle to the copy of the talk he gave to the Club: "The Nixon Connection: What Bismarck Would Have Done." Remarks of Thomas L. Hughes, Woman's National Democratic Club, Washington, D.C., December 15, 1973.
15. "The Meeting of National and World Politics," TLH papers.
16. Thomas L. Hughes, "Liberals, Populists, and Foreign Policy," *Foreign Policy* 20 (Autumn 1975).
17. Walter F. Mondale, with David Hage, *The Good Fight: A Life in Liberal Politics* (Simon and Schuster, 2010), pp. 168–70.
18. TLH, interview with author, September 2017.

19. Richard Immerman, *The Hidden Hand: A Brief History of the CIA* (John Wiley and Sons, 2014), pp. 115–23.

20. Thomas L. Hughes, "Carter and The Management of Contradictions," *Foreign Policy* 31 (Summer 1978), pp. 34–55; Thomas L. Hughes, "The Crack-Up: The Price of Collective Irresponsibility," *Foreign Policy* no. 40 (Autumn 1980), pp. 34–60.

21. Charles William Maynes continued to work in periods of grave illness and finally succumbed to his illness at sixty-eight. Tom Hughes eulogized him and celebrated his career in *Seven Eulogies*.

22. Thomas L. Hughes, "Up from Reaganism," *Foreign Policy* 44 (Autumn 1981), pp. 3–22.

23. Thomas L. Hughes, "The Twilight of Internationalism," *Foreign Policy* 61 (Winter 1985–1986), pp. 25–48.

24. Hughes, "Up from Reaganism."

25. Thomas L. Hughes, speech at Williamsburg.

26. Hughes, "Twilight of Internationalism," p. 33.

27. See Peter Baker and Susan Glasser, *The Man Who Ran Washington: The Life and Times of James A. Baker III* (Knopf Doubleday Publishing Group, 2020), for an engrossing account of Jim Baker's role in the Ford-Reagan-Bush foreign policy.

28. Hughes, "Two Decades in the Front Office," p. 94.

29. Ibid., p. 67. See Eric Lipton and Brooke Williams, "How Think Tanks Amplify Corporate America's Influence," *New York Times*, August 8, 2016, p. 1, 12, 13.

30. The Nixon Center is now called the Center for the National Interest and publishes the journal *National Interest*.

31. TLH, interview with author, July 2017.

32. Thomas L. Hughes, "Pro Patria per Orbis Concordiam": Speech delivered to Carnegie trustees and guests, Carnegie Endowment for International Peace, Washington, D.C., November 18, 1990.

33. Ibid.

Epilogue

1. Thomas L. Hughes, "The Power to Speak and the Power to Listen," in *Secrecy and Foreign Policy*, edited by Thomas Frank and Edward Weisbroad (Oxford University Press, 1974), pp. 28–37. The case was *United States v. Curtiss-Wright Export Company*, 229 U.S. 304 (1936).

2. Waldemar A. Nielsen, "Foundations and Foreign Affairs," unpublished manuscript, April 1973.

3. Jane's father, Joseph Casey, was a congressman for many years from Massachusetts whose career included running against, and defeating, John F. "Honey Fitz" Fitzgerald in the Democratic Party's U.S. Senate primary in 1942. Casey, however, lost in the general election to Republican Henry Cabot Lodge.

4. Kevin Diaz, "From the Attic to the Kaiser: A Minnesota Trove," *Star Tribune*, March 31, 2011, www.startribune.com/from-the-attic-to-the-kaiser-a-minnesota-trove/119035769.

5. Ibid.

Index

In this index Thomas Lowe Hughes is indicated by "TLH."

Acheson, Dean, 4, 80, 235–38
Adenauer, Konrad, 73, 94
Adzhubei, Alexei, 119
AIPAC (American Israel Public Affairs Committee), 252
Air Force reserve, 34, 44, 52, 54
Aitken, George, 49
Alekseev, Alexander, 117, 118
Allen, Richard V., 292
Allende, Salvador, 328
Alliance for Progress, 81, 97, 112, 118, 173, 199, 242
Alsop, Joseph, 64, 95–96
Alvarez, Everett, 192
American Foreign Service Association, 306
American Israel Public Affairs Committee (AIPAC), 252
Americanization of Vietnam War, 174, 205, 219, 232–33, 235, 249
Anderson, Rudolf, 145, 146
Angell, Norman, 304
Angleton, James, 254
Annenberg, Walter, 281, 288, 290–95, 311
Ap Bac, Battle of (1963), 155–56, 269
arms control, 64, 80–82, 148, 309, 320, 329

Armstrong, Hamilton Fish, 297, 299
Army of the Republic of Vietnam (ARVN): in Ap Bac battle, 155–56; and Buddhist crisis, 163; communism within, 157; data transmitted to MACV from, 153; disallowal of U.S. officers in, 173, 176; neutralist sentiment in, 174; reprisal attack led by, 205; subordination to U.S. operations, 246; and Tet offensive, 262, 267
Arthur S. Fleming Award, 102, 218, 290, 328
August 24th cable (1963), 163–65
Avery, Dorothy, 101, 150
Ayub Khan, Mohammad, 94, 149

Bailey, John, 45–46, 52, 62, 72
Baker, Pauline, 309
Ball, George: and August 24th cable, 163–65; and Cuban Missile Crisis, 138, 147; and Dominican crisis, 246; and Gulf of Tonkin Crisis, 180; and Operation Mongoose, 113; peace plan developed with TLH, 233, 235–38; political appointments of, 87, 91, 228; presentation style of, 234; as Stevenson's law partner, 70;

357

Ball, George (cont.)
  as UN ambassador, 252; on Vietnam War policy, 211, 214, 216–19, 225, 229, 232
Ball, Joe, 23, 24
Balliol men, 154, 324
battles. *See specific names of battles*
Bay of Pigs invasion (1961), 3, 84, 92, 102–03, 105–08, 120
Benedict, Steve, 23–24, 28, 39, 298
Bennett, W. Tapley, 242, 243
Benton, William, 37, 38, 45, 72, 287
Betts, Richard, 233
bipartisanship: in foreign policy, 5, 53, 207, 289, 328; in JFK administration, 83, 84, 162; in LBJ administration, 190, 275; in Nixon administration, 289
Bismarck, Otto von, 312
Bissell, Richard, 84, 102, 103, 109
Blanton, Thomas, 295, 328
Blatnik, John, 54–55, 68
Blight, James, 225
Boggs, Hale, 275
Bohlen, Charles, 125
Bolshakov, Georgi, 124, 138
Bowles, Chester "Chet": as ambassador to India, 35, 88, 109, 128; Bay of Pigs invasion opposed by, 105–08; *The Coming Political Breakthrough*, 71; criticisms of, 77, 79; and Cuban Missile Crisis, 128–33; death of, 34; at DNC kick-off dinner, 61; as foreign policy advisor to JFK, 58, 60–61, 63, 68, 74; in House of Representatives, 44–47, 51–55, 71–73; *The New Dimensions of Peace*, 37; political ambitions of, 37–38, 40, 58, 71, 77; and presidential election of 1960, 56–65, 67–76; press conference with JFK, 60–64; as secretary of state candidate, 60–62, 71–72, 76–77, 79–80; as special envoy to Third World countries, 108–09; State Department transition led by, 70, 79, 82–87; TLH on staff of, 34–35, 37–38, 46–47, 51–55; as under secretary of state, 87–89, 105–08; on U-2 incident (1960), 69
Bowles, Steb, 35, 36, 45, 72, 76
Branigan, Roger, 272
Braun, Werner von, 248

Bricker, John, 28
Brookings, Robert, 303–04
Brookings Institution: collaboration with Carnegie Endowment, 306; foreign policy and defense studies program, 286–87; intellectual climate at, 307; job offer extended to TLH, 286–87, 290; "Setting National Priorities" series from, 296
Brown, Pat, 61
Bruce, David, 72, 80
Brzezinski, Zbigniew, 274, 313–17
Buchanan, James, 9
Buchanan, Pat, 310
Buddhist crisis (1963), 157–60, 162–63, 169–70
Bundy, McGeorge: on coup against Diem, 172; and Cuban Missile Crisis, 126–28, 142, 147; on Dominican crisis, 246; as Ford Foundation president, 232, 252; "fork in the road" memo from, 214, 215; and Gulf of Tonkin Crisis, 188; INR's relationship with, 99, 105; on LBJ's relationship with Humphrey, 2–3; on national security team, 83, 87, 89; and Operation Mongoose, 109, 113, 114; retirement from government service, 232, 252, 259; as secretary of state candidate, 80; succession discussions, 218, 230–31; on TLH's promotion to deputy under secretary, 211–12; Vietnam trip (1965), 214–15; on Vietnam War policy, 2, 210, 213–18, 221–23, 229
Bundy, William, 80, 192, 209–13, 234–38, 256, 299
Bunker, Ellsworth, 269
Bureau of Intelligence and Research (INR): all-source intelligence utilized by, 95, 100, 326; on Buddhist crisis, 158–59; on CIA reform, 102–04; and Cuban Missile Crisis, 125, 135, 143; directors of, 1, 3, 92, 98–102, 105, 150, 153–54, 295; functions of, 100, 101, 154; and Operation Mongoose, 112–15; reorganization of, 100–101; reputation in intelligence community, 105; and Sino-Indian War, 149–50; and statistics war, 160–61; Vietnam analyses by, 156–61, 170, 174–77, 204, 212–13,

218, 246–47, 267. *See also* Hilsman, Roger; Hughes, Thomas Lowe "Tam"
Burger, Warren, 23
Busby, Horace, 270
Bush, Dorothy, 36
Bush, George H. W., 321, 323, 329
Bush, Prescott, 36, 38
Butler, Nicholas Murray, 304
Butler, Paul, 61, 67

U.S.S. *C. Turner Joy* attack (1964), 183, 186–88
Califano, Joseph, 251
Capehart, Homer, 120
Carmichael, Stokely, 227
Carnegie, Andrew, 297, 302–04, 311, 318, 320, 322, 324
Carnegie Endowment for International Peace, 301–25; board members of, 297, 300, 304, 308, 311; and Bush administration, 321; and Carter administration, 313–17; foreign policy reform efforts, 4–5, 301, 306; history and evolution of, 303–05; intellectual climate at, 301–02, 307; and Nixon administration, 310–13, 320–21; objectives of, 302–03, 308; policy advocacy by, 311; presidency of TLH at, 4–5, 102, 301–02, 305–21, 329; and Reagan administration, 318–21; research efforts of, 298; retirement of TLH from, 5, 15, 321–25; staff members at, 306–09, 329
Caro, Bob, 333
Carter, Jimmy, 4–5, 313–17
Carter, Marshall "Pat," 123, 126–28, 164
Carver, George, 156–57, 209, 259, 268–69
Casey, Jane, 18, 330–33
Castro, Fidel: Bowles on, 76, 107, 129; and communism, 117–20; and Cuban Missile Crisis, 139, 143, 148; and Ogaden War, 316–17; and Operation Mongoose, 108–15; sabotage campaign against, 110, 114–16, 118; threats posed by, 86, 102
Castro, Raul, 116, 119
Central Intelligence Agency (CIA): and Bay of Pigs invasion, 84, 102–03; in covert operations, 103–04, 149, 186; criticisms of, 99, 100; and Cuban Missile Crisis, 121–27; directors of, 5, 83, 105, 111, 242, 248, 314–15, 328; dual role of analyst and covert operator, 103; foreign policy influence of, 99; Hilsman-Hughes plan for reform of, 102–04; and Operation Mongoose, 110–15; sabotage activities of, 115, 118; Vietnam analyses by, 156, 174, 177, 212, 247, 249, 267
Chayes, Abe: and 1960 presidential election, 67; on Bowles's candidacy for secretary of state, 77, 80; as candidate to replace Bundy, 218, 230–31; and Cuban Missile Crisis, 136; as State Department legal advisor, 80, 87, 91, 105–06
Chennault affair, 283–84
China: communism in, 77, 79; and Sino-Indian War, 149–50; and Vietnam War, 154, 204–05, 211, 247, 251
Christopher, Warren, 314
Church, Frank, 205–06, 208, 333
CIA. *See* Central Intelligence Agency
civil rights: in Democratic platform, 67–68, 80; Humphrey on, 41, 207, 209; LBJ on, 180, 200, 226–27, 254
Civil Rights Act of 1957, 68
Civil Rights Act of 1964, 227
Clark, Joseph, 53
Clark, Ramsey, 254
Clark, Tom, 254
Clifford, Clark, 82–85, 213, 248, 267, 269, 275, 280
Cline, Ray, 189, 248, 295, 328
Cohen, Michael, 219
Colbert, Evelyn, 101, 150, 156–57, 160
Colby, William, 186
Cold War: arms control during, 148, 320; Bowles's predictions regarding, 71; conflicts following end of, 5; diplomacy in, 320; events leading up to, 30; prospects for world peace during, 303. *See also* Cuban Missile Crisis
communism: in ARVN, 157; and Castro, 117–20; in China, 77, 79; collapse of, 5; containment doctrine on, 226, 257; domino theory of, 171, 257; strategies for dealing with, 81

Index

Conein, Lucien, 166, 168–69
Connally, John, 267, 278
Connell, Bill, 42, 264, 271, 274
containment doctrine, 226, 257
Cooper, Chester, 237, 240–41
Corcoran, Tommy, 56
Cordier, Andrew, 147–48
Cornelius, Winston, 180
Cort, David, 29
Cotton, Norris, 79
Council on Foreign Relations, 296–300, 305, 307–08, 329
covert operations: CIA role in, 103–04, 149, 186; in Dominican Republic, 86; in low-intensity conflict, 96; Operation Mongoose, 108–15; in Vietnam War, 1, 176, 181, 184–90, 200
COVID-19 pandemic, 332
Cowles, John, 26
Cuba: alliance with Soviet Union, 86, 113, 115–18; military assistance for, 118–19; and Operation Mongoose, 108–15; severing of diplomatic relations with, 86; sugar embargo on, 113, 117; U.S. envoys to, 85; U-2 incident (1962), 145, 146. *See also* Bay of Pigs invasion; Castro, Fidel
Cuban Missile Crisis (1962), 116–48; Bowles-Dobrynin meetings on, 128–33; diplomacy in, 129–34, 138–40, 144; events leading up to, 116–20; ExCom deliberations on, 133, 135–37, 144–47; intelligence gathering during, 120–28; internal agency disputes during, 125–28; military options in, 133, 136–37; missile swap in resolution of, 131–33, 136, 138–39, 144–48; myths surrounding, 132; naval blockade during, 136–38; offensive vs. defensive weapons in, 122–24, 133; public opinion on, 138–40; Scali-Feklisov affair during, 142–44; TLH as public briefer on, 140–42
Cumming, Hugh, 99
Custer, George, 10
Cutler, Lloyd, 235–36
Cut Nose (Sioux warrior), 8

Dakota War of 1862, 7–10
Daley, Richard, 272, 278, 279
Davis, Angela, 227

DeBallios, John, 324
debate teams, 15–16, 20–21
Defense Intelligence Agency (DIA), 216, 249
de Gaulle, Charles, 73, 94, 167, 174
Democratic National Committee (DNC), 61–62
Denney, George, 101
DeSoto patrols, 181–84, 186, 189, 192, 205, 214
Dewey, Thomas E., 23
Diamond, Stanley, 232
Dillon, Douglas, 53, 55, 83
diplomacy: bilateral, 292; changing nature of, 3; in Cold War, 320; in Cuban Missile Crisis, 129–34, 138–40, 144; in Laos, 151; lone-wolf, 146; MMDBB metric to, 323–24; multilateral, 305; in Sino-Indian War, 149; summit diplomacy, 81; in Vietnam War, 173, 176, 217, 233
DNC (Democratic National Committee), 61–62
Dobrynin, Anatoly, 124, 128–35, 137–38, 144, 147, 239
Dodd, Thomas, 45, 201–02
Dole, Robert, 313–14
Dominican Republic: assassination of dictator in, 108; attack on U.S. embassy in, 243–44; U.S. interventions in, 86, 242–44, 246
domino theory, 171, 257
Dulles, Allen, 83, 84, 99, 102, 103, 105
Dulles, John Foster, 43, 52, 53, 304
Dungan, Ralph, 59, 81, 245, 252
Duong Van Minh, 168–69, 171–73, 176, 177

Eisenhower, Dwight: as Carnegie Endowment trustee, 304; foreign policy under, 97, 99; health problems of, 43; JFK on, 64, 69, 74, 97; MacArthur on, 46–47; New Look strategy of, 193; reelection of, 37; transition advice from, 151
Emerson, Ralph Waldo, 202
Erwin, Sam, 67
Etherington-Smith, Gordon, 177
Evans, Allen, 101
Executive Committee of the National Security Council (ExCom), 133, 135–37, 144–47

Fabian, Larry, 307, 324
federalism, 24–25, 28–31. See also Student Federalists
Federal Union Inc., 24–26, 28, 29, 31
Feklisov, Aleksandr "Foman," 142–44, 146
Feldman, Mike, 59, 71, 81
Fichel, Wesley, 159
Figueres, José María, 86
Flathers, Ila, 16
Ford, Gerald, 313–14
Ford, Harold, 209
Ford Foundation, 232, 252, 300, 329
Foreign Affairs (journal), 79, 296–99, 308
foreign policy: in 1960 presidential election, 63–64, 81; advisory roles in, 58, 60–61, 63, 68, 74; on aid and economic assistance, 51–53, 117, 152, 210, 236; bipartisanship in, 5, 53, 207, 289, 328; CIA influence on, 99; classified briefings on, 69–70; congressional role in, 52, 53; in Eisenhower administration, 97, 99; JFK's views on, 53, 64, 80–81, 86, 92, 96–97; management of contradictions in, 317; in New Frontier, 96–97; public support for, 6; reform efforts, 4–5, 301, 306; TLH's views on, 3, 5, 252, 258–60, 317–19, 327. See also Cuban Missile Crisis; diplomacy; Vietnam War
Foreign Policy (journal), 5, 297, 302, 308–09, 313, 316–17, 319, 329
"fork in the road" memo (1965), 214, 215
Forrestal, Michael, 99, 105, 151, 159, 163–65, 209
Fortas, Abe, 214, 246, 269
Frankel, Max, 95, 178–80
Fremont-Smith, Marion, 309
Frye, Alton, 305, 308
Fuchs, Klaus, 143
Fulbright, J. William: AIPAC attacks on, 252; as chair of Foreign Relations Committee, 49, 53, 194, 242; Gulf of Tonkin resolution sponsored by, 194; as secretary of state candidate, 80, 87; on Vietnam War policy, 205–06, 208, 239, 244

Galbraith, John Kenneth, 85, 87, 89, 109, 149
Gamble, Mary Morris, 39
Gelb, Leslie, 233
genealogical studies, 15, 19–20, 324–25, 330–31
George Washington University National Security Archive, 4, 295, 328
Gibbons, William, 244
Gilpatric, Roswell, 119, 147, 164
Ginsburg, David, 252–55, 275
glasnost, 320
Goldberg, Arthur, 66, 269
Goldwater, Barry: and 1964 presidential election, 180, 188, 203, 207–08; in Air Force reserve, 52; TLH's relationship with, 196–97; on Vietnam War policy, 188, 191, 192, 220
Goodwin, Richard, 59, 71, 76, 81, 109, 110, 199
Gorbachev, Mikhail, 320, 321
Gordon, Kermit, 286–87, 290, 296, 306
Gordon, Lincoln, 85, 87, 139, 242
Gore, David Ormsby, 94
Gospel of Wealth, 297, 303
Goulart, João "Jango," 242
Gould, Lawrence, 30–32
The Great Illusion (Angell), 304
Great Society: accomplishments of, 275, 278; coalition for enactment of, 173, 225; domestic consensus on, 328; programs features, 217; Vietnam War impacting, 251
Great Union (Cort), 29
Green, Theodore, 48–49
Greene, Fred, 101, 150, 189, 205
Gromyko, Andrei, 133–35, 138
groupthink, 103
Grove, Brandon, 89
Gruening, Ernest, 194
guerrilla warfare, 104, 150, 155, 181, 221
Gulf of Tonkin Crisis (1964), 175–95; attacks on U.S. destroyers in, 180–89; congressional testimony on, 193–94; and Oplan 34A, 176–77, 181, 185–92, 205; retaliatory strikes in, 1, 183–84, 187–92, 194–95, 205
Gulf of Tonkin resolution (1964), 192–94, 200, 244, 255
Gulf Wars, 322
Gullion, Edmund, 241
guns-and-butter strategy, 250, 251

Habib, Phillip, 268, 269
Halperin, Morton H., 269–70, 288, 295

Harkins, Paul, 152–56, 160–61, 166–67, 169, 176, 250
Harriman, Averell: and 1968 presidential election, 276–77; and August 24th cable, 163–64; and diplomacy in Laos, 151; as governor of New York, 55, 91; political appointment of, 87; as secretary of state candidate, 61, 72; and Sino-Indian War, 149, 150; in Vietnam War negotiations, 275
Harris, Fred, 271, 274
Harris, Louis, 64, 65
Harrison, Sig, 79
Harrop, William, 306
Hayden, Carl, 94
Heath, Edward, 293
Helms, Richard, 164, 227, 248–49, 259, 295, 328
Herrick, John, 181, 184, 186–87, 189–90
Herring, George, 233
Herter, Christian, 53–55, 69–70, 74, 76, 82, 85, 290
Hilsman, Roger: as assistant secretary for East Asia, 3, 101, 105, 150, 152; and August 24th cable, 163–65; on Buddhist crisis, 158, 159, 163; on coup against Diem, 163, 167; and Cuban Missile Crisis, 120–21, 135, 138–45; educational background, 98; on NIE 53-63, 157; on Operation Mongoose, 110–11, 113; personality of, 98, 99; political views of, 152; TLH's relationship with, 81, 98. *See also* Bureau of Intelligence and Research
Hiss, Alger, 304, 320
Hitch, Charles, 306
Ho Chi Minh, 154, 211
Hohenzollern family, 3, 15, 19, 20
Holborn, Fred, 59
Holbrooke, Richard, 316, 332–33
Hoover, J. Edgar, 83, 227, 246, 253–54, 293
Howard, Frances Humphrey, 289
Hufstedler, Shirley, 309
Hughes, Alice Lowe (mother of TLH): death of, 35; family records maintained by, 14; Lindgren family relationship with, 33; parenting practices of, 11, 12; political views of, 19
Hughes, Allan (son of TLH), 44, 294

Hughes, Burton (uncle of TLH), 11, 12, 32, 324
Hughes, Evan (son of TLH), 44, 294
Hughes, Evan Raymond (father of TLH): death of, 35, 44; educational background, 11, 32; FBI visit to home of, 20; Lindgren family relationship with, 33; parenting practices of, 11, 12; political views of, 19, 23; in public relations for TLH, 14
Hughes, Harold (Iowa governor), 275–76
Hughes, Henry (great-grandfather of TLH), 7–9, 11
Hughes, Jane Casey (wife of TLH), 18, 330–33
Hughes, Jean Reiman (wife of TLH): and 1960 presidential election, 76; on career path of TLH, 38, 40, 311; death of, 330; educational background, 35; marriage and family life, 36, 244, 251–52, 288, 294; medical community connections of, 243; political views of, 36
Hughes, John Henry (great-uncle of TLH), 9
Hughes, Marianne (sister of TLH), 14, 39
Hughes, Thomas (grandfather of TLH): educational background, 11, 32; historical works by, 8, 10–11, 289; influence on TLH, 12–13, 330; political views of, 19; on Sioux uprising, 7–9; Welsh ancestry of, 332
Hughes, Thomas Lowe "Tam" ("TLH" in this index): and 1960 presidential election, 58–62, 67–69, 76; and 1968 presidential election, 271, 275–81; in Air Force reserve, 34, 44, 52, 54; birth and early life, 11–14; on Bowles's staff, 34–35, 37–38, 46–47, 51–55; as Carnegie Endowment president, 4–5, 102, 301–02, 305–21, 329; as collector, 18–20, 245, 324, 331–32; and Cuban Missile Crisis, 120–29, 140–46; on debate teams, 15–16, 20–21; diary kept by, 20, 26–27, 48–50, 53–55, 62, 65–73, 76–77, 81; educational background, 13–16, 21, 27–33, 39; eighth-grade autobiography of, 13, 16, 18–19; family background, 7–13, 15; Fleming Award received by, 102,

218, 290, 328; foreign policy views of, 3, 5, 252, 258–60, 317–19, 327; genealogical studies by, 15, 19–20, 324–25, 330–31; and Gulf of Tonkin Crisis, 180–83, 188–89, 194–95, 200; health problems of, 39, 332; historical works by, 15–17, 20; hobbies and interests of, 3, 12, 14–20, 245, 324; on Humphrey for vice president, 196–97, 201, 202, 207; as Humphrey's legislative counsel, 40–44, 47–50; lectures given by, 257–58, 260–61; London appointment for, 290–95; marriage and family life, 18, 36, 44, 244, 251–52, 288, 294, 330; meeting with Fidel Castro, 316–17; musical career of, 14–15, 17–18, 330; and New Frontier, 89–96; on Operation Mongoose, 110, 113–14; peace plan developed with Ball, 233, 235–38; personality of, 3, 5, 11–12, 16, 19, 38, 302; political views of, 19, 23, 27; retirement of, 5, 15, 321–25, 329; on State Department transition teams, 83–84, 87, 209; as Student Federalist, 15–16, 18, 21–33; on Watergate crisis, 310–12. *See also* Bureau of Intelligence and Research; Humphrey-Hughes memo

Humphrey, Hubert: and 1960 presidential election, 55–60, 64–67, 70; and 1968 presidential election, 264–68, 271–85; and Carter administration, 315; at DNC kick-off dinner, 61–62; *The Education of a Public Man*, 226–27; foreign policy views of, 53; and Gulf of Tonkin Crisis, 183, 194, 195, 200; health problems of, 264; LBJ's relationship with, 2–3, 41, 48, 196–203, 208, 223–24, 263–64; loyalty oath to LBJ, 2, 201, 202, 216, 219, 222; as Minneapolis mayor, 24, 30, 38; personality of, 41, 47, 203, 256; political rise of, 23, 41; Salt Lake City speech by, 281, 288, 311; as Senator, 38–44, 47–51, 67; TLH as legislative counsel to, 40–44, 47–50; transition to private sector, 287; as vice presidential candidate (1964), 180, 196–203, 207–08; on Vietnam War policy, 208, 210, 216–21, 225, 281–82

Humphrey, Muriel, 49–50, 202, 208, 263–64, 270, 273

Humphrey-Hughes memo (1965): drafting of, 1–2, 219; events leading up to, 210, 216–19; historical assessment of, 219, 328; LBJ's reaction to, 2, 221–25; substance of, 219–21

Hurwitz, J. C., 261

India: and Sino-Indian War, 149–50; U.S. ambassadors to, 35, 88, 109, 128

INR. *See* Bureau of Intelligence and Research

intelligence agencies: barriers to work of, 110, 260; coordination of, 101, 103, 327; disputes among, 101, 125–28, 151–52, 247, 249, 326; politics and, 105, 120–22, 157, 258–59, 327–28; reform efforts, 102, 103, 327; TLH lectures on, 257–58, 260–61; transparency within, 100. *See also specific agencies*

intermediate range ballistic missiles (IRBMs), 121, 125, 134

International Court of Justice, 304

isolationism, 22, 25–26, 57, 300, 318, 326

Israel: and U.S.S. *Liberty* attack, 264; and nuclear weapons acquisition, 173; pro-Israel reputation of TLH, 252–53; and Six-Day War, 259, 264

Jackson, Henry M. "Scoop," 73
Javits, Jacob, 53, 141
Jessup, Philip, 305
Johnson, Joseph, 298, 300, 304–05
Johnson, Lady Bird, 202, 263–64
Johnson, Lyndon B. ("LBJ" *in this index*): and 1960 presidential election, 55–57; and 1964 presidential election, 180, 196–203, 207–08, 225; and 1968 presidential election, 264–68, 270–72, 277–84; assumption of presidency, 172–73; and Cuban Missile Crisis, 145; at DNC kick-off dinner, 61; and Dominican crisis, 242–44, 246; foreign policy team of, 172, 199–200; Humphrey's relationship with, 2–3, 41, 48, 196–203, 208, 223–24, 263–64; loyalty oath demanded by, 2, 201, 202, 216, 219, 222; national security team of, 2, 87; personality of, 48–49, 226–27; political failings of, 225–27;

Johnson, Lyndon B. (*cont.*)
   reaction to Humphrey-Hughes memo, 2, 221–25; as vice president, 70, 74–75, 145. *See also* Great Society; Vietnam War
Johnson, Tom, 278
Johnson, U. Alexis, 87, 104, 109, 111, 113, 164, 211–12
Jonas, Gilbert, 21, 40, 159

Kaiser, Phil, 91
Kalb, Marvin and Mady, 179, 310
Kampelman, Max: and 1964 presidential election, 196; and 1968 presidential election, 271, 274–76; educational background, 38; Humphrey's relationship with, 38–41, 43, 50–51, 56; in private law practice, 38, 245; in Reagan administration, 318; on TLH lectures, 261; on Vietnam War policy, 265
Kattenberg, Paul, 166–67, 170
Katz, Milton, 298, 305, 309, 329
Katzenbach, Nicholas, 91, 124, 253–55
Kaufman, William, 296
Kaysen, Carl, 113
Keating, Kenneth, 120–23, 207, 253
Kefauver, Estes, 43, 55
Kellogg, Frank, 22
Kelly, Kitty, 323
Kenan, Si, 252
Kennedy, John F. ("JFK" *in this index*): on arms control, 80–82; colonialism denounced by, 48; death of, 115, 172, 173, 197, 203; at DNC kick-off dinner, 61–62; on Eisenhower, 64, 69, 74, 97; family background, 57; foreign policy views of, 53, 64, 80–81, 86, 92, 96–97; inaugural address of, 93; national security team of, 2, 73, 83, 89; and Operation Mongoose, 108–15; personality of, 57, 62; press conference with Bowles, 60–64; and Sino-Indian War, 149–50; summit with Khrushchev, 80, 103, 107, 118; on U-2 incidents, 69, 74, 80, 81, 145, 146. *See also* Bay of Pigs invasion; Cuban Missile Crisis; New Frontier; presidential election of 1960; Vietnam War
Kennedy, Joseph P., Sr., 57, 77, 78, 80, 122
Kennedy, Robert "Bobby": and 1960 presidential election, 58–59, 68, 72; and 1968 presidential election, 265–67, 271–73; assassination of, 273, 276; Bay of Pigs review task force led by, 102; on Bowles, 107–08; and Cuban Missile Crisis, 122, 124, 137–39, 146, 147; as New York Senator, 207, 253; and Operation Mongoose, 109–10, 113, 114; as vice presidential candidate, 180, 197–98; on Wofford, 75, 80
Kennedy, Ted, 276, 278, 317, 333
Kent, Sherman, 156
Kerner Commission, 263, 275
Kerr, Robert, 48
Khrushchev, Nikita: Humphrey's meeting with, 50; JFK's summit with, 80, 103, 107, 118; on military assistance for Cuba, 118–19; on wars of national liberation, 97. *See also* Cuban Missile Crisis
Kiefer, Alois, 20, 21
King, Coretta Scott, 75
King, Martin Luther Jr., 75–76, 227, 253, 254, 263, 273
Kirkpatrick, Evron, 226, 274, 276
Kirkpatrick, Jeane, 274, 276, 318
Kirkpatrick, Lyman, 103
Kissinger, Henry, 274, 280, 288, 290–92, 295, 310–13
Kohler, Foy, 239
Kosygin, Alexei, 214, 216, 217, 225, 281
Kowalski, Frank, 52
Kreisky, Bruno, 139
Krulak, Victor, 167–68
Kuchel, Thomas, 53
Kucinski, Jane Casey, 18, 330–33

Lake, Anthony, 316
Lang, Janet, 225
Lansdale, Edwin, 109–14
Laos: bombing of supply routes in, 212–13, 234; diplomacy in, 151
Lawrence, William, 72
League of Nations, 22–24, 28, 304
Lefever, Ernest, 51
LeMay, Curtis, 197, 282
Levin, Richard, 331–32
U.S.S. *Liberty* attack (1967), 264
Lien, Petra, 16
Lincoln, Abraham, 8–10, 323
Lindgren, Emmy Lou "Clare": on debate teams, 16, 21; educational

background, 32; marriage of, 33; memorial service for, 33; as Student Federalist, 16, 21–28, 32–33; in Washington, D.C., 34, 39
Lippmann, Walter, 95, 96, 139
Little Big Horn, Battle of (1876), 10
Little Crow (Sioux chief), 9, 10
Lodge, Henry Cabot, 160, 162–66, 170–73, 176, 179–80
Logevall, Fredrik, 219
London, U.S. ambassador to, 290–95
lone-wolf diplomacy, 146
Lowe, Alice. *See* Hughes, Alice Lowe
Lowe, Margaret (aunt of TLH), 19
Lowe, Thomas (grandfather of TLH), 12, 15, 18–19, 330, 332
Lowe, Wilhelmina (great-grandmother of TLH), 19
Lowenstein, Allard, 51, 265, 271
Lowenthal, Jane, 324
loyalty oaths, 2, 201, 202, 216, 219, 222

MacArthur, Douglas, 46–47
Macomber, William "Butts," 83–84, 87, 290, 291
MacPherson, Harry, 245, 259, 270
MACV. *See* Military Assistance Command, Vietnam
Macy, John, 211
U.S.S. *Maddox* attacks (1964), 180–89
Magnuson, Warren, 94
Maguire, Robert, 271, 274
Mai Van Bo, 240, 241
Malinovsky, Rodion, 119
Mann, Thomas C., 199–200, 242, 243
Manning, Bayless, 299, 305, 308
Mansfield, Mike, 53, 205–06, 208, 225, 239
Manshel, Warren, 316, 333
Mao Zedong, 94, 257–58
Marcy, Carl, 49, 193–94
Marin, Munoz, 85, 86
Marshall, Thurgood, 254
Martin, Edwin, 87, 138, 139, 199, 242
massive retaliation doctrine, 96, 97
Maynes, Bill, 316, 317, 323–24
McCarthy, Eugene, 49, 196, 201, 264–66, 271–73, 278, 294
McCloskey, Herbert, 276
McCloy, John J., 134, 299
McCone, John: on August 24th cable, 164; on Buddhist crisis, 159–60; as CIA director, 83, 111, 248; and Cuban Missile Crisis, 120, 122–24, 128, 140; and Gulf of Tonkin Crisis, 190; on NIE 53-63, 157; and Operation Mongoose, 111, 113; personal advisory role of, 105, 123; on Vietnam War policy, 218, 229
McCormack, John, 197
McGovern, George, 49, 265, 273, 279, 300
McHenry, Don, 316
McLuhan, Marshall, 57
McMahon, Brian, 38
McNamara, Robert S.: on August 24th cable, 164; on coup against Diem, 166–67; and Cuban Missile Crisis, 147; as defense secretary, 83, 152, 249; and Gulf of Tonkin Crisis, 186–95; on Harkins plan, 152–53; INR's relationship with, 101; and Operation Mongoose, 109; and Pentagon Papers, 4; personality of, 99; presentation style of, 2, 89, 234; on Project Mayflower, 239; on statistics war, 160, 161; trips to Vietnam, 168, 177, 178; on Vietnam War policy, 2, 210, 213–14, 216–18, 229
McNamara-Taylor Report (1963), 168
McNaughton, John, 209, 215–16
Meissner, Doris, 309
Mendenhall, Joseph, 167–68
Meyer, Cord Jr., 31
Mikoyan, Anastas, 117
Military Assistance Command, Vietnam (MACV): on Ap Bac battle, 156; establishment of, 152; Harkins as commander of, 152, 176; transmission of data to, 153, 161; Westmoreland as commander of, 186, 246, 250
Minnesota Historical Society, 11
Mississippi Freedom Party, 202
Moise, Edwin E., 184, 189, 295, 328
Mondale, Walter "Fritz," 16, 271, 274, 313–15, 319–20
Monroe Doctrine, 129, 138
Moose, Richard, 278
Morgan, Thomas, 194
Morgenthau, Hans, 231–32
Morse, Wayne, 193, 194, 200, 206
Moscoso, Ted, 199
Moyers, Bill, 211–12, 218, 229–30, 232, 259

Moynihan, Daniel Patrick, 102, 218
Mundt, Karl, 21
Murrow, Edward R., 87
musicianship, 14–15, 17–18, 330
Muskie, Ed, 280

Nathan, Robert, 276
national intelligence estimates (NIEs): preparation process for, 247; SNIEs, 101, 125–26, 128, 212; on Vietnam War, 156–57, 218
National Liberation Front (NLF): in Ap Bac battle, 155; NIE 53-63 on, 157; peace talks involving, 236, 280–83; Pleiku attack by, 215, 216; spies and informants for, 153–54, 210; and Tet offensive, 262, 265–69
national liberation wars, 97, 257
National Security Action Memoranda (NSAMs), 175–76, 178, 205
National Student Association, 31
nativism, 66, 318, 319
NATO (North Atlantic Treaty Organization), 130, 133–36, 150, 228
Nehru, Jawaharlal, 94, 149, 150
neutralism, 22, 167, 172–74, 176, 210
Newell, Barbara, 309
New Frontier, 89–97; cult of youth in, 93–94; decisionmaking style in, 2, 89; domestic policy programs, 41; foreign policy agenda in, 96–97; media and, 94–96; paradoxes of, 90–94
New Look strategy, 193
new pluralism, 322
new world order, 321, 323, 329
Ngho Bui Diem, 283
Ngo Dinh Can, 168
Ngo Dinh Diem: and Ap Bac battle, 156; and Buddhist crisis, 158–60, 163, 169–70; coup plots against, 162–63, 165–72; death of, 171–72, 176
Ngo Dinh Nhu, 163, 166–71
Ngo Dinh Thuc, 158
Nguyen Cao Ky, 205, 256
Nguyen Khanh, 176–78, 193, 204, 214–15
Nguyen Van Thieu, 283, 285
Nichter, Luke A., 162
NIEs. See national intelligence estimates
Nitze, Paul, 64, 73–74, 81–82, 318
Nixon, Richard M.: and 1960 presidential election, 55, 73, 76, 78; and 1968 presidential election, 271, 274, 277–85; and Carnegie Endowment, 310–13, 320–21; foreign affairs experience of, 290; pardon by Ford, 314; resignation of, 313; State Department under, 287–92; as vice president, 55, 73, 77; on Vietnam War policy, 277–78, 282–85; and Watergate crisis, 310–13
NLF. See National Liberation Front
Nolting, Frederick, 158, 162, 167
North Atlantic Treaty Organization (NATO), 130, 133–36, 150, 228
NSAMs (National Security Action Memoranda), 175–76, 178, 205
nuclear weapons: balance of power in regards to, 119; as deterrence strategy, 96, 97; IRBMs, 121, 125, 134; NATO multilateral fleet plan for, 228; offensive vs. defensive, 122–24, 133; SAMs, 121–28, 135, 145, 146. See also arms control; Cuban Missile Crisis
Nye, Gerald, 22

oblique photography, 127
O'Brien, Larry, 66, 271, 274, 276–77
O'Donnell, Kenny, 198
O'Flaherty, Daniel, 309–10
Ogaden War, 316–17
Operation Mongoose, 108–15
Operation Plan (Oplan) 34A, 176–77, 181, 185–92, 205
Organization of American States (OAS), 118, 123, 138, 244
Ormsby-Gore, David, 94
Owen, Henry, 296

Packer, George, 332
pandemic, COVID-19, 332
Patterson, James T., 262
Peace Corps, 41, 43, 81, 92, 172
Pearson, Drew, 225
Pearson, Lester, 236
Pell, Claiborne, 90, 311
Pell, Herbert, 90
Pentagon Papers, 4, 295–96, 328
perestroika, 320
Peters, Charles, 66
Pham Van Dong, 174, 240
Plank, John, 101
Pleiku attack (1965), 215, 216

Pliyev, Issa, 136, 137
populism, 27, 258, 274, 313, 318
Power, Thomas, 154
Prados, John, 160, 295, 328
Prentice, Sterling "Coke," 32, 39–40
Present at the Creation (Acheson), 4
presidential election of 1956, 43, 46–47
presidential election of 1960, 55–87;
  DNC kick-off dinner during, 61–62;
  foreign policy issues in, 63–64, 81;
  Hughes-Sorensen negotiations on,
  58–62, 72; Kennedy-Bowles press
  conference in, 60–64; late moves in,
  73–77; margin of victory in, 76, 78;
  peaceful transfer of power following,
  77; platform for Democratic convention in, 67–68, 275; postconvention
  period of, 70–73; precampaign campaign in, 55–58; primary contests
  during, 64–67; staff coordination
  issues in, 68–70; State Department
  transition following, 70, 79, 82–87
presidential election of 1964, 180,
  196–203, 207–08, 225
presidential election of 1968, 264–85;
  candidate positioning in, 264–68,
  270–73; Democratic convention in,
  273–80; primary contests during,
  272; Vietnam War as issue in,
  274–85
presidential election of 1972, 300
presidential election of 1976, 313–14
presidential election of 1980, 318
presidential election of 1984, 319–20
presidential election of 1988, 321
Preston, Andrew, 163
Priess, David, 288
Progressive Era, 303
Project Mayflower, 233, 238–41

Raborn, William F. "Red" Jr., 242–44,
  248
race riots, 263, 264
Ramsbothom, Peter, 261
Rayburn, Sam, 51–52
Reagan, Ronald, 318–21
Reber, James, 127
reconnaissance flights, 121, 123,
  126–29, 146
Reilly, John, 223, 263–65, 274
Reiman, Jean. *See* Hughes, Jean Reiman
Reischauer, Edwin, 85, 87
Resources for the Future, 306

Reston, James, 106
Rhodesia, U.S. interference in British
  policy on, 293
Ribicoff, Abraham, 36, 45–46, 62, 72,
  141, 278–79
Richardson, Elliot, 286, 288–92
Riedel, Bruce, 149
riots (1968), 263, 264, 278, 279
Rockefeller, David, 297–300, 308, 313,
  314
Rockefeller, John D., 297
Rockefeller, Nelson, 55, 85, 141, 290
Rockefeller Foundation, 87, 88, 300,
  329
Rodriguez, Carlos Raphael, 316
Rogers, William, 286, 290–92, 295
Rolling Thunder bombing campaign,
  1–2, 216, 229, 235, 237
Romney, George, 294
Roosevelt, Eleanor, 67, 70
Roosevelt, Franklin Delano, 23, 30, 47,
  57, 96
Roosevelt, Theodore, 256, 302, 303,
  309
Root, Elihu, 302–04, 309
Rostow, Elspeth, 287
Rostow, Eugene, 255, 318
Rostow, Walt: and 1968 presidential
  election, 275; and Cuban Missile
  Crisis, 128, 136; as defense advisor,
  63, 64; as national security advisor,
  251, 252, 259; as policy planning director, 87, 154, 234; Taylor-Rostow
  Report on Vietnam, 104, 152; on
  transition task force, 82; transition
  to private sector, 287
Rowe, Jim, 56–57, 196, 198, 200–202
Rusk, Dean: and 1968 presidential
  election, 275; and August 24th
  cable, 164; on Chinese intervention
  in Vietnam, 154; on coup against
  Diem, 166, 167; and Cuban Missile
  Crisis, 126–27, 134, 138–39, 143,
  146–48; educational background,
  91; and Gulf of Tonkin Crisis, 180,
  182; on Humphrey for vice president,
  196; INR's relationship with, 102,
  104–05; LBJ's relationship with,
  229; on media relationships, 95; military service of, 245; and Operation
  Mongoose, 113–15; and Pentagon
  Papers, 296; on Project Mayflower,
  239; on promotion of TLH to

Rusk, Dean (cont)
  deputy under secretary, 211–12; as secretary of state, 84, 87–89; on statistics war, 160–61; transition to private sector, 287; trip to Vietnam, 178; on Vietnam War policy, 211, 214, 216–18, 281
Russell, Richard, 205–06, 208, 225

Salinger, Pierre, 95, 124
Salt Lake City speech (1968), 281, 288, 311
SAMs (surface-to-air missiles), 121–28, 135, 145, 146
Sarris, Louis G., 153, 160
Sather, Richard C., 192
Scali, John, 142–44, 146
Schlaberg, Charles Frederick, 19
Schlesinger, Arthur, 96, 139
Schulz, George, 320
Seaborn, J. Blair, 211, 241
Sharon, John, 77, 82
Sharp, Ulysses S. Grant Jr., 186, 190
Sherman, Norman, 265, 274, 284
Shipstead, Henrik, 22, 24–26
Shriver, Sargent, 75–76, 80, 83–84, 92
Sigismund of Brandenburg (ancestor of TLH), 330–31
Simes, Dmitri, 320–21
Sino-Indian War, 149–50
Sioux uprising (1862), 7–10
Sirhan, Sirhan, 273
Six-Day War (1967), 259, 264
Skillman, Adelaide, 11–12
Smathers, George, 77, 94
Smith, Earl E. T., 85–86
Smith, Jean Kennedy, 309
SNIEs (special national intelligence estimates), 101, 125–26, 128, 212
Solberg, Carl, 216, 280
Some Day (Hughes), 12
Sonnenfeldt, Helmut "Hal," 101, 125, 143
Sorensen, Ted: and 1960 presidential election, 58–62, 65, 72, 75, 81; and Bowles, 69, 71, 74, 108–09; and Carter administration, 314–15; and Cuban Missile Crisis, 146, 147; JFK as viewed by, 93; negotiations with TLH, 58–62, 72; political views of, 80
Soviet Union: alliance with Cuba, 86, 113, 115–18; dissolution of, 321; glasnost and perestroika in, 320; and Ogaden War, 316; U-2 incident (1960), 69, 74, 80, 81; and Vietnam War, 239, 281. *See also* Cuban Missile Crisis; Khrushchev, Nikita
special national intelligence estimates (SNIEs), 101, 125–26, 128, 212
Spellman, Francis, 78
Stassen, Harold, 23–24, 26
State Department: bipartisan cooperation between Congress and, 53; on diplomatic problems from U-2 incidents, 126; and New Frontier, 89–94; and Operation Mongoose, 110–12, 114–15; postelection transitions at, 70, 79, 82–87, 209, 287–92; reorganization of, 2, 88, 108; study of Vietnam War by, 4, 295–96. *See also* Bureau of Intelligence and Research
statistics war, 160–61
Steakley, Ralph, 180, 181
Stennis, John, 53
Stevenson, Adlai: and 1956 presidential election, 43, 46–47; and 1960 presidential election, 55–57, 61, 70–73; and Cuban Missile Crisis, 133, 138, 139; death of, 252; foreign policy views of, 85; as secretary of state candidate, 70–72, 76–77, 80, 82, 228; as UN ambassador, 86–87; on Vietnam War policy, 217
Stewart, Michael, 293
Stiles, Ezra, 330
Streit, Clarence, 24–26, 29–31
Student Federalist (journal), 28, 29
Student Federalists, 21–31; demise of, 30–31; epitaph for, 33; journal published by, 28, 29; leadership of, 21, 23–24, 26–30, 32; national convention of, 26–27; origins of, 15–16, 22–26; parties hosted by, 18; phases of movement, 28–29
sugar embargo, 113, 117
Sullivan, William, 20
summit diplomacy, 81
surface-to-air missiles (SAMs), 121–28, 135, 145, 146
Sutherland, Arthur, 327
Symington, Stuart, 53, 55, 57, 61–62, 64

Taft, William Howard, 302

Taylor, Maxwell: and Bay of Pigs invasion, 102; on coup against Diem, 166–69; and Operation Mongoose, 108–12; report on Vietnam, 104, 152; trips to Vietnam, 168, 177; *The Uncertain Trumpet*, 193; as U.S. ambassador in Vietnam, 180, 192–93, 204, 213–15, 229, 234–35
Taylor-Rostow Report (1961), 104, 152
Tet offensive (1968), 262, 265–69
Thant, U, 138, 139, 148, 217
Thatcher, Margaret, 294–95
Third World: Bowles's interest in, 54, 56, 80, 108, 129; civil wars in, 152; communist aggression in, 81, 151; economic assistance for, 52; research projects in, 257; TLH's interest in, 301; and world federalism, 25, 30
Thompson, Llewelyn, 125, 147
Tito, Josip Broz, 54–55, 94
Tran Van Dong, 211
Traverse des Sioux, Treaty of (1851), 9–10
Trilateral Commission, 313, 314, 321
Trueheart, William, 158
Trujillo, Rafael, 86, 108
Truman, Harry, 35, 41, 57, 61, 91, 199, 220
Turner, Stansfield, 315

Ungar, Sanford, 323
Union Now (Streit), 31
United Nations (UN): and Carnegie Endowment, 304, 305; and Cuban Missile Crisis, 138, 139, 143, 145; General Assembly delegation, 43; San Francisco Conference on, 23–24, 29–30, 140; U.S. ambassadors to, 86–87, 102, 252, 316, 321; U.S. leadership role in, 27, 28
United States Intelligence Board (USIB): and Cuban Missile Crisis, 121, 125–26; functions of, 101; meetings of, 105, 123, 248; NIE 53-63 presented to, 156–57
United World Federalists, 31
U-2 spy plane incidents: in Cuba (1962), 145, 146; in Soviet Union (1960), 69, 74, 80, 81

Valenti, Jack, 202, 240
Vance, Cyrus, 180–82, 275, 314
Van Dyck, Ted, 263–65, 274, 280
van Zandt, James E., 141, 142, 149

Viet Cong. *See* National Liberation Front
Vietnam War: Americanization of, 174, 205, 219, 232–33, 235, 249–50; Buddhist crisis during, 157–60, 162–63, 169–70; casualties of, 155, 269, 285; Chennault affair during, 283–84; Chinese intervention in, 154, 204–05, 211, 247, 251; covert operations in, 1, 176, 181, 184–90, 200; de-escalation of, 268, 270, 277; diplomacy in, 173, 176, 217, 233; escalation of, 1, 154, 191, 212–22, 328, 333; "fork in the road" memo on, 214, 215; guerrilla tactics in, 104, 150, 155, 181, 221; Harkins plan for, 152–56, 160, 161, 250; intelligence disputes on, 151–52; McNamara-Taylor Report on, 168; national intelligence estimates on, 156–57, 218; neutralist sentiment in, 167, 172–74, 176, 210; NSAMs on, 175–76, 178, 205; opposition to, 170, 177, 206, 220, 231, 251, 262–63, 273; path toward negotiations in, 232–35; peace plans for, 233, 235–41, 281–85; Pentagon Papers on, 4, 295–96, 328; policy reviews on, 166, 172, 179, 205–06, 211; and Project Mayflower, 233, 238–41; Rolling Thunder bombing campaign, 1–2, 216, 229, 235, 237; selective pressure campaign in, 168, 170, 176; stalemate in, 249–51; State Department study of, 4, 295–96; statistics war over data on, 160–61; Taylor-Rostow Report on, 104, 152; and Tet offensive, 262, 265–69; XYZ affair during, 241. *See also* Army of the Republic of Vietnam; Gulf of Tonkin Crisis; Military Assistance Command, Vietnam; National Liberation Front
Vo Nguyen Giap, 187
Volcker, Paul, 102, 218
Voting Rights Act of 1965, 227

Walker, Jenome, 309
Wallace, George, 271, 273, 280–82
Warren, Earl, 115, 225–26
wars of national liberation, 97, 257
Watergate crisis, 310–13
Waters, Herb, 40, 42, 50

Welsh, Bill, 276
Westmoreland, William, 186, 215, 246, 250–51, 257
Wheeler, Earle "Bus," 178, 180, 182–83, 267
White, Byron "Whizzer," 91, 253
Whiting, Allen S., 101, 150, 189, 234–37, 268
Wilhelm II (Germany), 15, 302–04, 312, 324, 331
Williams, G. Mennen "Soapy," 61, 87
Williams, Murat, 101, 242–43
Wilson, Harold, 94, 293
Wofford, Harris: and 1960 presidential election, 56, 65, 67–69; as Bryn Mawr College president, 33; death of, 333; educational background, 34; family background, 25; marriage of, 33; *Of Kennedys and Kings*, 83; Peace Corps work by, 92, 172; personality of, 24, 25; political ambitions of, 80; radicalism of, 20; on secretary of state candidates, 80; as Student Federalist, 21–28, 31–33; on TLH in foreign policy debate, 5; in Washington, D.C., 34, 39
Woman's National Democratic Club, 310–12
Wood Lake, Battle of (1862), 10
Woods, Randell B., 278
world federalism, 24–25, 28–31. *See also* Student Federalists
Wounded Knee, Battle of (1890), 10

XYZ affair (1965), 241

Yale University, 20, 331
Youngdahl, Luther, 41